DERBYSHIRE PAST AND

By

Alan Gifford

CONTENTS

Introduction	Page	2
The Distribution and Status of Windmills in Derbyshire	Page	4
The Design and Development of Windmills	Page	8
Derbyshire Windmills, As Seen by James Farey in 1808	Page	11
The Karl Wood Paintings of Derbyshire Windmills	Page	14
The Surviving Windmills of Derbyshire	Page	15
The Remains of Windmills in Derbyshire	Page	24
Some Vanished Derbyshire Windmills	Page	38
The Derbyshire Edges and Millstone Quarries	Page	97
Other References to Windmills in Derbyshire	Page	101
A Short Guide to Some Windmill Terms	Page	103
Bibliography	Page	105

INTRODUCTION

Being born and bred in Derbyshire it was perhaps inevitable that when I first became interested in windmills, back in about 1973, I should first look at the local mills. I soon found there were only two complete surviving windmills, but over the years have found the physical remains of about ten others.

It soon became clear that during the 18th and 19th centuries there were many more wind (and water) mills operating in Derbyshire. Evidence of the existence of the windmills was found in various places and the task was always to try and obtain confirmation. In some cases this was easily obtained but in others the trail is still weak. Over the years data on some 73 windmills had been found and recorded, but information on a further 13 is now included, bringing the total positive locations up to 85. More information has also been gained on some of the windmills in the first edition

The idea of committing this information to paper came during various talks on both wind and water mills that I have given to local historical and other groups when I was asked - 'Where can I read about these Derbyshire windmills?' The simple answer was – 'Nowhere!'

This book therefore seeks to rectify this and to make the results of my quest available to all. I generally limit the contents to post 1750, because prior to that the trail is much more diffuse. After some preliminary descriptive text the surviving complete mills are described, followed by the sites where there are remains to be seen, and finally the windmills that have now totally disappeared are considered.

The locations are given in terms of the nearest town, village or parish, as appropriate, and where possible, the National Grid Reference for the actual site is included. Where this has not been established, the reference refers to the approximate centre of the town etc. In every case there is a short description of the location of the windmill relative to major local habitations. The book concludes with a list of field names and other references to mills that may provide a basis for further investigation.

It was very gratifying that the first edition of this book was quickly sold out, with profits being used by Midland Mills Group to finance mill restoration work. The restoration to working order of Heage windmill has, however, greatly added to the interest in 'molinology' within the county, and Midland Mills Group, in association with Heage Windmill Society, felt the demand existed for a reprint. Profits will continue to be used for mill restoration and maintenance.

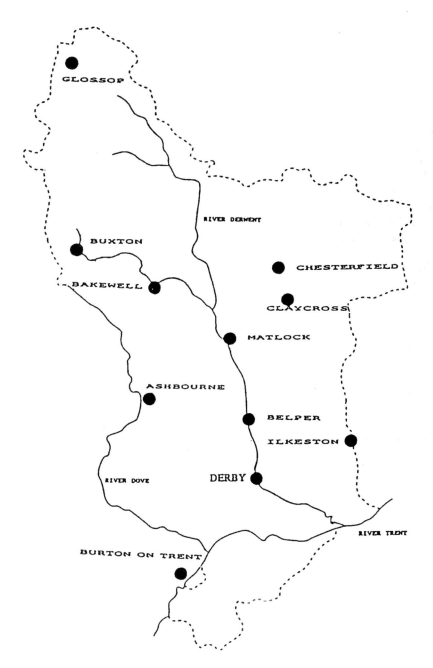

The Main Towns of Derbyshire Between 1750-1900.

THE DISTRIBUTION & STATUS OF WINDMILLS IN DERBYSHIRE

Unlike counties such as Norfolk, Suffolk, Kent and Cambridgeshire, Derbyshire has apparently little to offer in the way of a windmill heritage, but research has shown that this was not always the case. It is a medium sized county in a very central position in Great Britain which occupies approximately 2640 square kilometres (1016 square miles), stretching a maximum of 94 kilometres north to south and 58 kilometres east to west. There are three distinct regions, each with significantly different characteristics, as follows: -

1) The Peak District, which stretches roughly from Ashbourne across to Cromford and up to the Northern boundary of the county. This is an area of both limestone and millstone grit hills, with the River Derwent, flowing approximately north to south down the centre of the county, served by many tributaries. The milling requirement of this area was dominated by waterpower, with few windmills being present.

2) The Chesterfield Area, covers roughly from Cromford north and east to the county boundaries. In this area there was much mining and industry but, growing on the rolling countryside, were many crops which needed milling. The area was served by a mixture of both wind and water mills.

3) The Trent Valley, which is described as the area to the south of Ashbourne through which the Rivers Trent and Derwent flow, merging at Sawley. The River Dove meanders down the western county boundary to join the River Trent at Claymills and this largely flat and agricultural area was again served by many wind and water mills.

There were 81 mills and 10 sites identified in the county at the time of the Domesday Survey, however these must all have been water mills, since the windmill has not been recorded until after 1085 A.D., when the survey was completed. The number of water mills clearly increased significantly over the years, and from the late twelfth century, these were supplemented by windmills. Some horse and other animal mills were used in the county, and one was built in Derby as late as 1786. There are records of windmills in Derbyshire dating back to the 1600s or earlier and many cases of field names throughout the county, such as 'Windmill Close', for which we have no clear records of the mills themselves, or they may have been fields owned by a miller and not been the actual site of a windmill.

The main period for the building of windmills in the county appears to have been in the years 1780 to about 1835, with more limited numbers built after that date and with construction ceasing well before the turn of the nineteenth century.
The last known mills to be built were the twin towers known as 'James' and 'Sarah', at Riddings, which were erected in 1877.

Although some referenced contemporary newspaper reports refer to 'smock' mills these have all been identified as being tower mills. At the end of the eighteenth and in the early nineteenth century it seems therefore that the term 'smock mill' was commonly used to describe tower mills in this county. No evidence of the presence of a smock corn mill, i.e. of essentially wooden construction, has been identified.

Burdett's map of the county, dated 1767, shows 10 windmills in the county, whilst John Farey in 1808, listed a total of 45 windmills, referring to them as 'the main mills' (See Page 12). Greenwood's map of 1825 locates more than 40 but misses out some known to have been present at that time, in particular at Dale Abbey and Carsington.

Windmills, of course, require the wind to be blowing in order that they can operate and this in turn means that, since they are therefore always built on high ground or in open situations, they were exposed to the full fury of storms and gales. As a result numerous mills were lost or badly damaged during periods of severe weather, and rebuilding on existing sites was a common practice. Fire was also an ever-present hazard and many were destroyed or damaged with spontaneous combustion a continual source of concern. As a result of both the elements and fire the total number of mills at any one time was always changing and the actual peak number is difficult to determine.

The decline in the number of windmills took place steadily through the second half of the 19th century, probably largely affected by the increasing number of steam and roller mills, which offered much greater economy and which were often situated at ports to process imported corn. Using maps it is possible to follow the decline of the windmill in the county: the Ordnance Survey Map in 1880 shows there were 26 working windmills but this had fallen to only 9 when the 1895-98 edition was published.

Unlike many other counties, Derbyshire has not retained many of its windmills to the present time. In 2003 we have only two more or less complete Windmills left in the county: Heage and Dale Abbey; five windmills which have been converted into houses; and five stumps or ruins of tower and post mills.

WINDMILL LOCATIONS IN DERBYSHIRE

Complete Mills

DALE ABBEY* **HEAGE**

Significant Remains

BELPER	**BOLSOVER**	CARSINGTON	FINDERN*
FRITCHLEY	MELBOURNE	OCKBROOK	S. NORMANTON (2)
SPANCARR*			

Mills That Have Disappeared

ALDERWASLEY ALFRETON (2) ASHBOURNE (2)
BEIGHTON BELPH BOLSOVER* BORROWASH BREADSALL
CALOW CHELLASTON (2)*
CHESTERFIELD (3) *CLAY CROSS* CLOWNE*
CODNOR *CRESWELL* *CRICH (2)* DERBY (3)*
ECKINGTON EYAM* *HAZELWOOD* HOLBROOK
HORSLEY PARK *HULLAND* ILKESTON (2)
KILBURN KIRK IRETON LONG EATON* LOSCOE
MAPPERLEY MARLPOOL MELBOURNE MICKLEOVER*
MOSSBOROUGH MUGGINTON NETHERSEAL
NEWHALL NITTICAR HILL PLEASLEY
RIDDINGS (3) RIPLEY RISLEY SANDIACRE*
SAWLEY SHARDLOW SHIPLEY **SHIREBROOK**
SMALLEY SMISBY S. NORMANTON (2)
SPINKHILL* SPONDON *SWATHICK* *SWARKSTONE LOWES*
TEMPLE NORMANTON TIBSHELF WEST HALLAM
WHITWELL* *WILLINGTON* WHITTINGTON
WIRKSWORTH WOODVILLE

Summary

COMPLETE	2
REMAINS	10
DISAPPEARED	72
TOTAL	84

Legend to 2nd Edition

BOLD, ITALIC	-	NEW ADDITION
BOLD	-	MAJOR REWRITE
STARRED *	-	AMENDMENTS

6

SUMMARY & STATUS OF COMPLETE WINDMILLS & WINDMILL REMAINS IN DERBYSHIRE 2003

LOCATION	GRID Ref. (SK)	STATUS
Belper	353478	House conversion of tower mill (early 20th C.) with castellated top.
Bolsover	472712	Ruined stone tower, in very poor condition. Doors blocked up, no floors or cap, wooden upright shaft visible through window openings
Carsington	252545	Partially bricked up limestone tower, two courses of grit stone below curb level, no cap.
Dale Abbey	437398	Complete post mill, Grade 2* listed, brick built Midlands type round house, four spring sails, no shutters, all machinery in place.
Findern	302307	House conversion of tower mill (late 19th C.).
Fritchley	365532	Stone round house from post mill, holes in wall through which cross trees were removed.
Heage	367507	Fully restored (2002) ironstone tower mill, Grade 2* listed, six sails, shutters, two pairs of stones.
Melbourne	378245	Brick tower mill shell, concrete 'observation' platform replaces cap, no access.
Ockbrook	429357	One floor only of brick tower mill survives, no roof, used as store area.
South Normanton (1)	441569	Recent house conversion (1996), with additional, built on, living accommodation.
South Normanton (2)	442562	House conversion (late 19th C.) of small tower mill.
Spancarr	342660	Recent house conversion (1996) with conical, six sided roof. Kiln remains incorporated in building.

TOTAL – two complete windmills and ten with significant remains.
'**significant**' - arbitrarily defined as having more than 3 feet of structure standing.

THE DESIGN & DEVELOPMENT OF WINDMILLS

A post mill built in the nineteenth century was almost identical in concept to those built in the twelfth century. In fact the basic construction of windmills remained almost constant throughout that time although many refinements, such as fantails which automatically turned the mill to face into the wind and devices which regulated the sails with varying wind power, were introduced through the years.

The post mill is normally much smaller than the tower and smock windmills, having as a maximum two pairs of stones against as many as six pairs of stones in a large tower mill.

The post mill is a wooden box-like structure on which are mounted the sails and which is turned to face into the wind by a long tailpole projecting from the rear of the mill. The box is supported at its centre of gravity on a large cross timber, called the crown tree, by the upright post. This post is in turn held in place on two large cross timbers, called the cross trees, and maintained in a vertical position by four struts or quarter bars which then transfer the entire load equally to four stone plinths at their ends, beneath the cross trees. The actual process of turning the mill may be done by the miller himself, by setting a ring of posts round the mill and using these to attach a winding device using a chain and rope, but sometimes by attaching an animal such as a donkey to the pole. Turning the entire structure was a slow and tiresome business and, being made with many exposed timbers, the post mill was easily damaged or rotted by the elements. It was however a relatively cheap and 'portable' structure which could be sold to the highest bidder and moved to another location.

Some time in the fifteenth century the tower mill was invented, possibly in the Aegean area. In this type of mill the main component is a vertical cylinder-like structure made of brick or stone. This is of course, stationary, but on its top edge sits a cap or roof which carries the windshaft onto which is mounted the sails. The complete cap and sails assembly can be turned into the wind as a complete unit, independent of the tower. The cap rotates on a track or kerb and horizontal wheels, running on the inside surface of the tower, are often used to keep it centred. The cap and sails are held in place by their own weight. They can be turned by a number of methods, chosen by the builder of the mill. These include a long pole, attached to the cap, reaching down to the ground level, which was pushed or pulled by an internal winch, or by an endless chain to ground level, passing over a drive connected to an internal rack gear at the top of the tower, which would drive the cap round.

These methods of turning the cap were often replaced by a fantail; an automatic cap rotation device, which was invented by Edmund Lee in 1744/45. He fitted to the cap a device, known as a fan, which rotated in the wind, and which is connected by gearing to a track on the top of the tower kerb. The fan is 8 to 10 feet in diameter and has eight, ten or more blades. If there is no wind the fan remains still and the cap remains stationary. When the wind catches the fan blades at an angle, the fan rotates until it is in line with the wind, when it ceases to turn.

In so doing the cap and sails are slowly turned such that the sails face into the wind. Fantails may also be used to turn post mills, but there is no evidence of this application in Derbyshire. Originally the sails were known as 'common' and consisted of a light wooden framework upon which the sailcloth could be adjusted by tapering the end, to form a sword or dagger-like point. The mill had to be stopped and each sail set individually, a difficult and slow task in bad weather or high winds.

In 1772 Andrew Meikle developed another important invention - the spring sail, which enabled each sail to be set in a matter of a few moments - a matter of concern when economics of the operation was important. The spring sail consisted of a series of canvas-covered shutters, individually hinged at the ends, which were connected together through cranks to a rod running the length of the sail. When the rod moved, all the shutters opened and closed together. At one end of the rod was a large helical spring, the tension of which could be adjusted by means of a lever at the extreme end of the sail. The tension is adjusted such that the sails 'spill' the wind through if it gets too strong. This can be done in a few moments although the mill still has to cease operation whilst each sail is moved to the ground level in order to reach the lever. The shuttered sail is somewhat less efficient than the common sail and many mills adopted the compromise between efficiency and convenience - they fitted two common and two spring sails.

A further development in sail technology was the invention in 1807 by William Cubitt (later Sir William), of the patent sail. As its name implies this was protected by letters patent in the British Isles. Patent sails used shutters, similar to those in spring sails but with a significant improvement. The shutters on each sail are connected by a rod joined to a 'bell crank' assembly in the centre of the sails. The wind shaft was drilled down through its central axis to provide a longitudinal hole along its length, through which a metal 'striker' rod passes and which is connected to the bell crank assembly. When the rod through the windshaft is moved in or out, the sails are opened or closed. For the first time all the sails could be adjusted at the same time, without stopping the mill operating. Further innovations included the addition of weights to a chain hanging from the tail end of the striker rod. By adjusting the weights, it became possible to set the mechanism to allow the shutters to open if the wind became too strong for safety, but to remain closed if the wind was at a lower strength. With the combination of the fantail and patent sails, the operation of the windmill became much more automatic, making it possible to work many more productive hours when conditions were favourable.

Most tower mills in this country had four sails but a few exist with five, six or eight sails. Heage windmill is a fine local example of one with six sails. Four sailed mills can continue to work with only two sails remaining, whilst six sailed mills can work at lower output with two, three or four sails. Five sailed mills must stop work if one sail is damaged. Only one eight sailed mill remains, at Heckington in Lincolnshire.
There were never many of them, possibly because they produced more power than was needed or because maintenance costs were high. Almost without exception, post mills were only fitted with four sails.

The mechanisms inside the mill are the result of many years of development and the basic arrangements are similar in all mills. The wind shaft, made of wood or cast iron, carries a large toothed wheel known as the brake wheel, around the circumference of which is a large metal band brake, applied by moving a rope operated lever from the floors below. The wind shaft is inclined at about 8 to 15 degrees to the horizontal and via an iron pintle, fits into a journal (or bearing) that takes the thrust and axial loads of the sails. On small mills the brake wheel drives a single pair of stones through another toothed gear called the stone nut. On larger mills a wallower is mounted at the top of a large upright shaft which may pass through several floors to the stone floor, depending on the size of the mill. On the stone floor another gear wheel called the great spur wheel fits on the upright shaft and drives two, three or four pairs of stones through yet other gears called stone nuts. In some small mills another gear wheel, similar to the brake wheel, is fixed at the tail end of the wind shaft and this can be used to drive another pair of stones. Provision is always made for the stones to be put out of gear.

The stones, which are about 36 to 60 inches diameter and which weigh up to a ton each, are mounted in a wooden casing, or vat. Only the upper, or runner, stone rotates, driven by the quant, (stone drive spindle), on which the stone nut is mounted. The separation of the stones is sometimes regulated by a centrifugal governor, which by a series of levers, raises or lowers the upper stone and allows the fineness of the flour to be regulated. This arrangement allows the mill to continue to operate in the optimum manner, regardless of changes in the power or speed of the wind.

Corn is fed, either directly or from bins on the floor above, into a hopper to which a chute or shoe is attached, and which is mounted above the vat. The corn moves slowly down the chute, vibrated by direct contact with a square stone drive spindle, known as the damsel, and falls at a constant rate into the eye, or central hole of the upper stone. By changing the angle of the chute, the amount of grain falling can be regulated. A simple automatic device tells the miller when the hopper is getting empty. This works by a slack leather strap, nailed across the inside of the hopper at one end and attached to a string and bell at the other. Whilst there is grain pressing on the leather the string is kept tight and the bell is silent but when the level falls, the strap moves and the bell rings, alerting the miller that more grain must be added.

Other devices may be used to clean or dress the grain and flour produced, or to raise the sacks of grain to the top of the mill prior to grinding, but the interested reader is advised to seek further information elsewhere. (See Bibliography). There is however little doubt that the hard experience gained by millwrights over the centuries, in constructing both wind and water mills, provided them with the essential knowledge that enabled them to meet the demands of the Industrial Revolution in the 18th century.

DERBYSHIRE WINDMILLS AS SEEN BY JAMES FAREY IN 1808

We are indeed fortunate that a notable traveller and agriculturist of the early years of the 19th century, James Farey, visited Derbyshire and, as part of his impression of the county as a whole, included notes on contemporary wind and water mills in a book published in 1813 entitled 'Agriculture & Minerals of Derbyshire'. Seen from the eyes of this agriculturist he was convinced that water mills were 'a dreadful nuisance' and suggests that 'the damage done to adjoining land in flatter counties by water abstraction much exceeds the gross rental of the mills'. He admits that in Derbyshire less damage is caused because of the generally rapid fall in the valleys, but also because of the practice of placing a weir across the river or brook course, and taking the water to the mill via a goit or feeder, controlled by a sluice or shuttle.

We do not however gain much information on the windmills of the county. He simply comments that 'some are of considerable dimensions'. He does however give the names of 45 mills, which were said to be working at that time and which are listed in the following Table. This list is of great value to the molinologist in that many of the place names can be readily related to available records, although in some cases nothing now remains, or has been traced.

The windmill list was made in 1808, and of the windmills listed, eight: Alderwasley, Clowne, Heanor, Knitaker, Smithsby, South Normanton, Spinkhill and West Hallam were shown on Burdett's map of the county, published in 1791, but which was surveyed over the period 1762 to 1767. Karl Wood however painted or drew 12 of the listed mills during the 1930s. (See Page 14).

Farey's section on mills concludes by reporting on the appearance of steam driven mills in the county. In those early days of steam engines they were generally being used as auxiliaries to watermills during the summer, when water was in short supply. He gives examples of such mills being at Blackwell (Park Mill), Dronfield, Measham, Mosborough, Pinxton, Wirksworth, etc. He also notes that the flourmill at Measham was built by the late Joseph Wilkes and was used at night, powered by the same engine which, in the day time, worked a cotton mill.

Steam power was soon added to some windmills to enable them to work when the wind was not blowing, so Farey clearly saw the start of the steam power revolution. In a few short years, steam made the wind and water mills relics of the past, and brought to a close the long dependence on these power sources for the provision of flour and other cereals.

In the subsequent text reference is made to 'Farey' where a particular windmill was included in his listing.

DERBYSHIRE WINDMILLS LISTED BY J. FAREY IN 1808

ALDERWASLEY	ALFRETON	ASHBOURNE	BELPER
BELPH	BELSOVER	BREDSALL	CALOW
CHELLASTON	CHESTERFIELD	CLOWN	CODNOR
DALE	HEAGE	HEANOR	HOSELEY
ILKESTON (2)	KIBURNE	KNITAKER	LONG EATON
LOSCO	MELBOURNE (2)	MICKELOVER	NEWBOLD
NEW BRAMPTON	NEWHALL	OCKBROOK	PINXTON
PLESEY	RIPLEY	RISELY	SHIPLEY
SMALLEY	SPANCAR	SMITHSBY	S. NORMANTON
SPINKHILL	SWATHICK	T. NORMANTON	TIBSHELF
WEST HALLAM	WHITTINGTON	WIRKSWORTH	
			TOTAL 45

'Early C19th millwright at work'

'Views of Rural Occupations - 1807'. W. H. Pyne. Published by Dover.

12

THE KARL WOOD PAINTINGS OF DERBYSHIRE WINDMILLS

Karl Wood was born in 1888 in Nottingham. He moved to Gainsborough in Lincolnshire shortly after the 1914-18 war, and continued to live there for over 30 years. He became an art Master at Gainsborough Grammar School and was the organist and choirmaster at the local church. He undertook a wide variety of artistic commissions, some of which can still be seen in the area.

He clearly had a great obsession with windmills and travelled widely, sketching and painting them as he saw them. His first known mill painting was in 1926 and he continued to paint a total of 1394 windmills, 88% of which were painted in the 1930's. For example, in the August school holidays of 1933 he painted 84, of which only one was in Derbyshire. On some days he painted 6 to 9 mills up to 20 miles apart! The 1930s must have been very rewarding to a mill enthusiast, since many mills were still working.

The quality of the paintings varies enormously; some being excellent and detailed, whilst others are quite poor, lacking any detail. He painted a total of 21 windmills in Derbyshire between 1931 and 1940 most of which are of an acceptable quality.(See Table overleaf). He left Gainsborough in 1951 and retired to Morayshire in Scotland where he died in 1958.

Reference is made to his paintings, where they exist, in the gazetteer section of this book.

Viewing is now by arrangement with: -

The Keeper of Collections
Lincolnshire Museums
Usher Art Gallery
Lindum Road
Lincoln
Telephone 01552 527980

DERBYSHIRE WINDMILLS PAINTED BY KARL WOOD
1931 TO 1940

PARISH	GRID REF.	DATE PAINTED	USHER REF.
Ashover (Spancarr)	SK 3563	12. 05. 38	77. 1856
Bolsover	SK4771	07. 04. 32	77. 924
Carsington	SK2554	27. 12. 32	77. 745
Dale Abbey	SK 4063	11. 04. 32	77. 933
Findern	SK 3130	08. 04. 32	77. 926
Fritchley	SK 3653	09. 04. 32	77. 929
Heage	SK 3750	27. 12. 32	77. 1210
Mapperley	SK 4343	11. 04. 32	77. 932
Melbourne	SK 3724	08. 04. 32	77. 758
Mickleover	SK31 34	08. 04. 32	77. 925
Ockbrook	SK 4236	11. 04. 32	77. 934
Somercotes (Riddings) (3 Mills)			
a) West Mill	SK 4253	09. 04. 32	77. 930
b) East Mill		29. 06. 39	77. 1959
c) Leabrooks		17. 04. 40	77. 2014
South Normanton	SK4457	? . 11. 31	77. 841
South Normanton	SK 4457	26. 06. 39	77. 840
Spinkhill	SK4578	24. 08. 33	77. 1396
Swarkeston (Chellaston)	SK 3728	08. 04. 32	77. 928
Temple Normanton	SK 4267	05. 07. 34	77. 1472
West Hallam	SK 4341	19. 04. 32	77. 931
Whitwell	SK 5376	07. 04. 32	77. 923

Karl Wood's Childhood in Derbyshire

The paintings and drawings of Karl Wood perhaps owe something to his early childhood in Derbyshire. His grandfather, Timothy Wood, came from Lincolnshire and his youngest son John Radford Wood, became a market gardener in Melbourne, in the south of the county. There he married a Harriet Salsbury, and they settled in nearby Kings Newton.

Karl was born in August 1888, although there is no record he was ever baptised. It is therefore possible to speculate that during his many wanderings around the countryside and the lanes to the south of the small market town, that he saw the tower windmill at Melbourne and the impression this left with him led to him, in his later life, undertaking the mammoth task of painting or drawing all the then standing windmills in the country.

THE SURVIVING WINDMILLS OF DERBYSHIRE

Derbyshire is fortunate, despite having few surviving windmills or even many remains, to still have one of the finest post mills in the country, known as the 'Cat and Fiddle Windmill', at Dale Abbey, near to Derby. A tall post mill mounted on a Midlands type round house, it has suffered many reversals in fortune, but despite this, it still serves to remind us of the many post mills which stood in the county.

To the north of Belper, the village of Heage is proud to have its own tower mill, a little to the north west of the village centre. This squat, six-sailed, stone tower mill has been recently restored and dominates the skyline of the area.

DALE ABBEY, (Grade 2* Listed)   SK 437398

The village of Dale Abbey is about seven miles north east of Derby, some two miles from Ilkeston. It is well known for the spectacular remains of its Abbey, as well as for its Grade 2 listed post mill which stands on a rounded hill top about 100 yards north of the A 6096. The origin of the name, 'Cat and Fiddle', is not clear.

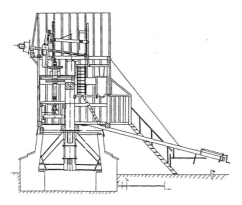

A Sectional view of Dale Abbey post mill.

The actual date the mill was built is unclear, although carved in an upper cross tree is the date 1788. This may be the date when the mill was built but it also could have been made from a piece of wood from an earlier mill, since it was common practice to use timber from old mills.

It was offered for sale in the Derby Mercury of 14th April 1830 as follows: -

> 'Post mill in good repair and full working order at Dale Abbey - for further details contact Mrs. Buckland, the owner. The mill, with everything attached to it, will be sold and the materials taken away if the consent of the landlord cannot be obtained for occupation before 25th March next.'

The mill must have been sold and the necessary consent obtained since the same post mill still stands in Dale Abbey.

It was initially built on a mound on top of the hill, as an open trestle construction. The sandstone roundhouse was added in 1841 to provide additional storage capacity. There are four external buttresses into which the cross trees protrude. The floor of the round house is below ground level such that free access can be obtained under the cross trees. It was eventually converted, at a date unknown, into a Midland type post mill - that is the lower edge of the buck structure runs on small iron wheels on a track on the top edge of the round house, affording much greater stability. In 1912 the mill was purchased by Stanton Iron Works Co Ltd. - later Stanton and Staveley - and for many years was ably maintained by them, often using their apprentice labour for the work. In 1941, Rex Wailes presented the Windmill Certificate of SPAB to the company, in recognition of their great efforts to preserve the mill.

The wooden cross trees are 14' x 14" and 14' x 12" and the junction with the four quarter bars have all been recently reinforced with steel plates and angle sections.
The main post is 21" diameter at the crown tree and blends out until it is 29" square at the horned base. The mill is turned into the wind by a winch on the tail pole the rope of which was, until about 1987, attached to a circle of equally spaced vertical posts around the mill. In 1994, these had been replaced by steel rings which were set into concrete in the ground. There are four sprung sails which are fully shuttered and which are 6' 9" wide at the tip and are mounted on 6" square stocks. These are carried on a cast iron wind shaft and are mounted in poll ends, 12' x 10", with a 4" diameter knob on the front for lifting purposes. The neck journal is made of granite. The wooden 7' 4" diameter brake wheel has recently been replaced following the tailwinding of the mill in 1987.

The drive to the stones is through a cast iron wallower with 22 teeth, via the wooden upright shaft which varies in diameter from 12" down to 9 ½". The iron great spur wheel has 48 teeth at 3¼" pitch, which drive onto the stone nuts, which have 20 wooden teeth. The stones are mounted on a hurst frame in the front of the mill. There are one pair of peak stones and one pair of French Burrs, each 4' 8" in diameter, and these can be regulated either by hand tentering or by centrifugal governors. The sack hoist, used to lift sacks of corn to the top of the mill, operates from a friction drive running on the inside of the brake wheel rim. A wire flour dressing machine, which carries the marks '**I N 1804**' is in an extension to the tail of the mill, and is driven from the brake wheel by a spur pinion at one side of the buck, via shafting. The flour produced was weighed on a steelyard, with a wooden beam, into the top of which is let a steel notched plate to locate the sliding weight.

A painting of the mill by Karl Wood in 1932 shows it as a complete and well cared for structure. It worked regularly up to almost the end of the Second World War when the drive to a pair of stones broke and was not repaired until after the war. The miller's name in 1857 was David Cotton but in Kelly's Directory, 1875, the miller is named as Stephen Smedley.

The mill was to remain in the Smedley family until it ceased commercial operation. It finally ceased to operate in 1952 on the death of the last miller, Stephen's son, George Smedley. His widow, Marjorie, continued to tend the mill she loved for many more years. The windmill, which was by now owned by the British Steel Corporation, was put up for sale by tender in 1982 and passed into private ownership once again, together with the adjacent mill cottage, at a price said to be about £30,000.

On the 27th March, 1987, at 2.15 pm, in violent north-west gales, the mill was tail winded and the brake wheel and windshaft blown out of the front of the buck. The brake wheel, which was already rather rotten, was smashed into pieces, as were the four spring sails, whilst the buck and other parts of the structure suffered considerable damage. With the aid of grants the owner, Mr Richardson, slowly toiled over several years to rebuild the mill and eventually, in 1993, the work was completed. The mill was again opened to the public on National Mills Day, May 1994, and can be visited by the public. The mill stands on private property, but prior arrangements to visit it may sometimes be made by writing to the owner, Mr. Richardson.

In January 1995 the wind once again damaged the mill and two sails were blown off although the stocks held fast. She stood in this condition for a number of years, but at the end of 2002, she has been repaired again, although no shutters have been fitted. The repainted sails gleam in the sunlight, but it is not known if the mill is operational.

The Cat and Fiddle post mill at Dale Abbey on National Mills Day, 1994.

HEAGE, (Grade 2* listed)   SK 367507

Standing in a very striking position, on the brow of a hill overlooking Nether Heage, some two miles to the north east of Belper, is a stone tower mill.

The squat building, of local ironstone, is 24 feet in diameter and has a stone plaque by the entrance door marked **'WSM 1850'**, the significance of which is not clear. The mill is built on a small mound and an entrance below could have enabled carts to back right into the building for loading and unloading. The first indication of the mill is in an advertisement for a tradesman in The Derby Mercury of 16th June 1791: -

> 'Heage windmill to be erected, any mason inclined to undertake the stone building to attend at the mill, all materials laid down in place.'

Soon after, on 20th September 1798: -

> 'To be let - complete smock mill with fantail, two pairs of stones, good dressing machine - made to plans approved by Mr. Wass - standing in good situation at Heage.'

Mr. Wass may well be a member of the Wass family that operated South Normanton post mill for many years.

The mill was advertised in the Derby Mercury in 1816, offering for lease in Heage 'a dwelling house, a smock mill and four acres of land'. However, tower mills were commonly called smock mills in Derbyshire (see Belper for comment on this). Particular note should be taken of the above request made in 1791 for a mason to build the mill. This must change the, often expressed, opinion that the 1850 date on the door pillars represented the date the mill was built.

There was a small stone building alongside the mill, which was used for the kiln although the roof had fallen in during the 1960s. One report suggests that a woman who entered the kiln to turn the corn was burnt to death when her clothes caught fire!

In 1850 the brothers Isaac and Joseph Shore purchased the mill, trading as millers and grocers. No clear photographs or paintings pre-1894 have been identified. One photograph, probably dated about 1870, shows the water mill and steam mills which were owned by the Shores, nestling in the valley, whilst right on the edge of the picture is the windmill, at that time fitted with four sails. Careful examination of this, and of the debris visible around the mill in the photograph taken after she was tail winded in 1894, suggests that the original mill probably had a boat shaped cap, similar to the one on Ockbrook mill, which is illustrated on page 33.

Note: The photograph referred to in the first edition of this book, which shows a windmill with an Ogee cap, had been wrongly attributed to Heage. It was in fact Belper windmill.

The old four sail tower mill at Heage was tail winded in 1894.

When the rebuild was commenced it was decided to replace the four sails with six patent sails, presumably to obtain more power, although in other respects the mill was externally similar. The work was carried out by George Chell, a millwright from the nearby village of Crich. A house there carries a plaque bearing his name and trade. The windshaft and the six-arm iron cross were cast by the Butterley Company of Ripley and were fitted out with six patent sails. The new ogee cap, complete with a ball finial was made by a local carpenter, George Spendlove, of Heage. The 20' 2" diameter ogee cap turns to face into the wind on an iron curb supported on 24 cast iron wheels and is maintained centrally by 6 truck wheels running on the edge of the curb track.

The brake wheel is of wooden clasp arm construction and had 60 wooden teeth at a pitch of 4¾". The circular wooden upright shaft of 15" diameter at the top and 17" at the bottom, drives the iron wallower which has 45 teeth. The Great Spur Wheel originally had 70 cogs at 3" pitch, in two staggered rows. The reason for this most unusual feature is not clear but whatever it was, the cogs had been sawn off long ago and replaced by sections of iron teeth, bolted onto the wooden framework, which have now disappeared. There are two pairs of 5' peak stones with conventional wooden vat etc. The stones are mounted on cast iron tentering arms, manually adjusted.

In the cellar there were three brick columns that were added about 1910 to provide additional support to the floor beams and machinery in the mill above.

Note: Following the insertion of new ground floor beams in the 1970s restoration, these became redundant and have subsequently been removed.

The mill continued to be in regular use until 1919, operated by Joseph and Enoch Shore, the sons of Thomas, and later by T. J. (Tom) Shore. It worked in conjunction with the nearby water and steam mills in the valley to the west of the windmill, which were under the same ownership.

In 1919 the fantail was severely damaged in a gale, most of the blades being lost. The damage was serious and presumably in line with the economic situation of mills at that time, the mill closed down. It became almost derelict, drawings and photographs in the 1930's showing it with the sail bars hanging down in a totally neglected manner. A report in the Derby Evening Telegraph in 1934 reports that the mill was up for sale by auction and includes a contemporary photograph showing that the fantail was missing and that the sails were not complete. Care was needed, it was said, when entering the mill because some of the floors were rotten. The view, taken from the nearby road, shows the adjacent Windmill Cottage and mill standing in an area completely devoid of the trees and vegetation that presently surround the site. Karl Wood painted the mill in 1932, standing without the fantail and with the derelict kiln alongside.

The wreck of Heage windmill in 1967, prior to restoration by
Derbyshire County Council.

It was struck by lightning in 1961, and a photograph in 1967 shows only the remnants of the sails and a stub where the fantail and its staging had been. Derbyshire County Council placed a preservation order upon the mill by in 1966, and they later became the owners.

Heage tower mill after restoration in 1972.

Over the next few years, the millwrights, Thompsons of Alford in Lincolnshire, carried out restoration work. New floors, sails cap and fantail at a cost of £7,500 were made. The new sails were hoisted on the 15th March 1972 and a skeleton fantail without any boarding was fitted.

Two sails were replaced in 1997 but shutters were not fitted at this time. Close examination of the structure had revealed serious problems, with erosion of the stonework, especially on the west side, and water ingress into the mill, occurring regularly through the cap and around the curb.

Through the early 1990s members of the Midland Wind and Watermills Group carried out some essential maintenance work and painting to try and stem the decay, but they soon realised that a major programme of work was required.

21

Local people became involved and an informal group, then known as 'The Friends of Heage Windmill' was formed in late 1995, leading to the establishment of a more formal steering group, 'The Heage Windmill Society' (HWS) in May 1996. They entered into a partnership with Derbyshire County Council and other local councils with the objective of restoring the mill back to working order. To further this aim HWS then sought and obtained charitable status in 1997, reforming the 'Friends' as a separate, but supporting body, to operate the mill.

The vat and hopper prior to the 2002 restoration.

In parallel with this, the mill was carefully surveyed, both inside and out, and a work programme for a full restoration was developed and costed. With this data to hand applications were made to The Heritage Lottery Fund, English Heritage, WREN (Waste and Environmental), and other bodies for grants for the work. Match funding was pledged by many organisations. Meanwhile the 'Friends' volunteered significant labour input and embarked on an extensive fund-raising programme, whilst Heage Windmill Society itself operated a major sponsorship campaign. Eventually, in 1999, notice was received of sufficient grants being awarded for the work to be able to start. Legal problems associated with a new access route from Chesterfield Road, flooding, and then the national outbreak of foot and mouth disease put all on hold. However contracts for the millwright works were let to Dorothea Restorations, and to Beighton Constructions for the building works, the total cost of the work at the mill being in excess of £380,000

Eventually, on the 10th July 2001 the cap was lifted off. The masonry of the tower was then refurbished. The remains of the old kiln were rebuilt and have been fitted out as a visitor centre.

In parallel the cap was stripped and rebuilt in the traditional manner, the aluminium covering being scrapped, whilst the internal machinery was overhauled and realigned, including a major rebuild of the great spur wheel. Here the wooden structure was reinforced and new cast iron gear segments were fitted, to mesh with the stone nuts. The wooden brake wheel was also strengthened, and cast iron segments to mesh with the existing wallower gear, were bolted on. Meanwhile volunteers from the Friends of Heage Windmill manufactured 24 new roller assemblies on which the cap turns and also made 129 new shutters (including some spares) for the sails. They also carried out major landscaping, dry-stone walling, and site clearance work, all during the very wet winter of 2001-2.

The cap was refitted on March 11th and the sails were returned on April 24th, complete with a full complement of 126 shutters. The basement of the mill had meanwhile been refurbished and converted into an interpretation centre, with a display showing the story of the mill. The completed mill was formally opened on May 27th 2002, by TV personality Kathy Rochford, and soon after visitors began to arrive to see the only working windmill in the county. In the near future it is planned to mill corn.

The old access route to the mill, past the miller's cottage, has now been closed permanently.

During the winter of 2002/3 the sack hoist was repaired and a new flour dresser was purchased and installed on the meal floor as a preliminary to milling flour at Heage, after a lapse of 84 years.

Heage Windmill is now open to the public every weekend and Bank Holiday from April to October. More details can be obtained by phoning the windmill on 01773 853579.

General note on the terms 'smock' and 'tower' mills in Derbyshire.

The above 18th century advertisement refers to the sale of a 'smock mill'. Smock mills are very similar in construction to tower mills including the provision of a cap which can luff (or turn) to present just the sails into the wind. The significant difference is that the main constructional material is wood, not brick or stone. No mills, other than post mills, which were made substantially of wood, have been recognised in Derbyshire during this research.

Clearly, since the mill at Findern is still standing and is a brick tower mill, the terms 'smock.' and 'tower' appear to have been interchangeable in the county during the 18th and early part of 19th century. Examples of this usage, other than at Findern, are demonstrated in adverts relating to Belper (1801) and Bolsover (1799 and 1821) etc.

THE REMAINS OF WINDMILLS IN DERBYSHIRE

Scattered throughout the county are the remains of some of the once proud windmills that dominated the skyline in past years. In order to describe them as 'remains' an arbitrary decision has been made that this description would only apply when some part of the actual mill structure can be recognised. Using this definition therefore there are 12 sites where all or part of the main structure of a windmill can be recognised. There are other sites, Netherseal, for instance, where the hedge enclosure for the post mill and a few fragments of millstones can be recognised. At Eyam the site of the tower mill demolished in 1877 is still marked by a pile of stones from the tower that have been used to form a raised flowerbed.

A tour of these 'windmill remainder' sites will take the reader into some of the very attractive locations in the county.

BELPER   SK 353478

The market town of Belper is on the A6, about 7 miles north of Derby and is more famous for the Strutt's Cotton Mills which were driven by water power than for windmills.

There was a tower windmill however, high above the town, off Windmill Lane, which was built in 1796 and which ground the corn for the town. In 1801 it was offered to let (Derby Mercury) as follows: -

> 'To be let, Smock wind mill, almost new, two pairs of stones, dressing machine, apply Samuel Linam, Heage'

Note the use of the word 'smock' to describe this tower mill. (see previous for comment).

An old undated print of Strutt's North mill at Belper, shows the windmill high on the skyline, isolated from the houses of the town. A blurred photograph, taken prior to 1891, shows the mill to be similar to the one situated close by at Heage. This photograph shows it to be a squat tower mill with three floors, a dark ogee cap and a fantail and staging. Like many mills it had two common sails, the canvas of which is wrapped round the stocks, and two spring sails. This system was often adopted as a compromise between cost of installation and the speed of setting the sails.

The mill was listed by Farey in 1808, and appears on Greenwood's map of 1825, but surprisingly does not appear on the Ordnance Survey map of 1839. An advertisement in the Derby Mercury in 1851 informs that the mill was equipped with a pair of French and a pair of Derbyshire stones, a flour machine and a drying kiln. In White's Directory for 1857 the miller was Daniel Morrell. The 1884 Ordnance Survey map shows the mill to be disused, and in 1891 all the machinery was removed and the tower was converted into a house, which is still occupied.

A recent visit to the site showed the mill to be about 24' diameter at the base, to be painted white and with a castellated brick top, but no cap.

The owner confirmed that 'apart from a few heavy beams' there was no equipment remaining inside the building.

Belper tower mill as a house conversion in 1994.

BOLSOVER **SK 472712**

Bolsover is situated about 6 miles east of Chesterfield, being a parish of some 1611 inhabitants in 1851. In that year two millers are listed in White's Directory, Alfred Bunting and Thomas Smith, but it is not possible to establish which of the two known mills they operated.

A corn tower windmill at Hill Top, Bolsover, was built, it is believed in 1793, the date being carved above the door. An advertisement in the Derby Mercury of the 2nd May 1799 read as follows:-

> 'To be sold, newly erected Smock mill at Bolsover- occupier
> William Burrows, with the miller's house, Drying kiln, counting
> house and six acres of land.'

The actual sale is not recorded, but in 1803, it was owned by Richard Parker and later, by Martha Pearson of Sheffield. It was sold again in 1821 with an advertisement as follows: -

> 'For sale, smock mill, drying kiln, stable, small house and bakehouse
> nearby. Five and a half acres in the possession of Joseph Cuthbert. One
> pair of French stones and one pair of Grey stones.'

Mr Cuthbert was listed as the miller from 1835 until 1854.

Towards the end of the nineteenth century one of the sails was damaged in a gale and a vertical steam engine was added, built into the basement of the mill, with the boiler and chimney standing outside. About 1906 the boiler burst, soon after a patch to cure a leak had been added, but two men who were in the mill at the time were not hurt. The boiler was destroyed and, probably resulting from the damage incurred, the mill fell into disuse.

The cap was lost and for a long time the upright shaft has rested on the stone work at the top of the tower. The windshaft was unusual in that it is one of the few recorded wooden windshafts with a cross in the Midlands. There were two pairs of stones, one French and one grey, originally fitted with governors on the first floor and a single pair on the second. Eventually the floors gave way and most of the stones, gearing and machinery ended up in an unholy pile in the base of the mill.

Karl Wood made a painting of the mill in 1932 that showed the windowless stone tower, without a cap, but with evidence of the cross on the windshaft and the brake wheel still visible.

In 1990 planning permission was given to clear the area for housing and a new road was built passing close to the base of the mill, but requiring the preservation of the truncated version of the still surviving chimney from the ill fated boiler and the tower itself. At that time many items of the mill mechanism were visible in the pile of debris within the base of the mill. The housing and the road, Mill Close, have been completed but the stone tower of the mill itself, at the end of 2002, still remains. It stands in a sad condition, closely surrounded by just a low enclosure wall that contains much building rubbish and other debris. The doors into the building are blocked off. Through the frameless window openings, the wooden upright shaft, with a universal joint about 10 feet from the ground, still leans against the inside wall. Access into the tower is not possible. The stonework of the tower is in poor condition, with numerous cracks appearing, and the pointing is, in places, nonexistent. It could soon become a hazard.

Bolsover tower windmill in the housing estate, October 2002.

It is a great pity that steps were not taken at the time of the development on the site, to ensure that the mill tower itself, was preserved for future generations.

26

CARSINGTON PASTURE SK 252545

CARSINGTON PASTURE

The stump of this tower windmill still stands, just over a mile from the village of Brassington, to the south of the road leading to Wirksworth. It is high up in the Peak District hills and is in a very isolated situation. It probably dates back to the 18th century and is one of the few small stumpy tower mills remaining in the country. The actual date it was built is not known although it may have been during the 1780's, based on a very worn inscription in the jamb of one of the doors to the tower. It does not appear on Burdett's map of 1767 but is shown on the Ordnance Survey map dated 1839. It was out of use by 1887, being shown on the Ordnance Survey map for that year as 'Windmill - Corn (disused)'. No records of millers, names or of the mill being advertised have been found.

Carsington tower mill, standing high on the moors above Wirksworth.

The limestone block tower is about 22 feet high, 18 feet internal diameter at the base and 15 feet at the top. The top two courses are of millstone grit blocks, immediately below where a cap would have fitted. The batter on the walls is much steeper from about 15 feet from the ground, giving an unusual profile. This shape is very similar to the round house found on many windmills, however no traces of any stones piers, which would have supported the trestles of a post mill, are present, almost certainly confirming it to be a tower mill. The two opposing doorways and the staggered window openings all have millstone grit framings, suggesting that, it was owned by a wealthy person. One of the doorways has a fragment of an old millstone forming a doorstep into the mill.

All openings have, however, been walled up for many years and internal access is not now possible. There is no equipment remaining inside, although there was a fireplace inside the tower, the flue of which can be seen, on the south side of the tower, near the top.

Old millstone used as doorstep at Carsington.

FINDERN
SK 302307

This tower windmill is to the north-west of the village, some six miles south of Derby. It can easily be seen on the high ground to the east when heading south on the A38, being painted white and nestling in a group of poplar trees. It is not clear when the mill was built. It is not shown on Burdett's map of Derbyshire in 1767 and, rather strangely, it is not listed by John Farey in 1808, in spite of an advertisement in the Derby Mercury of 5th October, 1797 offering its sale, as follows:-

> 'To be sold by Auction - A smock mill at Findern, one pair of French stones, one pair of grey stones, dressing machine etc. Enquire of Mr Thomas Lovatt of Findern.'

It was again offered for sale in 1814, as part of an Estate, being described as 'a substantial Wind corn mill'. Included in the list of tenants is Mr Lovatt. The mill is shown by the symbol on both Greenwood's map of 1825 and the first edition of the Ordnance Survey map in 1836. The miller, between 1832 and 1861, was a Mr. William Coy and an account book prepared by him is held by Mrs. Torrington of Burnaston.

The following entries are included: -
'Findern Mill - to Mr Foreman in 1832

Jan 3	5 Strikes of Barley Ground	2s - 1d
Feb 19	4 stones Barley meal	4s - 8d
Oct 3	3 strikes Wheat	1s - 6d
Apl 18	2 strikes beans	8d

And in 1836   Total work for year   £4 - 6s - 10d

Settled - Wm Coy'.

Note - A Strike is a dry measure, generally equal to one bushel, or 8 gallons.

28

William Hodgkinson was the next miller. He was succeeded in 1874 by his wife, Mrs Eliza Hodgkinson, who was the last miller to be listed for this mill. The mill appears to have been working at the time of the Ordnance Survey map in 1887 but after this is described as 'old windmill'.

The mill features in a painting by Karl Wood made in 1932 which shows it looking much as it does at present when viewed from the north. No illustration of the mill with sails has been found.

Findern tower mill house conversion in 2002.

It was one of the first mills in the county to become a house conversion, probably about the turn of the century. The cap was removed, a conical slate roof installed and a two storey house built up to the mill structure. Findern mill was for some years, until 1998, the home of the then Member of Parliament for South Derbyshire, Mrs Edwina Currie, and at the time of writing it still remains in the Currie family.

FRITCHLEY   SK 365532
The mill is located about half a mile east-north-east of Fritchley village, on the north side of the road.

Simmonds reports that a Sun Fire Insurance Policy No 615507 dated 5th June 1793 on Joseph Bowmer of Fritchley includes: -

'Wind Corn Mill at Fritchley - timber, £150'

This indicates the mill was built before 1793 and it first appears on Greenwoods map of 1825 but it may have been the one referred to when a Mr Elijah Hall, in 'The report on the trials for High Treason', Oct 1817, held at Derby after the Pentrich Rebellion, was reported to 'have a mill a quarter of mile from his home'. The Ordnance Survey map of 1836 does not show the mill whilst in 1880 it is described as 'disused'.

Fritchley post mill c.1870.

A photograph, above, shows it to be a post mill in the late stages of decay. It had no roof, was lacking most of its cladding and was standing on a stone round house. Two common sails were still in place and the brake wheel was clearly visible. Alongside was a cottage, apparently in good condition, but the roof on an attached outbuilding had collapsed.

Some of the millers listed for Fritchley are: -

Elijah Hall	1817	Eliza Hall	1829
John Hall	1846 –1855	George Fletcher	1862
James Slack	1864 -1887		

At the present time only a part of the tall stone roundhouse survives and large holes have been knocked into the walls above the stone piers for the cross trees, presumably so that the valuable, heavy timbers could be extracted for other use. There is no sign of the cottage.

MELBOURNE
SK 386252

Melbourne is a small market town, some seven miles south-east of Derby. It has had two windmills, a water mill and a steam mill.

Burdett in 1767 did not indicate there were any windmills in the town but Farey listed two in 1808. They also appear both on Greenwood's map of 1825 and on the first Ordnance Survey map in 1836. There is no trace of the early post mill on Ticknall Road, which is described in the section on mills that have disappeared.

Melbourne tower mill c.1900.

A second windmill is still standing as an empty shell on what was known as Charnel Hill, Melbourne Common and which now forms part of a recreation area owned by the Severn Trent Water Board, at Staunton Harold Reservoir. It was built in 1797 at a cost of £100 with a further £159 being spent on it a year later. A survey of Lord Melbourne's estate in 1808 refers to 'the windmill, recently built with brick at Lord Melbourne's expense'. At that time the miller was William Peat and the value of the installation must have been recognised since more money was used on improving the installation, for example £362 was spent in 1815-16.

Only one advertisement that appeared in 1846 and offered the mill to be let has been found: -

> 'To be let - windmill on Melbourne Common, three pairs of stones and
> five acres of grassland, apply F. F. Fox.'

The mill became disused by about 1880 and stood derelict for many years. A photograph taken about 1905 shows the brick tower, complete with a rounded cap and a large window, but no fantail. The mill is obviously past its active life and the sails, which reached close to the ground, are seriously damaged. One pair are common and there is no evidence of 'patent' mechanisms so the other pair were probably spring adjusted. Karl Wood made a painting of the mill in 1932 and showed it in similar condition to the photograph, the sail backs still being in place. In 1934 a photograph taken by Eric Tuxford shows the mill had lost both the cap and the sails. In 1963, when the reservoir was being built, she was converted into an observation tower. Instead of a conventional cap, a strange open concrete flat roof with a gallery below was added. Access into this windmill tower 'observation post' was non-existent.

31

The viewing tower on top of Melbourne tower mill.

In 1992 plans by Severn Trent to incorporate the tower into a new visitor centre were vigorously opposed by local bodies and the plans were significantly modified. The mill tower has since been included in a visitor centre which opened on 27th June 1994, but there is still no internal access.

OCKBROOK   SK 429357

About 5 miles east of Derby is the village of Ockbrook. The site of a windmill is just to the east of the village, close to the Ock Brook and located on Windmill Farm.

A windmill at Ockbrook is listed by Farey in 1811-13 but does not appear on Burdetts map of 1767. It is shown on an Enclosures award map of 1773 as 'Windmill Farm'.

The Derby Mercury records that on December 26th, 1811,

> 'A Gang of frame breakers broke into the house of Mr. Hunt at Ockbrook
> Mill, they took 35 notes, of which 20 were worth a guinea.'

There is reason to suppose that the men were acting under the pretence of relieving Framework-knitters. This example of robbery thus gives the first indication of the mill.

The Parish survey of 1826 then reveals the following information: -

'Brick and tiled Dwelling House, Stable, Drying Kiln, pigsty, also a brick-built windmill and a small barn in the field, together with the yard, garden and orchard and three fields, totalling nearly 16 acres and occupied by John Cook, the owner.'

The tower mill was advertised for sale in the Derby Mercury during October 1833 and July 1834, being described as a ' Smock Mill' (see Heage).

Glover's Directory 1827/29 has John Cook as the corn miller and a freeman, and he was still the miller in 1855 when Thomas Hunt took over and operated the mill until it closed. The Ordnance Survey map of 1880 shows the mill to be disused but Kelly's Directory of 1880 still lists a 'Mr. Herbert Hunt' as the miller. One of the problems of old data!

Reports and photographs dated about 1890 show that it was a four-storey brick tower mill, with a loading door on the first floor. There were only two sails shown but the iron canister was for four sails. The shuttered sails appear to have been sprung, there being no evidence of 'patent' equipment. The cap was boat-shaped, unlike most others in the area which tended to be ogee-shaped, and in the absence of a fantail, the mill was probably turned by a chain wheel and rack, although there may have been a tail pole. The mill however was clearly out of use since part of the front of the cap covering was missing and the brake wheel could be clearly seen.

Ockbrook tower mill with two sails and part of the cap missing, in 1890.

Karl Wood, in 1932, made a painting of the remains and this shows two floors of the brick tower remaining, to which was fitted a pitched roof, a door on the first floor closed off by a corrugated iron sheet and a stable type door swung open on the ground floor.

There appears to be a lean to, single storey, brick building up to the tower. Most of the mill has now disappeared and only the base of the tower survives.

Currently the mill has been reduced to a brick annulus, about 14 feet in height with no roof or covering such that rainwater can get into the walls. One of the millstones has been built into a path and a portion of another has recently been found in an adjacent hedge bottom. The local parish council is currently seeking to get the walls listed to ensure their preservation.

SOUTH NORMANTON SK 442569

South Normanton lies about 3 miles east of Alfreton, very close to Junction 28 on the M1 motorway. In 1851 it had a population of 1340 and was a centre of coal mining. It has had at least four windmills in the last 250 years, of which, unusually for Derbyshire, two survive. (See next section for details of those that have gone).

1) Fordbridge Lane, (Grade 2 listed) SK 441569

This four-storey stone tower mill shell stands on the west side of Fordbridge Lane, just across the road from St Michael's Church near the centre of the village.It is not listed by John Farey in 1808 and first appears on a map in 1835 but is not on the 1836 Ordnance Survey map. It was built on land owned by the Gill family, probably in the 1820s and was offered for sale by auction in the Derby Courier in Sept 1843: -

> 'Farm and Grist Mill. A freehold farm and tower windmill. The mill has patent sails and grey and French stones - with drying kiln.'

The mill continued to work, sometimes with members of the Gill family as the miller, until at least 1880 when the Ordnance Survey map designated it as a 'Windmill (corn)', so it was probably still working at that time.

All was soon changed however for shortly after it was purchased from the owner by a local authority 'to build a water works' which would provide water for the inhabitants of South Normanton. The sails and cap were removed and a large iron storage tank mounted on top of the tower in their place. At about the same time three thick iron bands were fitted round the tower at approximately the floor levels.

The tower mill in Fordbridge Lane, South Normanton
with the water tank in place in 1975.

The tank was still in place in 1975, but by the early 80s, it had been removed and the mill stood as an empty cap-less shell, apart from a few floor beams that could be seen through the upper windows.

Modern housing encroached upon the mill tower, and its isolation was shattered, and for many years there was no access inside. Access was eventually gained to the interior, during a planning application, but no mill machinery remained, only a large diameter pipe, which had carried the water up to the storage tank, and a few beams. In 1996 planning permission was granted for a house conversion, with a built-on two-storey attachment to provide additional space. The cap was replaced with a conical structure, not typical of windmill structures, but which ensured the preservation of the tower.

House conversion of the tower mill in Fordbridge Lane, South Normanton, 2002.

2) Normanton Common SK 442561

This small tower mill was built on Normanton Common, at a time when it was an isolated place. Today it carries a busy local road and behind Number 47 Normanton Common is located a mill house conversion, known locally as 'The Mill House'. It is about 200 yards back from the road and takes some finding.

It does not appear on the 1836 Ordnance Survey map or on the 1840 Tithe map, and was first shown on the Ordnance Survey map of 1880. However it must have been built some years before that date and the listings of millers for the town may indicate it was built about 1850 to 1860. The windmill was owned by the Gelsthorpe family who provided some of the millers for South Normanton. Unfortunately for us it is not possible to always relate the millers to a specific mill in the village.

It was shown on the 1905 Ordnance Survey map, and sometime about then it was converted to become part of a house. It stands as a cement-rendered brick tower which is 2 storeys high and about 24' diameter at the base. It is quite sharply-waisted, suggesting that it may have had its height reduced at sometime. It is surmounted by a peaked, octagonal-tiled roof. No machinery remained inside the mill in 1995.

SPANCARR, (Grade 2 listed) SK 342660

This is a stone tower windmill with an associated kiln building still standing on the high moors, to the east of the B6015 Chesterfield to Matlock road, north of the village of Kelstedge.

In 1807 the windmill was erected jointly by James and Matthew Beresford of Hazelhurst Farm, Matthew paying James £14 for a half share. The mill is included in Farey's list in 1808 and it appears on most maps since that date. In 1816 the mill, standing in a field known as New Close, became the sole property of James but by 1823, a Mr Francis Elliot was the miller and occupier. At this time £500 was spent on repairing and improving the windmill with money borrowed from Robert Summers of Alfreton.

In 1836 it was put up for auction and Summers bought the mill for £100 from George Berresford, presumably the son of James. The 1841 census did not include Francis Elliot although his wife and two sons were listed. In 1860 the windmill and the associated 15 acres of land were valued as being worth £1200. The windmill was referred to as a smock mill and there was mention of a drying kiln being included. Milling remained in the Elliot family until at least 1888, although the sails were removed and the mill operated from a steam engine.

The isolated gritstone tower, about 34 feet high and 23 feet diameter at the base, is four storeys high and had no cap or sails. There were no floors or machinery inside and nothing is known as to how it was equipped. Unusually there were four fireplaces inside the building, with flues passing up inside the walls; it must have been a very cold location! There is a stone building alongside, believed to have been the kiln and granary store, and another building, which housed the steam engine, has gone.

No illustrations of the mill in operation have been found and a painting by Karl Wood, in 1938 shows it much as it appears today except that he includes a small lean to type building which may have housed the steam engine and which has now disappeared.

For many years after the cap disappeared, the mill, now designated with a Grade 2 listing, stood open to the elements, although the kiln retained its stone roof. Planning permission was granted in 1989 to incorporate the tower and kiln into a house conversion, which was completed about 1996. It is unfortunate that the replacement cap, a six-sided conical structure, did not replicate any recognised design of working mill caps but the work did ensure the preservation of one of the few complete towers that remain in this area.

Spancarr windmill during house conversion, July 1995.

The remains of the kiln are in the foreground.

SOME VANISHED DERBYSHIRE WINDMILLS

There have been quite a large number of other windmills in Derbyshire, which, sadly, no longer exist. They date back to before 1760, with the last of them being built in 1877. Changing industrial practices in the latter part of the 19th century led to their demise. In some cases they were moved, some were destroyed by fire or the elements, others were demolished, some were abandoned and just fell down, being gradually removed piecemeal. Many of the sites noted have now been built over, so nothing can be seen, but in some cases, the field locations can be visited and the generally excellent sites enjoyed.

ALDERWASLEY   SK 317526
The windmill at Alderwasley, some 5 miles north-north-east of Belper, was close to the Bear Inn on the Belper to Wirksworth Road, located on high ground, some 860 feet above sea level. The lane leading to the village from this road is known as 'Windmill Lane' and the mill stood in a field at the junction of the two roads, called 'Windmill Piece' which was directly opposite 'The Fish Ponds'.

This mill is clearly shown on the Burdett map of 1767 and is included in the list of Derbyshire mills by Farey in 1808.

A sale notice for the mill appears in the Derby Mercury in July 1773. It is not shown on Greenwood's map of 1825 nor on the 1836 Ordnance Survey map.

It seems therefore that the mill was erected before 1767 but disappeared sometime between 1811 and about 1835. The 1841 Tithe map shows a field name 'Windmill Piece' in this location but does not show the mill. No names are known for the millers at Alderwasley, nor is it clear what type of mill it was, although it is highly probable it would have been a post mill.

ALFRETON   SK 408539
At least two windmills worked in the small town of Alfreton, some 10 miles north of Derby.

1) Hitch Hill   SK 408539
This mill was located behind Watchorn Church, just off the A61, within a raised circular earth mound that was about 3 feet higher than the surrounding fields. This mound was in the form of an annulus, with an outside diameter of 45 feet, an inside diameter about 24 feet, with a hollow central area. There was a pathway of stones laid on the top of the mound but no trace of the mill foundation has been identified. However the Enclosure Award Map of 1816 shows this mill to be a 24 feet diameter tower mill and in 1824 the owner (possibly the miller) was John Cressey Hall.

38

The mound may have been built round the mill to prevent flooding and could also have been used as a platform from which the sails were set. Some pieces of well-worn Peak millstone, which must have come from the mill, were found in the mound.

2) Sleetmore Mill   SK 415539

On the area known as Windmill Hill, to the north Side of Sleetmore Lane stood Sleetmoor Mill. It was probably built in 1790 and may have been the one listed by John Farey in 1811. It appears on the Enclosure Awards map of 1816, also in the Alfreton Survey of 1824 and figures on Greenwood's map of 1825, but not on the 1836 Ordnance Survey map, although 'Windmill Hill' is marked.

The mill had been originally built with common sails but was fitted with two spring sails about 1870 to provide some automatic adjustment, but these were much heavier than common sails. It worked until 1908 and was demolished in 1925 when Sleetmoor Hall was built.

In discussions on the paper 'The Windmills of Derbyshire, Leicestershire and Nottinghamshire', (P. H. J. Baker and R. Wailes), Newcomen Society Journal Vol. 33, 1961, Mr Dan Taylor, who was the son of the last miller, was reported, in 1949, as saying that he well recalled the post mill. He said this had a round house without a curb, two spring and two common sails, a pair each of Peak and French burr stones, a four grade flour machine and, in the gears, box wood cogs, which were lubricated with neatsfoot oil from a bottle. He asserted that a mill without a round house was not rated. In proof of this he cited an old map showing Mill Lane, but no mill, though a mill was well known to be standing there but, because there was no round house there at the time, in the eyes of the rating authority no mill existed.

ASHBOURNE   SK 180463

The small market town of Ashbourne, 13 miles north-north-west of Derby, had at least two, possibly three, windmills as follows: -

1) Windmill Lane   SK 179471

On Windmill Lane, at Town Head, about a quarter of a mile out of the town, to the east of the main road leading to Buxton.

An advertisement in the Derby Mercury, 19th January, 1792 offers the mill for sale by auction at the Wheatsheaf Hotel: -

> 'New erected tower windmill for the grinding of corn, complete with two
> pairs of French stones: standing on a piece of land called the Low Top
> Pingle, near to the town of Ashbourne.'

There were a series of very similar advertisements over the next two years that additionally advise that there was a 21year lease associated with the mill which had 18 years left to run. This therefore suggests that the mill was built in about 1790 or 1791. An advertisement, again in the Derby Mercury in 1811, indicates that the mill was to be removed, as follows: -

> 'For sale by auction, all the materials from a windmill at Low Top, Ashbourne, including one pair French stones 4' 6" and one pair of Derbyshire stones, 4' 8", dressing machine, troughs and sack tackle.'

It is not clear why the mill was dismantled when clearly the lease had still not expired, but this could have been associated with possible bankruptcy of the owner and an inability to sell as a working mill. A windmill is listed for Ashbourne by Farey in 1808 but it does not appear on Greenwood's map in 1825 or on the first edition of the Ordnance Survey map in 1836.

The windmill may however be the one which is shown on the distant skyline in an etching of views of Ashbourne, drawn by E. Dayes and included in J. Aitkin's '50 miles around Manchester', which was published in 1795. The location shown appears to be further along Windmill Lane than Low Top but this may well represent artistic licence. Unfortunately this etching does not give any details of the mill.

Another distant view is shown on an etching by J. Farrington in 1817, but this again does not add to our knowledge. The mill clearly had quite a short life and no trace remains on the site at the time of writing.

Some confusion existed in the local press in 1979 (Ashbourne News Telegraph) when, in correspondence about the windmills of the town, it was identified as a '50 foot high tower, used to pump water to four farms'. This clearly refers to a wind engine that was used up on the ridge.

2) Ashley Windmill   SK 173465
The second windmill at Ashbourne was further west, north of the A52, on a site adjacent to what is now the hospital, off Belle Vue Road. This mill was not used for corn milling but was used to power a colour pigment and paint manufacturing works and an associated tobacco processing plant.

In 1838 Simmons reported that 'a newly erected windmill called Ashley Mill at Ashbourne was to be sold or let, complete with all machinery necessary for manufacturing colours'. He also records that in the London Gazette of May 11th, 1847, 'William Ellam, a bankrupt, of Ashbourne will sell Ashley windmill, Ashbourne, under a Fiat of Bankruptcy'.

The mill is well described in an advertisement in the Derby Mercury in 1847: -

'To be disposed of by Private Contract. The machinery and works of a spacious brick Tower windmill used for grinding colours, situated at Ashley, adjoining the town of Ashbourne, in the County of Derbyshire, comprising sails, fan dome covered with zinc, upright shafts, spur wheels driving wheel, two pairs of edge runner stones, two mixers, with gearing complete, five pairs of colour stones, four pairs of paint stones, hand crane, two iron pumps, quantity of models and various other items used in the manufacture of paint.'

Note - It is possible that the models referred to above were wooden patterns for the cast iron work contained in the mill.

This description gives a clear impression of a large tower mill probably made of brick, with a domed cap and complete with fantail. Unfortunately no illustration of this mill has yet been identified. The mill is not shown on any maps by the mill symbol but the first edition of the Ordnance Survey, dated 1839, does mark 'Ashley Mill' in the location described.

Mr. William Ellam was operating the mill in 1837, but her life must have been short and she was presumably demolished, with the equipment being moved elsewhere after the 1847 advert. There is presently no evidence of a windmill on the site, although the location, in previous times, must have been very suitable.

3) Possible Post Mill, site unknown.
A white post mill, standing on open trestles, complete with fantail and with four sails, apparently in working order, was photographed by H. E. Simmons in 1935. In the Simmons collection held at the Science Museum Library it is described as being at 'Ashbourne in Derbyshire'. No other evidence of its existence in the county has been found and its identification as 'Ashbourne' is in some doubt. The mill appears to be very similar to the one at Drinkstone in Suffolk.

BEIGHTON   SK 434826
There was a post mill in Beighton, presently known as Waterthorpe, a village in the far north of the county, close to Sheffield, which for some time was in Derbyshire.
During October 1791 a series of advertisements in various newspapers covered the sale of the mill. These read: -

'A windmill for grinding grain at Waterthorpe in the parish of Beighton, late in the possession of John Marshall, deceased. One pair of French Stones and one pair of good black stones, with all other machinery and utensils necessary. Good Granaries above.'

Simmons reports the London Gazette of April 19th, 1831, included a notice to the effect that 'the corn mill at Beighton in the occupation of Mr John Staniford, was feloniously entered by a person or persons who stole some flour and then set fire to the mill'.

The actual location of the presumed post mill is not shown on any maps and it seems that the above fire was the end of the mill, for no other information has been found.

BELPH
SK 536755

The hamlet of Belph is in the parish of Whitwell, about 10 miles to the east of Chesterfield, in the north of the county.

Although a water mill is shown on Burdett's map of 1767, no windmill is depicted. John Farey, 1808, includes a mill at Belph in his list of 45 working windmills of Derbyshire. It is also shown on the Enclosure Award map of Whitwell, dated 1814 as an open trestle post mill.

Later maps do not show the mill and it would appear that the life of this mill was quite short, maybe less than 20 years. The presumed site has been covered over by spoil from the adjacent colliery.

BOLSOVER
SK 479706

There had been another windmill in Bolsover, other than the tower mill described earlier. This was a post mill, which was built just off Wilbeck Road.

The post mill was evidently standing in the 18th century since Simmons reports: -

'Royal Exchange Fire Insurance Policy Number 147513.
29th September 1795, Joseph Jessop, of Bolsover, in the County of Derebyshire on a wind post mill, timber built, situate in Bolsover aforesaid £100. On standing and going geers therein £100 in trade in same £100.'

This is gives us some indication of the value of a post windmill at that time and the value attributed to its trade. The 'standing and going geers' clearly refers to the machinery of the mill, rather than the structure

Only one mill is shown on Greenwood's map of 1825 and on the Ordnance Survey map of 1836. The later 1895 and 1906 Ordnance Survey maps both refer to mills as the 'Old Windmill' and the 'Mill'. The site of the previously described post mill refers to the former, although it was clearly still working at that time. It was built before 1800, since an advertisement in the Nottingham Journal, 21st November 1800 reads: -
'To be sold - A post mill standing on Bolsover Moor, near Bolsover.
Lately erected and in good repair - Enquire of Mr. Bagshaw.'

It is believed to have been a large open trestle Post Mill which had two pairs of stones, flour machine and a sack hoist. One of the sails was split longitudinally, by lightning during a storm and for its last years of life it worked with only two sails. It is not clear when the mill was built or was finally demolished.

BORROWASH SK 422345

Borrowash is a small village about 5 miles east of Derby on the main road to Nottingham. Burdett, in his map of 1767, did not show a windmill but one is however shown on the Ockbrook Enclosures Map of 1773, as an open trestle post mill, owned by Mr. S. Collernbrook. It is not listed by John Farey in 1808 but is located just north of the Nottingham road at 'Shacklecross', on a local map in 1826. A mill is shown on the Greenwood maps of 1825 and 1835, and it was advertised for sale in the Derby Mercury on the 15th September, 1830 as follows: -

> 'To be sold by auction a dwelling house and garden, also windmill and land of about 1½ acres in the possession of Mr. R. Foss of Borrowash.'

Piggott's directory of 1835 lists Robert Foss as one of two millers for Borrowash. However no miller's name is included for Borrowash in the 1857 White's Derbyshire directory, and the mill had disappeared altogether from the 1880 Ordnance Survey map.

BREADSALL SK 376394

Breadsall is a village some 3 miles north of Derby, on the road to Heanor. The windmill is not shown on Burdett's map in 1767 but John Farey lists one for Breadsall in 1808 and the Enclosure Award map of 1817 shows it to be in: -

> 'an ancient inclosure called Windmill Croft, belonging to Thomas Walker, miller.'

There is a triangular piece of land which stretches from the old Mansfield Turnpike (the present A608) down to Stanley Road, bounded on the eastern side by the footpath running down the hill, behind the Windmill Inn, which still stands on the main road.

From a series of advertisements in the Derby Mercury between 1827 and 1832 there was for sale, in addition to a Windmill, a Public House called the Windmill Inn, a newly erected messuage (or dwelling house) and in 1831, a brick kiln and sheds.

The windmill had three pairs of stones, a shulling mill and an adjoining drying kiln. In the adverts of 1831 the windmill was described as a 'Tower Windmill' whilst in 1832 it was called a 'Smock Windmill'. In 1832 Thomas Walker Jr. was the occupier.

It probably appears on the 1836 Ordnance Survey map, standing to the west of the Windmill Inn public house, athough the symbol is indistinct. The Windmill Inn remained in the hands of the Walker family for many years but the mill seems to have been regularly sold or let. In 1835 George Wood was the miller and the mill was again advertised for sale in the Derby Mercury on 31st January and 7th February, 1838: -

'At Breadsall Hill Top - a windmill, 3 pairs of stones, also a new Steam Mill with 8 HP Engine, 2 pairs of stones. Enquire on the premises, or to Mr. Samuel Henchley, 2 Derwent St, Derby.'

The new steam corn mill was built at the lower end of Bridle Road (the northern end of the footpath) on land that had belonged to Thomas Walker. Two years later the steam mill was again offered for sale in the Derby Mercury on 11th and 25th March 1840, but without the windmill

The 1841 census records Thomas Walker as the miller, presumably at the windmill, but in 1851 he was listed as a farm labourer and no miller is given for the windmill, however Joseph Bennet worked at the steam mill. White's directory of 1857 lists the miller at Breadsall as Eliza Gerrard, not making it clear which mill she operated. By the second half of the century steam corn milling had taken over and no more millers were listed for the windmill, probably signifying that she had ceased to operate.

She had probably been demolished by 1887, since it does not appear on the large scale Ordnance Survey map of that date.

CALOW   SK 417703

Calow is a village situated about 2 miles to the east of Chesterfield, the windmill site on Bole Hill being some 1/2 mile to the south of the village. Bole Hill has been the location of at least one windmill in the last 200 years. A windmill at Calow is included in Farey's list of 1808 and is shown on Greenwood's map of 1825, and also on the 1840 Ordnance Survey map, being designated by the mill symbol and by the name 'Calow Mill'.

A non-specific advertisement in the Derby Mercury of 10th December 1812 offers: -

'To be sold - Newly erected Post Windmill , one pair of French and one pair of grey stones, dressing machine - short distance from Chesterfield.'

This could well be Calow Mill although there were others in the area, such as New Brampton, that might fit this description.

According to Simmons, in 1836 The Doncaster Gazette reported: -

'On Monday night last a stack of hay and a barn near the windmill at Calow were burnt down', thus confirming its presence.

Little more has been found about its life until, in 1843, it hit the headlines, in the Derbyshire Courier of April 22nd, 1843 as follows: -

'**FIRE AT WINDMILL.** On the 15th, at about one o'clock in the morning the windmill at Calow was discovered, by a man named Bestwick, to be in flames. On account of the sad ravages of the fire he was unable to impede its progress or to save any of the property within.

It appears that the mill had been working the previous day, up to 12 o'clock at night, when all appeared to be right; but it is conjectured that, from the long run it had, the shaft had become hot from the friction through want of grease, and had so ignited.

We are sorry to say the mill, machinery and about 30 loads of wheat and flour were entirely consumed. The unfortunate owner was the occupier, Mr. Amcoates of Warsop, who had only recently purchased the property.

The mill was entirely destroyed and the damage is in excess of £200, a great loss to the owner who is not insured.'

The following week the paper made a correction: -

'We stated last week that the windmill burnt down was owned by Mr. Amcoates. We were misinformed. It was occupied by William Marshall, who is the severe loser from the fire. The machinery was well oiled at 10 o'clock the previous night and three hours later the mill was in flames.'

The mill does not appear on subsequent Ordnance Survey maps and it is not clear if it was ever rebuilt.

CHELLASTON   SK 380295

Chellaston is a village about four miles to the south of Derby, on the road to Melbourne. It adjoins the parish of Swarkestone and Swarkestone Bridge, famous for its connection with Bonnie Prince Charlie.

There were two windmills on the edge of the village, about 150 yards apart; one was actually in Swarkestone parish and the other in Chellaston.

For convenience they are both considered under 'Chellaston'.

A sketch in the Gilbert Thompson Notebook, No 2, dated 1889, held by Derby Local Studies Library and reproduced over by their kind permission, shows the two mills. The mill in the foreground, which is obviously disused stood in Swarkestone parish, whilst the other appears to be still in working order.

Old Mill at Chellaston.

1) Swarkestone Mill
SK 381297

This stood in a small orchard, behind 'Windmill Cottage', on Chellaston Hill. Presently only a pile of stones, built into a rockery in the garden survives, together with a few fragments of millstones.

Access to the land was initially granted on 27th March, 1793 when Joseph Dawson leased the land to Isaac Orme. An indenture in December 1794 records the following transaction: -

'Sum of two hundred pounds of good and lawful money for piece of land lately purchased by said Isaac Orme from Joseph Dawson, with the windmill for grinding corn, lately built by Isaac Orme upon Little Close.'

In an indenture of release dated March 1798: -

'Joseph Sanders and Thomas Grime agree to pay £655 for absolute purchase of dwelling House and Tenement windmill.'

They clearly wished to quickly sell it again since in April 1798 an advertisement in the Derby Mercury offers the mill for sale, as follows: -

'For Sale - a new erected brick freehold messuage and windmill, with two pairs of stones, dressing mill, in complete repair, with stable and croft etc, situate near the Grand Trunk and Derby Canals, in Swarkestone, late in possession of Isaac Orme - Apply Mr. Grime of Swarkeston.'

46

For a few years there is no more information until in September 1817, the will of William Elkin , miller, evidently an owner of the windmill , includes bequests: -

> 'My messuage dwelling house or tenement windmill for grinding corn,
> and the stables, in parish of Swarkestone, in close called 'Little Close' to
> my wife and £300 to my son Francis and £100 to my son William.'

A mill is recorded by Farey in 1808 and one figures on Greenwood's map of 1825. By the time of the first Ordnance Survey map of 1836, two mills are shown. The 1880 Ordnance Survey map shows this one as an 'Old Windmill.'

In December 1834 the windmill and close of land were conveyed from Robert Shipton to Sir George Crewe, Bart., and it seems that the windmill did not operate long after that date. In a document recording this transaction it is noted that Isaac Orme, referred to earlier, had gone 'bankrupt'.

The sketch shows the mill as a three-storey tower mill with a damaged ogee cap and ball finial and with only the fantail staging in place. The sails are common but there appears to be one or more sails leaning against the tower.

Karl Wood made a painting of this mill in 1932, which shows it to be reduced down to one floor and a basement and the owner of the cottage, in 1983, recognised this as 'the brick structure I had to demolish because it had become unsafe'. There are several pieces of millstones in paths of the cottage.

2) Chellaston Mill   SK 381298
This stood behind the Mill House, in the grounds of Mount House on Chellaston Hill overlooking Swarkestone and a few yards from the previously described mill.

It was a brick tower mill, probably built about 1827 for a Captain William Manfull, who was born at nearby Calke in 1773. He enlisted in the Light Dragoons as a private soldier in 1793. By 1805 he was a sergeant, and had risen to the rank of Captain when he retired in 1825. He took up farming, owning 18 acres of land, and had this second windmill built in the village, close to the existing Swarkestone Mill. It is very unusual that a retired cavalry officer should not only have built a windmill, but that he became a miller himself, being listed as the miller from 1829 to 1841. Members of the Manfull family worked the mill for some 50 years.
The mill does not appear on Greenwood's map in 1825 but both mills are clearly designated on the 1836 Ordnance Survey map. It does not appear to have been advertised at any time. Alexander Manfull, presumably a son, is named as the miller at 'The Hill', in 1857, though whether that was the name given to the mill is unclear.

Chellaston mill about 1970.

This mill is the one in the background of the Thompson sketch and appears to be in working order with four shuttered sails and a fantail. There is no suggestion of a chimney that might suggest it to be engine assisted.

It was shown as still working on the Ordnance Survey map in 1887 but was 'old' in 1899, and had disappeared from later maps. There is no evidence of the mill on the site in 1995, however there are still two complete grey stones set in the lawn and path of the house.

Millers at Chellaston (it is unclear at which mill)

1829 - 1841	William Manfull	1841	John Wilson
1841 - 1860s	Alexander Manfull	1860s - 1870s	Hiram Manfull
1860	William Cox	1881	John Pollard
1888	George Buckingham, steam miller and farmer.		

CHESTERFIELD   SK 385711

In 1857 Chesterfield was an extensive market and borough town, with six dependent townships and a population of 12,318. It lies 25 miles north-east of Derby, on the old A61 trunk road to Sheffield. Its milling requirements were served by a number of wind and water mills.

1) Holywell Street   SK 383714 approx.

This post windmill, which was very close to the centre of the town, appears to have been built about 1787 by a miller, Mr Thomas Olerenshaw. However he did not work the mill for long since two years later his widow advertised the property and, subsequently, the windmill: -

'Newly erected large Post Wind Corn Mill, standing within the Borough of Chesterfield, late in the possession of Thomas Olerenshaw, deceased: two pairs of French stones, dressing mill. Situation a good one for a windmill. Built about two years ago.'

A further advertisement shortly after notes 'there are 20 years of the lease to run'.

This mill does not appear on any maps and no further advertisements have been found suggesting that it may have been sold and dismantled for erection elsewhere.

2) New Brampton   SK 372710 approx.

New Brampton is about one mile west of the town of Chesterfield, and a windmill is first mentioned in the poor Rate Book for Brampton in 1800: -

'Windmill and kiln, annual value £12, assessed at 6 shillings, owner Mrs. Spillings, occupied by George Bainbridge'.

In 1813 the type of mill becomes clear through an advertisement in the Derby Mercury of 25th March as follows: -

'To be let - A complete post windmill, situate at the Brickhouse, near Chesterfield, occupied by Robert Botham.'

Brickhouse was a small area of Brampton and included a public house of that name. It was further advertised, this time for sale by auction, in the Derby Mercury of 29th September, 1814: -

'Post windmill, near the Brickhouse, Brampton, containing pair of French stones and one pair of grey stones. The mill is well timbered and lately repaired and painted.'

New Brampton is one of the working mills listed by John Farey in 1808 but the mill does not appear on Greenwood's map of 1825. However the Ordnance Survey map for 1836 does show 'Walton Mill' in New Brampton, but this may be a watermill on the River Hipper as no windmill symbol is shown. There is no more information on this windmill and it may well also have been sold and moved to another location.

3) Club Mill   SK 372717

Club mill was a tower mill which was built about a mile to the north-west of the town centre, just on the boundary of the borough. It is probably the mill listed by Farey as 'Newbold'. It appears to have been built about 1800 when, as a result of the Napoleonic wars, flour was very expensive.

A number of corn mills were built by Sick Clubs at that time, in order to provide members with cheaper flour, and the name 'Club Mill' possibly arises from this connection.

However the windmill was sold to a private individual, William Townsend, in 1811, but still appears on the 1836 Ordnance Survey map as 'Club Mill'. It does not feature on later maps and its operational life is unclear. There is no evidence of the mill on the site at the present date.

CLAY CROSS SK 395633

This windmill is first shown on Sanderson's map of 1835 lying just to the east of the main road through the village, just to the north of Thanet Street. It is clearly marked on the Tithe Map of 1841 and appears to have been a small post mill, standing in a small plot of land belonging to a Joseph Hayes, who is listed as the miller between 1841 and 1846.

Elliott Thomas became a miller in Clay Cross in 1857 and no others have been established to date. It is unclear when the mill ceased working, but by the time of publication of the 1880 Ordnance Survey map the mill had gone, being replaced by a house called 'The Poplars'.

A steam mill must have been located elsewhere in the village, as Mr. R. Thorpe was listed as a 'steam miller' in 1876.

CLOWNE SK 488755

The village of Clowne is in the north of the county, some 8 miles east-north-east of Chesterfield and had a population of 600 in 1857. Burdett's map of 1767 does not show a windmill at Clowne, but one was operational and included in Farey's list of the working windmills in the county in 1808.

The miller in 1829 was William Woodhead, who was still in charge in 1857, but was succeeded shortly afterwards by his son, George who then worked the mill until at least 1871. After 1871, until 1900, the miller was recorded as Samuel Hatfield and thereafter entries relate to a nearby steam mill. The long ownership by the Woodhead family and by Mr. Hatfield probably explains why no advertisements for its sale or lettings have been found.

It is shown a short distance to the west of the village on the 1836 Ordnance Survey map, being designated 'Clowne Mill', complete with the windmill symbol. It appears on subsequent Ordnance Survey maps but in 1880 had become 'postmill - disused' and last appeared on the map for 1887.

CODNOR SK 420495

The village of Codnor is on the A610 Alfreton to Nottingham road, about 5 miles from the former town. It had a population of 1890 people in 1851. Although there is a water mill shown on Burdett's map of 1767, no windmill is identified in the village of Codnor.

Farey however lists it as a working mill in 1808 and it appears on Greenwood's map of 1825, but not on the first edition of the Ordnance Survey map in 1836. Simmonds however reports that a Royal Exchange Fire Insurance Policy No. 180933, dated 7th January 1801, covered Henry Kirkland of Codnor as follows: -

> 'His post wind grist mill house situate a distance from his dwelling house at Codnor aforesaid, timber built £300. On the standing and going geers, millstones and machinery £50. Warranted no steam engine.'

Later in the London Gazette, of May 16th 1834: -

> 'Joseph Pearce, late of Codnor parish of Heanor, Derby (sued and late a partner with Michael Shaw, as farmers and millers, at Codnor and Loscoe, said parish of Heanor) lately a labourer, an insolvent debtor who was discharged from the gaol of Lenton Pereval, Co. of Nottingham. Creditors to meet to choose an assignee.'

So the mill was in place in 1801 but, by the evidence of insolvency above, had probably disappeared before the 1836 map. Codnor windmill apparently had quite a short life - although a 'corn miller - John Buxton' is listed in the village in 1851.

CRESWELL   SK 5274

The village of Creswell is in the north of the county, some eight or nine miles to the east of Chesterfield. The exact location of the mill has not been established from maps, but a mill was there, since an advertisement in the Doncaster Gazette October 3rd 1834 offers: -

> 'To be sold by Private Contract. A post mill situated at Creswell, near, Barlbro', Derbyshire, containing two pairs of French stones and a dressing machine. Apply to Mr. Robert Butcher, at Creswell.'

The first entry in a directory for Creswell concerns William Butcher (1828-9), followed by Robert Butcher, miller between 1835 and 1842 and the last entry noted was for Mrs. H. Thorpe, in 1864.

CRICH   SK 3541

The Peak village of Crich is some 4 miles north-east of Belper. No evidence of the mills survives on the ground but clear information has emerged to confirm that there were a number of windmills, in and around the village.

The first record is from the Wooly Manuscripts, held by Derbyshire Record Office.

In these we can find:-

'In the year 1757 Thomas Dodd of the Pothouse built a windmill, in close in Plaistow, just opposite the said Pothouse, whence ye close became 'Windmill Close'. The said close had formally been in three closes, then called the Nether Close, the Long Lands and the Square field. This windmill was pulled down and carried away to Four Lanes End by Johnathan Kendall in 1764.'

A Bill of Sale in 1773 offers: -

'For Sale - newly erected windmill with all machinery, gears etc., intact, situate on the road between Crich and Whatstandwell.'

The first Ordnance Survey map of the area, published in 1836, does not pinpoint the location of the mill but does carry the name 'Crich Mill', just above the road between Crich and Whatstandwell. It has to be a windmill, since there is no water in the area.

A report in the Derbyshire & Chesterfield Reporter, September 15th 1842 advises: -

Windmill Accident – On Saturday last, whilst Mr. Burton was working his mill, which is situated in Crich Carr, a boy, about eight years of age, the only child of Mrs. Mather, of Crich Carr, took shelter therein during a heavy shower of rain, which, when over he (the boy) was sent away by Mr. Burton. Shortly afterwards the boy returned during another shower of rain and was allowed to shelter as before, being again sent away when Mr. Burton resumed his employment. In a few minutes afterwards Mr. Burton was informed that the boy had again returned and by some means had got upon the stage erected round the body of the mill, and was knocked down by the tip of one of the sails, his skull being seriously fractured. He was immediately conveyed home in Mr. Burton's cart and Mr. Hall, surgeon, Crich, was called in, to whom, for his great attention to the case, too much praise cannot be given. Although all surgical aid possible was exercised by the above gentleman, not the slightest hopes are entertained of his recovery.'

Comment - This was clearly a tower mill, since the text refers to 'the stage', a feature only found on tower and smock mills, the latter type not being present in Derbyshire.

An announcement in the Derby Mercury of 20th July, 1842 advises: -

'**For Sale** – 11/96th parts or shares in 3 closes and a windmill thereon contact Thomas Wheatcroft.'

Shortly afterwards on the 2nd July, 1845, the same paper has on offer: -

'To be sold The Trust property of the late William Smith, Upper Broom Close with windmill, Little Broom Close and Nether Broom Close.'

The Tithe Award Map of 1847 contains the information presented below, together with some further data given to the author in 1983 by Mrs. Wragg of Crich, in the third column.

It is often not clear if fields called 'Windmill Close'etc. actually carried a mill or were just owned by the miller.

Plan Number	Description	Other Information*
308	Windmill Meadow.	Behind Wakebridge Farm on the ridge up towards Shirestone Cross.
583	Windmill Close.	No data.
847	Upper Broom Close Windmill (owners Thomas Wheatcroft two thirds, Sm,ith and Dodds one third. Occupied by Thomas Wheatcroft, baker).	Below Penrose.
1303	Windmill Close.	No data.
1368	Windmill Close (owner John and Ann Bacon).	No data.

Finally the Derby Mercury for 21st February 1849 carried a report: -

'**Total destruction of Corn Mill by fire** on Friday 16th inst a windmill belong to Mr. John Burton of Manchester, and lately in the occupation of Messrs. John and William Sykes of Crich, situate in Crich Carr, in this county, was totally destroyed by fire. The proprietor had been drying the cylinders and other apparatus belonging to the mill, which were in a damp state.

About 11 o'clock he was aroused from his bed to witness the fire, which was so intense no efforts could be made to arrest its progress. After about an hour the sails, together with great beams of wood, came down with a tremendous crash, leaving the mill a wreck.

The drying kiln adjoining the mill was not damaged, being to the windward side of the blaze. Mr. Burton was insured.'

Comment - This is obviously the mill referred to in the windmill accident above. It is not clear what the "cylinders" referred to above, were used for - perhaps they were part of a dressing machine.

Advice was received from the occupier of the house called 'Penrose' in 2002 that his garden contains 'a large quantity of burnt timber and charcoal', supporting perhaps the report of the fire given above. It has not been possible to relate millers listed in various trade directories to any of these windmills.

DERBY   SK 351367

The county town of Derby has, since the earliest times been a place of some importance. The Domesday Book lists fourteen mills but this was many years before the invention of the windmill and they all must have been water mills.

A number of early references to windmills exist, the most infamous of which was to 'Windmill Pit'. This was close to Burton Road, in the vicinity of Mill Hill Lane, where in 1553 a young blind woman, Joan Wast was, on religious grounds, burnt at the stake.

There are a number of old fields in the area with windmill names but for which, in most cases, all records of the mills have long since disappeared. Some details are available of three windmills.

1) Windmill Hill Lane   SK 333368

There was a windmill on the north-west side of the town, just off the Ashbourne Road, where a steep hill rises and which now joins the city ring road, near the old Territorial Barracks. Windmill Hill Lane is shown on Burdett's map of 1767 and the symbol for a windmill lies in a triangle formed with the Ashbourne road. The windmill is believed to have been located on the site of St. Barnabus' Church, radbourne Street, which was built in 1896.

In 1774 an advertisement in the Derby Mercury offers: -

> 'To be let - a newly erected Smock mill for grinding corn, one pair of French Stones, one pair of grey stones. Dwelling house a short distance from the mill, all standing near the Turnpike gate on the Ashbourne road. Enquire James Webster, maltster.'

The mill was again on the market in the Derby Mercury of 22nd November, 1781, this time offered for sale by a Mrs. Webster, who was presumably the wife of the above James Webster: -

> 'A windmill, house and large close near Derby adjoining the turnpike to Ashbourne.'

Farey does not list a windmill for Derby in 1808 and it is not shown on Greenwood's map of 1825. The first Ordnance Survey map, in 1836, refers to 'Windmill Lane' in this locality but does not show the symbol for a mill. It would seem therefore that the mill had gone perhaps soon after 1800. The name of 'Windmill Hill Lane' survives to the present time.

2) Depot Mill, New Normanton

New Normanton was a small village about one mile to the south of Derby, on the lane leading to Stenson. As noted above, Farey does not list a mill in the town but there clearly was a windmill in this village in 1816, as witness the following notice in the Derby Mercury of the 1st August: -

> 'On Friday last, Thomas Hardy, in the employ of Messrs. Walker and Co., being engaged in taking down part of the windmill at their lead works in the town, fell therefrom and was killed.'

It is shown on both the Greenwood and the Ordnance Survey map of 1836 as 'Depot Mill'. The Depot White Lead works was off Normanton Road and was a predecessor to Cox Brothers Lead works, which was still operating in 1960.

The windmill was offered for sale by auction in the Derby and Chesterfield Reporter, 4th May 1855, as part of the sale of the Depot Lead works, but the advertisement gives no more information on the windmill. It does however refer to the works as being 'late of Messrs. Cox and Co.'

The windmill is not shown on the large scale Ordnance Survey map of 1880 and must have gone by that date. However a report by St. James' Church school, dated 1920, source unknown, included the description of a walk through St James' Parish, written in about 1880 as part of a history lesson. This mentions 'there was a windmill at the top of what is now Chestnut Avenue', tending to confirm that the windmill had gone by that date. There is still a public house on the nearby Dairy House Road, which is called 'The Windmill' but any connection has not been confirmed.

Mr Douglas Gifford, brother of the author, who worked at Cox Bros. Lead Works between 1949 and 1951 recalls a tower windmill with equipment inside. The windmill was by then without sails and had a flat roof. The mill was situated within the works, near to the junction of Normanton Road and Mill Hill Lane, about ½ mile to the south of the town centre. He describes it as essentially brick built, some 50' high, about 30' in diameter and with walls 2 feet thick at the ground floor level.

The wooden upright shaft was still in place and two pairs of large diameter horizontal stones, together with several pairs of smaller stones, were belt driven by a single electric motor. These were still being used to grind the white lead, used in the manufacture of lead paints, to remove any traces of metallic lead, using a continuous supply of running water.

Grids of cast lead sheet were placed on top of earthenware pots filled with acetic acid. The pots were loosely covered and stacked in rows with wood planks above and with the interstercials filled with spent tan bark.

Fermentation took place, producing carbon dioxide. Basic lead acetate was formed which reacted with the carbon dioxide to produce basic lead carbonate. Grinding removed any unreacted metallic lead.

Walker's had started business as iron founders, in Rotherham, but went into white lead production in 1778. They built their first factory, complete with windmill, at Elswick, on the banks of the River Tyne, another in Islington (with two windmills), all to be followed by the Derby venture

There therefore appears to be some confusion regarding the location of the windmill, or were there perhaps two? However Chestnut Avenue and the site described above are only a few hundred yards apart along Normanton Road and further work will be required to resolve this confusion.

In the light of the confusing evidence the following is therefore speculated for this site: -

The Depot site was acquired by Walker's in 1792 and was sold by them, to Cox Brothers in 1838. Cox's subsequently sold this site in 1855 and the windmill thereon was demolished some time before 1888. Cox's then built a new factory (in Normanton Road) a short distance away and it is conjecture that a new windmill must have been built at that time on the new site. At some date, possibly at the turn of the 19th century, the cap and sails were removed and the tower converted to use electricity, the tower being still used in the lead processing cycle. It may then have been truncated at some time but was still in use into the 1950s, the actual date it was demolished being still unknown.

3) Littleover - Chain Lane   **SK 342326**
The evidence for a windmill at the junction of Chain Lane with Burton Road, to the south of the town is limited. However in 'Littleover and its Church', by A. B. Scott published in 1916 the author states that, 'there was a windmill at one time in the field on the west side of Chain Lane, between the lane and a clump of beech trees, in that part of the field called Mill Close.'

He refers to a deed of 1721, which included 'Mill Close' but this source has not been identified. The area described was formerly occupied by the Forte Crest Hotel but has recently been subject to housing development. It is situated just off the Burton Road, on an area of rising ground, and would have been an excellent position for a windmill to be built.

The windmill does not figure on any maps nor is it included in Farey's 1808 list of Derbyshire windmills, but the Tithe Award of 1848 identifies nearby 'Near Millstone Close' and 'Far Millstone Close'.
It may be that this windmill dates back to medieval times and should be excluded from this present work. In view of the doubt it is included for the sake of completeness.

ECKINGTON

Eckington is in the north of the county, some 7 miles south-east of Sheffield. It had a population of almost 6000 in 1857 and was a well-known centre of scythe and sickle manufacture.

The date of building the windmill at Eckington is not known and one is not included in Farey's list of 1808. The windmill does not appear on any maps but, in 1826, a mill in the village was assessed for the Poor Rate (held by Derbyshire Records Office) at 3s-5d, described as follows: -

> 'Part of the Church field, with windmill and house, occupied by George Wilson.'

The mill and house were for sale in 1828 and were subject to a lease of 99 years, starting from 1825, at a rent of £4-4s-0d. The mill was bought by a Mr. William Wilson possibly a relative of George Wilson, however, in January 1832 disaster struck and the mill was burnt to the ground. This event was reported in the Derby Mercury as follows:-

> 'The windmill at Eckington, belonging to Mr Wilson, was set fire to on the night of 19th January, by some wicked incendiary and was entirely burnt to the ground. It had not been used for near a fortnight nor had there been any lights used in it. Every effort was made to save the property but the entire machinery and everything inside the mill were destroyed. Part of the wooden steps leading to the mill were the only things that were unburnt.'

The fact that wooden steps survived the fire is a clear indication that the mill was in fact a post mill. The destruction by fire of post mills was not uncommon, (see the entry on Marlpool windmill).This calamity appears to have been the end of both the windmill and William Wilson who, in 1838, had his land and remaining property sold, he being an insolvent debtor.

EYAM

This is probably one of the most northerly points in the county that a windmill was built. Certainly it was one of the very few wind-powered mills that occurred in the essentially hilly and mountainous areas of the Peak District, since this is a region with bountiful supplies of water. The date this stone tower mill was built and why it was built is unclear, (see later). No advertisements have been found concerning the sale or letting of this mill. It is not listed by Farey in 1808, and the first map on which it is shown is Greenwood's of 1827.

In 1853 Dr. Spencer Hall observed in his book 'The Peak and the Plain': -

> 'It was a tall windmill and was constantly flinging round its long dark sails in the air.'

In 1857 White's Directory records that William Hall was the miller, but in 1876, no miller is given. It is not clear exactly what were the main crops to be ground in the mill but they may well have been barley and oats, rather than wheat.

Painting of Eyam windmill by John Plant, 1877.

Mr John Plant who lived in the village was a local artist and poet. One of his paintings, made in September of 1874, is now in Eyam Museum. On the reverse side, written in copperplate handwriting, it says: -

'The old mill is at rest, the sails are all furled'

The 15" x 10" painting clearly shows the windmill with an adjacent barn and cottage. The painting was used as a basis for the village well dressing in 1961. A tall slender mill, it had five floors and an ogee shaped cap and stood in a quiet country lane. The cladding on the cap was partially missing. There was a fantail frame and four shuttered sails, one of which had broken off, confirming that the mill had reached the end of its working life when the painting was made. There is some evidence in the painting that the mill may have used roller-reefing sails.

The mill was demolished about 1877 and it is said that the stone from the tower was used in the building of the Church School in the village. In 1995 the adjacent barn had been converted into a house, the owner commenting that 'all the cracks and crannies were full of grain when we opened it up'. In the garden there is a small pile of stones and rubble - the end of another windmill.

The following is an abstract from a poem, 'The Old Windmill' by John Plant, probably written about 1877 when the mill had been sold to be demolished.

Can you grumble if I fail
When the wind has snapped my sail
Only put me new ones on
And the grinding shall go on

The Restoration of Heage Windmill

The New Access Road

The Sails Come Off

Followed by the Cap

Which is Lowered to the Ground

The Wallower Gear Exposed

The Scaffolded Tower

Assembling Curb Roller

The Brake Wheel

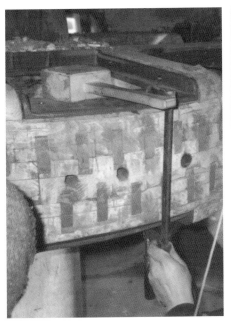

Reinforcing the Great Spur Wheel

Working on the Cap

A Working Party

A New Governor is Fitted

Dressing the Millstones

The First Sail is Lifted

The Sponsored Shutters

Opening the Windmill – May 2002

If you let me have your grain
You shall have it back again
And when I have made it meal
Fear me not - I will not steal.

If the miller will be true
All is right for me and you
Unless parleying, I am sold
Bartered for the love of gold.'

Discussions with Eyam History Group members have suggested that the mill may have been built to meet the needs of local miners. In the early 19th century the population of the village was much larger than at present and each miner had his own strip of land on which to cultivate crops, often including oats. The Lord of the Manor, who held the mining rights would also control milling in the area and it seems the mill might have been built to satisfy the local mining population's need

The village of Eyam, famous for its connection with the plague in the 17th century, is about 5 miles north of the market town of Bakewell. The windmill was located on Windmill Lane, about a quarter of a mile west-north-west of the village.

HAZELWOOD   SK 333460
This unusual windmill was in a field at Hazelwood, just above Belper, located between Godwin's Lane and the Chevin Road to Farnah Green, close to a public footpath. The site is marked on a 1906 Ordnance Survey map as a wind pump.

It was a rather strange smock mill-like structure, with a wooden tower, apparently covered with small wooden panels, surmounted by a very small cap. A long tail pole stretched down to the ground, and there were four sails, each with a leader board (a board fixed to the front edge of the sail to direct the wind onto the cloth or shutters), and with open bays, which might have had shutters at some time.

The structure was located in the middle of a field, with a ridged stone building close by. It is in fact the only smock type of windmill that has been found in Derbyshire. The mill was built just before the end of the nineteenth century and had a wooden frame, covered externally with a reddish coloured felt-like material. She was used to draw water from a deep well into a storage tank in the nearby building.

The windmill was demolished shortly before the 1939 war, but the building with the tank inside, was still standing a few years ago.

Hazelwood Wind Pump

Nothing has been found about the actual machinery that was located inside. From the tank, water was then pumped by an engine (nature unknown) up to a nearby large house, probably Hazelwood Hall, which at that time was owned by a Sir John (Commander) Aligne, who lived there with his three sisters.

HOLBROOK   SK 366453

Six miles north of Derby, high above Duffield on the last ridge of the Pennines is Holbrook Moor. There is no windmill shown there on Burdett's map in 1767, but there is one clearly marked on both Greenwood's map of 1825 and, right on the eastern edge, on the first edition of the Ordnance Survey map dated 1836. Farey does not include the mill in his list of working mills in 1808.

Mr. Robert Sheldon is listed as the miller at Holbrook in 1829 but no other records have been found. The Tithe Map of 1841 shows what is probably a post mill, located in field number 2. The mill does not appear on any maps after 1880 and it seems that its life was probably less than about 50 years.

HORSLEY PARK
SK 377439

Horsley Park is about 5 miles north of Derby, between Coxbench and Kilburn. No windmill is shown at Horsley on Burdett's map of 1767 but John Farey includes a mill in his 1808 listing of Derbyshire mills as 'Hosley' and it is assumed that this is an old spelling of the village name since no other similar connection has been made.

It is not however shown on the 1836 Ordnance Survey map and we can conclude that the mill's lifespan was short. It may have been a post mill that was moved elsewhere.

However the fact that there was a mill is borne out by the Tithe Award of 1844 which records a field as:-

> 'Mill close - Four acres.'

This tends to support the fact that the mill had disappeared within about thirty years of the Farey listing. No other information has been found and the exact site is not known.

HULLAND WARD
SK 266475

Hulland Ward is a small village on the Ashbourne to Belper road. The windmill was situated on the west side of a small lane leading to Biggin, on what is now called Windmill Farm. There was a water mill very close by in Biggin.

The mill was probably built about 1830. She is not listed by Farey and does not figure on Greenwood's map of 1825 but is shown on the Ordnance map of 1836. She was advertised for sale in the Derby Mercury on the first of March 1843 and was described as follows: -

> 'Newly erected stone built windmill with excellent new machinery, two pairs of stones, gearing for three, dressing. Close of land called Little Common Piece - occupied by Mr Richard Wilcockson. The mill is admirably situated for wind and neighbourhood ensures constant work.'

There was another advertisement in the same issue of the newspaper for the watermill, again occupied by Richard Wilcockson, so they were probably used as a working pair. This is not so uncommon since for instance Heage also was operated as a combination of a wind and a watermill. In 1841 Richard and George Wilcockson were occupants of Biggin water mill.

This was taken over by Mr. Anthony Buxton about 1850 but it is not clear if he still operated the windmill or indeed the date when she ceased to work. She is not shown on the 1880 Ordnance Survey map but the water mill continued to operate for many more years.

ILKESTON

The town of Ilkeston is on the eastern county border and is situated about 5 miles to the west of Nottingham. On Burdett's map of 1767 it is shown as a very small village with a water mill and two adjacent coalmines. There are no windmills shown in the area but there is, however, evidence that there were subsequently at least three in the town.

1) Lawn Gardens   SK 464423 approx.

This mill was probably located about half a mile north of the town, in an area known as Lawn Gardens. Farey in 1808 lists two working windmills in Ilkeston, but which they were exactly is not known.

There is an advertisement in the Derby Mercury in 1817 which, unfortunately, is not specific as to which mill it refers: -

> 'Ilkestone - sale of windmill complete with two pairs French stones, dressing machine - late occupation of Sarah Sills.'

The life of this mill is not well documented, in fact the most positive information is given in what might be seen as its obituary. It suffered the fate of so many post mills and was destroyed by fire, the last moments being described in a book, 'A History of Ilkeston', published in 1880 by Trueman and Marston.

> 'A flour mill in the occupation of a man named Morley, formerly standing on a space now occupied by Lawn Gardens, took fire early one morning in 1831, at 5 am. The whole building was a mass of flame that lit up the whole district. Fire raged until only the walls were left. At daylight hundreds of people came to see the effects of the fire which was thought to have been caused by the axle of the sails being too hot from want of oil.'

This description does not make clear the type of mill (strangely referred to as 'a flour mill') but clearly it was a windmill and, by the way it burnt, probably a post mill. No references to the millers, other than poor Morley and possibly Sarah Sills, referred to above, have been found.

2) Hungar Hill (Field Mill)   SK 465420

This windmill, believed to be a post mill, was on the outskirts of the town, about half a mile to the south and near to the junction of what is now the A609 to Nottingham and the road to Stanton-by-Dale.

The advertisement dated 1817, given above, could well apply to this mill but no positive connection has been made. It appears on Greenwood's map of 1825 and on the first Ordnance Survey map of 1836, but thereafter is absent from maps, the area being designated 'Field House'.

According to a report in the Ilkeston Pioneer of 3rd August 1934, this mill was moved and relocated on Derby Road in about the middle of the nineteenth century, the timing approximately coinciding with the appearance of a windmill in that location. **(See below)**.

3) Derby Road   SK 458413

Situated a few yards to the north of the A609 leading from the town to Derby, this post mill was about 1 mile from the town centre close to the Nutbrook Canal.

It is said that this windmill was in fact the one referred to above, at Hungar Hill, which had been relocated on the other side of the town, possibly to accommodate the building of 'Field House' but no written evidence to support this has been found.

It certainly does not appear on either Greenwood's map or the first edition of the Ordnance Survey in 1836 but is shown on the 1876 Ordnance map published in 1896, as a working mill, suggesting it was erected about the middle of the century. By the 1905/06 revision of the Ordnance Survey, published in 1908, it had become the 'Old Windmill'. It continued to appear in this form until the mid 1930s when it disappeared.

An advertisement in 'The Miller' of June 1885, advises: -

> 'To be sold - a good Post Mill at Ilkeston, Derbyshire, to be removed off premises, with four spring sails, one pair French and one pair grey stones, spur gear etc.'

It was not sold and moved however since a photograph at about the turn of the century, which is held by Ilkeston Reference Library, shows the windmill as a complete post mill with a porch extension at the rear complete with a brick roundhouse which has external buttresses. The overall appearance is almost identical to the 'Cat and Fiddle' at Dale Abbey which is still standing. The four spring sails are in place, one pair having seven bays for shutters whilst each of the others has eight. The ladder and tailpole are in place and a man is climbing up to the buck suggesting it could have been still working.

Another photograph taken about 10 years later again shows the mill and whilst the buck, roundhouse and ladder are still complete, the sails have gone. In the early 1920s a further photograph shows that it has lost the ladder and that the roof of both the buck and the porch were obviously badly damaged.

A notice on page 21 of the catalogue of the sale of the Duke of Rutland's Ilkeston estates in September 1920 completes the demise. This offers two enclosures of grass with buildings. These are further described as a stable and the remains of an old windmill.
It concludes by stating that the site of the old windmill would make an excellent site on which to erect a residence. Presumably the mill was sold and subsequently demolished.

It has not been possible to tie millers in Ilkeston to particular windmills and this was made even more difficult by the presence of both the water mill and a steam mill in the town.

KILBURN
SK 382455

The village of Kilburn lies about 8 miles due north of Derby, just off the A61 Alfreton main road. An advertisement in the Derby Mercury of 21st March 1821, offers for sale in Kilburn: -

'A freehold dwelling house and capital smock mill, one pair of French stones and one pair of Grey stones, dressing machine etc. in complete repair, together with 18 acres of land, all newly built and in good repair.'

By 1829 it is again on the market, this time to let, in an advertisement in the Derby Mercury of 4th March: -

'Tower wind mill, 2 pairs of French and 1 pair grey stones, dressing machine, corn screen, all in good repair - together with a stone house and 19 acres of land.'

This again confirms that the use of the term 'smock' is not in line with current convention and also advises that another pair of French stones have been added since 1821. The mill is shown on the 1836 Ordnance Survey map as 'Kilburn Mill' (no symbol), and does not appear on any maps after 1879.

KIRK IRETON
SK 265508

The village of Kirk Ireton stands at about 600 feet above sea level and presently the site virtually overlooks Carsington reservoir, being situated just off the Duffield to Wirksworth road.

There is not a windmill at Kirk Ireton in Farey's list of 1808 and it does not appear on Greenwood's map of 1825. A windmill is however shown on both Sanderson's map of 1835 and on the Ordnance Survey map of 1836, just east of the road leading from the village to Callow.

It was adjacent to a public house which became known as 'Windmill Inn' and an advertisement in the Derby Mercury of the 19th of February 1840, offers for sale in the village: -

'A smock windmill, 3 pairs of stones, drying kiln, together with all requisite machinery and public house with 2 acres of land - enquire Wm. Gretorex, Sherburn Mill, Wirksworth.'

Windmill Inn subsequently became a private house and the windmill had disappeared well before 1880. No records of any millers have been found and there are no signs of the mill today.

Note - Sherburn Mill is a water mill, still in existence at SK 293478.

LONG EATON

John Farey in 1808, lists a windmill at Long Eaton. In almost every other case supportive evidence has been found for the presence of a mill, wherever he has indicated the presence of a windmill in Derbyshire. However, despite considerable search no reference to a windmill in Long Eaton has been found other than the Farey list. Farey may not have conducted all of his survey personally and may well have used some information supplied by others. It is just conceivable that the mill, described in here as Sawley, and shown on the 1836 Ordnance Survey map midway between Sawley and Long Eaton (about 2 miles) had been reported to him variously, by different individuals as Long Eaton and also as Sawley - there is no way to find out.

LOSCOE

Loscoe is a village about a mile north-west of Heanor and south-west of Ripley. There is no windmill indicated here on Burdett's map in 1767, but Greenwood's map of 1825 clearly shows that a windmill was situated on land to the east of the village known as Loscoe Fields, close to a small lake and stream. The windmill also appears on the 1836 Ordnance Survey map as 'Loscoe Mill'.

Little has been found about the mill but an advertisement in the Derby Mercury of 6th March, 1844, concerning the sale of a water mill on the nearby stream states: -

> 'For Sale - Loscoe water corn mills with three pairs of stones - windmill nearby with two pairs of stones.'

In the same newspaper 10th September 1851 the mill is for sale as: -

> 'Post Mill with French and Grey Stones - apply T. N. Starbuch.'

The mill was therefore a post mill with two pairs of stones and probably did not have a round house, since this is not mentioned. It has not been noted on later Ordnance Survey maps and may have been removed after the 1851 sale.

LOWER PILSLEY

This site lies about one and a half miles to the east of Clay Cross, adjacent to Park House Green. The mill is marked as 'windmill', together with the small windmill symbol, on the one inch Ordnance Survey Map published in 1897, at a point locally known as Hagg Hill. No other record of the mill has been found it and it is not marked on earlier or subsequent ordnance maps, nor on early maps by Burdett, Greenwood, Sanderson, etc.

No record of millers has been noted in any trade directories and yet it is most unusual for the Ordnance Survey surveyors to portray a mill on their maps without clear evidence being available at the time of the survey, noted as 1875-85. It is just possible that this could be a wind engine (pump) but this seems unlikely. Continued investigations are required.

Mapperley village is about half a mile to the north of the A609, the Derby road to Ilkeston. The windmill was about 200 yards to the east of the church, on a ridge overlooking the village. It was a post mill, which was similar to those at Dale Abbey, Ilkeston (Derby Road) and West Hallam, so much so that one could wonder if they were all built by the same millwright. The actual date she was built is however not known.

It does not appear on either Burdett's map of 1767, on Farey's list of working mills in the county produced in 1808. It is first shown on Greenwood's map of 1825 and again on the first edition of the Ordnance Survey map in 1836.

The mill was advertised for sale in the Derby Mercury on the 22nd of September 1847: -

> 'Sale of Mapperley Windmill. By Auction - At Mapperley, a wind corn mill with drying kiln, late of Mr. T. Martin.'

Thomas Martin was the miller until his death shortly before this date. It continued to operate under the Martin family names of James and Martin, but it is not clear if they bought the mill or became tenants.

The windmill was for sale again in 1862 according to the Derby Mercury of 19th November: -

> 'For Sale - Freehold estate in occupation of Francis Martin. Includes five fields, post wind corn mill, drying kiln, farmhouse, etc.'

The uncertain future of the mill continued since, in the Ilkeston Pioneer of 8th November 1866, under a heading 'Mapperley mill', a variety of furniture, animals, farm implements etc. were offered for sale, along with 'winter eating of 20 acres of grassland with possession of the windmill up to Lady Day next'.

It is believed the mill fell out of use soon after this date as it was not working when surveyed in 1876-82, being marked as 'Old Windmill'. A photograph of the mill taken about 1900 shows the buck with much of the cladding missing, the round house overgrown with small trees and just one sail hanging forlornly down, the brake wheel is visible though vestiges of roof timbers.

Karl Wood made a painting of the remains in 1932 which suggests that the buck had been blown off the round house, the side girts and other timbers are shown upended above two pairs of stones, whilst lying underneath is the windshaft.

In a paper on 'The Economical side of History', probably written at the turn of the 19th century, Professor James Roger commenting on Mapperley village, wrote: -

'The only houses of any pretensions in the village were the Lord's, the parson's and the miller's, who by prescription, took a toll from all the inhabitants who were bound to grind at his mill, who was a busy and, according to the current report, not an over scrupulous personage in his dealing with his fellow villagers. Time has made havoc of three of these mills and they stand as dismantled wrecks of their former glory. The sails of the remaining mill may be seen sweeping round any day when the winds blow free. Twenty years ago all the four mills were in full working order.'

The working mill is assumed to be Dale Abbey whilst those that had deceased were probably Marlpool, West Hallam and Mapperley itself.

MARLPOOL   SK 442456
The village of Marlpool is on the A 609 Ilkeston to Heanor road, just outside Heanor itself. The symbol for a windmill appears on Burdett's map of 1767, on the road leading south from Heanor to Ilkeston, probably at Marlpool.

This is supported by an advertisement in the Derby Mercury in 1801 offering 'Windmill House' for sale, noting that there had been a windmill on adjacent land. Clearly an original mill had gone, either having been damaged beyond repair or been moved to a new site.

Another windmill was then built on the site but a report in the Derby Mercury of the 17th December 1828 advised that: -

'On the 4th of December, between the hours of 8 and 12 at night, a post mill belonging to Mr. Samuel Abbott was entirely consumed in a major fire, together with a quantity of flour and corn which were inside. The fire had started in the round house. No work had been carried out recently from which the accident could have arisen nor had any lights been used. It is concluded that this is the work of incendiaries.'

Subsequently a reward of 50 guineas was offered but it is not known if this was ever paid! In the same issue of the paper there is a letter from the owner, Samuel Abbott, appealing for help in his distress. He says the mill was one of the largest post mills in the county, which had cost more than 500 guineas, and it had contained over £150 worth of stock.

He had left it secure at 8 o'clock, but that it was set on fire by some malicious person. Flames were seen to issue from the round house and the mill was left a complete heap of smoking ruins. He further says that his wife, who was dangerously ill with an inflammatory affliction, twelve children and himself are all dependent on the mill for support and asks that gentlemen subscribe to help him out.

Help must have been to hand since Mr Abbott built another mill, believed to be a tower mill, in about 1830. Kerry, in his 'History of Smalley', 1905, refers to parts from the fire damaged mill at Smalley being taken to Marlpool early in the 19th century and these may well have been used in the new mill . The mill was assisted by an 8 H.P. steam engine. This new mill is shown on the 1836 Ordnance Survey map as 'Marlpool Mill', although the mill symbol is not given. It was shown to be working on the 1881 Ordnance Survey map, although no miller is given in Kelly's Directory of Derbyshire for 1875, and the mill had disappeared by the 1895 edition of the map.

However the Ilkeston Pioneer carried an advertisement in 1884 offering the 'old established corn mill and genteel residence,' to be let. It further advises that: -

> 'A good trade might be done by a steady persevering man, in pig food etc., and grinding flour for farmers in the neighbourhood.'

The problems of keeping a windmill operating commercially at that time are clearly seen by a further advertisement, in the same paper, during 1885. The mill was to be broken up and an auction was to dispose of the engine, boiler (24' long, and 3' 6" in diameter), and the whole of the gearing and machinery of the mill. Also to be disposed of were 'the sails and wind apparatus'. The life of yet another Derbyshire windmill was over.

MELBOURNE   SK 370245

The date when the post mill on Ticknall road, Melbourne was built is unclear but an advertisement in the Derby Mercury of 20th and 27th June 1782 must have referred to this windmill, since the other windmill on the Melbourne Common (described earlier) was not built until 1797. It read: -

> 'A windmill, in the Parish of Melbourne, in good repair, with dressing mill, two pairs of stones etc. Enquire Mr. Thomas Erpe of Melbourne.'

A further advert in 1788 again placed the windmill up for sale: -

> 'For Sale: - Windmill at Derby Hills, near Melbourne, with a new pair of French stones and grey stones, and a new flour machine. Enquire of Joseph Bailey at Melbourne.'

The mill appears in a number of adverts up to 1853 when the final one appeared clearly offering a post mill for sale, with two pairs of stones. No more was heard of this mill and it did not appear on the 1882 Ordnance Survey map.

Some years ago a circular mound was visible but no signs of the mill site can be found at the present day. The position would clearly suit the building and operation of a windmill.

The original windmill at Mickleover was built just south west of the village, south of the Uttoxeter road. It was sited in a large open field called Mill Field, before the Enclosures Act changed the landscape. A wind mill in Mickleover is listed by John Farey in 1808 and this may well be the one referred to by Samuel Hill a local baker who, in his will left to his wife, Penelope, 'all my property and my mills'. (It is not known which were his other mills).

Ordnance Survey map. In 1841 the miller was George Hill, a son of Samuel. The mill was apparently dismantled and moved in 1850 when the Derby Lunatic Asylum, later known as Pastures Hospital, was built on the site. The mill, or its main components, was moved to Common Road, later known as Windmill Close, off Station Road, Mickleover, at about this time. The three-storey brick tower had a very slight batter and later stood in a small yard.

Mickleover mill painted by Karl Wood in 1932.

In 1851 the Hill family still retained control of the mill, the miller still being George, whilst Thomas was a journeyman miller. By the 1861 census Thomas had become the master miller and in 1871 had added farming to his activities. The mill worked until about the turn of the century, as there was no miller listed by Kelly in 1895. Karl Wood, in 1932, painted the tower, without a cap and with the shears bare (see below). There are no windows or doors visible but a 1936 photograph shows two vertical lines of windows whilst otherwise quite similar to the Karl Wood painting.

She was shown as 'derelict' on a large scale 1956 Geographia map of the town of Derby. At some time part of the upper floors were removed and it was demolished in about 1973/74. The actual site now forms part of a housing estate, built soon afterwards, where roads in the area are named 'Mill Lane' and 'Mill Croft'.

MOSBOROUGH

A record in the Court Rolls of the Manor of Eckington, in 1802, notes that: -

> 'John Unwin, of Plumley Lane, millwright, had a messuage in Plumley Lane together with a newly erected windmill for the grinding of corn into flour.'

This windmill was built on a long, strip-like field, about half a mile to the west of the village of Mosborough, and to the south of Plumley Lane. The Mosborough Poor Rate Assessment schedule for 1856 includes field 1037, named as 'Windmill Croft', noting the presence of a smock mill*. There was a kiln included in the assessment and the owner was a Joseph Oates, The miller at that time was given as William Whiteley. The 1856 assessment notes that 'the windmill was not in a rateable state' and she had gone when the 1877 Ordnance Survey map was produced. No trace remains on the ground today.

*The description of the mill as a 'smock mill' almost certainly, in Derbyshire, relates to a brick or stone tower mill. (See comments on this subject under 'Heage').

Note. The site presently lies a few yards outside the county boundary but when the mill was operational, was within the county (boundary moved 1974).

Millers noted include:-

John Unwin	1802-1842	Joseph Unwin (son?)	1815-1823
Sykes and Hartley	1842 1846	William Whitley	1846-1852

MUGGINGTON

The small village of Muggington is about seven miles north-west of Derby and is some three miles to the east of the Derby to Ashbourne road, the A52.

The windmill does not appear on Greenwood's map of 1825 but is shown on both Sanderson's map of 1835 and on the first Ordnance Survey map in 1836 (as a tower mill). On the Tithe Award map of 1848 the windmill is adjacent to a house, in Windmill Field, about 200 yards to the north of the centre of the village. The associated schedule notes that the mill was owned by George Poyser but was occupied by John Ford who is later included in White's Directory, 1857, as 'corn miller and shopkeeper'. Kelly's Directory, 1876, has Joseph Holbrook as the miller at Muggington and also at nearby Mercaston, but it is not clear what type of mill was involved. No advertisements have been found for the sale or letting of this mill. It appears to have been built about 1830 but its life has not been established. No structure remains on the site at the present time but, in the grounds of 'Mill House', which sits on the brow of a rounded hill, are many hand made bricks, evidence supporting the presence of a brick tower mill in this village. It would have been an admirable site for a windmill!

NETHERSEAL

Netherseal is a village in the south of the county, about five miles south-west of Ashby-de-La-Zouch. The windmill was behind 'Windmill Farm', on the south side of Hunts Lane, about 3/4 of a mile north west of the village. The mill is not listed by Farey in 1808 but is shown on the first Ordnance Survey map in 1834 when it appears as a post mill, although at that time it was in Leicestershire.

It was offered for sale by auction in 1841 according to the Derby Mercury of 3rd November as follows: -

> 'Newly erected Post Mill with round house and seven acres of land, near the village of Netherseal.'

In 1843, under the Tithe Award, the mill and adjacent property was owned by Reuben Stevenson, with the family retaining control throughout its life.

It was worked until about 1905 (when it appears as a 'windmill' on the Ordnance Survey map), the last miller being Mr Fred Stevenson according to Simmons.
Millers include: -

1851	William Thorpe, aged 25 years, journeyman miller (meaning he was employed and did not own the mill).
1870	Thomas Stevenson, miller, born at Stretton.
1900-04	Frederick Stevenson - windmiller (and steam miller).

Several photographs taken at the turn of the 19th century give a clear picture of the mill. The white painted, horizontally boarded buck, which has a curved roof, sits on the top of a tall, slender, brick round house with external buttresses. The round house, most unusually, had four round windows just below the curb (assuming it was a Midland type mill). The skirt does not appear to be complete but the tailpole and ladder were still in place. There were four sails, two common and two spring, complete with shutters, mounted in a double poll end.

In 1994, the site, behind Windmill Farm, did not show any evidence of the mill structures, but a circular hedge enclosure, some 25 yards diameter, denotes its location. There are several fragments of broken grey millstones which appear to have been about 5' 4" diameter in the garden and also next door, at 'The Mires'.

NEWHALL

The village of Newhall is in the south of the county, some four miles east of Burton on Trent, which is in Staffordshire. The windmill was located about half a mile to the south west of the Burton to Ashby Road, the A50. A mill at Newhall is first noted by Farey in 1808 but appears on Greenwood's map of 1825, and on the first Ordnance Survey map in 1836, when it is depicted as a post mill.

It was offered for sale in the Derby Mercury of 17th August 1831, under a heading 'Windmill and Meadow Land', as follows: -

'Under the estate of Mr Humphry Higgett, deceased the undermentioned valuable property, All of the estate and interest in all that valuable CORN WIND MILL, most eligibly situated in the township of Newhall, in excellent repair and in the possession of Cantrell. Also the plot of land whereon the said wind mill stands. Held by lease which has 14 years unexpired at the rent of £5. The Lessee has the privilege of removing the windmill at any time during the term.'

The fact the windmill could be moved if required virtually confirms it to be a post mill. She obviously continued to operate in Newhall since in 1835/41 a miller is listed as William Kinnersley and Son. The date when the mill ceased to operate is not clear but the lease would have terminated in 1845.

NITTICAR HILL   SK 488786

The settlement of Nitticar Hill is just a very small group of buildings, about a mile north-east of Barlborough, on the A618 Clowne to Rotherham road. Little is known about a windmill which was built here. It was shown on Burdett's map of 1767 just to the west of the road and close to Barlborough Hall. It is listed by Farey in 1808 as 'Knitacre' but does not appear on subsequent maps.

Nitticar Hill Wood, which now approximately occupies the site shown by Burdett, was originally planted about 1830 and the mill must have gone by then. The mill was probably a post mill and its life of 50 - 60 years may have been typical of many small mills of this type.

PLEASLEY   SK 500645

Pleasley is a small mining village about four miles north-west of Mansfield, on the eastern county boundary. Close to the village, to the north-east, was a large cotton mill and the windmill was probably located some quarter of a mile due west of the village.

The mill in Windmill Lane was first listed by John Farey in 1808, when the name was spelt 'Pleseley'. It appears on Greenwood's map of 1825 and on the 1836 Ordnance Survey map, as a post mill, but had disappeared by the late 1860s, a colliery, built about 1870, being built over the spot. It is obviously not shown on the Ordnance Survey map for 1890. The miller between 1846 and 1862 was Samuel Fox but no other millers' names are known.

RIDDINGS   SK 428525

Riddings is situated about two miles north-east of Ripley, and had a population of 3300 in 1857 when it was a mining community. Records of three windmills have been identified in the village, although nothing is listed here by Farey in 1808.

1) Riddings

An advertisement in the Derby Mercury of 7th January 1829 offers a post mill for sale, as follows: -

> **RIDDINGS MILL**. To be sold by auction by Mr. Hopkinson on Wednesday 14th January at the house of Mr. Edward Cresswell, the sign of the Black Horse, Somercotes, near Alfreton a POST WINDMILL with one pair of Grey Stones and one pair of French stones, sack tackle and flour machine complete in good repair at Riddings in the parish of Alfreton, late in the occupation of George Taylor of Riddings who will show same.

George Sanderson's map of the area, published in 1835, but based on surveys carried out during the previous five years shows a windmill, just outside the hamlet of Riddings, in open country.

The location appears to be presently situated north of what is now South High Street and adjacent to Church Street but the area is now all built up and no trace remains of the mill which, as a post mill, was easily moved.

It has been suggested (Amber Valley Borough Council guide 'A walk around Riddings') that James Oakes (see later) bought the post mill, and the associated site in order to sink a colliery and to build the twin mills referred to later, but no evidence has yet been found to support this.

Karl Wood, in one of his paintings of the twin tower mills (ref 77/2041) shows what has been suggested as being the round house of a post mill, but the author considers this may have been the remains of a kiln.

2) Riddings, 'JAMES AND SARAH', Twin Tower Mills.

The last windmills to be built in Derbyshire were the twin tower mills, built a few yards to the east of Greenhill Lane, Riddings, in 1877, reportedly built at a cost of £17,000 each.

Most published information on these mills, has in the past, contained text to the effect that

> 'These mills were built by James Oakes, a local iron founder and colliery owner, and they were named 'James' and 'Sarah' after his wife and himself.'

It has now become clear (see bibliography) that James Oakes had died in 1868, before the mills were built, and that they were in fact, built by his bachelor brother Thomas Haden Oakes. Thomas named the mills after his parents, James (died 1845) and Sarah (died 1860), and was himself renowned as a great public benefactor in the community. It is just possible that the connection with 'James Oakes' stemmed from the company name.

James and Sarah tower mills c.1910.

The brick tower for 'James' was said to be 90 feet high to the top of the finial on the cap, 35 feet in diameter at the base and had eight floors, whilst 'Sarah' was certainly a little smaller, reportedly being just 67 feet high, with seven floors. This latter height, judged from photographic evidence, appears to be far too small. It would be difficult to believe that there was more than 10 feet difference in height.

Both mills were similar in shape and construction, and had domed ogee shaped caps, similar to that at Heage, complete with ball finials, eight-blade fan tails and unusually for the area, open galleries both above the second floor and surrounding the cap.

Simmons reports that Rex Wailes had noted that the mills had 'dead curbs', i.e. the cap was not mounted on rollers. The six-arm iron crosses were 15 feet across and were mounted on cast iron wind shafts, which were 16" diameter at the neck. 'James' had six patent, double sided sails, each with 24 shutters, whilst most records suggest that 'Sarah' never had sails fitted. This has always been ascribed as being as a result of a major error on the part of the unknown millwright (or maybe at the insistence of the owner), the mills were too close together to work properly. (See discussion at end of this section.)

A photograph inside one of the mills shows one pair of stones in a wooden vat, fitted with conventional furniture, with an iron stone nut and wooden cogs, but there must have been many more. The brake wheel is reported by Simmons to be one-piece cast iron, with segmental teeth bolted on. No other details on the internal machinery for these mills of relatively late construction, has been found.

Note. A recent booklet on these mills (see bibliography) suggests 'Sarah' had had sails fitted in 1877 but they were 'blown off' some ten years later and were never replaced. This has not yet been verified by this author and will be the subject of further research.

A photograph taken in 1910 shows 'James' working under wind whilst 'Sarah' has no sails or fantail. The sails were subsequently removed from James, in 1918. One mill, now believed to be 'James', continued to produce animal feed throughout the 1939/45 war, powered by a 24 HP oil engine.

The extensive outbuildings round the mills were used during the war as the headquarters of the local Air Scouts and Air Cadets whilst the ground floor of 'Sarah' was cleared and converted into a gymnasium for their use. On other floors instruction was given in radio, navigation and aero engines. At the end of the war the Granwood Flooring Company used the mill to store up to 600 tons of sawdust. Karl Wood visited the site three times, in 1932, 1939 and 1940, and his paintings show little change in their external condition. The wind shafts and iron crosses were removed in 1950, by detaching the bearings and letting the huge casting fall to the ground. Together with other internal machinery over 40 tons of scrap iron were cleared from the site. A photograph, taken at that time showed that the iron crosses and fan stagings had disappeared but surprisingly both upper and lower galleries were still in place on the two mills.

The site and the mills were sold in 1948 to a chemical company, Deosan, and they were initially used to house part of their processes. In 1961 the company needed to reorganise the site and to do this advised that they were planning to demolish the mills.

There was considerable local opposition but, in January 29th 1963, matters were brought to a head since in the early hours of that day a disastrous fire raged through 'James', leaving just a bleak shell. The end came shortly after, when the remains of both mills were demolished,, to be replaced by new factory premises.
By 1999 the operators, Deosan, had closed down and at the time of writing (late 2002) the site is being developed for housing.

A small plaque set into the wall outside the nearby Community Hall, and a 'time capsule' containing details of the mill embedded in the wall itself, are the only reminders of these once major landmarks of Riddings.

The stone plaque commemorating the twin tower mills at Riddings

75

Discussion.

As noted earlier the close proximity of the two towers and the fact that it has never been proved that 'Sarah' ever was fitted with sails has always been ascribed to a serious design error. In a private communication to the author, an alternative scenario has been proposed.

The Oakes family had a significant technical capability, operating both mines and an engineering works and, by the late 19th century, when the mills were built (1877), windmill technology had probably reached its zenith. We have no firm evidence to suggest that sails were ever fitted to 'Sarah', but if that was the case, 'How did they know they could not work?' They certainly would have operated satisfactorily when the wind was from specific directions - the prevailing wind perhaps? 'Were they ever designed to work together?' For the Oakes, and the unknown millwrights to have committed such an error of judgment at that time, would have represented a huge loss of face.

Is it possible that at the time they were built the industry was in such a turmoil, with the coincidental introduction of roller milling, that ideas were changing rapidly in the industry and it was decided sufficient production could be obtained from just one windmill, albeit supplemented by a secondary power source turning the second? Other questions raised include 'Why was one mill taller than the other?' 'Was the close proximity planned from the beginning, and was 'James' raised to ensure it got more of the wind?'

These thoughts open up a whole new area of research into the mystery of the twin tower windmills at Riddings and the reaction of other mills enthusiasts will be appreciated to this intriguing situation.

RIPLEY   **SK 410496**

Ripley is a small market town situated about 8 miles north-east of Derby. The windmill was at Peasehill, about half a mile to the south east of the town centre, and was known as Pease Hill Mill.

Ripley windmill at Peasehill c.1910.

76

This corn mill is not included in Burdett's map of 1767 but it is listed by Farey in 1808. It appears on Greenwood's map in 1825, and on most subsequent maps until it is recorded as 'disused' on the Ordnance Survey map of 1914. It worked in conjunction with an adjacent steam mill under common ownership. The death of Thomas Steeples, the miller, in 1892, brought to an end almost one hundred years of family operation and the mill was advertised in The Miller, June 6th 1892, as follows: -

> 'To Let, through death, Tower mill with patent sails, small steam mill, dwelling house and warehouse. Business established over a century. Address the Executors of the late T. Steeples, Pease Hill Corn Mills, Ripley.'

A winter photograph of the mill was taken about 1910, probably soon after it stopped working. This shows it to be a tall, slim, tower mill essentially made from stone block, which appears at some stage to have had a floor added to increase the height. This was achieved by the addition of a parallel-sided portion to the tower.
The domed cap had a ball finial and the fantail appears to have lost many of its blades. The four patent sails turned in an anti clockwise direction.

The mill was demolished in the 1920s and the site is now built over.

RISLEY   SK466362

The windmill was close to Risley village, about seven miles east of Derby, on the west side of Rushey Lane which runs north from the old A52 towards Stanton-by-Dale. This windmill is not shown on the Burdett map of 1767 but was present in 1798, as shown by an advertisement in the Derby Mercury of 23rd and 30th August and 6th September 1798: -

> 'To be sold by private contract, a windmill with two pairs of stones, machines, sack tackle etc, situate in the parish of Risley.'

In 1804 it was again advertised in the Derby Mercury of the 9th, 16th, and 23rd February as follows: -

> 'Estate at Risley - Messuage and barn 46 acres - a windmill on premises   to be sold with or without the estate.'

It must have remained on the market for some time because in 1810 the following advertisement appeared in the Derby Mercury of 15th March: -

> 'Sale of Risley mill, house on premises of Mr. John Fox, miller, near Risley, furniture etc, farmers and millers utensils.'

The windmill is included (spelt 'Riseley') in the list of Derbyshire windmills prepared by John Farey, 1808, and also appears on maps for 1825, 1835 and 1836.

The mill was again offered for sale in the Derby Mercury of 5th August 1835 as follows:-

> 'Post mill at Risley, sails, stones machinery, late in the occupation of Robert Elliott, field available if required, about five acres.'

No further information has been found and the site does not reveal any evidence of the presence of a mill.

SANDIACRE   SK 481356

Sandiacre is about 8 miles east of Derby where a post mill stood alongside the Derby/Sandiacre canal, on its eastern bank, close to the junction with the Erewash canal. It is not clear when the mill was built; it is not listed by John Farey in 1808 but does appear on the maps of Greenwood, 1825, and Sanderson, 1835.

The first Ordnance Survey map of 1836 does not show the standard windmill symbol in this location but does mark 'Sandiacre Mill' in the area adjacent to the junction of the two canals. This could however have been a steam corn mill, built at the same location, which was destroyed by fire in 1841 according to the Derby Mercury of the 21st July.

The windmill was advertised for sale in the Derby Mercury of the 12th and 19th March, 1834 as follows:-

> 'Sandiacre - For Sale. Post Windmill with grey and French stones, stone built warehouse 36 feet by 21 feet. A close of pasture land upon which they stand, 3 acres 3 roods, between and adjoining the Derby and Erewash canals. By order of the Assignees of John Thraves, a bankrupt.'

There is no further information on the mill and it may have been dismantled and taken away. It does not appear on the 1884 Ordnance Survey map, and no illustrations have been found of what must have been a very attractive location. The Plough Inn stood by the canal and the deeds show that in 1820 it was hired out together with the windmill, a farm building and several acres of land. Millers identified for this mill are John Thraves (1829-34) and John Radford (1841-57).

Nothing remains of the mill on the site today although the filled-in canal, which is now a footpath, passes by the spot.

SAWLEY   SK 482325

The village of Sawley is about two miles south-west of Long Eaton, on the B6540. A windmill is shown at Sawley on a map of 1825 and it is also shown on the 1836 Ordnance Survey map, but does not appear on the 1880 or 1896 maps.

The Derby Mercury on the 27th November 1794 reported that: -

'On Wednesday evening, at 6 pm Benjamin Platter, a journeyman miller, was robbed by two footpads near to Sawley Windmill.'

In 1801 it further notes that: -

'On 11th November Joseph Simpson, a young man employed at the windmill at Sawley got entangled in the machinery and was crushed to death'.

An advertisement on 2nd of January 1800 may also refer to the same mill, since no windmill is otherwise known at Trent Lock, which may just be the seller's address: -

'For sale - Post mill, one pair French stones and one pair grey stones, two machines - apply John Wagden - Trent Lock near Sawley.'

No other references have been found, but millers are listed for Sawley until 1861 and we must assume the mill last worked about that date.

The site is only about 200 yards from the boundary with Long Eaton and this may have led to Farey's confusion - see entry for Long Eaton. There are presently no remains in Hawthorne Avenue but the adjacent miller's house, in Tamworth Road, is still occupied.

SHARDLOW   SK 432303
The village of Shardlow lies about 5 miles south of Derby, on the A6. A lane wanders off to Aston-on-Trent and the windmill was located in a small field, just behind the village, on quite low-lying ground. This post mill was built about 1805, as witnessed by two advertisements in the Derby Mercury; the first in January 1803 concerned with raising the necessary capital to build the mill: -

'Auction Sale - Ten shares of £5-0-0 each in capital Wind Corn Mill at Shardlow.'

and also in July 1805: -

'Aston and Shardlow Union corn windmill at Shardlow will be let by private contract. It was lately erected and is in perfect condition, with proper stones, dressing machine and every other requisite for carrying out an extensive trade, either in batch or wholesale lines. Being close to the Trent and Grand canal offers opportunity to trade at Manchester and other markets.'

These advertisements indicate that the mill was in 'Union' ownership (see note below) and also that it was recognised that the canal system could be a means to open up the market.

It appears on maps in 1825, on the 1836 Ordnance Survey map and on the Tithe Award Map of 1850.

In 1851 the mill was offered for sale in the Derby Mercury of 5th November: -

> 'To be sold by Auction - Post mill, 2 pairs of French stones, recently painted - time will be allowed for removal of same.'

It clearly was not moved and continued to appear on maps until 1899 when it was designated as 'windmill - flour'. It disappeared shortly afterwards and was demolished about 1917.

H. E. Simmons reported in 1944: -

'I found the exact site, it seemed a poor position for the wind. My informant said a steam engine was used towards the end, as well as wind power. The last miller was Mr Draper, a little whiskered old man.'

He also recorded, from the London Gazette, May 28, 1850: -

> 'Edward Dawkins, now and for three years past of Great Wilne, miller and cowkeeper and for four years preceding of Shardlow, miller, an insolvent debtor. To appear at Derby on 15 June next for first examination.'

This last advertisement presumably explains why the mill was to be sold in 1851.
No illustrations of this windmill have been found to date.

Note. The principle of cooperative ownership of mills such as Shardlow and probably Chesterfield Club Mill was established at the end of the 18th century and during the Napoleonic war period.

The harvest had been poor for most of the 1790s and the miller's toll was not regulated until 1796 when some control of their profits was established. Unions or Societies, often established by groups of well meaning people, sought to ensure a supply at low prices for the masses. Few of these shareholders had experience of managing a business and they were often short lived. None the less, from this early start, emerged the Cooperative retailing concept in 1830.

SHIPLEY   SK 435445

Shipley Wood is on high ground, approximately 3 miles north-west of Ilkeston, and is now within the Shipley Country Park. A windmill at Shipley is listed as working in 1808 by Farey and it may be represented on the 1836 Ordnance Survey map, but the image of the mill symbol is not clear. The mill has not been identified on any other maps.

A report in the Derby Mercury for the 1st of June 1809 states: -

'On the 16th of May, during a violent storm a windmill at Shipley was blown down and the miller so hurt that his life was feared. He is now on the way to recovery.'

This report is contemporary with the publication of the Farey data but it may be that he collected his information well before the publication of his book or possibly that the mill had been rebuilt after the storm. If that was the case however, no further information on a mill at Shipley has been found.

SHIREBROOK   SK 532680 approx.

Shirebrook is a small village on the Nottinghamshire borders, about four miles north-east of Mansfield. For about 700 years the village was a township within the manor and parish of Pleasley. In fact Shirebrook had a greater acreage (1187 against 748) of arable land than Pleasley, when the Tithe map and accompanying apportionments were produced in 1841. This was the work of John Bromley, a surveyor and valuer of Derby, who was appointed by the Tithe Commissioners.

Bromley reported that in field 246, owned by Johnathan Robinson, named Mill Close, there was a post mill. This site is just a few yards from the county boundary and, whilst at the time of the tithe it was in open country, it now is on the edge of a moderately sized village. Evidently the mill had already been there for some years at that time since Johnathan is listed as the miller in Glover's directory of the county in 1829. It is not known when it was removed from the site.

No other records for this mill have been found and nothing remains on the ground.

SMALLEY   SK 408446

A little over eight miles north-east of Derby, on the road to Heanor, is the village of Smalley. Burdett does not include a mill here on his map of 1767 but John Farey had one in his list of working windmills in 1808. Two windmills are shown on both Greenwood's map of 1825, and on the Ordnance Survey map of 1836. One marked as 'Smalley Mill' and the other, by a windmill symbol, about half a mile to the south.

The Rev. Chas. Kelley, in his 'History of Smalley', 1909, provides some details of the windmills of the village. He records that in 1800 there were two mills in the parish. The first post mill stood at the top of Cloves Lane, on a knoll above Coppice Dumble and which was probably built about 1700.

About 1815 the tenant Mr. John Roe moved the mill from this location to one considered to be more convenient, alongside the mill dam in the village. It was far too sheltered however, and had to be replaced in its old location - at much expense. Kelley says the mill was demolished about 1856, although White's directory for 1857 notes that the miller was still Mr. John Potter.

The other post mill was working in 1800 and stood in 'Windmill Field', on the north side of Swine Hill Lane. It was built by Mr. Samuel Abbott, but was burnt down, and what was fit to be reused was moved to Marlpool. This incidentally was also burnt down in 1828 (see Marlpool). One might therefore wonder if this record confuses the two mills, which are in fact only about 4 miles apart and that the burning refers to Marlpool. No mills are shown on the 1879 Ordnance Survey map.

SMISBY   SK 343183

In the south-east of the county, almost in Leicestershire, Smisby is about 2 miles to the north of Ashby-de-la-Zouch. The windmill was about 250 yards up the lane from the A50, off on its eastern side, at Ann's Well Place, previously known as 'Annies Hole'.

It is on high ground with the land falling away on all sides. A modern bungalow now stands on the site, named 'Mill Farm'. There was a steam mill in the village and possibly another windmill (see note below).

It is not clear when this mill was built. The first record of the post windmill is by Farey in 1808, who calls it 'Smithby', but it appears on most maps subsequent to that date until, on the 1895 Ordnance Survey map it is shown as an 'Old Windmill'. It stood close to the Burton to Ashby tramway and would have been seen at work by passengers travelling along that route.

Only one rather poor photograph is known of the mill. It shows the mill, almost in silhouette, against a small building in the background. This makes it difficult to see if there had been a round house (but see below). It had a small buck with a rounded roof and was still complete with tailpole and steps. Two common sails and two spring sails were in place.

Simmons reports on a visit to the site in 1945. He notes that she was blown down in 1919-20 and that the mill stood on red brick piers, two being 5' high and the others 4'. There was a peak stone, level with the ground between the piers. In 1989 the writer found no signs of the piers although the millstone was still in the ground.

The windmill and the steam mill, appear to have been operated by the Bailey family virtually throughout their life. William Bailey was miller until 1829 when it passed on to Martha, then to Joseph (William's son) in 1850, then on to Charles Bailey, son of Joseph, until 1887. After this the records indicate that both the windmill and steam mill, were worked by Mrs. Ann Bailey until 1908, and finally, the steam mill only was operated by Thomas Bailey until 1928 - quite a family!

NOTE.   The 1883 Ordnance Survey map shows another windmill, marked disused, just off to the east of the Derby Road from Ashby and close to the village (SK 353189). No information on this mill has been found to date. It could have been a wind engine.

SOUTH NORMANTON

South Normanton lies about 3 miles east of Alfreton, very close to Junction 28 on the M1 motorway. In 1851 it had a population of 1340 and was a centre of coal mining. It has had at least four windmills in the last 250 years, of which two no longer survive. (See previous section for details of those that have some remains).

The two mills which have disappeared were both post mills, which were off to the north of the road leading to Alfreton, known as Alfreton Road.

1) The Old Post Mill   SK 439562

A number of early records suggest that the first post mill at South Normanton was built as early as about 1600/30, but no positive data has been found. Nonetheless the windmill is clearly marked on Burdett's map of 1767, well predating the known building of the second post mill. The Enclosure map of about 1804 shows a mill standing on the north side of Alfreton Road, opposite a lane now known as Birchwood Road. It was close to the end of its life however since an advertisement in the Derby Mercury on the 28th December 1809 offers the sale of the mill, by auction, in up to 30 lots as follows: -

> 'On the 6th day of January 1810, by Mr. Hickson. The ruins of a wind post
> corn mill, lately standing on South Normanton Common, near Alfreton, in
> the County of Derby; amongst which is a pair of excellent French stones,
> also three grey stones, an excellent cast metal neck with a remnant of a
> great many other appurtenances to the mill, which may prove to be useful
> to Millers and Carpenters as well as to farmers. The sale will commence at
> 12 o'clock at the mill and lots may be viewed at the mill any day previous
> to the sale.'

The wording of this advertisement must lead to the conclusion that the windmill had been seriously damaged, possibly blown over, and it thereby ceased to exist. No illustrations or descriptions of the mill have been found.

2) The Post Mill, (Grade 2 Listed)   SK442561

This better-known post mill was probably built about 1805. It is the mill listed by John Farey in 1808 and is shown on Greenwood's map of 1825 and on many subsequent maps.

Throughout its life, it was owned by the local Wass family. The miller from 1851 to 1871 was Ralph Wass who was succeeded by Thomas Wass, and who continued to operate it until he died in 1908. After that it fell into disuse and was never sold as a working mill.

Clearly when it was built it was in the open country but during its final years it became surrounded by houses, the framing of the mill eventually ending up in the garden of one of them.

A local inhabitant, Mr Norman Ludlam, who had worked as a gardener at the house, recalled that he had found a large stone, dated 1776, between the piers, which had possibly come from the early mill.

South Normanton post mill in the 1960s.

It was a classic open trestle post mill and stood on stone piers, which were about 3 feet high. The quarter bars were reinforced at the junction with the cross trees by large wedge shaped timbers. The roof was of rounded construction and the access ladder was off set to the centre of the mill. The crown tree was some 21" square. The wooden wind shaft was 8" diameter at the neck but increased to 20" at the brake wheel location. The brake wheel itself was of clasp arm construction and had 56 wooden teeth. There were two pairs of stones driven by wooden stone nuts mounted on wrought iron spindles. Two pairs of overdriven stones provided the output of the mill, one with a centrifugal and the other with a lag governor. In the tail of the mill there was a wire-dressing machine.

Millers at this post mill all appear to be from the same family, namely the Wass family. Records include Thomas (1803), John (1829-43), Ralph (1851-57) and another Thomas (1871-08), suggesting the mill worked into the 20th century.

Certainly the name Wass links with the advertisement on page 19 in respect to the building of Heage, where the 'plans are approved by Mr Wass'. One must wonder however what knowledge a 'post mill' operator would have which would permit his approval to be quoted for the building of Heage windmill, a tower mill!

The last days of South Normanton post mill prior to demolition in 1980.

A painting of the mill by Karl Wood in 1931 shows the roof of the buck exposed to the elements, apart from a few ribs. One sail still hung down from the poll end and the brake wheel is clearly visible. The steps and tail pole were missing, whilst much of the horizontal cladding of the framing had disappeared. A view by the same artist in 1939 shows the sail and all roof timbers to have disappeared whilst more of the ribbing of the buck is exposed. Photographed in 1946 by Frank Rogers all of the cladding had gone and the inside of the mill was empty, apart from the wooden windshaft which was inclined to the rear of the buck, lying over the cross tree.
The brake wheel had disappeared.

Over 15 years there had therefore been a significant deterioration in the condition of the windmill. The structure became increasingly parlous until, in March 1975 the then unlisted structure was, following the death of Mrs. H. S. Sampson, the owner, sold at auction for £12 to a Mr. Andrew Pugh of Matlock. A report in the Derbyshire Times, March 1975, under a headline 'Old Windmill doomed for the Chop' advised that the new owner was 'only interested in it for the wood'. Within a few weeks the Bolsover District Council had instigated a Grade 2 listing and the future looked better.

When seen in 1978 there was no cladding on the buck and only a wind shaft, lying within, survived of the mill's equipment. Over the next five years various plans for the mill's future were considered but in 1980 it was finally dismantled and put into storage.

For years the remains lay in Bolsover District Council's open storage yard, where they steadily deteriorated. Efforts by the council to get the mill re-erected in the grounds of the Midland Railway Trust, at Butterley, came to nothing. When they were eventually located by the author, in 1997, most were very rotten. They were removed from the site but eventually it was decided they were well past re-erection and all but a few small timbers were then burnt. A sad end for a listed structure!

85

SPINKHILL

The village of Spinkhill is about two miles north-west of Barlborough, just off the A616 Barlborough to Sheffield road. The windmill was an early stone tower mill, built before 1767, since it is shown on Burdett's map of that year, to the east of the road leading to Killamarsh. It is listed by Farey in 1808 and is present on both Greenwood's map, 1825, and on the first Ordnance Survey map of 1836.

No advertisements have been found for this windmill although millers identified were John Widdowson in 1795, William Scorthorn in 1841/51, and in 1856, Elizabeth Scorthorn, presumably his wife. The mill went out of use, probably in the 1860s, and was one of the earliest known conversions into a house, sometime in 1875-80. The Derbyshire Times, 14th April 1939, reported that it had been a house since 1879 and had lost its sails some ten years earlier. This became known as 'The Old Windmill House' and was in use until the mid 1950s, being demolished a few years later.

Karl Wood made a painting of this mill in August 1933. He portrays it as a stone tower, about two floors high, the top of which had been cut off obliquely at about 45 degrees and to the resultant slope of which a roof had been fitted. A tall brick chimney is shown running up the wall of the tower, which protruded above the highest point of the tower.

The remains of Spinkhill tower mill painted by Karl Wood in 1933.

SPONDON

Spondon village, which had some 2052 inhabitants in 1857, is three miles east of Derby, and this windmill was situated on Lock Road, about a quarter of a mile north of Spondon Church. It stood in a circular yard of what eventually became a cricket pitch, to the west of Loch Road.

It is first mentioned in the Derby Mercury of 19th May 1824 with a report that: -

> 'On Saturday last a son of Mr. Harrison of Spondon, seven years old, was struck on the head by the sails of the windmill there. His life is despaired of.'

The mill is shown on maps of 1825 and 1826 held by Derbyshire Record Office, and also on the Ordnance Survey map of 1838, as a tower mill. However it was probably a post mill, and was advertised for sale in the Derby Mercury of the 16th September 1846, as follows: -

> 'To be sold, piece of grass land of three acres with corn mill upon it, in the occupancy of Mr. Bennett.'

This is the last record identified but millers were listed until 1861.

| 1828/46 | John Bennett | 1846 | Mr. Coxon |
| 1851 | John Twigg (Sr.) | 1861 | John Twigg (Jr.) |

No illustrations or photographs of the mill are known.

SWARKESTONE LOWES   SK 336 298 approx.

Swarkestone is some four miles to the south of Derby and is at the north end of a medieval stone bridge which crosses the River Trent. The old main road to Derby continued more or less due north, along Lowes Lane, and on John Ogilby's map of 1675 a windmill is marked about three quarters of a mile from the bridge, almost at the top of the rise.

It is an area where there are a number scheduled mounds or tumuli; Lowes meaning a burial mound.

The map referred to is in the form of a strip, to be used by travelers, and the mill is clearly defined as a landmark, although nothing remains on the ground today. It is probable that the mill was in fact a post mill, since it would represent a very early date for a tower mill in the area.

There are two advertisements in the Derby Mercury in 1745, the first on January 4[th:]

> 'A new windmill, upon Swarkstone Low, enquire of John Constable of Hazelwood Mill, near Duffield.'

and in October the same year: -

> 'For Sale - a windmill standing in Swarkestone Low, in very good repair, enquire Mr. Matthew Smith, Derby.'

It is strange that if it was the same mill noted in 1675, it was advertised as 'new' in the first advertisement above. Maybe it had been refurbished. It is also of interest - why the change of owner or agent between the two adverts, only nine months apart? We shall probably never know.

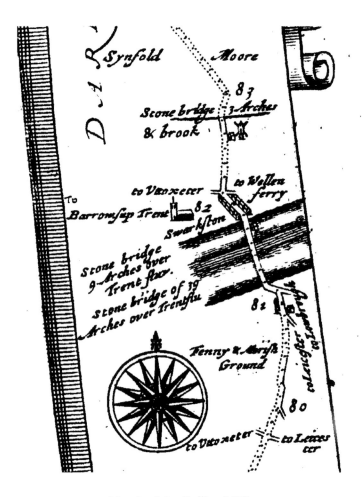

Map by John Ogilby, 1675

No windmill appears on Burdett's map in 1767 and it is not recorded on any map other than Ogilby's.

SWATHICK   **SK 365678 approx.**

Swathick is a small hamlet, just to the west of Wingerworth, a village some 2 miles south west of Chesterfield. This is the location of a windmill listed by Farey in 1808, but like the one he records as being in Long Eaton, no confirmation has been found on any old maps, advertisements or other records. There are no other known mills in the immediate vicinity of Wingerworth with which it might be confused. It remains somewhat a mystery and can only therefore be considered as being a 'probable site'.

Temple Normanton lies just south of the A617 Mansfield to Chesterfield road, about 3 miles south-east of Chesterfield. In 1851 the village had just 27 houses and 107 inhabitants. The date the tower mill was built is unclear but Rex Wailes reported that it was 'insured in 1796'.

Simmons noted the mill was covered by insurance with The Royal Exchange, on the 27th January 1798. This insurance was with John Coupe, maltster and miller, and related to the stock in trade in a brick or stone 'Smock Windmill', valued at £50. There was a warrant that there ' was no steam mill present'.

It was advertised about six times between 1800 and 1805, all of which basically offered to let a 'Smock Windmill, with shulling mill, a kiln and a malthouse'.

In 1806 there was a fatal accident at the mill, reported during November in the Derby Mercury as follows:-

> 'On Sunday last a young girl being near to a windmill at Temple Normanton was struck by one of the sails against her head, she died a few hours later.'

The mill is listed by John Farey in 1808 and appears on Greenwood's map of 1825 but not on the Ordnance Survey map of 1836. The London Gazette of October 29th, 1838, according to Simmons, reports that the former miller, John Spencer of Temple Normanton was declared bankrupt. He must have escaped this situation however since he was still the miller in 1846. In 1864,

J. Mills was the last known miller and the mill probably ceased operation about that time. Sometime later in the century it was converted into a house, which was occupied by two families, 'one up and one down'.

Karl Wood's painting in 1934 shows it to be of stone, four stories high and with a hexagonal, pointed roof. A chimney stack emerged through the roof and an upper door was approached via a flight of stairs. However, a year later, in 1935, it was the subject of a Ministry of Health enquiry seeking demolition. Commenting on the proposed action the Derby Evening Telegraph states: -

> 'The Society for the Preservation of Ancient Windmills has been little heard of in this part of the world but there are people in Derbyshire who are turning to it for assistance in saving the old windmill at Temple Normanton'.

It was however decided that the occupants must leave and the mill was in fact demolished shortly afterwards.

Temple Normanton tower mill painted by Karl Wood in 1934.

SATURDAY, MAY 12, 1832.

Windmill, Public-House, and Land,
AT TEMPLE NORMANTON.

To be Let,

AND MAY BE ENTERED UPON IMMEDIATELY,

A POWERFUL SMOCK WINDMILL, situate at Temple Normanton, in the County of Derby, containing one pair of French Stones, one pair of Grey Stones, Dressing Machine, Sacking Tackle, and Gearing complete.—Also a SHELLING MILL and DRYING KILN adjoining.

Likewise a newly erected PUBLIC-HOUSE, near the Mill, on the Turnpike Road from Chesterfield to Mansfield, and 17 Acres of good LAND, with a Barn, Stabling, Cow houses, and other Outbuildings.

All the above Premises are now in the possession of Mr. Rawlins, who will show them; and further particulars may be had of Mr. Cocayne, Tupton, near Chesterfield.

N.B. Temple Normanton is three miles from Chesterfield, nine from Mansfield, and in the neighbourhood of considerable Iron Foundries and other Manufactories.

Advertisement in the Derbyshire Courier, May 12th 1832.

90

TIBSHELF

Some four miles north-east of Alfreton is the village of Tibshelf. The windmill was on the outskirts at Nethermoor and served the 800 inhabitants of the village in 1851.

It was first reported by John Farey in 1808 as a working windmill and subsequently appeared on Greenwood's map of 1825 and on the first Ordnance Survey map, in 1840. Reference to the Tithe map of 1845 identifies it as a post mill without a roundhouse, situated in a field, about 100 yards from the lane leading off to Pilsley.

In 1857 George Cook was the miller and the mill probably went out of use soon after this. On the 1880 Ordnance Survey map it is marked as 'Old Windmill' and does not appear on subsequent issues.

WEST HALLAM

West Hallam is a village on the A609 between Derby and Ilkeston, about 3 miles to the west of the latter. There was both a windmill and a water mill in the village. The tall post mill was erected at the West Hallam village crossroads, on the site of the present Mill garage. The date, 1593, was formed by nails in the woodwork to the left of the entrance, but its significance is unclear. The mill is shown on Burdett's map of 1767 and it is listed by John Farey in 1808. It also appears on the 1836 Ordnance Survey map.

An old photograph shows the mill was built on a brick round house, with external piers for the crosstrees, and appeared to have had rollers between the buck and the round house. The large buck had a rounded roof and was approached up a steep ladder. There was no fantail fitted and no sign of a tailpole on the old photograph. There were no sails shown and the cladding on the buck had partly gone.

The remains of West Hallam post mill, in about 1900 - drawn by Jo Roberts.

The Heath family were the last working tenants and they fitted a steam engine on the north side of the mill some years before they left. When the father, William died in 1883, the business was carried on by the son, Gershaw, but very quickly, the trade disappeared and he had to leave. The end of the mill came in 1884 when an advertisement in the Ilkeston Pioneer offered to sell by auction: -

> 'West Hallam Mill, near Ilkeston. 8 HP Horizontal engine, 12 HP Steam Boiler, piping etc, dressing machine, corn screen, four pairs of stones, sundry useful articles for mills.'

The steam engine was moved to nearby Stanley but business there was no better and it was sold again. The windmill became increasingly ruinous and in 1902 the Rev. Chas Perry wrote an open letter headed 'The Plaint of the Old Windmill'. In it he describes how West Hallam mill had been a good and faithful servant for many years but now no one cares and she was falling to pieces.

The buck was removed in 1915 but parts of the round house remained until the 1960s when it was demolished to make way for a garage, 'Windmill Garage', which now stands on the site. When a painting was done by Karl Wood in 1934 only a fragment of the round house remained.

WHITWELL   SK 533 768
Located in the north of the county Whitwell was a large village in 1851, having a population of almost 1400. It is on the A619 Chesterfield to Worksop road, about 11 miles east-north-east of the former, and was in the Nottingham coal field.

The brick tower mill in Mill Lane, Whitwell, was built in 1829 and belonged to Mr. George Leggett, who lived in the nearby Mill Cottage, on Mill Lane. He was listed as the miller in 1834.

He was followed by a long serving miller, John Wilson, from 1839 to 1871. One wonders just how many times he climbed up the tower. She was advertised for sale in 1834 and the advert referred to: - 'An excellent smock Corn mill, built five years ago at a cost in excess of £600, Machinery by Leith and White. The mill has a fantail, two pairs of stones and a dressing machine.'

The mill is not listed by John Farey in 1808 but appears, just outside the village, on the 1840 Ordnance Survey map. An undated photograph included in the Whitwell 1000 Festival Guide, in 1989, shows the mill in working order. It had an ogee cap and four patent sails, although only two carried a full complement of shutters. A large inclined fantail was mounted at the rear and there was an auxiliary drive pulley visible on the wall. Two men were sitting on the fan staging.

Whitwell windmill c.1910.

A Karl Wood painting in 1932 shows the tower complete with ogee cap but without any sails. Adjacent to the tower was a small building, connected to the tower by an inclined wooden casing. This building had probably housed an auxiliary oil engine and the casing protected the drive belt to the pulley.

William Talland was the miller between 1881 and 1895 and, The Worksop Guardian in October 1950 , records the death at the age of 88, of William Tate, a native of Whitwell, who by trade was a miller and who had 'worked the old windmill at Whitwell for the late owner of the mill, Wm. Talland, who died in 1895.'

The sails were removed in 1912, the 1916 Ordnance Survey map showing it as 'Whitwell Windmill, Disused'. Over the succeeding years the mill became increasingly derelict. In 1964 controversy raged in the village as to the future of the, by now derelict mill, splitting villagers into 'Millites' and 'Anti-Millites'. A preservation group was formed in the village and funds raised to save the mill. A stay of execution was obtained but unfortunately the decision was taken to demolish the mill in 1965.

WHITTINGTON

Whittington was a village of 820 inhabitants in 1851, and is situated about two and a half miles due north of Chesterfield, in the north of the county. A stone tower windmill was built towards the end of the 18th century and was on an exposed ridge just to the south of the village. It is not included on Burdett's map of 1767 but is listed as a working mill by John Farey in 1808. It is shown on Greenwood's map of 1825 by a mill symbol and on the 1840 Ordnance Survey map simply as 'Whittington Mill'.

At an auction held in 1815 it was described in the Derby Mercury of 23rd March as: -

> 'A capital smock windmill, a small cottage and land. Mill contains one pair each of French and Grey Stones, flour machine, bolting mill worked by hand. Lately in the possession of John and Isaac Cundy.'

Simmons notes that in the London Gazette, August 8th 1818: -

> 'The partnership between Isaac Cundy and John Cundy, both of Whittington, millers and corn grinders, had been dissolved by mutual consent.'

Also in The London Gazette, March 25th 1820, a notice states: -

> 'There is a commission of bankrupt against Isaac Cundy, of Whittington, miller. To surrender on the 3rd of April.'

The split up of the partnership may have anticipated the subsequent bankruptcy. However the name 'John Cundy' appears as the miller at Whittington from 1815 until 1855, but this may include other members of the family with the same Christian name. The mill continued to work until about 1880 but by the 1895 Ordnance Survey was designated 'Old Windmill'. It was demolished about the turn of the century.

WILLINGTON (or EGGINGTON?)
SK 396305

On the 9th January 1710, Sir John Every, baronet of Egginton Hall, conveyed to Thomas Carter, of Derby: -

> 'a piece of enclosed ground on Egginton Heath, of some four acres also the wind mill thereon.'

Burdett's map of 1767 depicts 'Windmill House', close to what is now the A38 on what was the frontage to Burnaston Aerodrome, whilst Greenwood's map of 1825 has 'The Round House' marked in the same location. The exact position is not clear, but must fall within the boundaries of the new Toyota car factory.

The Enclosure award for Willington refers to a field in that area called 'Tween Mill Gate', perhaps confirming the one time presence of a mill close by. It is not clear however if the mill was in Willington or in Egginton parish.

It is probable that such a mill was in fact a post mill and may well have dated back to Elizabethan times. The 'Round House', as depicted on Greenwood's map, may well represent the brick enclosure often built round the base of such a mill .

Note.   **This site clearly predates Findern windmill.**

WIRKSWORTH   SK 274538
The market town of Wirksworth is about 3 miles south of Matlock and is surrounded by hills. A post mill, known as Wirksworth Mill, is listed by Farey in 1808 and whilst it is not shown on Greenwood's map of 1825, it appears on the 1836 Ordnance Survey as 'Wirksworth Mill', without a symbol. However it was built before 1799 since Simmons reports in that year: -

> 'Royal Exchange Fire Insurance Policy No 169576 Samuel Williamson of Wirksworth, miller; on his windmill house timber built situate in Wirksworth and having no kiln - £150. On standing and going geers therein £20; On stock in Trade £30.'

Another similar policy eight years later confirms the mill as 'a Post Mill, with no kiln or steam engine'.

> The windmill was located about a mile to the west of Wirksworth, near a spot called 'Godfreyhole', above a hamlet called Millers Green. An advertisement in the Derby Mercury in 1826 offered the mill to be let – 'complete with a pair of French and a pair of grey stones'.

In 1830, in the same newspaper, a notice appeared: -

> 'To windmillers - seeking a steady, unmarried man who is perfectly acquainted with the above business - Apply John Williamson at Wirksworth.'

It was again to let in 1833, so his quest for a steady man must have been unsuccessful!

There was an attempt to sell the mill by auction in 1846 when it was described as a 'Post Mill which draws 10 yards of cloth, 7' wide'. In 1848 the Tithe Award map showed the windmill in a large field, owned by Mr. John Williamson, presumably a relative of the above Samuel. The end is however registered in a major advertisement in the Derby Mercury of 17th October 1849: -

'The whole of the excellent machinery and materials in the above windmill and kiln, including pair 4' 6" French and 5' 0" grey stones (new) Dressing machine, pair sails (new), Wind shaft with cast iron neck and flanges, break wheel and break, crown and other wheels, regulators, quantity of good timber etc. Also a drying kiln, cast iron sparkstone, 3 feet square, stone runners and pot floor tiles, 2000 bricks and 28 large blocks of stone.'

It was not represented on the 1880 Ordnance Survey map and no illustrations have been found of the windmill, but from the above information it is possible to visualise what the mill must have been like.

WOODVILLE   SK 323190

Situated on the A50 Burton to Ashby-de-la-Zouch road, Woodville had extensive earthenware manufacturing facilities at the middle of the 19th century.

The windmill, known as 'Butt House Windmill', was to the east of the village, on the north side of the road.

The actual date this mill was built is unclear; Farey did not include it in his list of windmills in 1808 and it did not appear on Greenwood's map of 1825. It first appeared on Sanderson's map of 1835, followed by the 1836 Ordnance Survey map.

It therefore seems that the mill was built in about 1827/8. It is not on the 1895 Ordnance Survey map (which resulted from a survey in 1879/1883) indicating that it had been removed about 1880 after a life of 50 years.

Woodville windmill does not appear to have been advertised so the type of mill is not clear, although it was probably a post mill. White's Directory, in 1857 lists John Blood as a 'corn miller'.

In 1945 the adjacent Mill House was still standing but was reported by Simmons to be in 'poor condition'.

THE DERBYSHIRE EDGES AND MILLSTONE QUARRIES

Millstone grit, which is abundant in the hills of the Peak District of Derbyshire, was the source of many of the querns and millstones used in Britain over the centuries. It consists of a type of sandstone containing small quartz pebbles. The area in the north of the county from which the stones were extracted was well known to both wind and water millers all over the world, since many millstones, often known as 'Peak Stones', were exported to areas lacking suitable material. The quern stones, dating back to biblical times, represented the manual version of the powered millstone but were much smaller. They continued to be used long after wind and water power was available to turn the stones, because of the low cost.

The old quarries used by early millstone makers were fairly widespread in the north of the county, located at such places as Millstone Edge, near Hathersage, Stanage Moor, Curbar and Froggatt Edges. The stones were extracted and often completed in situ in quarries where the working conditions for the men involved must, at times, have been quite appalling.

Today much evidence of the industry can be found on the hillsides where the stones were extracted, with damaged or cracked stones lying where they were being made. In addition there are several hundred mill and grind stones abandoned beside the track through the Bole Hill Quarries (SK 248793), close to Surprise View, near Hathersage. The actual date of these stones is unknown but they have clearly been manufactured, collected together and then abandoned through lack of demand, possibly arising from the emergence of steam driven steel roller mills during the later years of the 19th century.

Transport of the stones, which often weighted in excess of one ton, in the days before modern roads were in place must have presented many problems to the quarry owners. In some areas there are still recognisable trackways linking the quarries to the local roads. However little is known as to how the stones were transported, although some evidence exists of rolling them in pairs, joined by wooden poles, and also of the use of sledges or skids. In the last hundred or so years of operation of these quarries, special wheeled wagons would undoubtedly have been used.

Millstone grit stones were considered during the 18th and 19th centuries to be inferior to the quartz French Burr Stones, imported from the Eiffel region of France. This type of stone normally only occurs in small irregular pieces and these had to be shaped and matched together to form the circular stone and then bound together with bands of iron, the back being sealed with plaster of Paris. Such stones produced a much cleaner white flour than was possible with the Peak stones which therefore tended to be used for the brown flour used by the poor and for animal feed. Often windmills had one pair of each type of stone.

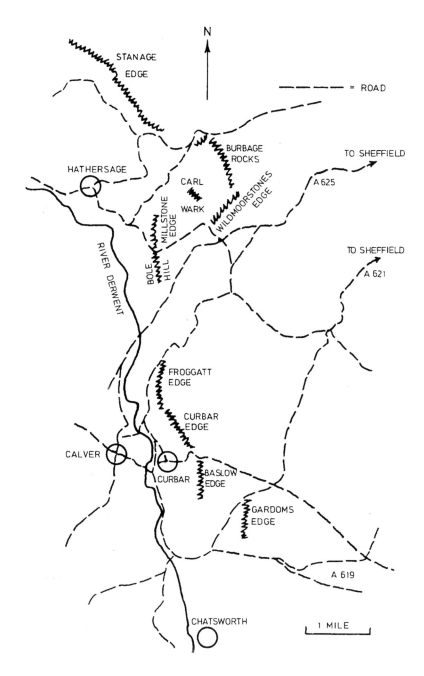

Map showing some areas of extraction of Derbyshire Peak Millstones.

98

A wide range of sizes of millstones was employed, depending on the power available and the required output, but typically they were between 3' 6" and 5' 0" in diameter and up to 13" thick, weighing over a ton when new. They had to be flat on the grinding face to better than one sixteenth of an inch and needed to be balanced to run smoothly. They operated best for the milling of flour at between 125 and 150 revolutions per minute.

The dressing of the stones is carried out by hand; the normal pattern being of 10 equal sections or harps, set out at a tangent to the eye, or centre hole, of the stones. The harps are sub-divided into lands and furrows, this being the work of very skilled craftsmen. The furrows are cut up to 3/4" deep, with a steep slope or arris on one side and a smooth slope blending with the land on the other. The surface of the lands may be still further cut to give a series of fine parallel lines, as close as sixteen to the inch in some cases. The bedstone and the runner, or upper stones, are cut to the same hand such that when the runner is turned over and placed on top of the bed stone, and the stone rotated, a cutting action ensues, rather like a pair of scissors. The corn is fed in at the eye or centre of the runner stone, and flour emerges round the periphery of the stones, being collected in a box like container known as 'the vat', and discharged into sacks at 'the spout'.

Each mill had at least one, but more often two pairs of stones and they represented one of the biggest single investments in the building of a mill. This expenditure had to be repeated every 10 -15 years as the stones wore out! The millstones had to be lifted and re-dressed about every three weeks when the mill was in full production and the miller had to care for his stones at all times if he was to be most efficient.

A sales bill for 1676 records:-

        'Sale of one pair of mill stones for windmill   £9 - 10s - 0d'

John Farey in 1808 gives more information:-

        'Pair of mill stones 5' 0" diameter   £ 10 - 10 - 0d'
and: - 'Pair of mill stones 5' 4" diameter   £ 12 - 12 – 0d'

Transportation of the stones represented a significant part of their cost. In 1722 a Derby source reported a pair of 'eighteen hands' millstones (72" diameter?) at the quarry was £2 - 10s with carriage from Offerton Edge to Derby, adding another £4 - 10s, a total of £7. On the road from Worksop to Chesterfield in 1737 a toll of 2 shillings per pair of stones was payable.

Simmons cites an advertisement in the Yorkshire Herald, March 6th 1779 when J. and A. Lowe of Hathersage 'advise their friends and the public that they make and sell all sorts of Millstones from the same quarry that their late grandfather had, which are equal if not superior to any millstones in England.'

An interesting insight into the importance of the millstone industry is shown by an advertisement in the Derby Mercury, 17th November, 1830, which reads as follows:-

SALE - BY MR ROBINSON

In consequence of the Burrs not reaching Nottingham in time for the sale it was postponed and will now take place on November 20th.
To Millers and Millwrights French Burr stones, on account of importance.
To be sold by auction, 500 French Burrs, in convenient lots, lately imported.'

This clearly indicates that bulk shipments of burrs, the segments forming French Burr stones, were imported by merchants, and were then sold in manageable batches to millers and millwrights.

Abandoned mill and grind stones, Hathersage.

OTHER REFERENCES TO WINDMILLS IN DERBYSHIRE.

In preparing this book it has become clear that the possibility exists that there were many more windmills in the county, perhaps spread over hundreds of years. This becomes clear when examining old maps and documents and noting the many occasions when the word 'windmill', or maybe more loosely 'mill', is used as a name in connection with fields, places or properties. It has not been possible to follow these up at the present time and the writer is grateful for input into this section from the late Don Paterson and Brian Radford who have made available their own collections of information. The list represents a selection of 'windmill references' where other supporting data has not been found to date.

In the following table only locations with windmill connections not referred to in the earlier part of the book have been included unless the data may indicate another mill. The data is not complete but serves to indicate areas for further research.

Location	Grid Ref	Comments
Alderwasley		Windmill Hill - Farey's mill?
Aston on Trent		Field Name 1750.
Ault Hucknall		Windmill Close.
Barlow		Windmill Close.
Blackwell		Field name - 1839.
Breaston		Field name - 1841.
Callow		Windmill?
Chaddesden		Windmill Hill - 1614. Another mill?
Chilcote		Reference in sale mid 17th Century.
Coal Aston		Field name - 1621 and 1766.
Cresswell		Windmill? Is this Elmton?
Crich		Numerous field names and sale records in 17th Century.
Derby		Mill Hill Lane.
Derby		Windmill Hill Lane.
Dethwick		Field name - 1699.
Dronfield Woodhouse		Field name - 1561.
Elmton		Shown on 1840 OS map?
Elvaston		Field name - 1762.
Etwall		Field name - not on 1839 OS map.
Findern		Windmill House – (see Willington/Egginton.)
Foremark		Windmill Hill, near Foremark Hall.
Grassmoor		Windmill? Little information.
Great Hucklow		Windmill Houses on Burdett map 1791.
Hartshorne		Windmill? - Little information.
Hazlewood		Advert in Derby Mercury 1744.
Hopton Moor		Windmill Pasture - 1638.
Kirk Langley	SK 290384	Windmill Close.

Kniveton		Molendine de Kniveton - 1349.
Longford	SK 233376	Windmill Field.
Little Hucklow		Wyndemilne House - 1607.
Long Eaton		On 1839 O/S - Sawley Mill?
Mackworth	SK 316364	Field name - 1770 Windmill Hill Wood.
Matlock		Dimple mine - water pumping windmill.
Monyash		Mine pumping windmill.
Netherseal	SK 269127	Windmill Hill and Close - may be same mill.
Newton Solney	SK 273248	Windmill field.
Norbury		Early field name - Windmill Lane.
Pilsey	SK 419629	Windmill Hill.
Repton Hill	SK 293260	Windmill Close, near Milton Brook Mill Hill on O/S.
Shirland		Windmill on Burdett map 1791.
Snelston		Windmill Hill.
Somercotes		Windmill?
Stanton by Dale		Windmill Pits - ? windmill on 1839 O/S.
Sutton Scarsdale		Mill Hill.
Tapton	SK391721	Windmill Hill, later Castle Hill.
Tissington		Field names of Old Wyndmilne and Windmill Field.
Unstone		Windmill Lane and Wyndhill.
Walton on Trent		Windmill Bank on early map.
Wensley		Field name - Windmill Bank.
Weston on Trent		Windmill Fields.
Woodthorpe (Common Side)		On Burdett's map 1791.

It is clear from the above list, and the many mills included in the main body of this book, that over the last 1000 years, the windmill, and the watermill have played a very important part in the life of Derbyshire. The role of the was very critical to that way of life since, unlike modern flour which contains preservatives and has a shelf life of over six months, the flour produced by the traditional windmill and watermill would only keep for perhaps up to four weeks, or often less. As a result grain was stored for long periods and then milled as required. As the transport system limited movement around the country, there was therefore a continual need for fresh flour to be produced at regular intervals. A major breakdown, or a fire in a local mill must have considerably disrupted the economy of the area.

Any information which adds to our knowledge of the above sites, and indeed to the other mills mentioned elsewhere in the text, will be welcomed by the author.

A SHORT GUIDE TO SOME WINDMILL TERMS

Bed Stone	The fixed lower stone above which the runner stone rotates.
Brakewheel	Mounted on the windshaft and drives the wallower. Brake acts on the rim.
Brake	Friction drive on to the brakewheel to stop mill.
Bolter	A Device to separate flour from bran. Consists of a rotating drum covered with fine cloth or silk and into which flour is fed.
Buck	The body of a post mill which is turned into the wind.
Burr Stone	Millstone imported from France, sometimes called French Burr.
Cap	Moveable top of a tower or smock mill which carries the sails and windshaft.
Common Sails	Traditional North European windmill sails, where cloth, sacking, or canvas is spread over a wooden lattice framework. Each sail is set individually to suit weather conditions.
Cross	Multi-arm casting on leading edge of windshaft to which the sails are attached.
Crowntree	The large horizontal beam which bears on the top of the upright shaft in a post mill and supports the buck.
Dresser	A machine which separates flour from the rest of the meal.
Dressing	The sharpening and grooving of millstones.
Eye	The hole in the centre of the runner stone.
Fantail	A device which automatically turns the mill to face into the wind.
Governor	Automatic device to regulate the separation of the millstones or which controls the speed of a machine.
Great Spur Wheel	A large gear mounted on the upright shaft which drives the stone nuts.
Grey Stones	Millstones made of millstone grit. Peak Stones.
Kiln	Structure with a drying floor of perforated ceramic or metal tiles below which heat is produced, normally by a fire. Grain is spread on the floor and dried to reduce the moisture content prior to grinding.
Main Post	Upright timber upon which the buck of a post mill turns.
Millstones	Stones in a mill used to break up and grind corn or other material. A pair of millstones comprises the Bed stone (fixed stone) and the Upper or Runner stone.
Neck Bearing	Front bearing of the windshaft.
Patent Sails	Shuttered sails which are self regulating.
Post Mill	A windmill where the body or buck turns on an upright shaft.
Poll End	Cast-iron socket on end of windshaft into which the stocks (sails) are fitted.
Roundhouse	Building which encloses the substructure of a post mill.
Runner Stone	The upper of a pair of millstones which rotates above the static bed stone.

Rule of Thumb	An ancient term derived from the old way of testing the quality of the grind by rubbing the product between the miller's thumb and finger.
Sack Doors	Sets of hinged twin trap doors which are set vertically above each other with the sack hoist chain or rope passing up between them. The doors, mounted on leather hinges, lift as the sack passes through and fall back by gravity. The miller counts the bangs to know on which floor the sack is located.
Sack Hoist	Device used to raise sacks of corn within a mill.
Sails	The main wooden structures which drive the machinery of the windmill.
Shoe	An inclined and tapering wooden trough which is fed with grain from the hopper, and is vibrated by the damsel, causing the grain to enter the eye of the stone.
Shutter	Pivoted or hinged panels on spring or patent sails. Often a wooden frame covered with painted canvas. Also called 'shades' in Lincolnshire and some northern counties. Vanes in Suffolk.
Stocks	Heavy timber beams to which the sails are attached.
Smock Mill	A tower mill which is made largely of wood.
Spring Sails	Sails constructed with shutters which open and close rather like the slats of a Venetian blind. They are connected to a spring, the tension of which can be set manually by allowing the multiple shutters, which are linked together in each sail, to open or close according to the strength of the wind.
Stone floor	The mill floor on which the stones are situated.
Striking Gear	Mechanism used to open and close the shutters in patent sails.
Tailpole	Lever used to turn the mill to face into the wind.
Tailwinding	When the wind catches the sails from behind.
Tentering Gear	Adjusts the distance between the stones, thus controlling the fineness of the flour.
Tower Mill	Main structure is made of brick, masonry or other durable materials; cap is fitted on top.
Upright Shaft	Main drive transmission of a tower mill, wallower and great spur wheel are attached.
Vat	Wooden casing which encloses a pair of stones.
Wallower	The first driven gear in a windmill.
Windshaft	Large timber or iron shaft which carries the sails and the brake wheel.
Wire Machine	Separates flour from meal into various fractions or qualities.

BIBLIOGRAPHY

MILLSTONES

Defoe, D., 'A Tour Thro' the Whole Island of Great Britain', Vol. 2, 1927 Edition.

Polak, J. P., 'The Production and Distribution of Peak Millstones from the Sixteenth to the Eighteenth Century', Derbyshire Archaeology Journal, Vol. 107, 1989.

Radley, J., 'A Millstone Maker's Smith on Gardom's Edge, Baslow'. Derbyshire Archaeology Journal, 1958.

Tomlinson T. D., 'Querns, Millstones and Grindstones', Hathersage Parochial Church Council, 1981.

Tucker, D. G., 'Millstone making in the Peak District of Derbyshire', Industrial Archaeology Review, Vol. 3, No.1, Autumn 1985.

GAZETTEER

Baker, P. H. J., & Wailes, R., 'The Windmills of Derbyshire, Leicestershire and Nottinghamshire, Part 1, Post Mills'. Proceedings of the Newcomen Society, Vol. 33, 1960/61.

Baker, P. H. J., & Wailes, R., 'The Windmills of Derbyshire, Leicestershire and Nottinghamshire, Part 2, Tower Mills'. Proceedings of the Newcomen Society, Vol. 34, 1961/62.

Brighouse, W. H., 'Windmills', Derbyshire Countryside, Vol. 32, February 1967,

Brown, R. J., 'Windmills of England', Robert Hale, London, 1976.

Burt, H. L., 'History of Riddings Windmills', Booklet, 1999, St. James Church, Riddings.

Crapper, C., 'Shirebrook Notes', Derbyshire Miscellany, Vol. XIV, Part 1, Spring 1995.

Farey, J., 'General View of the Architecture and Minerals of Derbyshire', published 1811-17.

Fraser, W., 'Field Names in South Derbyshire', Norman Allard & Co. Ltd., 1947.

Hall, S., Dr., 'The Peak and the Plain', 1853.

Hay, D., 'Derbyshire Windmills', Unpublished work in Chesterfield Public Library.

Johnson , M., 'Borrowash in the 1820's, Greenway Publishing, 1991.

Johnson , M., 'Ockbrook in the 1820's', Morley's Publishing, Ilkeston,1991.

Richardson , W. A., 'Citizens Derby', University of London Press, 1949.

Rodgers, F., 'Derbyshire', Breedon Books, 1994.

Sharpe, P., 'South Normanton, A Village of Considerable Extent'. Village Note Book, 1982.

Tann, J., 'Cooperative Corn Milling: Self Help During the Grain Crises of the Napoleonic Wars', Agricultural History Review, 1980.

Thompson, G., ' Diaries', Note Book No 2 - Derby Local Studies Library

Simmons, H. E., 'Records Relating to British Windmills and Watermills', 'Windmills of Derbyshire'. Held by the Science Museum, 1977.

NEWSPAPERS CONSULTED

Derby Mercury, Various copies of Newspapers held by Derby Local Studies Library.

Derby Evening Telegraph, Various copies of Newspaper held by Derby Local Studies Library.

Ashbourne News Telegraph, 'Windmill Debate is going on', Feb. 15th 1976.

Derbyshire Courier, Copies of Newspaper held by Derby Local Studies Library and Chesterfield Library.

Ilkeston Pioneer, Ilkeston Reference Library.

DIRECTORIES

Kelly's Directory of Derbyshire, Various years.

White's Directory of Derbyshire, 1857.

GENERAL READING

Gifford, A. F., 'Derbyshire Windmills', Midland Mills and Watermills Group, 1995

Gifford, A. F., 'Derbyshire Watermills', Midland Mills and Watermills Group, 1999.

Reynolds, J., 'Wind and Watermills', Hugh Evelyn, 1970.

Wailes, R., 'Windmills in England', Charles Skilton, 1948, reprinted 1975.

Wenham, P., 'Watermills', Robert Hale, 1989.

A Derbyshire County Council Greenwatch Award Certificate and a cheque for £600 presented to trustees of Heage Windmill Society in the 'Conservation of the Built Environment' Group for the restoration of Heage Windmill - May 16th 2002.

In April the work of restoring Heage Windmill was further recognised by a Civic Award 2003 Commendation for 'a project that has achieved an extremely high standard in design and contribution to the community or environment'. Of the 525 properties entered throughout the country, only 58 achieved this honour.

C18[th] Millwrights at work.

'Views of Rural Occupations – 1807'. W.H. Pyne. Published by Dover.

DERBYSHIRE WINDMILLS PAST AND PRESENT

A.F. Gifford. 2003

Healthy Loving

Relationships

Joe Hudson

CLARITY.NAME

First published by Clarity.Name, 2009
This revised edition first published by Clarity.Name, 2011

ISBN: 978-0-9563555-0-8

For additional content or more information about this book, visit:
www.healthylovingrelationships.com

For my family and Anna, Hannah and Aleks
with love.

Contents

Acknowledgements..*vi*

Introduction..*vii*

How to use this book...*ix*

Obstacles and new perspectives..**1**

What relationships mean to us...1

Lack of resources...9

Untangling values, beliefs and desires................................13

Our attitude to change..39

Internal dialogues and identity..48

Projections and prophecy..55

Fear (and general emotional turmoil) 59

A life changing journey..**72**

Spirituality and personal development 73

Self expression..75

Experimenting with ways of being and discovering the art of attraction...77

The power of contribution, modelling success and building rapport..80

Putting things into practice and the strange world of PUAs....86

Love and life in the clouds 91

But what is love?..94

The beautiful connection...**104**

The five keys..104

The glass melon dichotomy...114

Practice makes perfect (virtually)......................................121

Conflict..**129**

Conflict in a nutshell...129

Distinct modes of conflict..134

Observing, feeling, needing, requesting.................138

The role of judgements...164

Responsibility...184

Play conflict: fighting, arguing, joking...................195

To compromise or not to compromise....................203

Criticism, 'over-sensitivity' and the wall................208

Manipulation...212

Assertiveness 213

The effect of focus and self-interest......................216

Practical tips and further considerations.................**220**

First contact and conversations.............................220

Sex and the emotional impact................................230

Attitudes and the other's shoes.............................246

Evolution, competition and deception.....................257

Get your fresh roles here..265

Commitments and goodbyes 276

Final words..**284**

Subsection list..*288*

Index..*291*

Acknowledgements

Much of the credit for this book of course has to go to the partners, lovers and close friends who have been in my life, and those who still are, for the strength, joy and learning they have given me. Many grateful thanks to my friends, Tom Wilson, Andreea Cimpoiasu, Henrik Dahl and Nikki Krol, for their detailed feedback on previous drafts, which has led to this being a far more complete and clear book than it would otherwise have been. Thanks also to friends, James Tylor, Juliet Heylor, Kieron Taylor, Paula Tanti and Vincent Sieben for some good conversations and useful ideas about the book. Raphael Achirei I'd like to thank for his timely advice on layout and typography. To all my friends and family who have given advice and strong words of encouragement to get this book out there, thank you for spurring me on! There were times where I might have decided to make this book just one of the many things I'll finish 'one day', if it hadn't been for you. I'm also very grateful to my many brief acquaintances over the years, people who have somehow ended up talking about relationships with me, at all hours and in all kinds of places. Thank you for your inspiration, this book would not have been written without you.

For this extensively revised edition I'd like to thank my family, and in particular my mum, for their continued support and feedback. For fresh inspiration, encouragement, honest sharing and critique I'm very grateful to my friends, Aleks Zawierucha, Annelies Oosterbaan, Stania Diffey, Biljana Lipic, Aaron Davies, Ruth Pethybridge, Lily Brandhorst, Andy McNeill, Adie Liddiard and once again to Tom, Henrik, Vincent and Andreea. The cover design was the product of input from many friends, some of whom I've already mentioned, with particular thanks to Melanie Driver, Mike Jewell, Aaron Davies, Pieter Kops and my sister Esther Theaker. For their expert input and generosity with helping me to improve the NVC content, thanks to Rita Herzog, Sylvia Haskvitz, Jack Lehman and Alex Censor. Lastly, thanks to Clare Saxon for her hard work and skill in editing most of the long 'nearly final' draft.

Introduction

It has been a recurring event in my life – falling into conversations with people of varied age, appearance, character and background who are currently quite confused and frustrated in their personal relationships. They're just not relating in a mutually satisfying and comfortable way with the opposite (or same) sex and feel as if they're going around in circles.

I really empathize with this, since for a long period of my life I felt the same way. In these conversations about relationships, in recent years I've often ended up explaining some of my shifts in attitude, and the things I've discovered, or learnt from others and done, which have radically turned my world around in that area.

It seems that for all the wonderful things people do and are, all their energy for life and desire for happiness, there is this huge, murky undercurrent of frustration and confusion in our society, surrounding relationships. So many of us are wading around in it, trying to find someone to lovingly share part of our lives with, or to connect better with someone we're already together with. There's not very much light down in this undercurrent, yet on the surface we appear to be getting on with life and doing well.

It was while reflecting on the above that I offered to email a guy who I met at a festival in 2008, about some of the things I'd learnt. I don't even know if that 10 page email was ever read, but there was still so much to write, so I kept going.

I'm not presenting myself as having perfect, exemplar relationships here, and if your yardstick is the total number or length of intimate personal relationships had, then there are other more qualified authors. I'm just someone who has gained some useful understandings and overcome some challenging obstacles in this part of life. I've noticed that these are understandings that a lot of people, regardless of IQ or marital status, seem to lack and obstacles that continue to cause problems for many, otherwise successful people, late into their lives. The purpose of this book is to share in the most clear and accessible way what I know works in relationships, not just for me, but for a great many people – regardless of background, age or sex. Wonderful relationships can take all shapes and sizes, the guidance within embraces that fact.

The material in this book has been thoroughly field tested, so whether you're utterly lost in this area, or are generally doing OK and just looking for a few tips, there's a fairly good chance you'll find something in the following pages that will help.

This book often takes a foundational, holistic view and as such, although chiefly aimed at emotionally and physically intimate romantic relationships, will be useful for other sorts too, including friendship, family, professional or spiritual relationships.

Obviously 'relationships' is a subject not starved of literature, and many of the topics here have a shelf or two of books written on them. What I've aimed to do here is create something that is compact and easy to read, yet crammed full of genuinely useful information; something anyone could pick up, read in a couple of afternoons and feel a renewed sense of understanding, direction or confidence in this area of their life, whatever their troubles.

A significant chunk of what I've written focuses on the initial and prerequisite steps of a relationship; the meeting of people and building up of a beautiful connection. The steps we take and the perspectives we have in these first moments quickly mark out the scope of any future relationship. These moments are packed with chances to shape our own destiny and the challenges that arise this early often reflect those that occur further on in a relationship. While looking at these first moments of beautiful connections, I explore the building blocks of awareness, self-development and various attitudes that support and attract them – and, most importantly, allow these connections to develop.

What the later stages are of course depends on what you want. One thing I've noticed though is that people who have a strong foundation in the above (the connection building skills, helpful attitudes and personal development) tend to have much happier relationships when they find someone they truly want to be with.

Revised edition – In this expanded and revised edition there is additional focus on some of the key issues of longer lasting relationships: love, commitment (and over-commitment), understanding each other better and sharing needs, taking responsibility and compromise. A substantial section on conflicts – and resolving them peacefully – explores what they are, why we have them and related issues like judgement, blame, criticism, manipulation, anger and violent behaviour. Also throughout this edition there are many new and clarified examples.

Finally, if you've browsed a number of books on this subject you may have grown jaded with what appears to be a trend of 'positive thinking' advice such as: "It's all in your head, think positively → get positive results in your life." That can be hard to stomach if you feel trapped and tired of trying and failing.

The fact is, thinking differently does make different results possible. But to think truly positively (with all the optimism, confidence, peace and goodwill that implies), we must first gain a genuine acceptance and constructive understanding of our suffering, or inner conflict, not deny it. We must develop empathy with ourselves. It is that ongoing journey from empathy to health, love and well founded positivity that this book embraces.

How to use this book

This book is divided into five parts. Beginning at a more internal level we explore a wide range of common 'road-blocks' to getting where we want to be in our relationships, and how to pass them; starting with the question 'What is a relationship?' From here the book tells the story of how I learned to have the relationships I wanted, putting earlier ideas into a personal context. The next part of the book is all about what makes a connection with someone most beautiful (whatever the type of relationship) and things you can do to make those connections more beautiful in your life. The following part on conflict, covers this inevitable element of relationships in just about all its guises.

This part – which could equally have been called 'how to find harmony in relationships' – may provide a fair bit of food for thought. Finally we look at various stages of having a healthy, loving relationship, from first meetings onward, and explore a number of practical considerations along the way.

While I've aimed to have a natural progression from section to section, this book is organized so that it can be dipped into. Much of the content is inter-connected and as you explore the subjects of most interest to you, you'll discover your own path through it.

I've tried to write for people who have a range of beliefs about and experience in relationships. Inevitably then, while some bits will resonate with you, other bits may not seem relevant.

I make the assumption that if you're reading this book there are some things that you'd like to improve on in the area of your personal relationships. For some people it may be things like having less fights with their partner or feeling more confident in their sex life. For others it may be just having the courage to talk to people they find attractive or addressing their self-talk or not putting themselves down in front of others. Whatever your situation, if you keep an open mind while reading this book you'll get the most from it.

Of course, part of having an open mind is being open to trying new things – even if there is a chance they might not work out well. Mistakes are half of how we learn, so be willing to make a few of them, along with the successes, when trying out ideas in this book.

Equally, to be willing to learn (or to change) does not mean there was anything wrong with you in the first place. It's my belief that there is nothing 'wrong' with you, or anyone. There is only how we presently are, along with actions that work well and actions that work less well in meeting our needs. So I invite you to suspend any judgements of yourself (or others) while reading on. As the Persian poet, Rumi said: "Out beyond ideas of wrongdoing and rightdoing, there is a field. I will meet you there." It's there that love's roots grow deeper than in any other place I know.

Obstacles and new perspectives

So, what stops many of us forming happy, healthy and loving relationships?

Various things. In fact, just about anything has the potential to be an obstacle. Sometimes simply changing our perception removes these obstacles. Consider the analogy of a fly stuck in a room. There's a gap at the top of the window, but it flies repeatedly into the glass, because it has no perception of the glass, only that something is stopping it. The idea of this part of the book is to offer different perspectives on some common obstacles in the hope that they'll show up some of those 'glass windows' and help you find a way through.

We'll start with the seemingly simple question, "What is a relationship?" and then focus on specific aspects of how we relate to ourselves and others.

What relationships mean to us

What is a relationship anyway? The answer is, it's many things. In general, having a relationship means having a certain connectedness or association with something, in our case 'someone' else. The open-endedness of this simple definition reflects the enormous variety of personal relationships that exist. The way we see 'relationships' is important because it predisposes us to having – or *not* having – certain kinds of relationships. Our outlook has the potential to empower us, or to be a major obstacle in finding fulfilment.

Many ways to connect, but what for?

The qualities and flavours we seek in that 'connectedness' of a relationship varies a lot from person to person. We are all multifaceted beings and have the potential to connect in many ways with different people. What we look for, as well as what we find, is shaped by our experiences and our values, beliefs and desires.

Do you know what you want in a relationship at the moment? What qualities do you value most in a partner, lover or intimate friend? What beliefs do you have about relationships, how they should be and about yourself in the context of relationships? What do you desire to develop most in your relationships?

Although they're apparently straightforward and practical, the above questions actually cover a massive amount of ground and can be hard to answer clearly. Neither are any answers we may have, set in stone. Firstly, let's examine how you feel about 'relationships'; are they 'good' things? What's your general outlook on them? If it's not congruent with what you want, you're unlikely to get it! What are relationships there for and what opportunities do they give?

Clarify and acknowledge what you want

It's hard to thread a needle using only your peripheral vision – even if you 'know what it feels like when you've got it.' Seeing your goal clearly helps you take more precise and coordinated action towards achieving it.

To gain clarity, it can be very helpful to write down your thoughts and feelings – especially in terms of what you're looking for – regarding relationships. It's the process of writing that helps. When something is on the page it's easier to take a more objective view and identify conflicts or contradictions, or indeed strengths and opportunities, that we might not see if we just reflect in our heads. Writing a list of your current values, beliefs and desires is a good starting point.

When writing in this way, the key is to avoid judging your

thoughts and feelings, or vetting them before you write. The idea is to see what's actually going on in your head and heart, not what you think *should* be. When you can clearly acknowledge the situation, you can make a better decision about how to move forward.

Another great way of clarifying what you want, and moving towards it, is to visualize it. See section: 'Practice makes perfect (virtually)' for more in visualization.

Personal boundaries: supports or impediments?

How are personal boundaries (experiences we will not allow ourselves) connected to what relationships mean to you and the relationships you have? Clearly, some boundaries are a product of the thing you want to change, such as a low self-image or social phobia, and serve to hinder positive change. Other boundaries can act as support structures to help define, protect and develop the person you want to be. That in turn helps to keep a relationship healthy and loving, or to end it where that doesn't seem possible.

Your boundaries define the scope of relationships you can have, for better or worse. It's worth then examining your boundaries. Aside from any fear around them, are they helpful *support structures* or more impediments to personal growth? If it's the latter, many of the ideas throughout this book will help you redefine them.

The spice of life

It's useful to recognize that people will want different things from relationships. Maybe what you most need is some honesty, respect and genuine mutual affection. Or perhaps it's just to share humour and understanding, or other times adventure, or some support. Sometimes what two people want marries up beautifully, sometimes it's possible to find a happy compromise, sometimes it's not. With the right attitude we can enjoy, learn and contribute in each one of these connections.

There are many positive attributes that can be developed in a relationship too, such as: love, affection, honesty, understanding, respect, humour, discovery/learning, support, loyalty, adventure, mutual inspiration and so on. If we can appreciate the value in a wide variety of these positive attributes, rather than fixating on just one or two (or holding out for the 'perfect' match in a partner), this will help us.

It's my belief that a connection that helps to meet some of our needs in a mutual and respectful fashion is never a waste, however short-lived it may turn out to be.

A balance of give and take

If your focus on what you will receive from the other person over-shadows what you can *share*, build and give, then take a few moments to think about how your future partner will feel in that relationship. How will their needs be met? Does it seem mutually healthy?

Similarly it's possible to have an imbalance where you keep giving and don't make enough space to receive (e.g. by being a 'rescuer'). How do those relationships affect your energy and quality of life? Ultimately are you helping those people by allowing this imbalance to continue?

It can certainly be mutually healthy to focus entirely on giving, sometimes. Imbalance comes from letting the natural joy of giving be swamped by things like obligation or guilt: "I have to keep giving, I'd be *bad* if I didn't", a desire to be accepted: "I'll be rejected if I don't keep giving", or unmet needs for love and connection: "This is the only way I know how to get the love and connection that I'm starved of". Be wary of letting your giving behaviour be a way of avoiding resolving your own issues, or digging yourself deeper into them.

Being overly giving, or playing the rescuer role, can sometimes be a method to control others; by taking charge of another's life problems or nurturing a sense of dependency or indebtedness, we can potentially dis-empower someone.

By accepting our own needs as *equal* to those of the person we're close to, we're more likely to find a healthy, balanced and sustainable connection that can truly blossom. The process of developing empathy with others in a way that includes us, helps us to find this happy balance. (See section: 'Assertiveness', for more on this idea.)

There was a time when I wanted some angel of a person to come and 'save' me, to fix all the hurt and frustrations I had. When I realized I had to start being that person for myself, life started to get a lot better. The sections of 'A life changing journey' tell that story.

The weight of expectations

It's often hard not to have expectations when we meet someone we feel very strongly about. What expectations come into your relationships? As we will see later (see section: 'Projections and prophesy'), it's the *way* we look ahead that really matters.

At what point does an expectation stop being useful and just get in the way? To answer that let's take a closer look at what they are. We can have expectations for our-selves, for others and for relationships. As well as being about 'what will probably happen', they can also be about 'what should happen'. Expectations come in different weights too. A light expectation leaves space for other possibilities that would also be acceptable or favourable and isn't tied to a sense of inevitability or very strong 'future attached' emotions. A heavy expectation is pretty much the opposite; one that leaves little space for other acceptable or favourable possibilities and is tied to strong emotions about a possible future.

If we have any more of the heavy kind of expectation than is absolutely necessary we can easily feel trapped, overwhelmed, or like life is always going wrong.

It's much easier for a heavy expectation to 'get in the way' of exploring what life has to offer and really getting to know people than a light one. Light expectations are really more like anticipations; they are more about what we think *could* happen or would *like* to happen (or avoid), than what we think *should* or *must* inevitably happen.

With the light kind we've more opportunity to engage ourselves fully in the present – towards bringing about an outcome we want, while not setting ourselves up for major disappointment if things work out another way. This allows us to better "invest in the process, not the outcome" (a pretty smart philosophy of Srikumar Rao[1]).

'Light' and 'heavy' here aren't about the depth or length of relationship you're looking for. Whatever your desires and goals are – and however seriously you take them – whenever you look ahead, try doing so in a 'light' way. Allow for the element of chance and change in both your inner and outer worlds, because the future is uncertain. (Since people are complex, changeable things – and two together often even more so – I've found it's usually best to have few expectations.)

Strategies are not needs

Part of a personal relationship is expressing our needs. I feel it's worth talking very briefly here about separating 'need' (the most underlying values and desires) from strategies.

Getting more directly in touch with your underlying needs or values is very empowering, because it gives you a sense of deeper self-knowledge and also a lot more options! While

---

1 Srikumar Rao (2010) "Happiness at Work: Be Resilient, Motivated, and Successful - No Matter What By Srikumar Rao" ISBN: 978-0071664325

mistaking a strategy or a strong preference for a need can tie you into unhelpful patters. Let's take an example that presents a clear obstacle. We may have a need for emotional security or safety in our relationships and one strategy for getting it could be controlling or manipulating your partner, because it's easier to feel secure perhaps when you feel in charge. A more healthy, loving and sustainable strategy though, could be becoming more open in your feelings, learning how to listen well (so you understand people more deeply) and offering that same security and safety that you crave. recognize the need/value and then find the best strategy, for healthy and long lasting success.

Seeing this distinction between strategy and need can also help you deal with difficult behaviour from loved ones. We can understand "this is just a strategy, I know there's a need underlying it ..." and then focus on addressing that need, as we wish. When someone makes progressive, healthy changes in their behaviour, give them positive feedback by showing appreciation or affection, it helps! This isn't about trying to control someone with rewards, just helping them to find healthy, effective ways of relating to others through a natural expression of appreciation and affection, when you feel it. (We discuss strategies and needs more in sections: 'Untangling values, beliefs and desires' and 'Observing, feeling, needing, requesting'.)

Outside the 'what you should want' box

We are often subject to a lot of conflicting social pressures from different areas of society, regarding what sort of relationships we should seek and how we should feel and act in them. It's very important to have good guidance or examples to follow (which we look for wherever we can find them: parents, friends, partners, teachers, films, books, people we see, and even adverts).

However, popular (consumer) society is not always on a very enlightened track and tends to set its members up for repeated grief and frustration. And of course the same kind of pressures can come directly from our friends and family, as well meaning as they may be. For this reason it's worth asking yourself to what extent you agree with how things apparently *should* be. Without the above pressures, what would your healthy, loving relationship look like?

Relationships never happen in a vacuum

No relationship ever exists in a vacuum. It is never just two people together; there is always what surrounds them. *Our environmental relationships make up part of the meaning of any personal relationship, because we exist within our environment.* It's a simple idea, but one with far reaching implications. It goes beyond what you do with your living space, or where you spend your time, although that is very important.

Our lifestyle habits, the way we relate to whatever we interact with on a daily basis, and to nature as a whole, all define the mental and emotional backdrop for our personal relationships. Take, for instance, someone who spends large parts of their life interacting with the world as if it were a commodity source that provides an endless variety of disposable goods for their entertainment, and who lives in the kind of area where neighbours don't know each other. It's hard to see how that person would have the same perspective on personal relationships as someone who, say, lived in a more rural area, with a closer, calmer connection to nature and more shared spaces in the community. Of course, we're adaptable and it's possible to be happy or sad in either environment. Nonetheless the connections we have with our environment will tend to characterize our personal connections and also the problems related with them.

This book is about interpersonal relationships, rather than the environmental kind. However, it's worth giving some thought to the wider context, as the two cannot be fully separated in the complex web of our lives. And it's in this wider context that we may find various obstacles to having the relationships we'd really like. Thankfully, just like the personal kind, our environmental relationships can change too.

Lack of resources

Resources can seem like a huge obstacle to having the loving relationships we want. We may think we don't have enough money, time, good looks, intelligence, personality, etc. Let's consider each in turn.

Money: If you can afford to eat, have shelter over your head and can join the local library then you can work with that (if not then you probably have bigger things to worry about). Read on, it's all about attitude. If general money worries are taking up a lot of your energy though, it might be worth focusing on fixing them first.

Most of the ideas in this book can be applied for free or on the cheap. What about other people's perception of money? Sure, it's very attractive to some people. There is very often a strong appeal to financial security, especially to those who see their mate fulfilling the 'provider' role. But sometimes the desire for a moneyed mate is more about having a doting purse, or someone to validate a desire for status.

In much of the world, money, like status, is really an analogue for having material resources. Just how important material resources are, depends on the individual and to an extent the kind of relationship and commitment each person is looking for. The thing to remember is you can have all the resources you like and *still* have miserable relationships. What you have and share in your *character* counts for vastly more.

Time: If you really have to work all the time just to stay alive, or to take care of your responsibilities, then your options are a little more limited. Until you get a better job or occupation, finding someone en route, within work, at the shops or online could be a possibility (read on if this seems daunting). Otherwise, what are your priorities? If you can afford to make time, it's really down to you to do so.

Good looks: Are very much a subjective thing, and significantly influenced by how much you smile and feel comfortable in your own shoes. In any case, you'll find many couples that seem happy together even though one of them got a very generous share of physical beauty while the other got more of a bum deal. (I'm not just talking about those couple's where the latter happens to be stinking rich either.)

The way you relate to people is often much more important than how you look. But it's that initial, visual or bodily reaction that often sets the tone and scope of any first meeting. The message here is about making the best of what you've got. Just making a decent effort can take you a long way.

For example, if you're a bit heavier than you'd like to be, making an effort here would be committing to yourself to getting regular exercise and eating healthy foods according to your body's actual needs. That will help you look better and be healthier, which in turn is going to give your confidence and energy a big boost.

If you were born with a facial disfigurement or blemish for example, you know what a challenge getting past initial visual impressions can be. When I was 10 years old I had a prominent, brown birthmark below my nose removed, thankfully. A very minor thing compared to what many live with, but the playground reaction certainly gave me some perspective.

For some, there is pretty limited scope for changing appearance. The focus then is on developing those attitudes that make looks less of an issue in your life.

Interestingly enough, being 'freakishly' beautiful can also lead to its own acceptance problems; alienation and jealous aggression from others being just some of them.

It's worth noting that our visual appeal goes beyond our static appearance and is affected significantly by how we *move* and carry ourselves. This includes things like our posture, how we walk and generally what kind of energy or emotion we project when we use our bodies.

Intelligence: Can be a very attractive quality, depending on how it's used. There are things you can do to be intelligent without necessarily having a high IQ (besides, IQ is just one metric for a narrow interpretation of what intelligence is). Being honest with sensitivity, being respectful and taking the time to get in touch with your own feelings and needs and the feelings and needs of others are good examples of smart and attractive behaviour.

I would argue strongly that someone who does the above but is perhaps a little slow in other respects is much more attractive than someone who is awfully witty, can solve the Times crossword in five minutes but doesn't care to ask friends how their day has been, or is forever demonstrating their 'intelligence' at the expense of others. Intelligence is just one personality trait of many that can be attractive and it's one of those things where worrying about it just gets in the way.

Personality: This actually can be a real obstacle, but fortunately it's perhaps the area where we have the most opportunity to transform and develop. A big part of our personality is manifest through our attitudes to ourselves and others. If you are prepared to examine these things – paying particular attention to your habitual thoughts (internal dialogues) – and make some shifts, you can radically change the sort of relationships you have.

Etc.: Can you change it? Do you want to, and is it worth it? If so, do it! Otherwise worrying about it probably isn't helping, so concentrate on what you do have. One of the most valuable resources you can have (and which only depends on how much you decide to give yourself) is active commitment to your well-being and lasting happiness.

What is it about the way you look?

I'm going to spend a bit more time now talking about 'looks', or physical appearance, since, as a society, we spend so much time and energy either trying to improve it, or worrying about it. Sure, it's often the first impression you make, but why is it so important to so many people?

There are the evolutionary arguments; that being fit, strong and well endowed in the baby making and rearing parts being indicators of good mating choice. Then there are cultural and social arguments; that physical attractiveness reflects the norms and peculiarities of the culture you're in, so how you looks shows how well you 'fit in'. (Clearly there's a lot of variation here – depending on where you are, being plump, wearing designer labels, having an elongated neck or giant ear lobes may be ideal.) Then, of course, there's our personal preference, fitting in somewhere between those biological and cultural influences.

Accepting some cultural bias, the condition you keep your *body* in will make a statement about your self-respect and self-control. Sometimes it's that statement that is important to people, as much as the sensual appeal of being in 'good' shape. It's true, people identify with their bodies to different degrees. The fact remains though; our bodies are a rather essential part of who and what we are in this world.

Supposing then, for instance, the condition you keep your body in suggests your self-respect and self-control aren't very high. What would that say to someone you like about how you'd be in an intimate relationship? Are they things you want to say? If not, it's time to take action. Whichever way you cut it, as subjective as 'looking good' is, and as much as a smile helps, taking good care of your body is a smart choice.

Finally, all of the obstacles in this section largely come down to beliefs – which then lead to certain actions – and beliefs can be changed.

Untangling values, beliefs and desires

You meet someone with some kind of mutual compatibility and desire, you start spending time together and hey-presto, you're in a nice relationship. It should be simple then, right? I suspect you probably wouldn't be reading this book if things were working out quite so easily.

Two people who are in very similar difficult situations with a close personal relationship, or with forming one, can decide to take very different action. So then it's not just the situation that determines their actions; but very often it's their *actions* that determine their results. What else then decides our actions? It's our outlook and self-image, it's how we see ourselves in relation to others and the world and also our ideas about how people should relate. It's a question of mental perception. Our *thinking* tells us not only what is possible, but what is 'good', 'bad' or 'acceptable' too. It's in these areas that we become tangled and often end up going around in circles. This is why personal relationships are not so simple.

Relationships can be extremely complex and challenging, despite their fairly universal and simple aspects, such as wanting to share some kind of support and affection. How many people out there would dearly like to have someone they can really share their feelings with and have a good hug when they need, but somehow aren't finding it? I can tell you from my time working for the Samaritans and the many other individuals I've spoken to over the years, that it is a large number. (If you're not in that situation, then there are probably at least a few amongst your friends and family who are, even if they are not showing it.)

The basic idea: the way you think → the results you get, is not new. It's found in many places throughout history.

"Man is made by his belief. As he believes, so he is." - Bhagavad Gita

"All that we are is the result of what we have thought." - Buddha

"I the Lord search the heart and examine the mind, to reward a man according to his conduct, according to what his deeds deserve." - The Bible

"The appearance of things to the mind is the standard of every action to man." - Epictetus

"What we achieve inwardly will change outer reality." - Plutarch

"Remember, the entrance door to the sanctuary is inside you." - Rumi

"For 'tis the mind that makes the body rich" - Shakespeare

We also see the basic idea take a central position in some modern forms of clinical psychology such as Cognitive Behavioural Therapy (and variants), Transactional Analysis, Solution Focused Brief Therapy and Ericksonian Hypnosis.

Sometimes just believing, without *deliberately* taking action, can have physical effects. In pharmacology, the placebo effect, in which patients show significant relief from symptoms after a course of fake medicine they *believed* to be real, is well recognized. Indeed, new drugs are performance tested against it.

Naturally, the idea of what you think determining your actions and results, is also strongly embraced by countless authors in the modern self-help movement. Dale Carnegie, Stephen Covey and Anthony Robbins, to name a few.

Fine, so what you think can have a significant impact on the results you get. But how can we possibly go about undoing our seemingly intractable tangles in the thinking that can surround our relationships? Isn't this 'positive thinking' stuff all rather simplistic? Well, if we left it at 'think positive', or 'think more resourcefully', then yes it would be. To see how it's not just a simple case of 'thinking positive', we must understand the process of thought → action a bit more clearly.

It must first be acknowledged that, for some people, their circumstances or physical situation makes it especially challenging to develop healthy, loving relationships with others. For instance, those who have been abandoned by their family or whose friends or loved ones have died and who are isolated and not very mobile, or those who have lost most of their senses to illness or injury, or those who are imprisoned. Without such huge difficulties it's perhaps easier to see how your results come down to 'what's going on in your head'. It could be argued though, that the greater your circumstantial or physical difficulties, the *more* important your way of thinking.

"I understood how a man who has nothing left in this world still may know bliss, be it only for a brief moment, in the contemplation of his beloved." – a quote of Viktor Frankl[2], who wrote profoundly on his experiences in a WWII concentration camp, where over 1 million people were exterminated. He concluded that love is humankind's ultimate meaning and even in such truly terrible conditions it could still be found, and that love was indeed the key to survival. Another example is Nick Vujicic, a man born without arms or legs. He is able to share and receive great love with many thousands of people around the world, because he travels and speaks about making the most of the opportunities we all have.

Once you start to look, the number of examples in the world of people who somehow defy great hardships to find happiness, love and meaning in their relationships, just keep adding up. Perhaps the hardest obstacle of all to overcome is the mind itself – at least when it gets itself into a tangled state.

Some readers may find parts of the following material in this section quite challenging. It's like a kernel from which many other sections branch out. The ideas are grouped together here to provide more of the bigger picture, and some directions that

---

2 Viktor Frankl (1946) "Man's Search for Meaning" OCLC: 233687922

you may choose to explore further, or revisit at a later time.

Let's now divide the region of 'entangling thinking' into some smaller, more manageable areas – that together lead us to deciding what actions to take in our relationships. We will focus here on values, beliefs and desires (VBDs), which seem to cover a good stretch of the 'entangling region'. (There's no doubt our *feelings* can drive us to action and can be very conflicted. However, the origin of that conflict I believe lies primarily in our *thinking*.) Before we look at some of the VBD tangles that get in the way of us having the relationships we'd like, let's clarify what is meant by 'values, beliefs and desires'.

Values: Qualities, features, ideals, customs that hold meaning and worth to a person. Values are things that are appreciated and cared for and they can define a sense of 'good' and 'bad'. They can also be innate, like the valuing of sustenance, shelter, pleasure or affection. The kind of feelings that result from experiencing something you value include: appreciation, gratitude, contentment, joy and connection. Values are desirable but not always desired. That is, we often desire what we value, when we're not currently experiencing it. But when we already have something we value, then there is no urge, or desire to get it, even though it is still valued.

Beliefs: An idea of 'what is the case' which is held to be true, true on the condition of certain action being taken (i.e. a rule) or true in an ideal world ('I believe this *should* be ...'). Beliefs are a kind of persistent evaluation or judgement. When a belief is formed we weigh up different ideas and interpretations – taking into account what evidence we think we have – and make a judgement (consciously or otherwise). That judgement persists over time (until the belief is changed) thus affecting our future decisions. Like values, beliefs also influence our feelings.

Desires: Qualities, experiences or situations that we seek to gain or develop, either without conscious reasoning or explicitly to satisfy a value. The kind of feelings that result from having a desire include: anticipation, yearning, eagerness, agitation, hope, expectation and separation.

Going back to values, we see they cast a pretty broad net, including desirable feelings, innate 'needs' and certain types of belief and judgement. Values may also be desires where they are not currently being experienced. Yet they are a commonly recognisable idea concerning 'what really matters'.

Judgement and the tree of actualization

One feature that values, beliefs and desires have in common is the presence of judgement. Together VBDs form layers and branches of judgement that eventually lead to a decision of what specific action to take. Values and beliefs provide a sense of direction to the driving force of desire. In sub-section 'Knots not to keep', from page 27, we look at several examples of the tangles that these judgements can get us in – especially those deeply buried judgements which take the form of beliefs and certain kinds of values.

To get a better idea about these 'branches or judgement' lets first consider desire. From a desire for something arises the question of how to get it. The result is a plan or 'strategy'; collections of guesses and judgements on how best to accomplish that goal. On top of those are yet more strategies to fulfil bits of the main plan and so on, moving then into technique and subconscious habit. You could imagine the original desire being like the trunk of a tree with the main strategy creating branches which then split into smaller branches of technique and subconscious habit. E.g. "I want affection" → "I want a hug and kiss from this particular person" → "Say hello, request hug and kiss" → "Smile, step forward, open arms" → "Avoid head-butting or stepping on feet". Notice that as it blends into strategy a desire can become more *specific* (or rather bits of the plan become filled with desire). The desire acquires an object. This helps commit us to take specific action, but it can also lead to over-attachment to what was really just one potential option to satisfy the underlying desire.

Already we've found one mechanism of becoming tangled or stuck; getting wrapped up in just one potential way of getting what is at the root of our desire. It gets complicated because the object of desire may carry special significance that ties in with other of our VBDs, e.g. "I want affection from him/her *because* they're more trust worthy/attractive/available/...." We'll come back to this point later.

'Strategy' is not necessarily a premeditated plan, it may be subconscious or spontaneous. A strategy is simply a plan of action to minimise cost (essentially emotional pain) and maximise benefit according to our VBDs. This could be an internal plan how to change how we feel in a certain situation (e.g. by reasoning with ourselves or identifying with different ideas/persona) or an external plan/model about what and how to communicate. It could also be a plan for how to interact physically with something or someone. A strategy, then, can be taking an attitude as much as a set of concrete actions.

Looking at beliefs as past judgements that we have a persisting confidence in, we can see a similar tree-like structure as with desires. On top of a belief can be laid other judgements about how things work and are. E.g. "I believe I'm attractive." → "That person's smile meant they were attracted to me." These judgements, of course, feed into the strategy forming process and so to some extent also influence our desires, e.g. "I'd like to see more of that smile." → "Introduce myself." On the other hand, if we started with the belief "I'm not very attractive", we might interpret someone's smile differently, e.g. "They're probably just being polite." or "They've probably noticed something funny about my appearance" → "Look for somewhere to hide."

Beliefs can affect how aware and accepting of our values and desires we are. Imagine someone who believes that "People only like you for how you look", that "They'll just use you if you let them get close" and that "I'm not worth very much because people have hurt me so much in the past". As a result of these beliefs the values of self-protection and comfort may be particularly strong, which *could* (for example) lead to the desire for lots of food and the strategy of over-eating and becoming obese. At the same time the values of intimacy and vitality may be very subdued, or in painful conflict.

So above is another mechanism for becoming entangled; conflict within our beliefs can lead to certain important values being suppressed. This reduces our options for fulfilment and can lead to unhealthy habits which can reinforce those beliefs.

Now a picture starts to emerge. It is our values and beliefs that form our self-image and outlook and give rise to desires. Sometimes our self-image or outlook contains conflicts that lead to a lot of our desires being frustrated. Sometimes, due to these conflicts, we might not even be aware of our deepest values. If your actions are like the outer-most branches of a tree and your deepest values are like the roots, then it's as if the branches – which are our way of thinking – are strangling each other. Energy is blocked from getting to the roots and nutrients from getting to the leaves and so the whole tree suffers (see diagram on page 33). But how do we go about resolving such a situation?

Getting to the root: innate values

Returning to the question: "How do we resolve our VBD tangles?" we now have to go a level deeper and look at what truly lies at the roots of our desires to act in various way.

Abraham Maslow's famous hierarchy of needs[3], starts with basic physical needs and moves up through access to resources, then acceptance and finally at the top are needs such as morality,

---

3 A.H. Maslow. (1943) "A Theory of Human Motivation", *Psychological Review* 50(4):370-96.

honesty and creativity. More recent work, by Manfred Max Neef[4], Marshall Rosenberg[5] and others, suggests that there is a broader set of deep drives, needs or values that exist, not as a hierarchy, but as an interrelated collective. This idea is based on the study of many cultures and people in varied socio-economic conditions.

Taking the above as a starting point, it seems there are basically two types of value:

Innate values: values that exist without societal conditioning or having to learn what is good or bad, right or wrong.

Conditioned values: values that come from developing experience, beliefs and a sense of good and bad, right and wrong.

Innate values are more than just basic needs like food and shelter, or vague positive feelings like 'happiness' or 'satisfaction'. They include states of being, doing and feeling like: relaxation, affection, self-expression, respect, nurture, freedom, purpose, humour, understanding, commitment, love, contribution, kindness, enthusiasm, excitement, safety and many more. (Innate values are essentially 'needs' in the communication method known as NVC. See page 140 for further discussion of them.)

It's *because* a conditioned value satisfies an innate value that it matters to us, i.e. *innate values underlie all other values*. Or in other words, a conditioned value satisfies one or more innate value. This is a significant understanding, as our innate values have certain very helpful characteristics:

- **Innate values:** always have many ways of being satisfied or experienced – giving us more flexibility and freedom.

- **Innate values:** are not inherently conflicting – at this level of value there are no tangles.

4   Manfred Max-Neef, et al. (1986) "Human Scale Development: An Option for the Future", Development Dialogue, número especial (CEPAUR y Fundación Dag Hammarskjold). p.12.

5   Marshall B. Rosenberg (2003) "Nonviolent communication: a language of life" ISBN:978-1892005038

- **Innate values:** are universal, everyone understands them because they don't depend on conditioning – so it's easier to understand other people at this level.

What this means is that getting in touch with our underlying innate values gets us a long way towards resolving the tangles in our VBDs. (The 'Conflict' part of this book is a good companion to this section, as it continues in this vein, and also looks at the various effects of judging others in relationships.)

It's very easy not to be in touch with our innate values or just to jumble them up with our conditioned values. These higher level or overlying values (which are really collections of judgements/ decisions about what matters) have a *filtering* affect on our desires.

A desire starts out as a drive to experience an innate value, even if we're not always aware of it at that stage. It then passes through our conditioned values, then our other beliefs about how things work, who we are and what is and isn't possible. At this point the desire is object or situation specific – and possibly already in conflict with some of our beliefs and values. Now the desire moves into strategy forming and finally action (or inaction where no acceptable strategy is found). The diagram on page 22 illustrates this progression. The action arrow represents the final chosen path along the 'tree of judgement' previously discussed.

The entire path of our desire, from conditioned values, through our other beliefs to strategy and finally action, can be seen as a series of present and past persistent judgements. That means we can be fairly sure that our inner conflicts (and the outer ones they manifest) have something to do with our *judgements*. This is a 'good thing' because it means we can take control of our lives, if we take control of our judgements. It can also be a scary thing, because it lays the *responsibility* for our life and happiness squarely at our own feet.

Here's an exercise that may help you identify some of your innate values. Using the table on page 159 for inspiration (if it helps), think over your values and complete this sentence for each one: "I value/It's important to *the value in question* because it gives me *the innate value(s)*". Here are a few examples: "I value *a good sense of style in my partner* because it gives me *a sense of belonging, connection, stimulation and harmony*", "I value *being seen as flawless* because it gives me *a sense of safety, significance and acceptance*", "It's important to *be fresh and fragrant* because it gives me *relaxation, energy, a sense of respect, acceptance and hygiene*", "*It's important to be strong in the face of authority* because it gives me *self-respect, a sense of independence, self-worth and integrity and sometimes a sense of contribution*"

Filtering of desire, from innate values to action

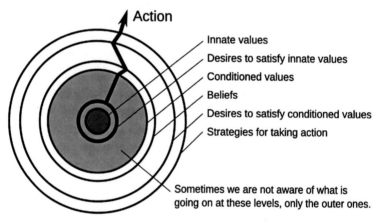

Obviously you might have many hundreds of values, so try to pick the dozen or so that affect you the most and work with those for the above exercise.

When doing this exercise be as specific as you can. (If you just end up with 'because it gives me *happiness, nice feelings, satisfaction*', then you're not a lot further from where you started.) It's a deceptively challenging exercise because it prompts you to look into yourself as well as avoid the temptation to answer in terms of believed consequences or judgements. E.g. "It's important for my partner to put the toilet seat down *because it proves respect, stops things falling in or germs getting out and because otherwise it would look horrible*." instead of identifying the underlying values of, say: *peace of mind, sense of respect (rather than 'proof of'), aesthetic harmony, protection,* etc. The previously listed beneficial characteristics of innate values can best be taken advantage of by directing your attention towards them – and away from inflexible and restrictive judgements. With your attention directed in this way it's easier to have the 'light' kind of expectations previously discussed in section: 'What relationships mean to us'.

Incidentally, how many of your values are beliefs about what others expect of you or about how they see you? As discussed on pages 7 and 70-71, these type of values can cause a lot of grief.

The previous exercise can also be used to investigate the more general type of self-beliefs that you have. It may surprise you to think that even the most crushingly painful of beliefs have some grounding in our innate values. E.g. What values could the belief "I am unlovable" possibly serve? There are certainly major values that won't be satisfied by it, such as love, significance and affection. But there are also some that may be, such as self-identity, certainty and understanding. Since conforming to the judgements of others can be a strategy for gaining acceptance, perhaps, perversely, the value of acceptance is also served by this belief (where it stems from judgements taken in from significant others).

Once you can see what innate values are satisfied and which are not, by some of your most painful beliefs, you may gain some distance and freedom from those beliefs (remembering the three helpful characteristics of innate values from page 20). Next, we explore more ways of helping such beliefs to change.

Beliefs, the gatekeepers to fulfilment

The process of identifying your innate values is one of self-empathy. However, just doing this may not be enough to let you escape your tangles – your beliefs may still tie you up. Taking a few of my own old ones for example, you may think: "I can see that I have these underlying values and maybe other people can find better ways of experiencing them, *but* what choice do I have, since I'm ugly, boring and undesirable? I'm just a shell, empty inside. Besides, people are generally stupid and selfish and not interested in helping someone like me."

The trouble with beliefs like that is that you believe them. How do you get around that? Beliefs can't be changed *directly* by choice, but they can be de-constructed until you are able to re-examine the original judgements that lead to the belief. By reassessing those judgements the belief may change. If you're focused and make good use of *new* ways of thinking that open up, it can work well. Otherwise this approach can lead to the 'paralysis of analysis', or limbo if your outlook and self-image become less certain. Sadly, such states can last for many years.

A related approach is to ask: "Is it *possible* my belief could be untrue, or my judgement inaccurate?" If we ask this question seriously it can allow us to explore other possibilities. *Progress relies on an open mind.*

Fortunately, beliefs – and the behavioural habits that grow from and reinforce them – can also be bypassed, and then changed with fresh new *experience*. This can be done by 'modelling success'. This process is actually the oldest form of learning and something we all, to some extent, do subconsciously anyway. However, the idea of it may feel uncomfortable or scary if you haven't used it consciously before.

The first step is to find someone else who does really well where you'd like to do better. Think 'role model', not for your whole life, just for the particular context in which you'd like to improve or are having difficulty with. That could be particular social situations or events, dealing with conflict, anger or disappointment, or feeling comfortable with intimacy, for instance. Then, having found your 'model', make yourself like a sponge.

At its heart, this idea is about learning what we can from

others. Through our youth, most of us have role models, or 'good examples to follow' – it's a very natural way of learning. It also explains why imitation is considered the sincerest form of flattery. But we often grow more fixed in our thinking with age and reject the doing of things as others do them, as a sign or weakness or dependence. The irony is, we can gain great strength, independence and understanding by accepting lessons from others, keeping an open mind and remembering to experiment.

Modelling success has two components, the internal and external, or the cognitive and behavioural. Each can be used independently, but together they are often synergistic, since one aspect naturally accompanies the other.

With the internal component we try to develop an empathy with that person we're 'modelling'. We take in their emotions, self-image and outlook, specific attitudes or thoughts that seem to have any connection with the area we'd like to improve in. This gives us a sense of their 'cognitive strategies'. The idea is to see how their way of thinking is connected to the good results they get.

With the external component we look closely at how that person behaves in the situation or context we're interested in. We take in their habits of body and voice, posture, mannerisms, phrases, etc. This gives us a sense of their behavioural strategies.

Now we use this understanding to 'adopt' some of *their* strategies (ways of thinking and behaving) that can also help us to better experience *our* innate values. This incredibly powerful technique helps you bypass your own limiting beliefs, long enough for them to shift with fresh experience. It helps free you to see what is *truly* possible.

It's one thing to entertain the idea that your beliefs might be inaccurate: "sure, theoretically, in a parallel universe, I might be a really attractive person"; but quite another to experience a contradiction: "I really noticed a positive change in how people related to me when I adopted some different strategies *(modelling success)*. Maybe I'm not so bad?" It is by adopting new strategies that we allow ourselves to experience such helpful contradictions.

In the words of Aristotle: "It is well said, then, that it is by doing just acts that the just man is produced, and by doing temperate acts the temperate man; without doing these no one would have even a prospect of becoming good. But most people do not do these, but take refuge in theory ..." i.e. it is by practising the way we want to be that we become that way.

The process of modelling someone else's strategies can also take place from only a brief observation. Simply catching sight or sound of how someone interacts in a certain situation can be enough to give us a clue about what might work well for us – and thereby open our eyes to a different way of perceiving ourselves and others. You can even apply this modelling process to something you read or hear about. Sometimes the cognitive side seems more useful, e.g. in finding ways to feel more comfortable expressing yourself freely. Other times the behavioural side seems more useful, e.g. borrowing someone's joke and the way they tell it, for a future meeting.

However, even when you have no interest in a specific instance of using a principle, you just want the principle itself, at first trying out someone else's external strategy can be the quickest way of really imbibing a new principle. Experiencing different examples of success (and contrasting it to failures) helps us to synthesize it.

There are many fears and objections that may come up with taking on someone else's way of doing things, e.g. that it's 'unreal' or seen as somehow inferior. These and more are addressed specifically in section: 'Our attitude to change'. Here, this powerful method of overcoming limiting or destructive beliefs is simply introduced. Without a doubt it's changed my life and relationships for the better. I have hope and confidence that if you have such beliefs, it will help you too.

Where does self-acceptance fit into the above ideas? Acting resourcefully on the desire to learn and improve does not require that you see yourself as inadequate. 'You' are not your strategies and your innate values are just as valuable and valid as anyone else's. Your choices (and how you direct your attention), whether they're inspired by anyone else or not, are entirely yours to make.

Of course the idea of modelling can be applied to yourself too. First by looking back at a time where you dealt with a challenge more successfully, with a different frame of mind. Second by looking forward and asking "If I didn't have this self-belief or fear, how would that me act?" and then just giving it a go. That might sound crazy, but if you can give yourself permission to lay down whatever baggage you're carrying for a moment, it can work very well.

Returning to the subject of beliefs, the specific habits of thinking that are internal dialogues (or 'self-talk') and in general the words we choose, have a profound affect on our outlook and self-image. These are discussed more in Section: 'Internal dialogues and identity'.

Knots not to keep

We talk more about how modelling success and adopted strategies can help you further on. But returning to the issue of tangled VBDs, here is a small collection of 'stories' based on conversations, personal experience and observations, which show various mixtures of VBDs and some of the relationship tangles that can result. It is by no means a complete collection.

Companionship, status and achievement:

"Life is about what you achieve and getting recognition. The more I achieve, the better the person I will attract. Having a beautiful relationship with a beautiful person is seen as part of being successful. The happiness in a relationship comes just as much from the admiration of peers as from the other person. My success comes from my total independence, yet I'm very lonely. But how can I make time for a true companionship and still be successful? If I rest for too long I will lose what I've built, which is always

what has made me feel important."

What it means to be strong and fear of intimacy:

"Needing someone to be close to you shows weakness. I am a strong person, so I shouldn't show signs of needing someone. I am safer at a distance. It takes a lot of strength to trust someone and still be safe. Perhaps I am not strong enough. But needing someone to be close, shows weakness. Also, that must mean if someone needs me, they are weak. I'm afraid of being needed. I would feel somehow responsible for their care and happiness. It takes a strong person to be needed ."

Loyalty, fear of rejection and trust:

"I value loyalty very highly in a partner, but it's so hard to find. People are always looking for something better. They'll leave when they see a fault or get bored, so it's best to make the break first. I'll probably never find someone who wants to stick around, so why give anyone the satisfaction of rejecting me?"

Self-worth and partner worship, or wanting to rescue:

"Loving someone is to dedicate yourself to them; therefore the more I do this, the more I show my love. I'm not deserving of your love so I'll try to compensate you by doing all that you need – so that you could hardly manage without me. You stay with me because I serve you; that is my best quality. Maybe one day you'll love me back, but I don't think you really know me. I'm afraid to show myself, in case it's not what you want."

Commitment, personal failure and expectations:

"Relationships should be happy and long lasting. I'm not one to give up and accept the embarrassment of failure. Success requires dedication and taking the rough with the smooth. You never know when you'll find someone else, so even if I'm unhappy, it's always better to hang in there, things will change. Relationships should be happy and succeeding is worth sacrificing my happiness for."

Rescue, dependency and proof of feelings:

"I'm not strong enough to take care of myself. When you fix my problems it proves that you love me. I need that proof. Because we are together, my problem is your problem (and maybe vice versa). I depend on you for my

happiness. I know whenever I share the pain from my past you will show me warmth and compassion. You see the beautiful person I am inside and want to rescue me. I have so much love to give you it's scary. One day I will find you."

Contribution, responsibility for feelings and judgement:

"I want to have a relationship where we're truly contributing to each other's well-being and development. I value someone accepting me for who I am, but I find people are quick to judge and criticize me. I just can't stand someone telling me what's right, it's just wrong! It makes me feel undermined and inferior. There's often criticism hidden behind a suggestion or disagreement. It's really not worth trying if someone is going to be like that, they won't change. It's impossible to connect and grow if you're feeling defensive, so I just let them know they've ruined their chance and hope to find someone who doesn't judge, and wants to give 'me' a chance."

'Bad luck', self-protection and emotional dependency:

"I'm just unlucky. I never seem to find someone who's compatible with me. I know I'm fussy, but what's the point in pretending something has a future, when it doesn't? If you let yourself go with the wrong person, you'll just have your heart broken, or you'll break theirs. I don't want to risk that again. I need acceptance and security. At least by myself I get some of that. As soon as you commit to someone, you grow emotionally dependent. I'd like to settle down with someone, but there always seems to be something wrong. I just wish I wasn't so unlucky."

Sharing feelings, control and threat-focus:

"You can't be too careful. I'd like to think otherwise, but relationships are really just about getting what you want. You have to fight for your corner and stay in control. Never let on too much or too soon what you're really feeling – because then your weakness is known. It will just come back at you if they can use it to their advantage. I try to be trustworthy. I'm actually the most honest person I know, but people rarely want to open up to me. I guess that just proves my theory that honesty and trust are rare commodities. Sure, it's tiring and lonely living like this, but I didn't make the world the way it is."

A vicious cycle of post conflict intimacy:

"I'm always arguing and fighting with my partners. I find it so stressful, I wish it didn't happen so much. But I suppose at least I know they care. It's hard to control my temper. I get so angry when I think someone is being disrespectful or taking advantage. But then it feels so good when we make up and they're caring and sensitive. But the feeling doesn't last. They grow distant after a while and I can't tell if they appreciate the things I do for them. It must be my fault, but I don't know what to do."

The good news is that, to each of the above and similar stories, there is a path to disentanglement. It's just a matter of finding and then having the courage to walk it.

If you have some beliefs you're beginning to question, here's a thought experiment that may help you to unknot yourself. It's called 'the job interview'. Imagine your beliefs had to apply for the roles they play in your head. Your company, 'MyLife Co', needs to 'economise the workforce'. Picture yourself, the director, calling in each belief on your short-list to be interviewed.

You start with the request: "Please tell me what makes you a good fit for this company." Then, you try and make the case for the belief, e.g. "Well, because I'm true!" You go on and continue the dialogue, e.g. "That's what all beliefs say isn't it? Besides, there are many true things I don't necessarily need to spend much time thinking about – such as my mild intolerance to parsnips, for example. So what makes you different?" and so on. The character of the director in this experiment is of a genuinely caring person, but also someone who is prepared to make a tough decision, gets to the point and doesn't take any crap.

As you continue the interview you'll get a sense of the character of the belief. Is it one you wish to adopt? You'll also get a sense for how a belief that you're beginning to question, plugs into some of your innate values. Other interview questions you may like to ask could be: "What are your normal functions in/ Do you enjoy being at/How do you see the future of 'MyLife'?" Sub-section: 'Define your fear' from page 61, may help too.

Why does this keep happening to me?

Notice how the sort of scenarios in the previous sub-section can be self-sustaining. The internal logic and tangled half-truths in our VBDs and our – often unconscious – strategies for meeting them can create vicious cycles.

Sometimes the strategies we develop to protect us from our worst fears and to help us get what we want, fail repeatedly on both counts. Why is that? It appears to me that there are broadly three reasons for this repeated failure:

- **Contradiction** within our VBDs. Taking consistent, congruent action or even thinking clearly is tricky when you get pulled in different directions. Thus your results suffer.

- **Avoidance** of pain along the path to success. Avoiding a major fear or accepting the smaller pain of cutting an attempt short we block our path to achieving what we want and to personal growth.

- **Partial confirmation** or false confirmation. Where our strategies result in giving us just a little of what we want, or appear to somewhat protect us from harm we conclude (or hope) that by carrying on in the same way we'll get better results eventually.

So we put a 'cap' on our success. The elements of CAP (Contradiction, Avoidance and Partial confirmation) are co-dependant. Take for example a contradiction of beliefs: "If I'm in a committed relationship I should spend a lot of my time with that person." and "We should allow each other to do our own things and be independent." One strategy for dealing with this contradiction is to give up a lot of time to be with your partner and try to subdue the need for independence, where it conflicts, because it feels less important. This works until your neglected *desire* for independence wells up and you have to take some time out from the relationship, or you become depressed. So what stops you from seeing the shortcomings of this strategy and finding a better balance? The fact is these beliefs and this strategy don't exist in isolation, they are supported by other VBDs which are *partially* met or confirmed, and particularly fears with your partner you're 'putting yourself above them' and being 'selfish'? Supposing you value safety in relationships very highly and taking time for yourself seems to present a risk to that, especially when your partner complains about it? You want to avoid the pain of risk and of feeling selfish. Given your outlook, you're doing the best you can. Thus it is our whole landscape of VBDs that allows such conflicts to nest.

In summary, when we experience a contradiction in our VBDs, and thus are at a point of risk, our strategy kicks in to 'protect' us from the bigger anticipated pain, in a way that doesn't actually help us long term. It does this by removing us from the path of risk (and potential change) and returning us to 'safe' ground. Our view of reality is 'confirmed' since we *felt* compelled to act to avoid *directly* facing a big fear or taking a seemingly big risk (e.g. rejection, humiliation, being judged, uncertainty, or facing responsibility). Maybe we also got *some* taste of what we wanted. So then why change our view or behaviour? Instead, our strategies become more engrained and our fears go on plaguing us. So we fail to see that it *is* those very strategies tied to our conflicting VBDs that are bringing about our unhappy experiences.

Besides the above mechanism for becoming stuck in strategies that don't serve us well, there may be more general resistances to change that block progress. We look at some of those in Section: 'Our attitude to change'.

So far we've explored the processes that take place from our inner-most drives (our innate values) through to the actions we take. We've also looked at some of the ways we can become ensnared in our own thinking along that path. Continuing with the tree analogy, the diagram on page 33 brings these ideas together.

The tree of actualization

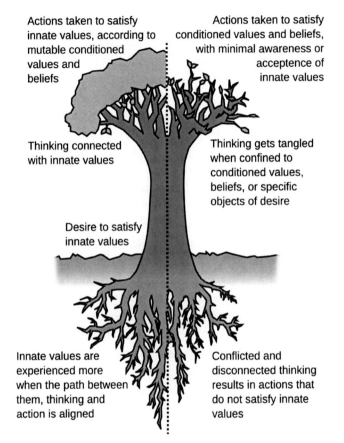

Actions taken to satisfy innate values, according to mutable conditioned values and beliefs

Actions taken to satisfy conditioned values and beliefs, with minimal awareness or acceptence of innate values

Thinking connected with innate values

Thinking gets tangled when confined to conditioned values, beliefs, or specific objects of desire

Desire to satisfy innate values

Innate values are experienced more when the path between them, thinking and action is aligned

Conflicted and disconnected thinking results in actions that do not satisfy innate values

The left side of the tree of actualization, shows the results of maintaining connection with our innate values as we are thinking on different levels and deciding what action to take.

The right side shows what happens when we lose touch with our innate values. Thinking chiefly in terms of conditioned values, beliefs and specific objects of desire, tangles easily arise. It's on this side that judgements such as *right, wrong, should, shouldn't* tend to be made and the heavier kind of expectations and obligations come into play. Judgement clearly has it's uses, but without that clear connection with our innate values, we can become locked in conflicted thinking, our beliefs and desires tying us in knots. It's as if the vascular system of the tree becomes constricted and we suffer from root to branch.

How do we lose touch with our most underlying values to begin with? I believe it happens gradually through a process of sacrifice and habit forming. It's not always possible to get all the things we desire and value in some situations, or we don't find a way of doing so. As a result we sacrifice some values in order to satisfy other values. But what starts off as a strategy to make the best out of a tough situation can form into habits and beliefs. E.g. "In order to be accepted now I need to do what people expect of me first and what I want last." → "What I want is not important."

Earlier in this sub-section the basic inclination to avoid pain was discussed in the CAP concept. This ties in with the strong innate value for safety or protection. In order to be 'safe' other values are sacrificed. Similarly, in order to gain, for instance, acceptance, significance or companionship, we may sacrifice many parts of our being. In this self-compromised state we take on the expectations or judgements of others, which often adds yet more knots to our thinking. Then, more successful strategies simply don't occur to us, or they appear impossible from our distorted, or blinkered perspective.

The strategy adopting process (modelling) described previously is akin to pruning the branches of our tree, so that it – and our relationships – can flourish once again, with our connection to what really matters most to us, restored.

Breaking the pattern

Don't worry, there is hope. As we've already outlined, once we notice the *patterns* we're falling into we can choose to explore *alternatives strategies*. These new strategies are outside the internal logic of our beliefs and conditioned values, but compatible with our desires for change and the innate values we'd really like to experience more. Change requires effort, especially where habit is involved, and this process will also likely have some risk of short-term pain, so keep in mind your wanted long-term gains and have courage. Frustration and pain can be your friends here, they will help you try alternatives. It may well be that what you are afraid of turns out to be either highly unlikely to happen, relatively harmless or completely fictitious. Or, that by altering your perspective, you are able to deal with your feared outcome effectively and without harm. (See section: 'Fear (and general emotional turmoil)' for more detail.)

Changing your strategies and behaviour is not about denying your feelings. Denying or blocking your feelings and trying to find happiness is like trying to navigate out of a dark forest without using the compass in your pocket; needlessly challenging. Instead, use your feelings (emotions) to guide you to your innate values and having found them, put yourself *fully* into learning effective strategies.

One consideration with this strategy adopting idea is "Just because it works for them, why should it work for me?" The truth is, it might not. But by treating it as an experiment, you get to find out. Also, if what they're doing doesn't rely wholly on some physical attribute you don't have, there's a fairly good chance you'll benefit from trying their strategies out.

We all have a common set of innate values, as well as largely the same innate body language for different emotional states. In the context of our particular model of success, we may also have cultural or other similarity which help us to relate to them. With so much in common it's hardly surprising that a great strategy for one person will often be just as great for another – once contradictory beliefs are overcome. In the words of Anthony Robbins, "Success leaves clues." Perhaps the most meaningful measure of success of any strategy is really how much more you're connected with and experiencing your innate values, as a result of that strategy.

The diagram below (page 36) shows how adopting such new strategies can allow us to escape old patterns. New strategies → new experiences. As new experience – including taking new perspectives on an old situation – accumulates it penetrates our self-image and outlook, and our beliefs and conditioned values change. As this happens and our tangles loosen, our understanding of those tangles will deepen.

Diagram showing the VBD – strategy-experience connection

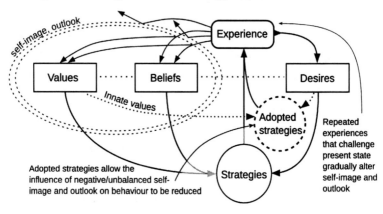

Let's follow this VBD diagram with a simple example: Sam really likes Alex, but is finding this very hard to show. One of Sam's self-beliefs is that they're unattractive and boring. Sam's usual coping strategy is to feign disinterest to avoid rejection, and to readily agree with others opinions so as to at least be somewhat pleasant company. Sam desires to be accepted and appreciated (accepting others and being appreciative are also some of Sam's *values*).

The usual result of this situation is that Sam gets drip fed those desires while having his/her beliefs reinforced. The feigned romantic disinterest creates some curiosity in others, which Sam feels, but it quickly fades as others get the impression they are unwanted. This gives a fleeting sense of being appreciated – which Sam associates with pretending to be disinterested – but it then confirms the belief of being unattractive. The habitual agreeing with others results in 'agreeable', yet ultimately boring company. This gives some sense of acceptance but also confirms the belief of being boring. This loop of: [→ belief and value → strategy → experience →], is shown in the left side of the previous diagram.

Eventually Sam, despairing with frustration, considers what can be done to improve the situation. Learning about the idea of modelling success, i.e. trying out other people's strategies that are especially successful, Sam finds an acquaintance, Bernie, who is particularly good at making friends and catching people's interest.

After studying Bernie's habits of body, voice and speech, and learning about his/her attitudes, beliefs and internal dialogues, Sam then adopts some of these behaviours and ideas as *new strategies*. This is the loop on the right half of the previous diagram. Sam's frustration helps him/her to gain 'escape velocity' from self-limiting beliefs, overriding fear and giving strategies *contrary to those beliefs* a chance of success.

Bit by bit Sam's adopted strategies result in different, more positive experiences, which are like splashes of warm water on the ice of long held contrary belief – of being unattractive and boring. What starts out as shock that things could be different, turns to relief and a sense of personal power. Gradually those unhelpful beliefs change, as Sam finds ways to integrate those strategies into his/her character. They are now Sam's own strategies. Sam now finds it possible to express those feelings for Alex with ease and confidence.

In the modelling process, Sam noticed many things about Bernie. Physical aspect such as how they held eye contact a little longer, how they were more physical and enthusiastic when they said hello, or their flirtatious habits, complemented the mental aspects. E.g. "Well Sam, the way I see it, if someone doesn't like you, that's their issue. I just give them the *opportunity* to know me. It's all good, and I enjoy not knowing how things are going to turn out. Luckily for me, people seem to find that attitude attractive."

As Sam *experiences* the results of adopting each of these strategies, more light is shed on *why* things were turning out the way they were, and why they're now changing. So, it's not that Sam becomes dependent on acting like Bernie. Rather the particular *shifts of thinking and action* that allow change to happen are experienced, and Sam is then able to mould and integrate those shifts with his/her own character.

VBDs, the foundation of your relationships

In conclusion, our VBDs determine the kind of relationships we are able to have. They are the topography over which our thoughts and feelings flow and they are the foundation on which our relationships are built.

Through a relationship many of our VBDs may develop and help to further enrich our life and the life of the person we're having a relationship with. Having natural harmony and support between our values, beliefs and desires allows relationships to be more fulfilling and less problematic. Getting to this state involves more deeply understanding what our values are and questioning our beliefs. Also by realising that there are many ways of satisfying what lies at the heart of our desires – that any plan or object of desire is only one possibility – we do ourselves a big favour. Then, if we adopt alternative strategies, where our current ones aren't working well for us, we allow genuine personal progress to be made. The following sections expand on some of the complexities we've touched on here.

Our attitude to change

What do you think about change in yourself and in your ways of doing and seeing things? Is it desirable, or even possible?

If what you've been doing so far hasn't lead to the relationship(s) you'd like, what is it that stops you from having a true commitment to personal change (if you currently lack such commitment)?

To know whether you can change you need some idea of what 'you' is. Besides your consciousness and without getting too metaphysical it seems there are a few elements involved, such as your memory, values, beliefs, desires and habitual strategies. Your character and even your experiences are shaped through these elements. It seems clear that your circumstances can alter many of them, but what control can you have? It turns out, rather a lot.

Your outlook makes choices for you

Let's consider our self-image and outlook. (Outlook being the way we tend to see and interpret the world and others - leading to ideas of what the future holds). If our outlook and self-image are firmly rooted and such that we quickly judge what's in front of us, a sort of self imposed blindness can take hold. Used to seeing ourselves and others a certain way, anything that doesn't slot into our outlook can easily pass us by or confuse and upset us.

Where our outlook is already tinted a certain colour, the things that occur to us from it will often lead to it being reinforced. This is because we more easily blot out things that have a very different 'colour'. Think of trying to shine a blue light through a piece of red glass; not much will get through. Similarly, consider giving someone the opportunity to be trustworthy when we take the view that people can't be trusted, or accepting generosity when you take the view people always have a selfish motivation; it will be hard. This is why commitment to change is needed.

To a large extent our outlook reflects the way we see ourselves. With our self-image, we may have thoughts such as 'when I was young I had this traumatic experience' or 'my parents were really messed up' so 'that's why I am this way'. Of course, early emotionally charged experiences and parental influence can have a profound effect on us. But if it's something we truly want to change, we can! It's by using the very real power we have over what we do in the *present*, in a committed and consistent way, that change occurs.

Giving away your power through blame

Blame, or rather holding on to it and using it as a channel for venting our present life frustrations and unhappiness, can really hold you back. I've personally wasted a lot of time (years) and energy blaming people or circumstances for my unhappiness in the past. Yes, we are affected by our environment and the people in our lives. But by continually offloading what we don't like about ourselves and our lives onto things that are in the past, or outside of our control, we are disempowering ourselves. We are rejecting that real power to change our lives in the present.

Thoughts such as: *"It's not my fault, I had no choice. It's ... fault I am the way I am"* or *"It's not me, but other people who need to change"* perpetuate the power of the subject of blame, whether it's a person, event, accident or circumstance.

If you share the above kind of disempowering views, try substituting something like: "I acknowledge how these things have affected me in the past and the pain they've caused me." followed by "Now I give myself freedom to find harmony in my world. I release that pain and without resentment step beyond it into a self-guided way of being and the life of my choosing." Say it to yourself a few times, out loud, and see how it feels.

Studies have shown your brain is plastic

From a scientific perspective, it has been conclusively demonstrated that the brain has a high degree of *life-long* 'neuroplasticity'. That means your brain can *re-wire* itself, well into adulthood. In the 1960's, Dr Paul Bach-y-Rita developed a device which enabled blind people to 'see' through the skin of their back[6], connected to an array of actuators hooked up to a video camera. Since then it has been shown that by receiving sufficiently stimulating *new experiences*, people who've suffered a severe stroke can actually regain the skills they lost, including language, mountain climbing, or even scientific research.

Your brain is extremely flexible, it just needs to be provided with different inputs (new experiences) to start adapting. If it seems like, following whatever past experiences, your brain's wiring is a bit 'iffy', give it what it needs to change, pick some new strategies and allow yourself some fresh experiences.

Being 'true to yourself' and 'behaving as if'

One very powerful way of creating inner change is to *behave as if* you've already made it. By creating experiences that don't fit with parts of your current self-image and listening to the feedback you get from the world, step by step, your self-image can grow to fit your adopted behaviour. (It needn't be a giant leap, but big steps can help to imprint a new perspective.) Now, if we try to apply this idea, two adages may come to mind:

1. "If you try to be something you're not, you are untrue both to yourself and to others."

2. "I should be accepted for who I really am."

Parts of these adages are rightly valued and guarded, because at the core of developing deep and loving relationships are:

---

6   P.Bach-y-Rita. (1967) "Sensory Plasticity" Acta Neurologica Scandinavica, 43:417-26

a. Wanting to connect with people in a genuine, authentic way that reflects your true feelings.

b. Wanting to be appreciated for the genuine things you see and value in yourself.

The danger, however, with 1. and 2. above (and similar statements) is in the 'who you really are' bit. If we see our 'true self' like a stone sculpture, fixed from some point in the past, then we can easily cheat ourselves out of a happier, more loving life.

How did we develop the personal qualities we already have in the first place? As babies we started with pretty much zero identity. We observed, experimented and learned from our experiences. After trying out different ways of behaving, we stick with the ones that seem to work well for us at the time. Our 'true self', therefore, is more like a story; one that continues to be written until we stop exploring.

It's true that at key periods in life, such as adolescence, many people establish parts of what becomes a firm sense of identity, and when those periods pass, development (of our sense of who we are) slows or even stops. What is it that makes us think that at this point, change is no longer possible or desirable? Supposing the things we came to believe about ourselves when we were actively developing (and it is an active process) don't serve us well in later life? Practically speaking, aside from the scientific possibility, can we pick up the pen and continue the story of ourselves from where we left off? The answer is 'yes', providing you have the courage and determination to do so.

It takes courage because you could be undermining some self-beliefs you've built up over many years and, to some degree, you're stepping into the unknown. It takes determination because old habits of mind and body die hard. This kind of change requires effort. It's not that convenient and there is no 'easy-cook ready-meal' option. Sorry. However, it does get easier once you've built up some steam in the direction you want to go. Looking at it another way, what else is effort for – if not to make changes? Actually, once you feel some momentum in exploring what it is to be you again, making this effort can be very exhilarating.

It's not only how we deal with the present or look to the future that can change. Even the experience of our memories can be transformed when, through altering our perspective, we come to understand the meaning of past events differently.

How does 'being true to yourself' fit into the 'behaving as if' idea, and other self-development concepts?

The first step is to realize that 'you' *is* a truth that changes as the days go by. From our body, to our attitudes, skills and knowledge, to the ways we relate to ourselves and the world as our fortunes change; we change without even meaning to. To seek or be open to inner change, then, is not to accept personal 'fault'. It's simply embracing the nature of life.

The second step is to realize where the value – and danger – in 'honesty' (and of course dishonesty) lies.

Honesty allows us to experience relationships more directly and richly than if we were separated with some pretence or deception. Some types of honesty are far more important than others to make that relationship experience a healthy and loving one. Especially important is honesty with our *intentions* and *interests* and the every-day honesty of meaning what you say and sticking to your word.

Dishonesty with intentions or interests reflects poorly on a person's character and makes any relationship a difficult and ultimately broken one. If, however, we take the attitude that *any* and *all* feelings must be shared with someone we feel close to, then the situation can easily become claustrophobic, or like a counsellor/patient one. This is not a good thing for a balanced and mutually supportive relationship. People do want the truth from you, but they often don't need or want the whole, unabridged truth, as it can be overwhelming.

Applying this understanding to a common example, let's take

'improving confidence' (similar could be said for other changes you may want to make). Supposing Billy, or Bill for short, notices something about someone which they really like and respect, e.g. how they look or smile, how they treat other people, the way they speak, the care they take over doing something well, or their walk, etc.

Lacking the confidence to make a connection, normally Bill would just think about them. But *this* time Bill decides to model success (see page 24) and go ahead and make that connection, even though part of them is feeling scared and wants to run away. Bill says something like: "Hi, I noticed your smile, I like how it suggests calmness with a hint of mischief" or perhaps "Hi, I noticed the care you take over wrapping your scarf, I like your attention to detail". According to their response Bill then strikes up a short conversation, arranging a meeting in the near future, where they can get to know each other better. See sections: 'First contact and conversions' and 'Attitudes and the other's shoes' for some more ideas on how to do this.

When we take the kind of step Bill did and try something different, what's happening in terms of being genuine and 'true to yourself'? The table on page 45 lists the major points.

Now, of those two lists in that table, which for you is more important? Actually, we can see there's quite a lot of authenticity and honesty in that left column, alongside its positive, pro-active outlook. It's vital here to separate *acknowledging* a feeling from your *choice of how to act* on it. I'm not advocating denying feelings of fear or discomfort. On the contrary, accepting – and then taking responsibility for – those feelings is the way to transform them.

Psychologist, philosopher and author Virginia Satir, known for her work on managing change (amongst other things), writes on 'living humanely': *"... a person who is real and is willing to take risks, to be creative, to manifest competence, to change when the situation calls for it, and to find ways to accommodate to what is new and different, keeping that part of the old that is still useful and discarding what is not."*

you are being true to:	you are not being true to:
Your genuine like and respect for that person (your interest). Your intention to share those good feelings and connect (more than just *wanting* to).	Your lack of deep confidence and inner calm (you're trying to behave like you *do* feel that way). Wanting to run away because you feel afraid or awkward.
Meaning what you say. A belief that self-expression and happiness is worth some risk.	A desire to be seen exactly as you currently are. Saying *everything* that you feel.
A desire to grow and learn by trying out other ways of being.	A belief that your character/personality/self is fixed in stone.

Making change stick

Continuing the previous example on confidence, let's put ourselves in Bill's shoes. What would happen if you continued to model success in the same way? Essentially one of two outcomes:

1. The process of *behaving as if* you have that confidence and inner calm actually brings those qualities into you.
2. You remain at a stage of only behaving as if you really feel those qualities.

What leads to 1. above? The *emotional significance* of the *risks* you're taking combined with the positive feedback you get from people helps, bit by bit, to imprint your new habits of behaviour – or adopted strategies. As you turn an adopted strategy into habit, it becomes more of a subconscious way of being. Where feedback is less positive you take an attitude of continual learning and improvement (see section: 'Fear (and general emotional turmoil)'). As you become more deeply confident, you perceive less and less risk in approaching people you find attractive; then that confidence is just "the way you naturally are". This is the result of consistently activating the natural feedback process between new experience and self-image (see diagram on page 36).

Obviously outcome 1. above is what we want, but what would lead to 2.? Several things. Overall I'd say it's being fixated on the 'you are not being true to' side of the previous table. The attitudes and habits in the following list will also make it hard for you to create lasting inner change (of any kind, not just confidence) by adopting better strategies or 'behaving as if'.

- Not being committed enough to see it through. It can take lots of repetition to imprint part of a new self-image. If you're thinking: "*what's the point, it'll never work*", then you're absolutely right, it'll never work – if you think that way. Consider how reluctance to take action allows so many sad things to continue in this world. Take action; define your future.

- Being too deeply affected by rejection. Feeling your whole being is de-valued, when it's probably only a part of what you *communicated* that was not liked on that occasion (if it even had anything to do with you).

- Being obstructively self-analysing (think "*the paralysis of analysis*"), or allowing fear of failure to pin you down and deny you the chance of success.

- Being too proud to accept the usefulness of having a role-model for a particular area of your life. Distracted by thoughts like "*I don't want to be like anyone but me*", you miss the point that 'you' is something that you have the privilege to change – alongside all the other natural influences on our being.

- Thinking: "*If I change, people won't accept me any more.*" It could be true, but if there's a strong bond, or you grow more content and at peace inside, then it's more likely they'll get used to it. Typically, the more content and peaceful you become in yourself, the more attractive you are – especially to those who share these inner qualities.

- Thinking: *"Why should I change? I'm sick of thinking there's something wrong with me. Aren't I OK as I am?"* I firmly believe there's nothing wrong with you. However, developing your way of being, does not have to imply fault in how you were or are. To embrace change is simply to embrace life.

Of course, initially this 'behaving as if' process may feel (and maybe occasionally seem to others) a little strange as you get used to it, but you're taking steps towards a better, happier way of being. So, have courage and continue to see yourself where you want to be, as you flower more into your ever evolving, true, potential self.

Applying this attitude to change, it's not that your past vanishes, the grooves of our old patterns take time to wear away, it's just that we make new grooves to run along.

In summary, your authenticity of intent to be a better, happier person will grow into the authenticity of those qualities you're developing. Don't get tied down with fretting "this isn't really me", give yourself the *freedom to grow*.

Personal boundaries can also be connected with how much we allow ourselves to change. We discuss them more on page 3.

What's to lose, what's to gain?

If you're unsure whether you really want to make a particular change in your life, take a moment to think about it now. Imagine how doing nothing about it would affect your life. What would it be like 6 months from now? What about 1 year, 2 years, 5 years? What's on your mind, what sort of place are you in, what are your relationships like at each of those points in the future? Let the feeling really sink in for a bit. Now, shake it off and imagine how your life would be if you made that change now. See yourself there, 6 months, 1, 2 and 5 years from now. How would your world change? How would you feel? For a minute or so walk around in that world 5 years from now, having already made that change. Compare *that* state with the no change state you imagined before. After this exercise, what you want to do should be a lot clearer. Ultimately, chance takes effort. You have to decide if it's worth it.

Another thing that can strongly affect our resolve or impetus to make positive changes in our lives is our 'internal dialogues'. If, when we recognize we're unhappy and feel we'd like to change, we moments later tell ourselves things that reflect a belief that "we are where we deserve to be" or that "we can't change", then it's like our right leg is trying to walk forward but our left leg is jumping back. So then when we land on our face we have our negative beliefs reinforced. That's really going to scupper our chances of happiness!

Internal dialogues and identity

Faced with certain situations we say to ourselves: "you're such a.../I am a.../I can.../I can't.../I'll always.../I could never...". We are making an identification with ourselves (or having an internal conversation under-pinned by one or more of these statements). These *reinforce* the opinions or beliefs we have about ourselves. They are like mantras, repeated over and over, sinking in and colouring our mental space and our idea of who we are. It's worth really taking note of what we're telling ourselves because it really makes a difference to our quality of life. If it's not helping you be the person you want to be, then it's time to change track!

If you suffer from any of the issues mentioned so far, picture yourself, if you will, in a café. You've just met someone you find very attractive. You caught each other's eye in the queue perhaps and there happens to be only one free table, which you both sit at. You've exchanged a 'hello' and a smile. Suddenly a voice kicks up in your head (these are examples from my own past and what friends have shared, please substitute your own):

"What are you doing? *Hello?* You're going to humiliate yourself again. Do you really want that? They're far too beautiful for you. You're making them uncomfortable. S/he doesn't want to talk to you. You'll probably have nothing in common anyway. You could try to make them like you, *trick* them into liking you, but then you'd be a deceptive creep, just the needy, shameful, sex starved, social failure that you are and *always will be.* Besides, you're *boring.* You can't possibly hide all the problems you have. Better just *pretend* you don't like them now before they reject you, as per usual."

Phew, toxic stuff isn't it? Shake it off.

Rhetorical question: Would that dialogue help you in the situation? Would it help you relax and take in what's around you? Would it help you connect with them in a comfortable yet exciting, playful, inquisitive and spontaneous way?

I'm guessing your answer is no! Your personal demons may not be as vitriolic as above, maybe they're more apathetic, or defeatist: "I just can't do it!" or "It's just a matter of time before I screw this chance up." Perhaps they're more fearful: "They'll only hurt me." or "The only person I can ever trust is myself." Whatever they are, I urge you to start addressing them, today.

Imagine someone who didn't normally have this issue suddenly hearing that previous internal dialogue whenever they met a person they were attracted to. How would that affect their attitude and relationships? Not good right?

So far we've talked about self-identifying internal dialogues and how they affect our sense of self. What about the habitual dialogues we have about other people, that aren't *directly* about us ("s/he is ...", "s/he will ...", "you are ...", "typical ..." etc.)? Actually these also affect our sense of self in the moment and often reflect a self-belief. Sometimes it helps to judge and generalize, that's lift, but doing so in this way, with habituated dialogues, often just obstructs forming deeper, more beautiful connections with people (especially if those dialogues are verbalized). Therefore it's also crucial to address these types of dialogue.

Strategies for transformation

So, negative internal dialogues, what do you do about them? Several things have helped in my experience:

Acknowledgement: "Yes I actually do say those things to myself. Now *why* am I doing it and what can I do about it?". Also, start to take note of when you are doing it.

Notice that the dialogues are almost always *subjective interpretations of possible reality*, not actually factual statements. Remember *there is always an alternative interpretation.*

Discussion: Talk them over with yourself, a trusted friend, counsellor, or the Samaritans. Talking things through can shed useful light on your personal knots.

Writing them down: It can be really helpful to see the things you tell yourself in black and white, right in front of you. It takes the dialogue out of your head. It gives you some room to move and a clearer view, which can help you find the understanding and resolve to release those dialogues that are holding you back.

Assertive disagreement: Is the habitual statement something you don't *really* agree with? Then be assertive in your disagreement. Actually, even if you still somewhat believe what you're telling yourself, try assertively disagreeing anyway. You may find it feels good and opens the possibility in your mind that things may be different. Here is one way of getting started with this process:

Imagine you're saying what you usually say to yourself, to a friend. Imagine them responding in a submissive or non-assertive way. An unpleasant feeling, no? Now switch roles and imagine them saying the same thing to you. E.g. "You're obviously not very together. You're always forgetting things and leaving a mess behind you." At this point, imagine how you could respond in a straightforward, assertive way that disagreed with that statement – and its underlying assumptions/beliefs. E.g. "No, that's not right. It's normal and human to forget things or create a mess sometimes. I can be very organized and mindful and some of the things around me are just beyond my control." Isn't that a nicer feeling? The more you step into that assertive voice the better and easier it gets.

Finding alternatives: By shifting your view to being less final and condemnatory, leaving the door open for both acceptance and positive change, feelings of anxiety and personal failure will diminish. Beyond just disagreeing with a negative statement, if there's a quality you'd like to have more of but your negative statement or dialogue detracts it, find another statement that affirms or promotes it and say that instead. Let that statement *support* you. If you're really not feeling the quality you'd like to develop at present, instead of: "I'm confident/playful/passionate/...", you can say "I am *becoming more* confident/playful/passionate/...". Then, find something (even if it's small) to do each day that demonstrates and reinforces that view.

Translating the judgement: If an unhelpful dialogue is really something you still firmly believe, assertive disagreement and finding alternatives may be hard. One way of addressing that belief is to get in touch with your feelings and unmet needs *behind* the self-judgement. E.g. If we habitually say: "I'm a nobody" we might 'translate' that judgement into: "I'm currently *feeling* very disconnected, fragile and hopeless, because my *needs* for acceptance, respect and affection are not being met, and I don't know what to do." This alternative way of relating to ourselves is exceptionally powerful and discussed more in the 'Conflict' part of this book.

The "Can I be ..., but *sometimes* ..." question can also help you find alternatives. For instance, if you often tell yourself that you're stupid, ask yourself: "Can I be an *intelligent person*, but sometimes make a silly mistake?" Forming a question with this structure around a self-judgement can help you gain perspective and more self-forgiveness.

Experimenting: Once you've found an alternative dialogue or way of relating to yourself, put it to test. You can start with the past. Recall a situation where you've said something to yourself that created or re-enforced unhappy feelings. Note those feelings. Now, substitute your new alternative into that situation. Observe how you see things differently and how your feelings change.

One great use of experimenting is 'reality checking' your habitual self-talk with people you know. It could be that some characteristics or challenges you consider peculiar to yourself turn out to be quite common. An effective approach used in the cognitive-behavioural school of psychology is to take the statement which sums up your self-belief and ask: "If that was true, what results would you expect to see?" Often these are very real fears that you have. Then the idea is to do a controlled experiment to field-test the hypothesis – hopefully gaining positive experiences that *disconfirm* the predicted results and *undermine* the negative self-belief. Section: 'Untangling values, beliefs and desires' goes much deeper into related ideas.

Here's an everyday example of using alternatives that I've found helpful and you may wish to experiment with.

Sometimes when we walk past people in the street we might get distracted by unwanted thoughts about something negative they may be thinking about us, or seem to be generally giving out to the world. Or we just see something that we dislike about them and fixate slightly on it. It can become a habit. I've found that if, when I first notice someone, I *immediately* look for some little thing I *like* about them and just let my mind appreciate it for a moment, that *completely* breaks this pattern. So simple. Note, it could be anything you like, the tiniest detail, from the shape of their neck to the sound of their shoes on the ground. (If this seems a little contrived, is it any more contrived than having a default negative thought or reaction to people?)

Being mindful: *Watch* when unhelpful internal dialogues occur. Our power to change our lives is always in the present. To be fully in the present we must let go of evaluations/judgements and simply observe. Mindfulness is participatory observation. Whatever thoughts are flowing through your mind, whatever feelings you're having, simply turn your awareness to them and *observe* without trying to push them away or bring them closer. Just by separating your awareness out from your self-identifications, evaluations and associated feelings – *without trying to change anything* – your mind will start to gain freedom from old patterns of thought.

Buddhists cultivate a similar mindfulness to this through meditation. But we can benefit from mindfulness whatever our physical activities or spiritual beliefs. Being still and quiet is not necessary to be mindful, although being so can be helpful to get a taste for the experience.

Your body, an emotional organ

Taking a step back now, you may notice these internal dialogues don't happen in isolation. There will be an associated emotional state and a *physical* state (posture, rate of breathing, muscle tension, perhaps subtle facial expressions) too. These aren't incidental, they are instrumental. Our brain, and so our mind, is inseparable from our body. What we feel is reflected in our body – and what our body *does* is reflected in what we feel.

So, if you have an unhelpful internal dialogue, notice what your body's doing, in detail, and alter it. If your chest is sunken and your breathing shallow allow your shoulders to relax back and breath deeply and calmly. If your hands are clenched, let them relax to your sides or lap. If your brow is furrowed and tense, slide your finger up the middle of your forehead and imagine cool clear water running over it (or whatever works for you) leaving the muscles around your eyes soft and relaxed.

After altering your body state in this way you will notice the dialogue either stops, changes in tone or seems very faint and distant. If you keep doing this (every time your mental state begins to slip to a place you don't want it to go), eventually you'll just do it naturally without thinking about it.

Of course the tensions we hold in our body don't just affect how we feel, they affect how other people feel about us too. Those tensions may be hard to let go of though if we're entrenched in a certain 'protective' state of mind. When we feel this way it's often because we have a fear of something and are focusing on what we don't want.

Your words become what you see

We've talked about dialogues, but what difference do individual words make? It turns out, quite a lot. We think in the language we speak, so it follows that the words we pick define the scenery and begin to lay the possible future tracks for our train of thought. When we think of a word, we not only think of its written meaning, but also of its personal meaning and associations. With some words (or phrases) we will have strong memories, emotions and beliefs associated with them. Those experiences (or mental processes) may trigger the word, but the word will also trigger or reinforce the experiences in our mind.

Let's look at an example or two of how words can shape our inner landscape. What can we tell from this dialogue? "Ah, *dumped* again. Did I *not deserve* a better chance? Oh well, just another *wasted* 3 months." This person is upset, perhaps they are also feeling hopeless, disappointed and frustrated. The words: 'dumped', 'not deserve' and 'wasted' portray a particular frame of mind. They suggest that the person thinks of themselves as rejected and unworthy and has certain beliefs that dismiss the entire time spent with someone as a waste, when that relationship comes to an end. While it might be *one* way of expressing their feelings, does the use of such words help or hinder that person in changing their disempowering perspectives? Sometimes it's certain key words in our dialogues that hold power over us and changing those words allows our outlook and self-image to grow in a more positive direction.

Here's another dialogue: "Does s/he *love* me? I just can't tell. I'm so anxious about it. Is it *true love*? Do I *love* them?" Here the issue is with the word 'love'. While referring to a central, sustaining experience in human life, it's also a notoriously nebulous concept. As we discuss later in section: 'But what is love?', one way of avoiding being pinned down by a word is to focus more on the experience and where we'd like to go with it – and worry less about the label.

Projections and prophecy

This section looks at how the mental projections we make for the world and others can have a real effect on the way things actually turn out – leading sometimes to self-fulfilling prophecies. (For key distinctions between observing and projecting, see section: 'The glass melon dichotomy'.)

The ripples of our outlook

In sections: 'Our attitude to change' and 'Untangling values, beliefs and desires', we discussed the idea of our outlook acting as a filter to what we're actually aware of (and thus influencing the outcome of events by limiting our choices). Here we look also at how that outlook – and the projections that come from it – affects the impression and feelings of others.

This effect naturally arises through what we communicate with our actions, words and body-language. Our outlook is also a window for others to look in. But how can we appreciate the *link* between certain projections and certain outcomes?

It seems to come down to focus. You have an idea of how things will turn out. If you strongly expect it, you will be actively looking for signs to confirm that expectation. It is this searching, or rather the trail it leaves, that creates effects. Essentially, our evident choices about what to pay attention to, communicate our outlook and projections to others, who then react in light of that knowledge. Now here are two examples, the first showing how the above process can be a big obstacle, and the second how it can be a great help.

Supposing we meet someone and we project into the future: "I really like this person. But people I really like usually end up deceiving me, taking me for granted and then leaving. Why should this be any different? *I can see it already.* What is it about me that people take as an invitation to do this?" (Note how our projections may contain habitual internal dialogues.)

As the relationship progresses and this projection, or story, persists, we'll be looking for evidence to confirm it, even if that's just responding to the other person with the fear of it in the back of our minds. This in turn creates an uneasiness in the other person. They think, "I think this person doesn't trust me, or suspects my motives. It's hard work sharing my feelings with this person, because I think they're often doubted. I feel disconnected. Maybe I'll try not sharing my real feelings so much, maybe things will improve gradually."

At this point we sense a slight withdrawal from them, which only serves to support our projection of eventually being deceived and left. Part of us now is already giving up on the relationship, and we don't make the same effort to be there for the other person that we used to. This in turn leads them to have a sense of disconnection and even rejection from us. Not feeling the love they used to, they may grow lonely and less hopeful. They respond in kind by making less effort in the relationship, as it seems to make little difference now.

This combination of mistrust, disconnection and less support or concern from us, leads the other person to spend more time with friends. At some point they find a friend who really seems to accept them and has a refreshingly positive attitude. Naturally, things progress. Only they can't possibly tell us about it. That would only confirm our suspicions. They feel guilty, but don't want to leave us, because they really care and think maybe they can put things right. However, because we're always on the lookout, we somehow find out what's happened. There's a conversation. They're sorry, they try to explain, but we only hear excuses. They leave, saying "we just weren't right for each other". Once again, it seems we're proven right; deceived, taken for granted and left. So the cycle repeats.

This doesn't mean you shouldn't share your thoughts of the future if they trouble you. Discussing a worry with someone, with an open mind, although it may not be easy, shows trust, honesty and a desire to see things differently. This leaves a *very* different feeling than inadvertently letting someone know that to you that worry is already a forgone conclusion.

On the flip side, positive, optimistic and constructive projections can be helpful, even if they are not totally warranted by past experience or 100% 'realistic'. In the same way that a negative projection will often beget its reality, so will a positive one help to bring itself about.

As an example, suppose again that we meet someone we really like but instead project: "I really like this person. I can see us forming a close bond, being able to talk about anything and being playful and affectionate together,"

Naturally we'll be searching for confirmation of these projections, and since this is a positive outlook, probably by looking for opportunities to experience it. The other person thinks: "This person seems able to trust me and feels really comfortable around me. They don't seem to be hiding anything.

It's easy to be affectionate and playful with this person, I feel good around them."

We take the other person's reactions as confirmation of our outlook, which makes us very happy and encourages us to continue being this way. In turn this confirms to them, that we really are who we seem to be. How it works out from here depends to a large extent on what we're both looking for.

Notice how simply *looking* for positive outcomes, helps to *create* them. We are making ourselves more receptive and welcoming to the outcomes we want. When we project a positive outlook it can be quite contagious and it makes it easier for people to connect with us.

Smart projections

Clearly we live in a world where everything doesn't always work out happily ever after, and there's certainly no substitute for being a level-headed observer of people. However, while things might not turn out as well as we imagine, hopefully the powerful *influence* of projection on what becomes reality is clear. The smart choice then is to focus more on outcomes we'd like, than those we wouldn't.

What can you do if you're in the habit of making unhelpful projections? I would suggest a similar approach as for internal dialogues. Also try actively searching for evidence of the thing you're worried about *not* happening, allowing the projection to then shift to the *positive* extension of the thing indicated. E.g. "It seems they're not being disrespectful/insensitive/dishonest/..." → "It seems they're being *respectful/sensitive/honest/...*".

The most helpful projections are ones that encourage us to take positive, affirming action and which do not load anyone else with responsibility for our own happiness.

Fear (and general emotional turmoil)

Fear of rejection, intimacy, ridicule or judgement and emotional issues such as self-loathing, shame, bitterness or resentment, and low self-esteem (to name a few) are massive blocks to happiness in relationships. I know because I had a serious case of most of these.

In previous sections we've talked about different ways fears and emotional turmoil can be created and manifested, through negative self-talk, projections and conflicts within our values, beliefs and desires. Here we'll look at what that fear and turmoil is saying, and specific ways of overcoming it.

Fear and turmoil, along with anger and despair, share a certain emotional space. At one end is utter hopelessness, at the other is rage. The common message of the feelings in this space is that we have pressing needs (see page 159) that are not being met. We don't feel peaceful or resourceful here; it's a place where we're either fighting against some pressure or giving in to it (or yo-yoing between those two states). The fact is, within this emotional space we're much *less* likely to find a sustainable way of meeting our needs than outside it. But while it can be hard work to shift our inner state, our suffering can also give us the momentum we need to turn things around.

In a nutshell, the solution is to keep an open mind about what those things that are leading to our anguish really mean, and to keep taking those first steps of action that allow change to happen. We must seize opportunities to transform our emotional state, and see a future without that pain. How can you define yourself outside of that negative emotional space? Section: 'Distinct modes of conflict' contrasts the kind of threat-focused state described above with a more constructive way of dealing with inter-personal conflict. You may find the ideas there are also applicable to inner-conflict.

We pick up the reins of our own torment where we identify

with the message. It's really incredible how we can take the hurtful messages from early experience and carry them with us for many years, re-affirming and reinforcing them long after those original messages have been forgotten by everyone else (if they ever spared a thought). Yet the reins are in our hands only for as long as we hold them. Changing how we make judgements and understand responsibility (see the 'Conflict' sections), are powerful ways to alter our emotional state and lay down weight we'd rather not carry.

Sometimes a lot of anguish comes from simply not knowing what to do. For instance, at one point in my life, even though on some level I felt I could tell when a woman liked me, I had utterly no idea what to do about it. Sometimes, out of the blue and having barely had a proper conversation, I'd give a woman who'd shown some interest in me a hand made gift – I enjoyed making my own origami designs. It always resulted in the same reaction from them; complete shut off, which compounded my frustration, confusion and fear. At the time I didn't have the awareness to see this reaction as a reflection of various factors, including social norms and, especially, what I was communicating.

We communicate through what we do as well as what we don't do. In my case I clammed up, couldn't hold eye contact for more than a second and walked with a sunken chest. In other words I didn't hold personal contact, or my own space confidently. At the time, I felt despair, trapped in my confusion and fear. Because I didn't see a way out of it I was bitter, with a growing dislike for myself (except when I was being creative or clever) as well as for other people. Inevitably my behaviour left clues about these facts, which were less than appealing to others.

I share my own experience above because it's a prime example of the way we can block our own path to meeting our innate needs, such as affection, understanding, trust and many more. It is our habits of internal (e.g. "I'm just a socially handicapped, emotional failure") and external (e.g. our posture and voice tone) communication that bind us and reinforce our fears.

Within some intimate relationships similar emotional turmoil, and symptoms of it, can exist. Of course it can be more subtle, for instance in the mounting pressure of avoiding direct conflict over some long-standing issue, or in the panoply of unhappiness caused by manipulation or power-play. These situations and more are explored in depth in the later 'Conflict' sections.

In overcoming fear, your personal resources are invaluable. When you have areas in your life that you're confident in, these can provide a stepping stone to cross over your fear in other areas. More positive experience; more fuel for inspiration and confidence. It can also just be a matter of sharing what you love more and allowing your enthusiasm to create new connections, both in your mind and with other people, which cut through fear. (If you don't feel there is really anything you are well developed or confident in, don't worry, that can be changed!)

Define your fear

Many fears wither under the light of close scrutiny. It's when they are part hidden or ill defined that they are most powerful. How can we conquer something that we can't get a solid grip of?

By clearly defining our fears we also *confine* them. If we don't they will sprawl behind our vagueness. Suppose, for instance, we have a fear of public displays of affection. How can we pin that down? Well, is it stronger in the presence of strangers or people we know? Are there specific thoughts that go with the fear, about judgements people may be making? If so, what judgements specifically? Or is the fear more about something that might happen to you? Are there certain internal dialogues or memories linked with the fear? What is the worst outcome? And so on.

After getting more specific about a fear, we can get a better idea about its possible consequences, their likelihoods and how to manage them. How, for instance, would people making judgements about you on a particular occasion for kissing in public materially affect your life? Would any effect be short or long term? Would you have any control over the effect, and how would you cope with it? Now considering those factors, how would you score the possible *cost* (negative consequences), on a 1-10 scale, of taking a certain action and your feared outcome happening? 1 being a minor irk, 10 being a life-shattering catastrophe. See how as we answer each of these questions we cut down the area the fear occupies, or casts its shadow over. The fear is literally getting smaller as we put it in a box.

Now, in contrast, what would the direct and indirect *benefits* be of taking a certain action (that part of you would like but is afraid to do)? What would *change* if the action worked out well? How would you score the potential positive impact on your life or your relationships on a 1-10 scale? 1 being like a flat greeting, 10 being a profound and lasting gift of joy. It may help you to draw a table: put potential negative outcomes of taking a certain action down one side, positive down the other. Put an impact score beside each outcome. Total up each side and compare.

After thoroughly evaluating a fear as above (considering the chances and consequences of different outcomes, and how you might cope with them) we're in a much stronger and more resourceful position to decide what action to take. It's a lot easier to feel calm and self-dependent in such a position, and therefore easier to re-frame a fear into 'a positive opportunity with some associated but manageable risks'.

One – *sometimes over-sensitive* – function of fear is to protect you by immobilizing you or making you run away. Thus you may encounter some resistance as you start to define your fears, because even taking a sober look at a fear goes against its program. See from page 66 for more on re-framing.

Rejection, the truths and the unknowable

Fear of rejection seems to be a major trap for a lot of people. It can also be a trigger or reinforcer of other issues. Defining this fear, as invited in the previous sub-section, we might begin by asking: "Is it more to do with needing to be liked or more just not wanting to be alone?" and "In what situations is the fear strongest?" Following the process through will hopefully significantly reduce or even remove the fear. But rejection is a tough one. It may be that certain *beliefs* need to shift before we can be free of our fear of it. One key thing to remember about 'rejection' though, is what it relates *to*.

Every day we all make choices about what we like or dislike, or want more or less of. It's part of human nature and we make these choices with limited information and not as objective judges. In fact we are very subjective creatures with our own characters, stresses, needs, fears and desires – especially when it comes to other people. (See also section: 'Attitudes and the other's shoes'.)

If you've ever felt that someone has *'rejected you'*, it may have felt as though your whole being and worth was being devalued. That can leave us feeling very raw and vulnerable. If, though, we keep in mind the above broader picture, we may get closer to the truth: that as a result of what they were feeling *at the time* and their own personal situation, plus what *limited* part of ourself we *communicated*, they chose to end the connection, *at the time*.

Adding detail to and broadening our perspective in this way shows us that there are lots of factors involved; some we have no control over (e.g. sometimes people are just having a hard time and it's no reflection on us) and some we do.

If it seems like others are consistently not welcoming the quality of connection you'd like with them, then know that we have the ability to constantly develop as people and we have lots of options to alter what we communicate. If we can take this to heart then 'rejection' becomes much less a blow to the heart and more a reminder that we're alive and in a world where current needs and desires don't always match up. Actually 'rejection' can help us navigate towards becoming a better, happier person if we choose to learn and not run and hide from opportunities that might in fact turn out well.

One substitution you may find helpful to make: *"They don't like me"* → *"Maybe they don't like what I'm communicating, or maybe they're having a bad day?"* (Remember they only have the little, filtered bit of you that they're seeing to go on).

It may be that we have an opportunity to actually find out what's going on for the other person when we hear a rejection. Learning what someone's feelings and needs are which differ from our own in such situations can really help us take that broader perspective – and possibly even find another way of relating that works for everyone. See section: 'Observing, feeling, needing, requesting' for more on this idea.

Even those occasions when someone really seems to enjoy giving you the cold shoulder without apparent concern for your feelings, help. You can use such occasions to help you decide who you'd like to spend time with, or you can use them to uncover the underlying unmet needs of the person and show understanding. Rising to the level of empathy in such situations can bring you real relief, and they may thank you for it one day too.

If you really want to get crazy and turn rejection on its head you could even say, *rejection is just a blessing in disguise*. On top of the valuable lessons to be learnt, whenever one door closes another one often opens.

Knots, self-love and taking action

I share a little more of my past here in the hope that some readers will be able to relate some of it to their own lives. When I look back to my general emotional state not even 10 years ago, although I was slowly moving forward, it often didn't feel like it. All the anguished things I was feeling seemed to be tied together in one giant, unsolvable knot; was I resentful because I was lonely, or lonely because I was resentful? I was spending a lot of energy on blame but it didn't seem to be helping. As soon as I felt I was beginning to loosen this resentment spot I'd slip round to the side that was fear of intimacy and rejection and push the person away, which tightened the knot back up.

It was quite an insidious situation really. Doubly so when you consider that the sense of certainty (having my negative beliefs 'confirmed') and the emotional blanket of self-pity it gave me can be quite addictive. These are things you can build a grand and elaborate fortress of excuses around.

It seemed after a certain point of talking about it I was just digging into old tracks (although talking was very helpful in seeing the tracks more clearly). Many things helped but it was the realization of how strongly our physical state affects our emotional state and the power I had in the present moment to change that, which really let me escape the dark place I was in.

Although I did feel pretty sorry for myself I had enough determination to overcome my weaknesses and buried underneath the self-loathing enough love to keep going. If you're struggling to find that determination and love though you may find it useful to consider three things:

a. As a human being made of the same stuff we all are, you're just as entitled to peace and happiness as anyone else.

b. A person's inner world can be a barren and lonely place, no matter where you live or what things you have, or even how many people love you. You're not alone and there will be many people out there who are similarly hurt, confused and lonely, even if they don't seem it at first.

c. It's just a series of decisions on your part as to how long you stay in this inner state (and maybe if you take action you can help some others along with you).

People respond powerfully and positively to those who *take care of themselves* as well as looking after others. Whatever size steps you can manage, just go ahead and do it, despite how unhappy you may feel! Look around for examples to follow if you're stuck. (See also section: 'Our attitude to change'.)

As Buddhist teacher Thich Nhat Hanh put it: "Sometimes your joy is the source of your smile, but sometimes your smile can be the source of your joy." This idea, which we've already explored from different angles, can be summed up as 'self-actualization through action and openness to change'. It is through taking action and having in mind where we *want* to be that we arrive there. Whatever issues you have wont just lie down and take it, they'll twist and block where they can, but the strangle-hold will loosen with fresh experiences.

While still fully acknowledging them, there are times when we need to be strong in how we *respond* to our emotions, and treat them as a *signal* for doing things differently. Sometimes it takes the movement of action for our mind to stumble upon the right path.

If you're in a real funk and you take positive action, you're training yourself to be resourceful, and also more receptive to love. Similarly if you continue to not take action, you're training yourself to accept defeat and suffering as normal. This is why, while it's never too late, the longer you leave it, the harder it gets. It's also why the more frequently you take that first step of action the easier it gets.

Once you know which of your needs or innate values are not being satisfied, in your current situation, you're at a strong advantage in figuring out which first steps to take. See sub-section: 'Getting to the root: innate values' from page 19 to read more about why.

Lastly, if you have supportive friends and family, they're a blessing. Let them help, they are there for you.

When your fears happen

There will be times when some of our fears are, at least partially, confirmed. How do we deal with this? Well, first we have to recognize what opportunities we have. There is the opportunity to let the fear take a tighter grip on us, and there is the opportunity to examine the situation more deeply and learn from it. How able we are to take the second option depends on how much control we've already given to the fear. If we've already 'defined our fear' then we'll immediately be in a much more well prepared position.

Mindfulness, as described in section: 'Internal dialogues and identity', really helps to see under the surface of our fear with a steady mind. When we do this and take an attitude of continual learning and openness to change, our fears often dissolve, revealing what were really gifts in disguise.

Suppose we have a fear of intimacy combined with a fear of being alone. We become friends with someone we're attracted to and we feel torn between these fears. So we keep that person at a certain distance despite part of us wanting them to be closer. If we calmly pay attention to what's going on in our head when those fears kick up, we may see, for instance, an underlying fear of inadequacy. If we keep that mindful state and just *observe* when we share some things about us which we're a little self-conscious about, we might come to think they don't see much wrong with us after all and allow them closer. But what if, when things become more intimate they suddenly pull away, saying they're uncomfortable with the situation? Is this *really* a confirmation of our fear?

Suppose we suspend judgement (and doing that does require practice) and simply enquire why they're uncomfortable. It could be that something troubling in their life has happened, that has nothing to do with what they think of us, and by staying in the present we have a chance to offer support (and so the gift is revealed). It could also be that their feelings for us have changed. Pages 280-282 look at ways of dealing with this possibility more resourcefully.

The calm and detachment that mindfulness brings allows us to be less disturbed by things not working out as we wanted. It also makes us more able to focus on the positive opportunities that come with taking certain risks. Continuing the theme of mindfulness, section: 'The glass melon dichotomy' explores a way of being accepting of yourself and others that helps to strengthen positive connections and avoid falling pray to fears.

Fears about openness and intimacy

A point on fears and openness: At first thought they may be two things you'd like to keep as far apart as possible. However, sometimes, sharing a fear with a person we care about can deepen a mutual emotional connection, because sharing it demonstrates two powerful things: trust and honesty. Not only this, getting a fear out in the open can help release it – and even avoid inadvertently bringing it about (see: 'Projections and prophesy').

More widely speaking, intimacy comes from people opening up (think "into-me-see"). Fear of intimacy is often fuelled by a fear of inadequacy. If you don't believe that you're worthy of the love that you'd like, then showing yourself to someone you feel strongly about would seem to invite the pain of rejection and the confirmation of your believed inadequacy. Repetition forms part of the solution; repeated, *progressive* sharing of 'self', as you'd like to share it: thoughts, affection, feelings and needs. You *can* re-frame 'rejection', find inner acceptance and learn again how intimate, loving connections are built.

When you have the courage to share your true feelings, thoughts and needs, there's an element of vulnerability. Even if we're completely at ease with our inner state, we could still be exposing ourself to potential injury or attack, or at least disappointment. So then, *vulnerability is a prerequisite of intimacy*. If we want intimacy we must be prepared to take a chance with something we cannot control.

A curious experiment

Here's a 3 minute experiment you can do right now which demonstrates the powerful principle of *changing your emotional state by changing your physical state.* This principle can help you out in many challenging situations. Find a quiet place.

To start, take a deep breath and recall a time when you were really enjoying the moment, the most free and joyful time you can remember. As much as possible, put your body in the state it was in then; the posture (how were your shoulders, head, hands?), the breathing (how deep, how fast or relaxed), the muscle tension/relaxation and your facial expression. Spend a few moments here, there's no rush, and really take notice of your body and how you feel.

Now the difficult part. Come back to now and, just for a minute, recall a time where you were utterly miserable or overcome with fear, a *really* bad time. Put your body in the state it was in then; the posture, the breathing, the muscle tension/ relaxation and facial expression. Once again, take notice of your body and feelings.

Now the interesting bit. Shake off that bad feeling, and when you're ready, remembering exactly how your body just was, every last detail, go back into that *unhappy physical* state you were just in, but think of the *happy memory* you had before. Without letting your body state change at all, try to *feel* that happy memory. How do you feel? Not as happy as before?

Now, finally, clear your mind and change your *body* back to the happy state you had at the beginning of this experiment, in every detail. Keeping your body perfectly in that happy state, recall your unhappy memory. Keeping your body, facial expression and breathing the same, how does that unhappy memory feel now? Interesting, no? You have the power to free yourself in the present moment.

Relating to this idea, here's another quick tip for changing your mood. Shake and bounce about for 5 minutes (put a your favourite music on if it helps) and let yourself smile while you're doing it. Get your heart pumping. Then, stretch out. You may have your favourite stretches. One I like is gently bending forward from standing, stretching out the hamstrings and hips, then stretching your whole body up, reaching for the sky! Repeat your stretches several times and feel the change.

The alternative interpretation

"What's the alternative interpretation?" This question is another great way of improving your mood and freeing yourself from fear. There's always an alternative way of seeing things, and often pausing and taking another look from a different perspective can make a huge positive difference to how you feel around others (and thus also how they feel around you).

You can treat it as a game if it helps, e.g. "If I was to think up some alternative, more positive interpretations for why they said that, or did this, what would those interpretations be?" Have fun with it. There are countless variables that affect the actions of other people (and events in general) and others don't necessarily see things how we do, or know what we know. But that's easy to forget sometimes when we allow our mental projections to masquerade as an accurate portrayal of reality.

As well as an infinite breadth of alternative possibilities we also have depth to explore. Suppose we're talking to someone, either in our personal or professional life, and they proclaim, for instance, "I know what's best here!" If we're not in agreement and would have liked more dialogue, we might wonder, did they say that to us because they think we're just here to follow their orders and they don't value our opinion? Or, did they say it because they think we're pressuring or competing with them and they're trying to defend their position? Or, maybe it was because they've had an extremely frustrating day and their fuse has worn right down? Or, perhaps they're simply so pleased and confident about their idea they've just forgotten to take our view on-board?

The above four interpretations have three types of focus: what someone's thought processes are relating to us, what events may have influenced their actions, and what their thoughts relating to themselves are. A fourth type of interpretation might be something like: Maybe they said "I know what's best here!" because they'd really like a greater sense of significance and respect and they're feeling flustered or tense because they're not getting it? Or, maybe it was because they feel desperate or anxious to find some resolution and certainty to the situation? Here, the focus is on the driving factors of feelings and needs.

Together these different types of focus give depth to our alternative interpretations. All types of focus can be useful in understanding why something happens (or doesn't happen). But now we can see, that point of focus that tends to result in the most fear and emotional knots – *what someone else thinks of us* – is only a rather small area within the space of possibilities and understandings of why anything is said or done.

When we practice considering interpretations of different kinds – especially those focused more on what's going on for the other person – we're doing two things. We're bringing freedom to our thinking and we're also training our empathy skills or emotional intelligence. Both of which are extremely helpful for healthy, loving relationships.

Of course, considering different interpretations to any given situation is something our brains (with their 100 billion neurons) are rather well equipped for. Like many of the suggestions in this book, this one is something you do anyway. It's just that the conditioning we go through, in many cultures, can leave us pretty rusty – or very narrowly focused – in this area of considering the alternatives. However, by applying this useful habit consciously and more often, we can rediscover our natural talent for it and reap the benefits.

Whether it be in forming a relationship, or during difficult times in an existing one, if you make a habit of asking "What's the alternative interpretation?" it might just change your life.

A life changing journey

Everyone's journey will be different. I describe mine here since a personal account is usually more engaging than a series of abstracted ideas. Although the keys to having good relationships could be boiled down to a small set of attitudes and principles and left at that, these attitudes and principles were only made *real* for me through my own experiences. I hope that by sharing these, you can more easily find a way of making some of these principles and attitudes real for you.

At the time the following events begin, not all that many years ago, I didn't have the insights or experiences that led to the ideas and advice in the previous part of this book. So what did I do about it? Since many of my emotional needs were not being met and I didn't know what to do about it, I got even more depressed. I didn't look after myself, I formed more twisted views of the world, men and women, and it often felt like I was sinking into an ever darker place. There was even a point where I literally stopped speaking to people for almost a year because I felt so emotionally isolated and conflicted. Part of me was desperately trying to unravel the tangles in my mind. Then several things happened in my life that helped me move forward. The focus here will be on those transformational points.

Before we dive in I should say that, for all of us, this journey of inner and outer change has no clear ending; it's one that branches out and invites re-examination from time to time as life unfolds and lessons are learnt and forgotten. The story in the following pages is one that encompasses a great deal of change over the years it covers.

For me, the question of how to have fulfilling relationships and how to have a fulfilling life can't be treated in isolation. It's difficult to have one without the other. So for this reason, the answers are inherently broad in their scope.

Spirituality and personal development

One of my clearest memories from my childhood is standing at the bottom of my driveway, between two large sandstone pillars and making a decision. It seemed to me that there were those that went through life agreeing with others, capitulating to avoid a struggle, then there were those that stood independently and were their own guide, come what may. I felt a need to choose what to be and I chose the latter. It seemed like a choice between living and only half living.

I don't recall what lead up to it now, but I doubt I'll ever forget that moment as a 7 or 8 year old boy. In the years since, it's made me a richer and stronger person. As well as a source of personal development, I would also describe it as one of my earliest spiritual experiences; spiritual in the sense of having a clear sense of self and my connection with a greater whole.

Fast forwarding through many formative experiences and times where I drifted from and then back to that boyhood decision, I arrive at university. It was here that I felt the trajectory of my life begin to take a positive turn in the area of personal relationships. Having drifted once again from the way I wanted to be, I found the Hare Krishnas. For the few years I spent with them, before going my own way, they had many good and lasting effects on me.

One such effect was the ability to communicate with people (and especially women) while having a broader, deeper perspective – one that wasn't totally blotted out by worrying about what the other person thought of me. I still had a lot to learn and a lot to unlearn, but this was a big step. One of the things their scriptures, the Bhagavad Gita, teaches is that we are all sparks of God, the same in quality but different in quantity with the whole. Taking this sort of view on board can help you to move out a little from the confines of your own personal demons. What is a social phobia between 'sparks of God', however tiny?

I'd never felt particularly nourished in the company of people who chiefly like to get drunk, watch TV, think about getting laid and who meet the world with a mix of indifference, fear and aggression. This seemed to cover a lot of people I was around at university (including me at times). That was perhaps a stilted and superficial view, but at the time I lacked the perseverance it can take to get below the surface. Now here, with this bunch of dancing, feasting and chanting devotees, I'd found people who actively encouraged my love of thinking and celebrated being the odd ones out in society. They encouraged me to develop my sense of identity and I feel a deep gratitude to them for salvaging my life.

While much of this book is related to personal development of one kind or another, the above really highlights the kind that helped me most at that time. That is, I was developing through association with something bigger than myself. This expansion of identity not only broadened my horizons but allowed me to lay my baggage down to rest for a while too.

Also at that time, taking up Jiu Jitsu really helped develop my confidence and comfort with physical closeness (comfort with emotional closeness was still a much harder nut to crack). Who'd have thought that learning how to turn someone upside down in 30 different ways would be so helpful in life?

So, pursuing things that lead to personal enrichment, a sense of belonging and growing comfort in myself was absolutely indispensable in my journey towards having healthy, loving relationships. If you think you lack some of these things, it may be that religion or spiritual practice could help, or you may prefer a club or society with a common interest you can really share, where there's a sense of supportive community and belonging. Some good places to explore for options are the web, local paper, community centre, café notice boards and library.

The more we grow, both as individuals and as parts of a greater whole, the more we have to share in any personal relationship.

Self expression

It was then, while spending time with the Hare Krishnas, that I began to write poetry. After my first poem addressed to Krishna, I began to write about all the conflicts and confusions I saw in my mind and heart and in the faces and actions of the people around me. Doing this was a huge releasing, deepening and enriching force in my life.

Release, recognition and unity

I learnt a lot from careful, focused observation of my own state of being and that of others. Tangles were beginning to unravel! After a while I began to write more about the states of being and qualities I wanted to *develop* in myself. I believe this meditation on those things really helped bring them about. Several times I've looked at what I'd written a few months previously to find I'd really stepped into what I'd written about.

I began to get a much needed sense of connection with, contribution to and respect from other people from my poetry, so after a few years I started to perform my work. That really helped me develop a confident presence and voice amongst groups of people. Through this continued passion for writing I've met many interesting people and had some beautiful relationships I might not otherwise have had. (Similar can be said now of my passion for Argentine tango; be warned, it's a highly addictive dance!)

One thing that sharing my writing has shown me is how similar people are in many ways, in the joys and the struggles we have. To read this timeless idea in a dusty old philosophy book is one thing, but to have so many, by appearances very different, people say "I could really relate to that poem, thank you" leaves a real impact.

Often after I'd performed some poetry, people would come up

and tell me how brave I was for sharing such intimate things. I appreciated this, but for me it wasn't brave. Through the process of distilling these things into 'just the right words' I'd come to terms with them and to some extent, exorcised their binding power over me. And the more I shared the more I realized I wasn't alone in the challenges I was facing. I'd found a way of bridging focused introspection to the outside world, and so became less locked in my own mind – and more positively and peacefully disposed to other people. In retrospect it seems that sharing some of my deep feelings and ideas through poetry helped me to be more comfortable with emotional intimacy. It was a way to let people in.

It's amazing how willing a lot of people are to open up about what they struggle with when you do the same. I learnt a lot about romantic relationships this way, even before I'd ever had one, just listening to other people's stories. Probably because my writing was often about personal struggles at this point, I heard a lot of stories of relationships that continued in misery or ended likewise. On quite a few occasions I remember reflecting to myself "Ah, I'll try to avoid that approach when I have a relationship!" I also realized more now that my parents weren't as uniquely messed up as I'd thought.

Find what makes you feel alive, then share it

When you develop and share something you're passionate about some of that passion can spill over. It's an attractive quality. Just talking about what you love to do can bring a lot of energy, interest and enthusiasm into a conversation.

I'd recommend giving writing a go, even if you don't share it with others; it's an especially powerful tool of self-discovery and expression. But writing may not do it for you. It may be making music, singing, painting, dancing, sports, martial arts, juggling, designing, computer programming, clothes making or any number of other things. But there'll be something (or many things) that, when you try and persist with you'll find you feel more alive and more in touch with yourself. If you haven't found it yet, find it now, you'll be glad you did!

This isn't about being super talented or having to have a 'gift' for anything, it's about having things you do that you can really express your individuality and develop yourself through – things that help you in some way connect with yourself, the world and other people.

So, to recap, from not being happy at all, I found a group of people that gave me a safe space to both discover more and develop who I was and wanted to be. As a result I started to change my way of thinking and grew more confident. I then began to explore and share my situation and my challenges through creative expression. This in turn resulted in more confidence, insight and good personal connections, as well as the simple joy in the expression itself.

Experimenting with ways of being and discovering the art of attraction

There's a lot of advice out there on the art of attraction. When I started joining online dating sites for example, a mailing list called 'Double your Dating' mysteriously found my inbox. I didn't agree with much of the general tone, but the content did open my eyes to how some of my personal experience and observations could be explained. It spoke of the importance of not being supplicating, of offering challenge and humour, and of getting past the harmful idea that you somehow have to buy an attractive woman's attention, with gifts, compliments or servile behaviour.

Some particularly helpful content included situation-specific social skills, emotional dynamics (having more than one emotion in your communication), building sexual tension (through playfulness, flirting and being in control of yourself), seeing yourself as the prize as much as them (although now I believe it's more helpful just to do away with the idea of prizes altogether) and presenting yourself well (being clean, dressing well). Such useful advice in fact, that once I applied some of those elements I began to get some face to face flirting; well, it was a start!

While this section talks about some very useful things I learnt at the time, for more in-depth detail on how attraction can be developed naturally, see section: 'The five keys'.

Small steps, taken often

At the beginning, just being able to walk past a beautiful woman on the street and share comfortable eye contact and a smile was a major, major development for me. I made a habit of doing this whenever I was out and then saying a simple "hello" if I felt like it. It felt very good.

If this is a challenge for you too, I *highly* recommend making the same habit. Just focus on getting a sense of relaxed confidence into your *body,* without any expectations for acknowledgement, a smile back, conversation, date, or their future undying love. Work on building calmness in your eye contact and resisting the temptation to immediately glance away. Remember, there are 101 reasons why someone may not want to meet your eye or smile, most of them are not about you, so don't worry about it. Your aim is simply to develop a sense of natural ease and normality in this first stage of making contact with someone – as only practice can give you.

A note on eye contact: It builds emotional intensity. If you can make it comfortable, it helps 'chemistry' to spark.

As well as getting used to initiating eye contact, online dating really helped me blossom. Rejection hardly matters when there's several dozen other profiles that take your fancy! You have room to experiment and find yourself. (See section: 'Our attitude to change' and 'Get your fresh roles here'.) Over a couple of years I probably wrote hundreds of emails, changing my style until I found something that felt good for me and got *consistently positive responses* from women I was interested in.

I don't need you to like me

One excellent general rule is: Don't place too much importance on the initial and medium stage outcome of any one connection with someone, because you know you have the confidence and openness to connect with someone else you also like before long. (See section: 'Our attitude to change' for an example of developing confidence and related issues.)

I developed many long running and interesting online relationships with intelligent, attractive women, went to some amazing parties and had a few one-to-one meet-ups. However the women I actually met at this stage didn't usually attract me physically that much (maybe related to the fact that I was still struggling to maintain feeling good about the way I looked myself). Still, as a way to develop my conversational and flirting skills/playfulness, online dating was invaluable.

It's OK to experiment (but keep moving forward)

Although I found, with developing rapport and attraction online, it mostly boiled down to things such as humour, confidence and openness, it took a fair bit of experimenting to get comfortable expressing those qualities in my own way. It's natural to experiment like this – think of how children behave, trying out different approaches and attitudes, gauging the response and changing accordingly. They are developing themselves. Sometimes the things we learn as children or later really don't help us in finding happiness in adult life and need to be unlearnt, through becoming aware of them and then experimenting further to see what does work.

A word of caution: if a real face-to-face relationship is what you want, I would suggest practising your social skills, both with instant messaging and face-to-face, and make sure the personality in the wording you use doesn't stray too far from how you can be and want to be in real life.

Also, if you're not just looking for a pen pal, don't spend too long emailing or text messaging each other. Remember there are lots of other profiles online, life is short and most people joined because they wanted some kind of real-life relationship. So, ease off on the long, life-story emails (if you're that way inclined), get talking on the phone quickly, then if you like how they both look and sound, arrange a relaxed meeting in a safe place.

This isn't just about sexual chemistry, but also basic physical and verbal rapport. What we communicate in these channels can be quite different from our writing. It's only really at this stage of being face to face you have a fair idea of relationship prospects. It might be scary meeting new people, but practice and positive learning from your experiences is how it gets easier.

When I was at this point in my life, the decision to really give myself permission to experiment with different ways of being was invaluable, (online dating is one easy way to do that) as was setting myself achievable, interim personal targets – and working on them! (See also, section: 'Our attitude to change'.)

The power of contribution, modelling success and building rapport

Things were going fairly well. I was enjoying some good conversations with women I found attractive, getting out and meeting more people, but my relationships never went any further. Face to face with people, I still felt trapped by fears, negative self-image and a lack of understanding. Thankfully, around that time, I had the opportunity to hear a tape of Anthony Robbins, a world renowned 'life coach'.

I listened to that tape for perhaps an hour and let the ideas work through my mind over the course of the day. Just in that short time I got a glimpse of the radical changes in my state of being that were possible with only a small shift in thinking and acting. The exercise that really struck me and was to turn my world around demonstrated the principle of emotional/physical anchors. Anchoring is a blindingly simple concept in NLP[7], which Anthony Robbins builds on in his material. The idea is that our emotional and physical states are very strongly connected, and particular physical states (posture, breathing, expression, muscle tension) are associated with particular emotional states. This means in a certain physical state it's much easer to feel the emotions associated with it and a lot harder to feel the ones not associated with it.

Many people intuitively understand the idea of anchoring to some extent. You probably know that if you relax your shoulders and smile it's a little easier to feel happy. But not so many people know just how empowering the concept can be, if you really pay attention to your anchors in particular moments.

The exercise on page 68 takes you through the same exercise that helped me in that tape. If you can, I recommend finding an audio copy of 'Giant Steps' by Anthony Robbins. There's something about the man's seemingly boundless energy and desire to serve that helps the message come across. Soon after the demonstration of anchoring, came this simple idea (as I remember it): *imagine yourself without the particular issues you're struggling with, imagine you've already overcome your challenges. How would you act, how would you be in your body? Imagine it and then just do it.* I thought to myself, 'that sounds simple enough as an experiment, I could try that'.

That evening I remember standing at a bus stop somewhere in

7 Neuro Linguistic Programming. NLP, developed by Richard Bandler and John Grinder, is a synthesis of complementary schools of thought including Gestalt psychotherapy, linguistics and hypnotherapy. It is often thought of as a toolbox for developing excellence and better interpersonal and self-rapport.
I've also found "Way of NLP" by Joseph O'Connor & Ian McDermott (ISBN: 0-00-711020-0) to be a useful reference.

London and noticing I was ill-at-ease. There were some men and women around, about my age, and despite what I'd already learnt, making positive, relaxed, confident contact with people I didn't know was still a struggle. It wasn't that I felt I *needed* to, I just wanted to be *able* to. I remembered the idea from the tape and I stepped into that alternate me. I might have asked for info on the next bus or just smiled and said 'hi'. I don't remember the words now, all I remember is the new sense of freedom.

My above experience was also an example of 'modelling success', an extremely powerful idea in NLP (with parallels in other therapeutic interventions), expanded on in many parts of this book and especially page 25. In this case I was the model. The experience really introduced me to the magical power of role play. Here, I was behaving as if I'd already made the change I wanted to make – as if stepping into a role. With the right approach, eventually your new way of doing things becomes 'just the way you naturally are'. This idea is discussed in detail in section: 'Our attitude to change'. To get the most from it, it's vital to also address your inner dialogues.

One of the basic tenets of NLP is: 'The map is not the territory.' This means the way you happen to see things is *not* the complete picture of what you could do and be – if you expanded your awareness and allowed change to happen.

A valuable tool box, body and mind aligned

Counselling had been useful in helping me clarify what the problems were, somewhat, but NLP (or a certain adaptation of it) really booted me forward and gave me some powerful tools for the rest of the way. I booked an Anthony Robbins weekend in 2004. At the time it was a big investment for me. It was phenomenal. The memory of 12,000 people, beaming, practically floating across the colossal hallway with new found confidence, direction and positivity at the end of it is still strong.

One of the key ideas was how body-language not only

powerfully affects your own emotional state but that of others as well. I learnt about how to relax my speaking voice, letting it become naturally lower, and use mirroring to build rapport (getting on well with, having trust and feeling 'in tune' with someone).

Relaxing your voice might seem like fairly basic stuff, but when you go from holding all the unhelpful identifications, fears and frustrations you have in your speaking voice, to not doing that, it makes a *big* difference. Taking this step helped me in just about every social situation, including my poetry performances!

How do you relax your voice in this way? Through repeated conscious effort, in time turning into unconscious habit. As you move towards conveying a sense of ease, confidence and gentle strength through your voice, you'll notice some big changes in the way you feel and how others see you.

Look into the mirror of rapport

Mirroring is where you adopt a similar posture, physical attitude or speaking style to the person you're communicating with. The result tends to be a gut sense of commonality, trust and understanding: rapport. Mirroring can be extended into dialogue by noticing the senses, 'submodalities'[8] or metaphors someone uses and reflecting those back in your way of communicating.

Mirroring can build rapport from either a neutral or negative starting point. For instance, you can use it to overcome a dismissive attitude by playfully imitating someone and letting them notice. Doing this can show a kind of understanding and confidence, which tends to make people more receptive and alive in the present moment. This approach is most likely to work when you let the warmth of your intent shine through your imitation.

---

8 Submodalities are sensory perception qualities used for analogy in expressing thoughts and feelings. For example: "I'm moving further away from that situation". The sense is visual and the submodality is distance (near/far). You might say in response: "So, where are you moving closer to now?" to mirror the language.

Mirroring can be used consciously of course, but it is often done subconsciously. So (in either case) this means you can get an idea that someone wants to get on with you if you notice them mirroring you.

Interpersonal communication itself is a kind of mirror. We can see reflections of everything we communicate in the other person's reactions. The idea in NLP is that the meaning of a communication *is* the response it elicits. So to convey meaning effectively we must develop understanding of how our *way* of communicating is interpreted.

Contribute your way to fulfilment

The importance of contributing to others cannot be stressed enough. Tony Robbins made a fine example and I took this to heart. When we're doing things to enrich the lives of others (without asking for, or expecting anything back), we get a tremendous sense of well-being and growth. It turns out that when we feel this way and do these things, we're also more attractive to people – especially ones who really know the value of contribution.

This is about more than being polite and holding the door open for people (although that can make a difference too); it's about being willing to give our time, emotion, creativity, material resources etc. freely, to help someone in need or to build a richer, deeper connection.

Like smiling, contribution can be infectious, and there are countless ways to do it: volunteering for charitable organisations, care home or prison visits, environmental or conservation work in and with the community, giving blood, teaching a skill, listening to a person who needs to get something off their chest, feeding hungry people, calling a friend who might appreciate the contact, making an unexpected and useful gift for someone, being supportive for a loved one, giving encouragement and celebrating someone's personal success, and so on. It feels great to contribute;

it's an action that spreads fulfilment in both directions.

Of equal importance, is contributing to ourselves. On a basic level this means looking after your body and mind and doing things that are healthy and strengthening for them. It also means giving yourself time to relax and enjoy the beauty in the world, and giving yourself the freedom to grow.

One of the great things about making the act of contribution something that we value in ourselves, is that it gives us opportunities to be valued by others and work with people who are moving towards a common goal.

Know what you want, and that you can get it

I'd always had a reasonably clear (if flexible) idea of what I was looking for in a partner. But my NLP experience clarified the qualities that developing in myself would get me closer to actually finding it. I now had a clear path to action; the ingredients of success now seemed within reach.

It really helps to know what you want from a relationship – emotionally, physically, socially and intellectually. It also helps to be able and willing to give, not necessarily in the exact same way, but on the same kind of level as what you'd like from your partner. If you can commit to giving in that way, and also to valuing what you have to give, then I believe you will succeed.

If you're not sure what you want, spend some time reflecting on the qualities you most enjoy and feel attracted to in people. Now considering the people who have them, which qualities are *they* attracted to? Are those qualities compatible with your values, and if so, how can you best develop them more in yourself?

It may be helpful to break things down into areas, e.g. physical, emotional, social, intellectual, or values and beliefs. What qualities or characteristics in each of these areas really draw you to someone? Which are most important to you? Are these qualities contradicting each other or conflicting with you in some way? If the answer to that last question is yes, see section:

'Untangling value, beliefs and desires'. Finally, knowing what you're looking for, beware the fallacy of perfection, it will only make you lonely and sad.

Putting things into practice and the strange world of PUAs

When I returned from the NLP weekend I felt very different. My old habits of body-language, conversation and internal dialogue had shifted enough for me to see the way forward: Stop doing self-defeating habitual things that say "go away, I'm not comfortable", or "I'm not worthy, I don't like myself". Start making more of a positive influence in the world and to the people around me, and spend more time with those who already have success where I want it!

Taking a risk and welcoming opportunity

A few months after the event, I was feeling a real lack of contribution to and connection with the world outside me. It was then, following a chance encounter with a kind and drunkenly forthright medical student, that I made a decision. I was out playing my djembe late one night and some people raising funds for comic relief asked me to stop and play to draw people's attention. I agreed and while I played, a guy sat down next to me and then gave me a half-hour lecture on why more should be done for local good causes. He talked about the things he did and how he wanted to organize a music event but hadn't yet succeeded. This seemed like an opportunity wearing a garish neon outfit and slapping me in the face.

I resolved then to put on a music and performance art fundraising event for local charities. I saw it both as a great way to contribute and as a way of meeting interesting people and enriching my social skills.

I had zero experience with event organising, but over a couple of months with help from a like-minded friend it all fell together nicely and the event was a huge success on all fronts. I felt a real glow of purpose, achievement and well-being. I decided to make it a monthly thing. With the generous contribution of many people I ended up running it for over 2 years before handing it on.

As an aside, I noted people's response when I told them what I was doing and asked if they'd like to help with the running of the event. An especially common response was "I'd like to, but I wouldn't have a clue how, I have no experience or contacts." Relatively few people responded in the fashion "Yes, I'd love to. I don't have experience but I'm keen to learn!" It's this kind of open minded, pro-active attitude that makes the difference between many events like this happening or them remaining an idea in someone's head. (The same can be said for many relationships. It takes someone to make a bold step into the unknown and see how things pan out with a positive attitude.)

While I was running the event I soon noticed the musicians with a certain following seemed very confident, popular and relaxed off stage. I watched how the male ones were with women. Lots of body and eye contact, kissing on cheeks, touching shoulders or backs while sharing relaxed smiles. These were things I never did. I needed to change that.

Since I was now a promoter and event organizer, I thought now would be a good opportunity to incorporate some of that behaviour into my way of doing things. It felt strange and incongruent the first few times, but soon became second nature. I was a changed man. Just this step gave me a huge sense of personal power and release.

Who wants to be a pick up artist?

As I incorporated the things I observed in 'men hot women went for', (for me, 'hot' is a type of chiefly physical attractiveness;

i.e. slim, toned, pretty, graceful) lo and behold 'hot women' began paying me a lot more attention. It was a rapid and exciting learning curve. Incidentally, some of my female friends who have had similar difficulties attracting the kind of men they'd like, have found the same principles useful.

At this point a book called "The Game" by Neil Strauss, about the underground world of pick-up artists (PUAs), came out. There are some very real dangers of becoming a hollowed out slave of seduction, walking down that path (as the book itself warns); some of the stories and principles in it, however, helped me take things further while keeping my integrity. Many of the ideas were simply ways of indicating that you are at ease with yourself, unafraid of beauty or rejection, playful and not just 'one of the crowd' or an 'approval seeker'.

Sometimes it's useful to have a framework to build around. There was a big emphasis on modelling success and building on it with your own individuality – and the critical importance of lots of practice interacting with people you find attractive.

It is by getting this practice, in communication and I would say also in different relationships and sexual experiences, that you will come to a point where you really know what works for you and what doesn't. In addition, as your confidence, experience and personal skills develop (as they will with practice), the more likely you are to be with someone you really want to be with – and not just because they'll have you – which makes for happier, healthier relationships!

Soon I was doing things like entertaining whole tables of attractive women I'd only just met and getting the numbers from the hottest women in bars and clubs after dancing with them. At parties I'd start massage circles with the most attractive women there, who I'd just met, and have them ask for more at a later date and offer me their numbers. When I went out in the evenings I was often the one being bought drinks. You get the idea.

(A note on massage. I'd done several afternoon workshops on

various sorts; technique is useful, but the most important thing is to listen carefully with your hands to the body you're massaging. Anyone can do it and it's a very natural thing to share.)

I'm positive until proven otherwise

One of the really useful shifts in attitude I made was to always assume that a woman I found attractive was interested in me, *whatever their initial response*. A lot of people don't know how to handle sudden attraction. It scares them, they assume the worst in people, or aren't socially confident and push people away to hide the fact. "Oh, she turned 180 degrees and made a point of not looking in my direction – she must really like me, she's probably shy or perhaps she's had a lot of guys come on too strong recently, so is being cautious. Or maybe she just forgot to brush her teeth before coming out and is afraid I'll smell her bad breath if I approach?" See how it works?

Realistically, this assumption of attraction is not always accurate. But making it rarely does any harm if you're respectful and often does a lot of good, by giving you confidence and them another chance. If it turns out they're already happily in a committed relationship or that your feelings aren't mutual, so be it, but that's no reason not to enjoy that first meeting. Consider that *there is always an alternative, more positive interpretation for any reaction.*

How do you tell if someone is firmly not interested? First, give them the benefit of the doubt and make a clear and good effort to build some rapport (taking careful note of the various possibilities outlined in section: 'Attitudes and the other's shoes'). If, after that, you get some of these reactions: they appear to make no effort to continue the interaction, make excuses and leave without showing interest in meeting again, or, obviously, tell you they aren't interested in a non-playful way, then you can be fairly certain they're not interested.

It's true some people like to be chased, but if they want

something more than just another admirer they will give you some opportunities to be more than that. It can be fun to chase, but beware of indulging in more than a light-hearted and playful way in this game, otherwise what you chase is likely disappointment and frustration.

Authenticity is always possible

One question that sometimes comes up is: "If you have a detailed, conscious understanding of how to build rapport and 'chemistry', how can you still be spontaneous and 'authentic'? Doesn't it all become just steps in a plan to satisfy some desire?" It's an interesting question.

In the context of learning new, more fruitful patterns of behaviour, in the initial phases some thought, planning and hypothesis testing is certainly helpful. Once ingrained understanding is acquired you may then have the option of 'creating attraction' in a detached, calculating or manipulative way. However, this is no more so than your option of just letting that understanding be a reliable second opinion, that pipes up when you're about to do something particularly ill-advised – while you just get on with expressing your natural spontaneity and sincere feelings. The choice you take reflects your general regard for the feelings and well-being of other people. Section: 'The beautiful connection' goes more deeply into using such knowledge naturally and respectfully.

Congruence is the key

At this point in my life I'd blown my fear of approaching and developing rapport with gorgeous women clean out of the water. I now had what some would call 'serious skills'.

Was it satisfying? Yes, it was. However the women I actually slept with and sometimes had short relationships with, were not really the sort I was most physically attracted to, although there was always something I admired or loved about them. There was always a sense of mutual contribution.

Still, I felt like I had to 'apply the rules of the game' for women I felt very drawn to physically to be attracted to me, and thus I was not fully congruent or comfortable. I was also rarely that interested in the person behind the beautiful body and so nothing developed.

I knew the sort of woman I really wanted to find; one who turned my heart and mind on just as much as my body. So on I went until...

Love and life in the clouds

I met a woman on a train coming back from Brighton late one evening in June. She sat in Lotus posture at the end of the carriage. I approached and sat down on the opposite side of the gangway (even though just about every seat in the carriage was free).

She was stunning, in so many ways; beautiful, warm, passionate, intelligent, funny, confident, sensual; I don't think I'd ever met a woman quite like her before. We spoke for just 10 minutes before her stop. I got her number, we text and called each other frequently, and shared poetry while our feelings raced on. When we met up later that week we were in each other's arms and enjoying each other very fully in a park on a sunny Friday afternoon. I was blown away. It seemed she was too. My first love.

I knew then, whatever came of this, I'd always be just fine being with the sort of woman I wanted to be with. I had a clear sense of arrival. This is what life could be like, I had experienced it; as well as finding her, I had found the me I knew I could be.

It was a short relationship. She left to teach in India three weeks after we met. I learnt a lot about myself during that short time. It felt like I truly came to life, my feelings of all kinds had become so intense and sweet. Inspiration was suffusing me. I was even ready to move to India to be with her.

The painful blessings of separation

I learnt even more as we drifted apart. It was painful, but I learned how to take things slowly and that other connections can have a similar quality and intensity, although each one is a different journey.

I remember distinctly, about a year later, having a massage and suddenly recognising that quality of connection I'd felt when she'd massaged me. Some months later when a woman I was dating stroked my back in a light and playful way as we walked home, I recognized a similar warm giddiness I'd felt with my first love when she had touched me so. Then, in subsequent relationships, I found similar moments of wonder, gratitude and shared humour. So it was not a height never again to be reached; I could move on.

One thing that held me up for a while was holding onto anger and pain. Beside the gratitude and love I felt, I was also angry towards my first love for, as I saw it, letting me drift in uncertainty for so long. It wasn't until we came face to face again, the winter of that lovestruck year, that I realized how I'd been holding onto these feelings. I came to see too that at the time I wasn't quite ready for more than those few weeks with her. It was all as it was meant to be.

In an effort to analyse and grow out of my heartbreak, I came to examine again what I was feeling around women and what made for the best connections.

Even with my first love I'd still at times follow the principles of attraction as I thought I'd understood them rather than my natural inclination.

Initially this learning and changing of default/gut response can be very necessary and helpful in stopping you from shooting yourself in the foot. But there comes a point where once you've fixed the problem habits, you need to let go of any rules and routines and allow your spontaneity to flow – which again can be a very attractive quality.

The best and deepest moments I had with her had been those moments of flow and spontaneity, of creativity and openness, of trust and warmth, not of distraction by rules.

One thing I noticed when I was up in the clouds of love was that I seemed to radiate that love outward. I seemed to project my inner satisfaction, peace and joy to anyone within a certain perimeter. This really affected the way people saw and related to me.

When you're not looking to take anything – because you already have your needs met – rather just to *share*, you exude a sense of joyful content and people are drawn to you.

Since that first love and the new emotional horizons it opened up, my relationships have been more satisfying, longer lasting and beautiful than before. We tend to attract people who mirror the dominant qualities in our state of being and as I have become more confident, relaxed and expressive, healthy, passionate and loving, so have the women in my life.

My time alone, after my first love, really did do me a lot of good. It made me see clearly, how sometimes the best thing for us is to spend time not in a relationship but reflecting and working on other aspects of our life. I feel strongly that the more we can know and appreciate ourselves independently, the more that can be shared and built within a loving relationship.

Since my first taste of it, I've also realized that with falling in love, as with many things, fortune really does favour the brave.

Echoes of the past

It can take a long time to remember what we once knew. In the case of my remembering an overriding confidence in expressing my emotional and physical affection, about 20 years.

I was around 5 when I decided to kiss a certain girl on the lips. We'd been talking by the cenotaph in the playground and she must have said something I liked, because as she stood there, about 10 paces from me, I had such a sense of certainty that I wanted to kiss her. I walked up to her, turned her around and kissed her without a second thought. I don't even remember her reaction. What stays with me now is the clarity of purpose and confidence I had – just as with my first love, 20 years later. Yet, very soon at that time in my childhood, that kind of confidence crumbled, undermined by the conflicted self-image and outlook that proved so hard to shake.

What happened? Who can really be sure? But various things had an effect I think, such as my father leaving when I was 5 and a half, and my picking up of some poorly functioning beliefs and coping strategies that some parents tend to pass on to their children – well meaning, as they may be. The point I want to highlight here is that courage in connecting intimately with other people is not something you're either born with or not. It can be learnt and it can be forgotten, and it must be maintained when you have it. But whatever challenges you face there is always hope for love, because it's already in your genes, it just gets covered over.

But what is love?

It would seem strange for a book on relationships (and especially one with the word in the title) to not address the question: "What is love?"

We've all considered it and heard many answers. Indeed it's a good conversation to have with someone we feel strongly about. On reflection we can see many types of love; love for friends, family, partners, lovers and fellow human beings. Love can be compassionate, romantic, lustful, joyful, affectionate, stern, sorrowful, unspoken, obsessive, possessive, selfish, platonic and religious. The Greeks had five words for different kinds of love and in fact many cultures have several words just for 'love' to describe its different facets. It's this kind of specificity that helps to avoid getting hung up, wondering "Is it love, or isn't it?"

In a philosophical context, love is a virtue that encompasses all of human kindness, compassion and affection. In religion, love tends to also form the basis of existence: "God is love".

Different loves sometimes go together, and 'love' is often what we make it – especially that head-over-heels, knock-you into-the-clouds love. We share certain experiences (particularly sex) with someone, and weird things happen to our brain chemistry that alter our perception. We become filled with inspiration, euphoria, feelings of well-being and often a strong desire to procreate.

From a biochemical perspective there are specific chemicals associated with specific emotional and mental aspects of love. For instance, a growing number of researchers over the last few decades have found that dopamine, a neurotransmitter, is a key component in the experience of romantic love.

Dopamine release in the brain leads to feelings of ecstasy, increased focus, desire and motivation. Higher amounts can result in anxiety, sleeplessness, or even obsession. Its influence differs according to what area of the brain it is present. In the mesolimbic pathway, for instance, dopamine has been found to increase general arousal and creative drive[9]. Clearly then the effects of dopamine have a lot in common with romantic love. Acting in concert with dopamine is norepinephrine, which stimulates the production of adrenaline and in high concentrations makes your palms sweat and your heart race, can increase feelings of joy, and reduces appetite[10]. Sound familiar?

Lust is most associated with the hormone testosterone. While

---

9   Flaherty, A.W. (2005) "Frontotemporal and dopaminergic control of idea generation and creative drive" Journal of Comparative Neurology, 493 (1): 147–153
10 Vieira, T. (2002) "When Joy Becomes Grief" AWHONN Lifelines, 6: 506–513.

the attachment and enduring affection of longer lasting relationships are associated with oxytocin, vasopressin and serotonin[11]. Interestingly, these chemical processes of love are not unique to humans. Research shows[11] they are a common feature of mammalian biology, found even in rodents.

So what does all this talk of 'love chemicals' mean? Is love somehow reduced to a narcotic adventure, or a mundane, impersonal chemical reaction? When considering the implications, let's not forget the bigger picture. These chemicals may be *part* of the process, but they are not the experience itself – mix them together in a jar and no one will feel 'love'. The influence of such chemicals on the firing and connecting of our neurons and the states of our bodies, cannot be separated from the context of our previous experiences relating to love and a particular person. Similarly, the quality of our experiences are influenced by our beliefs and values. Furthermore, a certain kind of love could be said to be a particular state of consciousness. But what is consciousness and how can we reduce love to a formula without also doing the same with that perennial mystery?

As magical as chemicals are, the full story of love requires more. To say "love is just chemicals in the brain" is like pointing to the moon and saying "oh, that's just reflected sun light". Of course, that's not to say an awareness of the related chemical processes is not useful. Indeed, knowing what a cocktail of dopamine and testosterone with an oxytocin chaser can do to your mind, can help you get a grip when love knocks you for six. Knowing more about this dimension of love might even help you relax and get more from the experience.

Knowing some of the differences in brain chemistry between men and women can help us each be more accepting of the other's nature. A man's tendency to be more sex focused more of the time can be understood by his higher testosterone levels,

---

11 Stein D.J., Vythilingum B. (2009) "Love and attachment: the psychobiology of social bonding" CNS spectrums. 14(5):239-42

relative to most women. While a woman's tendency to focus more on cuddling and bonding, more of the time, can be understood by her higher levels of oxytocin in combination with oestrogen, relative to most men. That doesn't mean we're entirely at the mercy of our brain chemistry, just that those natural influences are there. By accepting them we can reduce our frustration and confusion, and focus on working together.

Opportunity and the rewards of perseverance

The incredible and natural state of 'romantic' love is an amazing chance to share and learn. Although it is a *phase* of that love we have for a partner. Typically it will mellow and given time and the right mix of personalities, grow deeper and richer. This deepening can bring its own thrill and elation.

Some people, however, don't realize this, expecting a 'true love' to carry on being that hair raising, heart pounding ride it was at the beginning. Or, they realize that initial flavour of love is transitory, but the thrill of it is so much that they go from one person to the next as the highs pull and wane. They are addicted to love. For a similar reason some people may at the same time, genuinely, love a partner in one way and a lover in another – not that that automatically makes it fine for all concerned.

What type of love do you look for?

Possessiveness

What is it to be 'possessive'? Controlling behaviour and acting as the owner of someone, are traits, but possessiveness is the strategy. The driving factors are generally jealousy, a fear of losing our 'object of love' – and the emotional benefits they bring us – and a desire to feel more significant. The problem with this strategy is that it easily becomes destructive and tends to end in suffering for everyone.

It's natural to want to protect a close relationship – and to some extent you can do this by constraining the behaviour of your loved one. But freedom is something dear to us all, and a freedom snatched is a desire stoked. Personally I'm quite sensitive to this one. I can understand attachment, but I do not like to be 'owned' (nor to own). I tend to treat what I see as possessive behaviour, initially as a playful test of character. Failing that, it's time for some serious talks.

If you loved me then you would ...

"If you loved me then you would *do as I want*." To accept such an idea is to make love a kind of servitude and yourself a slave. But sadly this is the understanding for some people.

Even if no one gives us the above judgement we might still think to ourselves: 'I need to do XYZ to prove my love' or 'Doing XYZ is what it means to love someone'. Firstly, love, responsibility and obligation are all very different things, even though we may be in the habit of attaching one to another. Secondly, what could it mean to 'prove' love? Is it a formula or test? Though love – and its remnants – may be experienced in many shades, the most elemental and sustaining aspects of love are surely joy and compassion. Those things can only be experienced and freely, willingly offered, but never proven.

The idea of 'sacrifice' is often associated with love. Love (when it's *not* mixed up with obligation or fear of rejection) *may* lead to sacrificing something of great personal value. But again, the true distinction of a sacrifice made in love is that it is done willingly, without any sense of needing to prove anything, fulfil a duty or gain approval, or another's 'love' in return.

Acting as you'd like to be, can help you step into that reality, just be sure it's not motivated by that love-repelling state: guilt.

If what we mean by 'love' is essentially a mixture of joy, compassion and affection, then there may be moments where we *don't* feel like that towards someone – even though they remain an important person in our lives and other aspects of our bond remain intact. That's normal and natural in the ebb and flow of most loving relationships.

On the subject of showing love, it is indeed our actions that allow us to communicate our feelings. It's worth remembering that sometimes the simplest actions are the best. For instance, a great deal of love can be expressed with a hug, whether it be between parent and child, lovers, friends or even strangers. I highly recommend being liberal with your hugs.

What's in a word?

The word 'love' itself, can be an issue for some. It can carry a lot of weight and a lot of baggage. Whenever someone says "I love you", there are certain feelings and thoughts for them attached to those words; think of all the kinds and states of love we've mentioned. In fact, the emotional state of love will be (at least) slightly *different* from situation to situation. E.g.: saying goodnight, taking a romantic walk, laughing at a joke, saying 'I do', or farewell etc. The 'flavour' of love can range widely from warmth and affection to gratitude and admiration and from to lust and passion to loyalty and protection. The *meaning* of "I love you" therefore, is in the *whole* expression. Focus then not only on the words, but more on the tone of voice, facial expression and posture – along with the context – and you will get a clearer picture of someone's feelings when they talk of love.

With a clearer sense of the *way* someone is feeling 'love' for you, at that moment, it may feel OK to say "I love you too", if before it was difficult. Otherwise you can just say "Thank you", or, if their expression doesn't make it clear, "What does love mean for you in this moment?"

How do you feel when you say "I love you" (or think about saying it)? Do you say it in a spontaneous moment of up-welling feeling? Do you do it looking for reassurance from the other person that they love you too? Or perhaps you do it with the fear they will take your words as permanent and binding, when you're not sure if you'll feel the same way next week, or even later that day? If you know what the other person's attitudes and beliefs about love are, this will give you a clue to how they could interpret you telling them that you love them.

For some people 'love' is a huge word, for others, not so much. For this reason you may choose to either use a different word, be more specific in describing your feelings or, to avoid confusion, use the word 'love' more sparingly. The more experience I have of love the more I realize the value of discussing what love means and being specific when I share how I'm feeling it.

Is there a right time to say "I love you"? If you just met someone 30 minutes ago and you've just swapped contacts, that might not be a great time. But in general, taking into account the above factors, say it when you feel like saying it.

If you're declaring your love for the first time to someone, your chances of getting a positive response are higher if you are comfortable when you say it. Again, a good way of testing the water and avoiding misunderstanding is to first discuss the idea of 'love'. E.g. "Oh, so love is where you feel really joyful and affectionate around someone and care deeply about them. In that case, I definitely love you." Or "Oh, so love is where you feel an undying devotion to someone and no-one else. Hmm, not sure I feel quite like that, but I would like to have some commitment between us and to offer support and affection."

Beware the trap of trying to pin down and measure love, or using it to measure yourself, such as thinking of yourself as 'worthy' or 'unworthy'; it's the best way of distancing yourself from joy and compassion. Don't let the word get in the way of the reality.

Connected with the use of the word love, is making sense of someone's behaviour around you. E.g. if someone is very affectionate and attentive, we might wonder 'Do they love me?' Again, getting more specific about what that behaviour means for them, at that time and in that context will help you avoid confusion and general emotional tangles. For instance, we might ask: "When you show me this affection, I wonder what it is you're feeling. I'd like to know more clearly what these moments mean for you. Would you be willing to say?" Depending on the response, you could go on to ask how they would like things to develop, if that's on your mind. Just as the experienced meaning of a word can differ from person to person, so can the meaning of a particular behaviour.

A blinding flash of love

What does it mean to be 'blinded by love'? It's the rose tinted effect, which is often accompanied by extreme tunnel vision, where we simply can't see what's beside us and what we do glimpse is filtered through a heady cocktail of love chemicals. A similar blindness can result from someone meeting some of our powerful desires or giving hope to strong expectations. In any case, our brain finds ways of editing out any evidence which might threaten either our 'love addiction' or the fulfilment of our desires.

This blindness presents a real problem when there are serious spanners in the works (e.g. the other person not returning your affections, or using them to manipulate you). Unfortunately, I'm not sure there's a lot that can be done, unless you've at least managed to entertain the thought that you *just might* be in this love blinded state. In this case you may find it helpful to first write down all the reasons why you are good for each other. Be as detailed as you can. Then find someone who's a good listener and willing to help you explore those reasons and what they mean for you. (For ideas on how to avoid this state, see section: 'The glass melon dichotomy') If you already realize why you're not well suited for someone but still feel unable to break the connection, then explore your values, beliefs and desires. How is this relationship plugging into them?

It's interesting that what we call love has the potential to give us the most charged, yet tranquil clarity of perception and purpose, and also the most murky and tragic of delusions. It's that latter possibility, of course, that makes many people so afraid to 'fall in love'. The trick, I think, is to make it less of a fall and more of an ascent, with your eyes kept as open as your heart.

From cynicism and familiarity to continued freshness

"Pah! Love, shmlove." sums up some people's attitude after a few intimate relationships. How can we avoid cynicism setting in, or a lack of excitement or freshness as we experience different loves, grow familiar with the cycles of a relationship and find that some of our ideals didn't match up with reality? How can we treat new relationships with an open mind and open heart? Doing this depends partly on how we continue to carry our past relationships with us and partly on our focus in new ones.

Do we focus on the 'failures' or dashed expectations from the past, on what could, or should have been? Or do we focus on what good things were shared and learned? If it's the former, we naturally become jaded and tired of love. If it's the latter we sail forward with a stronger wind the further we go.

In existing relationships, as we gain more experience, what once seemed exciting and new often becomes familiar. We may then shift our values away from those fading appeals to more steady or mellow ones, such as loyalty, attentiveness, reliability, etc. We may also find continued freshness – in tandem with those steady qualities – in being with someone who continues to help us develop, in love, in ourself, life and understanding – and we for them. If we want this, our focus must be on attracting that kind of person; someone who is committed to continued growth and contribution, in whatever ways work for the individuals involved. Such a relationship, if it lasts, will require commitment and the willingness to make compromises – just like any enduring, healthy, loving relationship.

At the time of writing I have a space for such a person in my life. But I have a lot of happiness nonetheless since I share love with many people – even despite devoting 2 years of my life to writing this book, which I'm very grateful for. It may change, but my current personal belief is that, while there are many things you can do to help yourself (including getting out of the house more), finding this kind of person can't be rushed, so it's best to just enjoy the process.

Making sense of love that ends

Even the deepest of heart-felt loves can come to an end, even if everyone tries their best and even if you have both taken the time and effort to really get to know and support each other. Sometimes what you'd come to know as 'love' (beyond any initial infatuation), is no longer. It could be that somehow you've forgotten how to really touch each other, that routine has eroded the emotional bedrock between you, or perhaps life stresses have beaten down the bond you shared instead of strengthening it.

By gaining clarity on what's happened, it may be possible to rebuild a precious relationship. However, I'd like to offer the idea that sometimes people just grow apart, or their paths in life are bound to meet and then diverge and such a love that comes to an end was no less deep or valuable because of it. This is so even if it lasted for only a small fraction of your life (accepting that for one of you at least, that love might endure). The memories live on and the gifts of love and understanding resound and are there still to be shared with others.

In conclusion, I believe the more we understand our own feelings around love and unlock our fears of it, the more of it we will have to share and the more we will be able to accept.

The two greatest catalysts in my life have been love and loneliness. I have to say, I much prefer love.

In the following parts of the book we explore some key ways of maintaining a healthy, loving relationship.

The beautiful connection

I came to thinking that what makes a connection with someone most beautiful, romantic interest or not, are roughly five things. These points, or keys as you might call them, are all underpinned by one thing: a default positive regard for yourself and others. This positive regard can be more easily gained after addressing the various obstacles from the first part of this book, and from the accumulation of positive experiences that will result.

The five keys

♦ **Confidence and spontaneity** – sharing with ease your character and individuality in the moment. When you overcome hesitancy and tension in your communication (especially body language) you are infinitely better company; it makes relaxing and sharing so much easier. Confidence inspires confidence. When someone doesn't waste energy on habitually deprecating themselves (or others) and doesn't speak through apologies, but is comfortable enough to communicate clearly and directly, then a big part of a beautiful connection is already there.

When you're at ease and have positive self regard, you have more space in your mind for the beautiful and joyful thing that is spontaneity to develop, as well as more emotional space to really relate to and connect with others.

When you're comfortable being spontaneous it's much easier to express and develop your playfulness, affection, humour and creativity – all things that bring our awareness into the light of the present moment. (Rather than think: "right, I have to be spontaneous!", simply give yourself permission to express those natural sparks of playfulness, affection, humour and creativity, that are in us all – however deeply buried.) With spontaneity comes an element of unpredictability, which, in combination with the other keys, helps to keep things fresh and interesting.

♦ **Acceptance** – taking in without casting out, allowing time and space for a person to share themselves as they are safely. Rise above pretence and try and see what's actually there. It feels great both ways when we do this for someone and don't assume they will be, or are, this way or that way. *Acceptance implies the indefinite deferral of judgement.*

In the case of meeting someone, at any point you could decide you would like to end or pause a connection, or that you would like to continue and meet again. Better to make it a well informed decision. You can only do this if you don't block or distort your own view with insecurities and unconstructive habits of mind. Try to notice when you're distracted by your own reflections and projecting yourself onto someone else. It's *self*-acceptance (whether you are feeling positive and at ease, or quite the opposite) that underpins the acceptance of others.

This key is very much about accepting imperfections as integral to organic human beings and learning to really *listen*. How often do we hear: "I just want someone who understands me"? It's by listening well that we come to understand others better, and also notice more often their attempts to connect with us.

♦ **Honesty with humanity** – share openly but sensitively. It's much easier to feel comfortable with someone if you feel they're sensitive to your feelings, thoughts, needs and values, at the same time as being honest with their own. It's very refreshing to spend time with someone who, rather than just acting in accordance with the accepted popular norms, is much more interested in having authentic connections, sharing how they really are with the world and what really matters to them. It's also very refreshing to *be* this way.

Of key importance is finding a balance between how much, what and how we share of ourselves, with the needs and feelings of the person we are communicating with. If we lose track of rapport (trust with a sense of commonality and mutual empathy) and the other person's perspective – by *just* focusing on honesty – it's easy to over-share and overwhelm. This balance will be affected by...

♦ **Confluence** – where through conversation, play or other communication you find similarities that you can appreciate in each other. These could be shared *values, beliefs and desires*, which are expressed through a common passion, activity, skill, habit, understanding, goal or idea. It could also be a similar characteristic or emotional state.

The more confluence there is, the closer you tend to feel to someone. Literally, it means one thing travelling along the same path as another. Some beautiful examples of shared emotional state are: being comfortable with shared laughter, curiosity and interest, sharing eye contact, touch or a smile for as long as it feels good, and sharing moments of silence or calm without feeling a need to say something *(it's the space between the notes that makes the music)*.

♦ **Congruent divergence** – where we discover something new or complimentary in the other person (skill, habit, ability, knowledge, belief, experience, etc.); something *different* and of interest in the other and there is a willingness to share, receive, contribute and grow. Another way of looking at it is, having compatible and supportive differences of direction between you. This could just be a positive attitude when someone needs it, or it could be realized through sharing a joke, a massage, a new perspective, a practical act of service, or teaching a new skill. Essentially, this is the giving and accepting of gifts that help each other move and grow in the directions we want to. Look for opportunities to give in this way; embrace the value of our differences.

And the secret ingredient is...

You could view these five aspects as different layers of the same cake (there is some overlap). It's the attitude that really makes the flavour special. You might conceivably have all the above qualities, interacting with someone, without much compassion or genuine care for the well-being of the other. You could be considerate and sensitive without really caring much. The interaction might still feel beautiful or fruitful, but it would lack a certain warmth.

It's not about making everyone you meet the centre of your world. Rather, it's about allowing a real emotional connection to be made (if it's offered and wanted) and recognising that person as a fellow human being, which in many respects puts them in the same boat as you.

I've found when I've done this, my connections with others have been far richer. In practice (at least for me), this is something you approach many times from different places, forget and relearn. Over time we can gradually imbibe the ideas within the five keys if we make the choices to practice them as opportunities arise.

Contribution and gift giving

Contribution runs through every aspect of the beautiful connection: contribution by offering all the facets of yourself you wish to share for another's enrichment, your thoughts and feelings, your honesty and creativity; contribution through acceptance and the space to share and grow that it brings; contribution through shared pleasure and encouragement and contribution through gift giving, practical acts of service or sharing of skills. (They're all gifts really).

Why is contribution to others so important? In a nutshell, it makes you less of an island, gives you a feeling of positive connection with the rest of human kind and a deeper sense of self-worth. When we contribute we become part of something bigger than ourselves. Because of the enriching and strengthening effect contribution tends to have on relationships, the more generous our contribution to others is, the more fulfilled we become (providing of course, that we also respect our own needs and limited capacity).

If honesty is the thinnest, clearest window through which we can know each other, contribution is the magical element that can pass through it, allowing us to truly touch each other.

On the subject of gift giving, it's common to want to give physical, bought gifts to someone we feel attracted to, especially in consumer societies. Allow the various other gifts of contribution detailed above to come more into the foreground, especially in the early stages of relationships. They generally leave the best and most long lasting impression. This way you also avoid sending the message "I feel the need to buy you things in order to spend time with you", which is *not* a helpful one to send. If you have a strong desire to give something physical, sometimes creating a handmade gift is a great option. It carries a personal touch that's hard to beat. Physical gifts, made or bought, can be wonderful, life enriching things. Just be mindful of when they become a substitute for other types of emotional connection, a symbol of compensation, or not freely given.

Accept a gift because you want to accept it, give one just because you want to give it. Try to avoid expecting gifts or thinking you're obliged to give them. It's often natural to want to give something back; obligation only dampens or pressurizes this feeling. Expectation invites disappointment.

What does blame give you?

We'll go into the quality of acceptance a lot more in the next section, but I want to mention something here that is a particular hindrance to it and to beautiful connections in general: blame.

While blame can bind you to its subject, blaming is also a way of gaining distance from something. By holding onto blame and by dwelling on the past, we move away from the present, where the chance of change exists. Were we blame someone else we move them (as they are now) away from us by finding fault and again by dwelling on the past. Blame is a response (or strategy) that has its uses, but in loving relationships it is best minimised, or avoided altogether.

Something for every relationship (accept where three is a crowd)

Applying the ideas in the 'beautiful connection' will enhance just about any kind of relationship, but especially intimate personal relationships. (Indeed, the beautiful connection *is* an intimate connection.) I believe that where these five qualities persist, they form the roots and branches of such a relationship, helping it to be more healthy and loving.

These are things I've come to realize after having a fair number of relationships, falling in love and doing a lot of (on-going) reflection. I don't know how much sense it would really have made to me in an earlier stage of my life, beyond the intellectual, but I hope in any case you can get some use out of it, whatever point you're at.

In the specific case of more intimate relationships it's perhaps worth pointing out the obvious – that some people you take an interest in will not respond in a way that encourages a connection to develop, because they're involved in another relationship that takes up that space for them. This eventuality is not something to fear. The chances are they will be grateful for your interest anyway, if it is expressed along the lines of the above ideas, even though they decline any development. If fear of rejection is a major block for you, see section: 'Fear (and general emotional turmoil)'.

Where someone doesn't decline further development of an intimate connection between you, while letting you know they are already in a committed relationship, this poses some important questions, which we explore more in section: 'Evolution, competition and deception'.

Applying and re-examining the five keys

So, how can we apply these five key qualities more? It can help to ask that question in the moment, while you're communicating with someone you'd like a deeper connection with: "Can I appreciate more, or build on this quality with this person?" Perhaps take the one or two keys that appeal to you the most and work on those first, seeing how they change things for you.

But before we get to that point, what happens when we find certain, potentially desirable, ways of connecting with people challenging? A fairly common reaction is to try and mask or compensate for the difficulty by emphasizing other ways of connecting we feel more secure about. That's understandable, but in the case of the five keys balance is well worth pursuing.

Let's consider some possible scenarios where our style of connecting or relating is predominantly in one of the key qualities.

Suppose we're in our element 'being in the moment', spontaneous and confident. We might then find starting relationships comes fairly easily. But if we struggle with sharing what's truly close to our heart, as in the key of honesty with humanity, then our connections may lack a certain depth.

Similarly, if we tend to converse only about what's deeply important or highly emotional to us, neglecting to play in the present moment, then our connections may grow tense and tiring.

If we're extremely accepting of others, but not very forthcoming with ourselves, or find it hard to relax, then our connections may lack trust, intimacy, or excitement.

Let's say we're very focused on learning from each other and making the most of our differences, as in the congruent divergence key. If that's to the point where we're rarely still, or appreciate the similarities and the simple moments of togetherness (or confluence), then our connections will likely be fraught with pressure or anxiety.

Conversely, if we're very in tune with the similarities we share with someone and those moments of confluence, but find it hard to embrace our differences, then our connections may become stifling or dull. Thus, the five keys work best in combination.

It's not that we should strive for a perfectly even balance between the keys – it's natural to have favourite ways of relating to and being with others according to our character. Rather, if we can understand the benefits and be *open* to experiencing a little more of each of the keys, it will be helpful for our relationships. In that way we'll find our own balance.

Here are five questions that may help you get more in touch with each of the qualities of the 'beautiful connection' in your relationships. With each question look for *specific* answers that involve *actions* which help to clearly show what you wish to communicate, or otherwise bring about that quality.

"How could I share my character and individuality more in this moment, with the quality of confidence and openness to spontaneity?"

"Am I as open to accepting this person for what they are in this moment as I could be, and how can I make them feel more welcome to be themselves?"

"With consideration and sensitivity, how could I be more honest about myself, my feelings and needs with this person?"

"What things are there in our characters, experience, interests and understandings that we share and value, and how could I appreciate them more?"

"What things are there in our characters, experience, interests and understandings that are different and complementary and how could I appreciate them more?"

Notice how through these qualities we actually grow to really know the other person and see how we might enjoy spending time with them in the future, which is rather handy if you're looking for a relationship. Indeed, can you imagine being truly happy in a long-term relationship where any of these five qualities were missing?

The diagram on page 113 visualizes the beautiful connection concept. It shows the five key qualities, and alongside them the distancing and generally unhelpful qualities that tend to result from obstructing or denying the experience of that key. There is the idea of the qualities building on and feeding back to each other. Each block represents acting with that quality, embracing it and also recognising it in the other person.

I'd like to conclude this section by offering an alternative recap on these five keys or qualities.

In the order listed from page 104, in the first quality you're sharing your character and engagement with the present moment. The second is a reflection of that, where you support the other person in doing the same. The third adds a dimension to the first two – *truthfulness and sensitivity*, adding value and strength to them. Through the first three qualities we can naturally show a strong sense of interest in and openness to another person.

The fourth and fifth can be seen as flowing from the first three. After getting to know each other, how much there is of these provides a measure of compatibility.

It is when we appreciate the beauty and value in our similarities and differences that our connections really shine (and also tend to be longer lived). Where the two qualities of confluence and congruent divergence extend beyond the present moment they provide a means to really involve someone in your life on an ongoing basis, and for them to involve you in theirs. (Again that quality of honesty with humanity, from the beginning will help us appreciate these qualities more clearly and help avoid any issues snowballing). Doing things *together* that make you both feel more alive and whole, because they are rooted in these two qualities, is like a powerful 'relationship glue'.

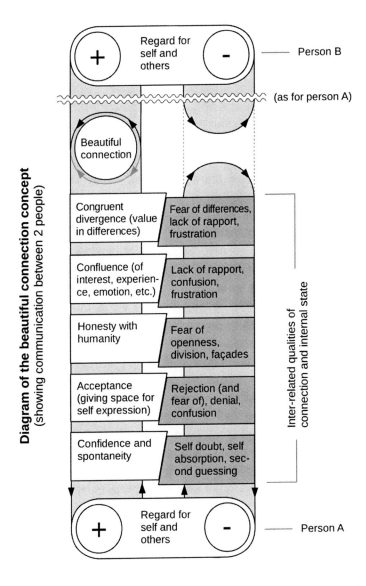

Diagram of the beautiful connection concept
(showing communication between 2 people)

Person B

(as for person A)

Regard for self and others

Beautiful connection

Congruent divergence (value in differences)	Fear of differences, lack of rapport, frustration
Confluence (of interest, experience, emotion, etc.)	Lack of rapport, confusion, frustration
Honesty with humanity	Fear of openness, division, façades
Acceptance (giving space for self expression)	Rejection (and fear of), denial, confusion
Confidence and spontaneity	Self doubt, self absorption, second guessing

Inter-related qualities of connection and internal state

Regard for self and others

Person A

Each of the five keys provide a channel for authentic self-expression and connection, in sharing ourselves and in learning about and showing real interest in another.

The glass melon dichotomy

This section is about 'acceptance' and what it means to really listen. Let's re-examine the quality of acceptance in the 'beautiful connection' with an analogy. Imagine you are walking past a shop window and something on the other side catches your eye: a big ripe melon, some sexy shoes, a trombone, whatever works for you.

Now in this moment, not only can you see this item, you can also see yourself, reflected in the window. This distracts you somewhat from the item. You start to wonder about your appearance and what that item might say about you.

If we're feeling negative we might think: "that fat melon reminds me of overeating and being fat – I don't like it", "those shoes say I'm cheap – they're not good shoes", "that trombone reminds me how I don't seem to stick at much and would only lead to disappointment – the trombone makes me sad", etc.

If we're feeling positive we might think: "that melon reminds me of my healthy post exercise smoothies and how great it feels to taste that energy – melons are good", "wearing those kind of shoes say I'm exciting – they make me confident", "that trombone makes me think of being creative and listening to my favourite music – that trombone makes me happy", etc.

Notice how both positive and negative reflections don't really have much intrinsically to do with the items themselves. They are expressions of our inner state and memories, which result in feelings that we then project onto the items. The melon, the shoes and the trombone are exactly as they are, unchanged, but our perception of them and our feelings about them are totally coloured by our own reflections or internal dialogues.

This can often be what happens when we meet someone. Our attention is drawn into our reflections and we ascribe the resulting feelings to the person; we *project*. Even though what we're feeling has to do with us more than the reality of who they are, still we think "you are ...", "you make me feel ...". You can see the glass window as our senses, our interface with the outside world, giving us the choice of what to focus on; our reflections, or what's out there.

Does that mean there will always be a glass barrier between two people? Though that separation between ourselves through our senses will remain, if we really focus away from our reflections onto what's beyond it, it can be as if the glass is no longer there. E.g. when I dance closely with someone and we're really listening to each other and the music, sometimes it's as if our movements become so attuned that they could be that of one being; the glass seems to vanish completely.

Don't miss the melon for the glass

Although reflection – in the sense we've been discussing it – and forming opinions on other's views can be extremely useful (helping us make connections, form new ideas and providing an avenue for self-expression), sometimes we miss the melon for the glass. The first thing we catch is our reflection and our attention goes no further. E.g. "I see your eyes are ..." → "my eyes are ..." → "you probably think ...", rather than continuing to be open to what their eyes, and the rest of them, are expressing. This behaviour is often linked to a habitual *internal dialogue*, or with longer term projections (or stories) we may have (see section: 'Projections and prophecy').

What would it be like if, when we met someone we liked, we did not dwell on our own passing reflections or our default assumptions? What if we really opened our attention to just taking in their way of being?

This is a real gift to give someone, to accept them for who they are (as far as you can tell) in that moment, and also a gift to yourself to see more of who someone is, by being more sensitive. In this way you can get a better idea of what your similarities and differences are and who you're being open, confident and spontaneous with.

One of the beautiful elements of this idea is how it helps you to appear confident without you even trying to. "I see they appear very confident" → "I feel nervous" → "They probably think ..." turns to: "I see they appear very confident" → "I notice how they move and speak and I continue to absorb the quality of their presence without self-reflection". If you relax while you're accepting their way of being, guess how that looks from the outside? Yes, that's right, confident.

Being clear on the difference between *projection* and *observation*, the empowering thing is, to make it a choice which side of the glass you focus on – recognising the potential for projecting our reflections and mistaking them for fact, or real observations.

You can be accepting and sensitive in this way from the moment you meet someone (it can be harder if we already know them, where we have pre-formed opinions). To do this more, it's useful to first recognize when you're not doing it. "OK, now my view of this person in this moment is obscured by my reflections on my XYZ, or how they possibly feel about XYZ".

When you recognize this pattern of thinking, as you will with practice, you can more easily change it. Then, when you have this awareness and exercise your choice of focus, it will be like bringing a sky-load of fresh air and light into your interactions with people.

The message here is not necessarily to 'reflect less' during our interactions with people. It could be useful to think about it as just *waiting a bit longer* before relating what we observe in others to ourselves (and then projecting). Or simply observing a little more before reflection, judgement and interpretation. The state of mind this concept aims to highlight is really a form of 'mindfulness', as practised in Buddhist meditation.

Projection is an invitation

There is a feedback effect with projection. Where we form an opinion, P, on what others think of us, inevitably this will, however subtly, colour the way we communicate. We are acting like 'someone who people see as P would act.' You could see it as playing a *role*. Unwittingly we are sending out an offer: "Would you like to play a role that fits the one I'm playing?" (or the one associated with how I'm communicating).

Just by taking on an idea of what others think we are, we're effectively *retransmitting* that idea as a statement: "This is how I am." Some people will attempt to help you see more clearly, but sadly, some people, stuck in their own unhappy projections, will see you as someone they can take advantage of – because of the clues you're giving out about how you see yourself. If the window we have into the world must always have some reflections, perhaps then it's a good idea to make them slightly gold tinted.

Here's an every day example of how our emotional state affects how we reflect and how we look beyond those reflections. Supposing you are walking down the street, one you often walk down. It's fairly busy and as you pass people, you pick up on their vibe and in the very awareness you have for each other's existence there is something communicated in your body language, eye contact or first expression. Perhaps you can even imagine what they could be thinking.

I was doing this one bright afternoon, not too long ago, when I noticed the vibes I was 'picking up' from people were not very positive, sometimes verging on hostile or dismissive. What was going on here? It's possible I just passed a string of people who were feeling particularly unfriendly. However, the next day I walked down the same road, similar time, and for some reason was reminded of some very beautiful moments I'd shared with someone in the past. I felt a deep contentment and gratitude and I couldn't help smiling.

Now as I walked past people, that instant of *recognition* seemed to *last longer* and I felt more warmth returned. The contrast struck me. The day before I'd felt quite tired, I'd not been sleeping much, but how can that explain it? Perhaps it was a combination of projections (and habitual roles) on both days.

What interests me is that on the second day my internal reflection (remembering those beautiful moments) became an *external* projection (I radiated happiness), some of which then came back to me – which helped me take a *better look* through my window into the world. So then, it's easier to peacefully observe someone (or something) that you have a default positive regard for.

On day two, those few who were still apparently not friendly, in that moment, seemed to glide past. My feeling was sufficiently secure (it was coming from a strong memory), self-contained and different from those people's feelings, for there to be very little scope for connection. Any interaction would have meant at least one of us shifting how we felt, or at least allowing in a reality very counter to our present awareness and focus. This kind of 'engagement blindness' is a well known phenomenon, beautifully demonstrated by Dr Christopher Chabris and Dr Daniel Simon's famous 'invisible gorilla' experiment.[12] Sometimes, for better or worse, it's almost impossible to see what lies outside our range of expectations – even if it's right in front of us.

Acceptance, from acknowledgement to disputes

Coming back to the idea of acceptance, we've seen that to be accepting we must cultivate awareness. The two qualities are inter-dependent. Awareness is useful in relationships for many reasons. One is that it allows us to acknowledge the other person when they're trying to connect with us – and show that we *accept* their connection. In the case of "hey, I'd like to talk/hug/do XYZ with you", that's fairly easily done. But actually there are so

12 Christopher Chabris, Daniel Simon "The Invisible Gorilla: And Other Ways Our Intuitions Deceive Us" ISBN: 978-0307459657

many little attempts to connect within most personal relationships, for instance: making eye contact when you're near by, preparing food or drink for one another, leaving a message, or just offering a touch. Noticing and responding positively to these 'little moments of togetherness', is a large part of what any lasting partnership is about.

How does this idea of acceptance and acknowledgement work in conversations? To be able to truly accept someone's ideas and feelings – not necessarily agree, just respect as their own and acknowledge – we need to be able to *listen*. By that I don't just mean taking in someone's words, but really looking through the glass.

So much unhappiness, frustration and 'hard work' results from people not knowing how to listen to each other in relationships. How many conversations about fairly basic things descend into acrimony, blame and general aggression, or end in one person feeling totally frustrated? The problem is essentially one of habit and interpretation. We judge and respond too soon. We sense some threat, pressure or accusation, *stop listening*, or raise our hackles and the conversation becomes a battle.

Simply focusing on that 'looking beyond your reflection' acceptance as we've discussed here, you will naturally find yourself listening more. Some more listening pointers are:

Make the choice to look through the glass for longer before responding. Allow your body-language to help someone feel welcome to express their feelings and relax. Let your tension drain away, relax your breathing and the muscles around your shoulders, stomach and eyes.

With disagreements, focus on feelings, needs and actual events instead of blaming, judging or interpreting the other's actions. Be responsible for *your* feelings and be constructive. On accepting responsibility for an undesirable event or action, this is more easily and constructively done without blame (dwelling on personal fault, guilt or shame). Rather, focus on understanding and then mending, where possible. NVC (non-violent communication) has some very useful ideas on conflict resolution. The above points, NVC and conflicts are covered in more detail in the 'Conflict' part of this book.

Listening often works best when it's an active process. You can engage someone with encouraging or supportive comments and sounds and by asking open questions, more than ones with 'yes' or 'no' answers. Understanding can be shown by reflecting back and summarising important points in your own words. Mirroring (subtly) voice tone and posture can also help, both you in empathizing and them in sharing more of their thoughts and feelings.

... and even while kissing

These ideas about acceptance and listening don't just apply to visual and verbal communication, but also to the physical kind. Imagine, for instance, kissing someone:

You're feeling good and completely absorbed in the moment. Let's say that you're not at all distracted by reflections like "Am I doing this right?", "Is my breath OK?", "Do they really like me?". However, the other person *is* distracted in this way. How does their kissing feel? Is it sensitive, responsive, passionate, playful? Or is it more tentative, distant or rigid? Now imagine that person, like you, is at ease and really absorbed in the moment. Through the contact, texture, shapes, sound and movement you are both really 'listening' to each other now. How does *that* kiss feel? Any better?

The connection of inner and outer acceptance

There's a nice, simple relationship between accepting yourself and being able to accept others, that ties in with the glass melon dichotomy. If you can accept yourself in a peaceful and loving way, the less distracting, self-conscious brain chatter you have to get in the way of accepting other people in a peaceful and loving way.

So far we've mainly talked about how to better accept others. Can we use the same ideas to better accept ourselves, to avoid premature judgement and allow space to get more in touch with who we are at any time?

In the same way that spending more time 'looking through the glass, beyond your reflection' helps us to better see what's 'out there', doing it with *self-observations* helps us better see what's 'in here'. Where before the glass was our senses, now there is only a frame containing our reflections or judgements. We have the choice to lay the frame down.

When we reserve self-judgement, there is no longer that screen dividing us from our actual feelings and innate values, so they have a better chance to surface. The idea is simply to spend *longer* observing our own sensations and feelings – with the same respect and default positive regard we would extend to those closest to us. It will help us feel more peaceful and loving, both to ourselves and to others.

The diagram on page 122 illustrates the glass, melon dichotomy concept.

Practice makes perfect (virtually)

Besides practising being how we want to be in real life, it can also be very useful to practise in our heads. Here we'll focus on a particular theme: developing imaginary scenarios where you meet someone you're attracted to and start communicating with them, visualizing a beautiful connection taking shape. Actually, it's fairly likely you do something like this already without thinking about it, just drifting off into a nice day dream now and then. If we take a more mindful and systematic approach to it though, this ability can be even more useful to us.

The glass, melon dichotomy

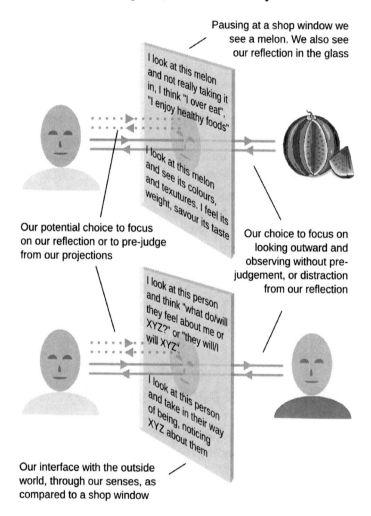

Pausing at a shop window we see a melon. We also see our reflection in the glass

I look at this melon and not really taking it in, I think "I over eat", "I enjoy healthy foods"

I look at this melon and see its colours, and texutures. I feel its weight, savour its taste

Our potential choice to focus on our reflection or to pre-judge from our projections

Our choice to focus on looking outward and observing without pre-judgement, or distraction from our reflection

I look at this person and think "what do/will they feel about me or XYZ?" or "they will/I will XYZ"

I look at this person and take in their way of being, noticing XYZ about them

Our interface with the outside world, through our senses, as compared to a shop window

A great way to do this consciously is to pick a situation that suits you, somewhere you like being and where you find other people. If it helps, decide what you're wearing, the time of day and other details.

Success is where preparation meets opportunity

What's the benefit of going over imaginary meetings? The idea is that through this practice we can, without risk, identify helpful and unhelpful habits of communication we have. This may be tending to steer the conversation onto a particular subject, or reacting in a certain way when we feel threatened somehow, or attracted, or anything else that may upset our balance. We can also try out *alternative* ways of behaving.

Now of course anything you think of won't be *exactly* like it's going to happen in real life (wouldn't it get boring?), but the feelings and challenges that come up will be similar. So by exploring possibilities like this you're preparing for certain types of situations. As Henry Hartman put it: *"success always comes where preparation meets opportunity"*. Such preparation is also very effective at reducing anxiety.

So, to illustrate how the process might work, here's an example scenario. (When you're doing this and you're looking for ideas you may find it helpful to use the five questions at the end of the section: 'The five keys'.)

You're at the supermarket and you notice someone nearby that you like the look of. What do you do? At this point a tree of possibilities begins.

Some first options: *a.* do nothing. *b.* make eye contact. *c.* approach and say something: "That's a nice coat. / Those look interesting, have you tried those before? / I don't suppose you know how to eat these?"

Now if you chose anything but *a.*, they react. Try to keep it as realistic as you can and be aware of where your projection is coming from. Does it reflect an old internal dialogue, or are you really aiming to put yourself in their head? It's OK to try out negative reactions, so long as you explore some positive ones as well. Remember, there's always an alternative interpretation.

Carrying on from your above choice of action, they might react: *a.* strange or shocked look. *b.* smile warmly. *c.* say something: "Thanks! / Yeah, they're one of my favourites actually. / That's a good question, it's puzzled me too. / Yes, you take your thumb and..."

Now this is where it gets interesting. For each of the possible reactions you've thought up, you can choose how you'd like to respond: "I'm sorry, have I surprised you? *friendly smile* / That's a nice smile. / It's really quite distinctive, can I feel it? / Oh, really? I thought you were the adventurous sort. / I had a feeling you might be knowledgeable of such things."

While you're doing this, pay attention to what you're doing with your body in your minds eye. What's your posture like? Where are you facing? They will respond to this. Also how does your body language feel to you? Practice this bodily aspect of communication, both with contact and without, just as much as the verbal. Talking about contact, how would you make a touch convey both gentleness and confidence? How would you massage someone's shoulders? Can you tune yourself into the tension you feel in their muscles, feeling how they respond to a light or firm touch? Now, how would you make eye-contact with someone in a way that said: "I like you, I'm comfortable in myself and I'm interested in seeing what we might share together"?

It can be a lot of fun thinking up different responses in imaginary meetings, and it soon gives you a sense of how much and how quickly the destiny of a conversation can change, depending on the choices and *chances* you take.

It's OK if it's just meeting eyes and a smile, but often after a few exchanges you can be swapping names and talking about the things you do in your lives. Then, taking our little example above, you might feel like saying: "Do you fancy taking a few of those funny fruit to share in the park with me?/It's been good to meet you, would you like to get together for a tea later this week?" etc.

If you come to a point where you're struggling to imagine anything but a negative reaction to a particular thing you might do, ask yourself: "Why would they be responding that way? If I were in their place, what would I think?" and, most importantly: "What would be a way of responding to that with calm strength and positivity?" Perhaps you've been tending to look at the glass more than the melon, or forgetting to consider the alternative interpretations? Or you may suddenly realize why or how you've been tripping yourself up in the past.

For more positive inspiration, when you're around people in real life, try just putting any thoughts about the impressions you're making gently to one side – visualizing your inner state as a warm and tranquil lake. The golden sunlight reflected from it is shining up into the sky. Let this warmth and light shine from you and see how it starts your connections on a different foot.

Now, when you feel comfortable, try initiating some of your scenarios in real life, and see what beautiful connections evolve!

As well as the above uses, we can also use visualization to work through interactions we've recently had and situations we don't like, in order to help us find possible alternative outcomes for the future.

Exploring qualities you wish to express

Beyond visualizing initial connections and future or past challenges, we can take a specific quality we'd like to express, or have more in our relationships and explore it in our mind. Section: 'The five keys', offers some example qualities, and we'll look at two other related ones shortly. The idea is to deepen our understanding of what a particular desired quality is and discover different ways of developing it. One question that may be helpful to ask yourself is: "How would expressing or having more of this quality affect the personal connections in my life?"

Try to consider the above question from both sides of the connection. What value would the quality bring to you, and what value would it bring to the other person? In this way we can more fully understand the nature of that quality. Then we can start imagining scenarios or strategies for bringing more of it into our relationships (or perhaps just with a particular person).

Support and affection

Continuing from the previous sub-section, let's say we pick *support* and *affection* as example qualities to explore. Starting with support, here are my own reflections on what it is and how it affects my personal connections.

Supportiveness is about allowing what you have to be a strength to others when you share intelligently, and helping what they have to be a strength to them when you listen. It's also about offering encouragement and affection liberally. Sometimes your giving helps others, but so can your receiving, at times when they wish to give to you. Mutual support brings people closer and creates warmth and trust in a relationship, if done with respect for your own needs and limitations.

Imagining some scenarios now, supposing someone dear to you was studying for an exam, or mourning for a lost friend. What would be the best ways of being supportive? Can you imagine how, in either case, you could be helpful while still allowing learning and natural feelings to run their course? Being supportive is often not about solving someone's problems. Contact, active listening, and understanding, followed by encouragement, are sometimes the best ways. Other times it could be what someone needs most is space to find their own way.

How does listening help you be supportive? Think what a difference having your feelings heard and accepted makes. To be offered advice or a well meaning pep talk without first having a sense of being *understood* isn't quite as effective. When someone takes the time to really listen to you, does it not seem like you're more valued? This combination of acceptance being understood and valued is very helpful in several ways. It can help difficult feelings or challenging situations be further expressed or dealt with, as well as giving you a sense that someone really cares. Thus being a good listener is a very supportive quality.

Affection is free food for the soul. For all the obstacles that can block us giving and receiving it, I believe it is perhaps the one quality most needed for emotional and physical health in a loving relationship. When people share affection with each other it brings joy, invigoration, and warmth to their connection. Affection conveys fondness or attraction, acceptance, significance, care and safety. It can also be a powerful stress reliever.

How would you show *simple* and *regular* affection for a loved one, expressing warmth and care with your gestures, hugs, and touching? Visualize it. It's amazing how such a simple act can make us feel so much more alive and happy. Words can also be used to great effect to express affection, although physical expressions, like hugging, are typically more potent. That's because touch has a more direct physiological effect, and there are usually less mental filters involved in understanding it.

On the subject of affection, hugging deserves a special mention. In the words of world renowned psychotherapist Virginia Satir: "We need 4 hugs a day for survival. We need 8 hugs a day for maintenance. We need 12 hugs a day for growth." Hugs, of course, far from being only for the needy or lonely, can make the happy even happier and the most secure feel even more so.

There are many types of hug and a hug can have many subtle or not so subtle qualities besides basic affection. A hug may be gentle, firm, consoling, friendly, erotic, calming, celebratory, perfunctory, tepid, enthusiastic, and many other things besides. With a hug there's often an element of vulnerability. Along with being preoccupied with the daily stresses of life, vulnerability is a very common reason for people not hugging as much as they'd otherwise love to. When someone says "I'm just not very physical" it doesn't necessarily mean that the longing to be held is not there. It may be reflecting a fear of rejection or judgement[13].

13 There are always exceptions. It's well known, for instance, that autistic people often don't like to be touched. There is evidence to suggest that the reason for that could be physiological (abnormalities in the cerebellum producing hypersensitivity to touch), while the natural human longing to be held remains present. Autism researcher Dr Temple Grandin invented the 'squeeze machine' to treat her own autism. With her invention, she and many others have been able to overcome their hypersensitivity and enjoy normal physical contact, including hugging.

Another reason for some people avoiding hugs is thinking that they're only for lovers or partners. This unfortunate belief can lead to a lot of unnecessary loneliness and unhealthy dependence. But let's not forget the case where someone simply isn't feeling affectionate in a particular moment. In any case, if someone communicates that they don't want a hug, that is to be respected.

One of my passions is dancing tango, which in some ways could be described as 'a walking hug'. This dance really highlights to me how rich and varied an emotional exchange hugging can be.

Getting back to affection, if you're not used to sharing it, build up from a smile. Incidentally, if affection is a challenge, taking small but regular steps to express it, besides strengthening your relationships, can help reduce any fears of physical intimacy.

I'd like to highlight the fact that both giving and receiving the two qualities of support and affection is an especially effective way of transforming feelings of loneliness. Loneliness is the antithesis of connectedness, and this entire book is about building better personal connections – but getting more of those two qualities in your life is a great place to start. My view is that it boils down to *freely offered* contribution; if you can do that, then your connections of all kinds will blossom and you will not be lonely. Now, there may be a whole slew of things that are getting in your way (see the first part of this book). But if you can start reaching out more, in small ways, to whoever you know or meet, being the first to offer a connection, then you'll notice positive changes immediately. Offering affection and a supportive presence (while not over-stretching yourself) are relatively straightforward and very commonly valued examples of reaching out and contributing.

Concluding the discussion here on practising different qualities of connection that we'd like more of, the other side of the coin is practising being *receptive* to those qualities. How well do you pick up on other's offers to connect (with affection, support, or other qualities) and how positively do you tend to respond? This is where 'the five keys', especially acceptance, can help.

Conflict

This part of the book looks at how conflict arises and how it is resolved in relationships. The central ideas of empathy, judgement (in its many forms, including blame and criticism) responsibility and compromise are explored in detail. Some of the questions that will be addressed include:

- How can conflicts be peacefully resolved with the best chance of everyone getting what they need?

- How can you understand and effectively deal with anger?

- What does it mean to be 'responsible', and is it possible to be so without blame and guilt?

- What is the role of compromise in relationships?

- What role do play-fights, play-arguments and joking have in relationships and when is 'play' not play?

- What does it mean to be manipulative?

- How can you have empathy in the face of criticism?

The following sections consider inter-personal conflict of various types, hidden, overt, physical, verbal and playful. We'll also apply and develop some of the connected ideas about internal conflict, introduced in earlier parts of the book.

Conflict in a nutshell

Conflict can mean arguing and fighting. It can also mean any kind of opposing thoughts, feelings or actions. Sometimes conflict can be a good source of inspiration and mutual contribution – we can learn a lot from each others differences. But sometimes conflict just seems to lead to suffering and more conflict. Indeed, we occupy a world where conflict of one kind or another is common and inevitable, and the paths to resolution are many, including: faith, philosophy, meditation, music, art, dance, humour, walking in nature, and countless forms of therapy. I believe all these paths tend to share a common ground – they provide some *relief* from a certain closed way of thinking. In the following sections we explore that way of thinking, alongside ways of shifting it, which open a path to peace, mutual understanding and joy. I hope you will find these ideas complementary to whatever methods you currently find useful.

You already know the solution

The simplest of good ideas are sometimes the hardest to apply. Most of the ideas in this and later sections are 'simple', they are things you probably understood perfectly well by the time you were 3 years old. But they are also ideas that are easy to forget, or to grow to see as 'unrealistic' or 'impractical'. The detail that follows is there just to help untangle the conditioning that may have obscured the true, practical, everyday value of such ideas. So if the common approach to resolving relationship conflicts of trying to decide who is *right* and *wrong*, and consequently who *should* do what, isn't working so well for you, read on. There is another way.

A lack of mutual understanding is a common catalyst of conflict, but what does it mean to be 'understood'? A sense of recognition seems to be key to it, but recognition of what? There's no doubt that we can be understood at different levels. Someone may understand what we desire or intend to do at a particular moment, but not know how we see that situation, or ourselves in it. E.g. **You want to cook me dinner and you intent to do so tonight**. Someone may understand what our opinion is about some matter, but not what we feel emotionally about it, or what it means to us personally. E.g. **You think tonight is the best day out of* *the ones we could have chosen and the ingredients you bought are the best you could get**. But at the core of our experience and sense of meaning in life are our feelings and our innate values or needs, and to be understood at *that* level often signifies the most to us. E.g. **You want to cook me dinner tonight because you want to show your love and appreciation. You really value spending quality time with me like this because for you it's part of sharing companionship, support and affection**.

Taking another example, if someone tells you: "You missed the coach to meet me at the station because you're a disorganized day-dreamer. I guess you're just reliability-challenged, oh well" and you *identify* with those labels you may think: "Yes, you've really seen me for what I am." Contrast that sense of understanding, however, with how you might feel if they said: "I guess you're probably feeling stressed because you missed the coach. I know you wanted to meet me when I arrived and help me with my luggage. Maybe you're feeling somewhat disappointed with yourself about that?" Is that response more deeply connected with the present and what you might be experiencing in that situation?

The words we use are part of what allows us to find those deeper connections and understanding within relationships. But arguably the most important form of showing understanding is with our body and our voice tone. These are the oldest and most universal languages. It's quite possible to have a very strong sense of understanding and acceptance, just sharing a look, sound or touch. Indeed, spoken language would often be hard to trust or understand, without these channels of communication working in tandem.

One reason why showing understanding without words can work so well is because it avoids expressing judgements, labelling, blaming or criticising the other person. Unfortunately in much of the world, east and west, these types of judgements are heavily engrained into how we use spoken language.

Before you were 2 years old, you'd probably already learnt how to understand someone else's feelings. But as we become conditioned with a judgement-rich style of thinking and speaking we can lose sight of this fundamental level of understanding and become wrapped up in our own internal dialogues. The problem is compounded with stressful lifestyles focused around material success and consumption. Such lifestyles pre-dispose us to thinking in competitive, threat-focused ways. We get angry or defensive more easily. (In fact this way of living is as unsustainable for our personal lives as it is for the planet.)

The alternative ways of communicating that follow, help to avoid the pitfalls of the above sort of conditioning and allow conflict to be more fruitfully resolved. But to be most effective they must be joined by alternative ways of thinking. Section 'Untangling values, beliefs and desires' explored the power of thinking differently in the context of internal conflict. It's really not much different with the inter-personal kind.

One of the key shifts in attitude and intent that leads to more understanding, acceptance and peace in relationships is described in section: 'Distinct modes of conflict'. Essentially, by focusing on working together (collaborating) when there are disagreements and looking for *mutually beneficial outcomes* (win/win instead of win/ lose or win/don't care) a lot of discord can be avoided. As we'll see, it's really not about being a saint or being a push-over. Neither is it about substituting carrots in place of sticks. Rather, this frame of mind allows our natural, often forgotten, emotional intelligence to come into full play – alongside our other ways of thinking – in a way that is squarely directed towards genuine peace.

Another major catalyst of conflict is thinking that we need something from someone, when in fact there are very often other ways of meeting our needs. It's true that, as social animals, we are dependent on each other, to a large extent, for our well-being. But when our vulnerability is followed to its routes it allows us to be more resourceful and more free. By embracing what lies at the route of our desire, we can avoid mistaking our underlying needs for a particular *strategy* that may involve a particular person.

Arguments

There are few relationships that are without the odd argument. Arguments or disputes – where some part of the conflict is out in the open – are one type of conflict that cause a lot of anguish for people. I have a vivid childhood memory of my parents arguing. I was sitting on the wooden steps, with a partial view into the kitchen. I could hear them yelling and I saw the plates smashing against the wall. I don't remember why they were arguing, but they often did. I just remember the fear, sadness, confusion and sense of hopelessness. Why do relationships get like that sometimes? It's a combination of factors, internal and external conflict and the roles we play. Arguments are not always so traumatic and they don't always have strong affects on others around. But unless we take care of our frame of mind, they do have a tendency to escalate.

Arguments generally start with a difference of thinking and are an attempt to establish the rightness, worth or awareness of a point of view. They are often thought of as a kind of fight, but arguments can be many things: habitual, explosive, violent, vicious, serious, diplomatic, peaceful, playful, polite, etc. The *uses* of argument also include: getting an emotional response where other attempts at intimacy fail, venting life stresses, or contesting authority, strength or boundaries. What kinds do you tend to get into?

Arguments can certainly be useful at times. They can help air important issues and find mutually agreeable solutions, make feelings clearer and resolve misunderstandings.

It's vitally important to allow space in a relationship for arguments to be had, or disagreements to be heard. Being evasive, or refusing to listen is likely to create feelings of *disconnection* and allow frustration or resentment to grow.

The kind of arguments we want to *avoid* though are those where someone is left with a sense of being unheard, forced, cruelly treated or treated without common respect. Doing the following should help prevent your arguments from descending into these destructive kinds and to stay productive:

Practice *acceptance* – especially listening – together with *honesty with humanity* (see section: 'The five keys'). These are traits we develop early in life, with our natural curiosity and openness. But the trials of life can lead to them being masked.

Develop empathy by *separating feelings from judgements* (which we'll explore shortly). Again, we already know how to do this, it is just a matter of remembering and beginning to untangle ourselves from our conditioning.

It turns out the above two elements provide a very powerful means of addressing many sorts on conflict in relationships.

Distinct modes of conflict

It seems to me that conflicts (in the general sense, including disagreements, arguments and fights) have essentially two modes or styles which can be entered into:

1. **Collaborative:** Working together to understand each other well and to find a mutually beneficial outcome to the conflict, takes centre stage. There is a strong will to be constructive and find a peaceful resolution.

2. **Threat focused:** The other party presents a threat to you or something you value and removing that threat takes top priority. Threat focused conflicts tend to be combative or defensive; it's *you against them*. It's very hard to feel peaceful in this mode.

If you're arguing over limited resources critical for survival and the other party is about to put a spear in you to make their point, then true, there's fairly little scope for seeking deeper understanding and exploring feelings. Sometimes it really is imperative to focus on the threat and avoid defeat. But if things aren't quite so dire there's probably the *option* to collaborate, or at least to attempt to. Incidentally, how can you be 'collaborative' if you're actually fighting someone? One option is to fight to protect rather than injure and then, if safe, to engage in dialogue. Another potential option may be to make the fight playful (we discuss play fighting later on).

Choices in communication like blaming, assuming a motive, demanding and criticising can *push* a disagreement into threat-focus mode; while choices like listening to and respecting the other person's needs and point of view and sharing feelings directly can help keep it in collaborative mode. Essentially, judgements can easily create opportunities for the other person to think they're misunderstood or threatened. Therefore it pays to know when you express judgements and to know how to express yourself without them. (As we'll discuss later, sometimes the appeal of judgemental communication is that it allows you to not express so much of what's going on for you.) The various kinds of inner-personal conflicts discussed in the first part of this book can also be strong catalysts of threat-focus.

The attacking or defending of threat focused conflict is not necessarily overt, it can manifest in subtle ways such as: deceit, jealously, manipulation, stubbornness and resentment.

Naturally it's possible to straddle the boundary; to make an effort to collaborate but keep one eye out for cheating or betrayal, half expecting it, and to see outcomes more in terms of who is winning or losing. Just as naturally, the results are mixed. See section: 'Projections and prophesy' for why it might not be the best option.

The prevailing attitude of working together for mutual good –

collaboration – can still exist even where some threat is present. It's a choice. Showing that you have this attitude – and that you trust the other person to take it too – is a powerful diffuser of fear and anger. Also, in a broader sense, when you take this attitude in conflicts you're collaborating towards a better relationship, with more understanding of each other and how to work together. The very act of creating a solution to a conflict together is a bonding process. Note that *collaborating* goes far beyond simply *cooperating*.

But the fact is, dealing with things in a threat focused way works, sort of. You can get by with it and even get a lot of the things that you want, with sufficient strength. It's just that it's often not the best strategy for the job, especially if you want things to end in peace, empathy and love. The diagram on page 217 illustrates this point. (For more ideas on changing your strategies, see sections: 'Untangling values, beliefs and desires' and 'Our attitude to change'.)

What happens when two animals fight a lot and one of them tends to lose? Besides the physical injuries the loser will tend to become submissive and even depressed. It's the same with people when their conflicts are like fights. It's also the case that there doesn't actually have to be a threat for there to be a 'threat-focus'. Just acting on a *sense* of one is enough to get the side effects discussed. In some cases a defensive reaction can actually *prompt* another person to 'attack', where they otherwise wouldn't. If they are also threat focused, defensiveness can be seen as antagonistic (e.g. "you're just playing the victim and fishing for sympathy so you get your way") or as an opportunity for victory – and for playing a known role (see from page 117).

We can learn from the above that standing up for what is important to you (being assertive, without being aggressive), is key to maintaining equality in a relationship and to securing or restoring a collaborative approach to conflict.

Resolving conflict is often written about while focusing on the art of persuasion and influence – how to get other people to do what you'd like and feel they're doing the 'right thing'. That's an appealing approach, if you already take the view that conflicts are 'you against them' and typically zero-sum games. I.e. the approach is often just a refinement of threat-focus strategy. The approach taken by this book favours collaborative solutions as the 'smarter way'. As we will see, although it's not the objective, influence is a natural by-product of the collaborative approach.

One habit that's very helpful in finding a collaborative frame of mind, is considering the alternative interpretations (see page 70) whenever we think about why someone acted as they did.

What is your body saying?

A brief note on body language: If you've read the rest of this book you'll know (if you didn't already) that whatever kind of conflict, it's not just verbal dialogue that matters, *body-language is key*. So use that most powerful and subtle channel for the message you want to communicate.

If you, for instance, want to send a message of calmness and positive intent – as well as help yourself feel those things more – try *relaxing* your breathing and shoulders, *softening* your voice and offering a *friendly* smile. Similarly if you're breathing heavily and your hands are clenched, it hardly matters what you're saying, the message is going to be 'anger/pain/frustration' (unless of course you're in a more amorous state). Make your body congruent with your mind.

Physical rapport building skills are as useful in conflict as anywhere else in relationships. Show with your *body* that you're ready to collaborate and it will be easier to do so. E.g. mirroring (see page 83) – not just in body but also in verbal language – can really help get a sense of common ground and trust. Sometimes that's needed before someone is willing to open up about their feelings and needs and work together with you.

Observing, feeling, needing, requesting

We'll now focus on conflict resolution and in particular an approach that epitomises the 'collaborative' approach, discussed in the previous section. 'Observing, feeling, needing, requesting.' These words mark out a straightforward four step process for communicating in a way that empowers you to resolve conflict, work better together and find more peace and love in your relationships. This process, developed by Marshall B. Rosenberg, is known as Nonviolent Communication (NVC) or Compassionate Communication. It has some common ground with Buddhism and other philosophical and spiritual traditions which emphasize compassion and understanding. Because of its effectiveness and direct, uncluttered approach, we'll explore NVC is some depth over the following pages. It is offered here both as a practical tool and as a philosophy which you may find valuable.

Is there *anyone* who doesn't want to be heard and understood, to be able to share feelings and needs without shame, to be able to take responsibility without blame, to give and receive joyfully without obligation, and to know the people in their life more deeply? And yet for so many people this seems like a very distant set of goals. NVC provides a simple and natural process to actually achieve them. The process has been used with great success in many areas, from marriage counselling, to treating unhealthy eating habits, to multi-national conflict resolution in the middle east.

NVC works by focusing on present feelings and needs and strategies for meeting them *mutually,* while avoiding judgemental communication, including blame, assuming motive, diagnosis, demands or threats. In the case of our own judgements and those we may hear from the person(s) we are communicating with, we look for the feelings and needs which lie *behind* them and focus on those. Expressing our observations and relating them to feelings and needs takes the place of exchanging judgements.

Requests replace demands or coercive behaviour.

At the heart of the NVC process – and indeed the 'working together with' attitude shift, previously mentioned – is the pursuit of *respectful empathy*. Empathy means the understanding of another person's internal state in terms of their feelings, what they want or need and what they think or believe. Psychoanalyst Heinz Kohut, described empathy concisely as: 'the capacity to think and feel oneself into the inner life of another person'. NVC focuses on the core empathic aspects of feelings and needs.

Because it's based on the natural abilities to empathize and work together that we all have within us, anyone can use NVC – there's no need to be a psychologist. In fact, even if we start with just identifying and expressing our own feelings without making judgements – and listening for the feelings of the other person(s) without focusing on any judgements – then we can avoid a large chunk of grief in our relationships.

Before we continue, it's useful to be clear on the central terms, so here are some working definitions:

'Observation' means sensing something that is independent of your opinion. True observations are free of judgement. It's easy to blend the two together without realising it though. E.g. "I get upset when I see/hear you being rude to me." How can you observe 'rudeness' when the same act will be 'rude' to one person and 'frank' or 'assertive' to another? It's more accurate to say "When I see/hear you do things that I *think* are rude I get upset." If we want to actually state our observation along with our feeling about it we might say: "When I hear you say my nose is big/my shirt is vile/I eat like a hyena, I feel upset." An observation can also be of a thought, e.g.: "When I remember you looking at me with that particular expression and sighing I feel miserable."

In the above rudeness example, the distinctions might seem fine or trivial, however, the difference they make is profound. When judgement is presented, not as opinion but as observed fact (i.e. confused with an observation or mixed in with one) the unhelpful effects of that judgement are multiplied. It gives people more impetus to argue and fight, or otherwise to think they are misunderstood or at fault and then to feel guilt or shame.

'**Feelings**' here mean distinct emotional experiences, separate from any associated interpretations of what they mean or what has happened or will happen and why. The table on page 160 lists a number of examples.

'**Needs**' mean strong desires or values *underlying* any strategy or plan of action. E.g. a strategy might be "I'd like to go to the beach with you today", where the need is 'companionship'. Needs are deeper than preferences. Feelings result when needs are met or go unmet. While there can be some cultural or gender bias, needs tend to be common to people; they are innate. This means it's not too hard to relate to each other, if we discover what our needs are.

Needs are aspects of our nature and every such aspect has the *potential* to be manifest in a wholesome and non-harmful way. No need is bad and in so far as self-realization is positive, so is seeking to meet a need. This leads to the profound understanding that however much suffering the *strategies* for meeting our needs may cause, behind every strategy, sometimes deeply buried, is simply *a positive intent to meet a natural need*. Remembering this tends to calm the mind and open the heart to compassion.

(Where certain actions or strategies lead to suffering, being aware of an underlying positive intent is not a *justification*, just a first step towards allowing responsibility to be taken fully.) The table on page 159 lists numerous examples of needs.

'**Request**' means expressing a desire for a particular action. The idea in NVC is that everyone's needs are served best when people act out of a want to enrich each other's life. This means if I make a request of you, *I only want you to do as I request if you're happy and willing to do so*. That rules out trying to make you feel obliged to say yes, or guilty if you say no. That's not to say some negotiation won't happen or that I won't try to make absolutely sure you understand my feelings and needs. It just means I only want you to agree to my request if it also meets some of your needs, whatever they may be.

Requests form the final stage of the NVC process: Observation → Feelings → Needs → Requests. The process is cyclical, so following requests (or needs, where there were no requests) would often be more observations which help to clarify what was shared or requested. This may result in more feelings being shared and so on, towards a peaceful resolution.

'Judgement' is the forming of an opinion, decision or evaluation by discerning and comparing. In NVC, judgements are essentially any kind of interpretation or evaluation about the world, yourself or other people, beyond identifying and expressing *only* your feelings, needs or direct observations. Judgement thus includes blame, criticism, laying responsibility, diagnosing, categorizing, assuming motives, and by extension making demands or threats.

In the NVC process the following types of *value-judgements* are necessary: identifying your feeling – 'I feel ...', identifying your need – 'I have a need for ...', or judging the effectiveness of something in meeting your need – 'This action/strategy/plan/ idea/situation/object/... helps/doesn't help meet my need for ...'. These value-judgements are distinguished from other kinds that make statements about a perceived objective truth or a commonly accepted truth, such as *moral judgements*: e.g. 'This action/strategy/ plan/idea/situation/object/person is right/wrong/good/bad'. From this point when the word 'judgement' is used please take it as referring to types other than the above value-judgements.

Do the previous descriptions of judgement and observation appear restrictive? In some ways they are. But the *apparent* economy of communicating without judgement can help to express what really matters in a more direct way than would be possible with all the baggage that tends to go with judgement.

On the flip side you could say that communicating chiefly in terms of rights and wrongs, evaluations, categorisations and other judgements, plasters over much of the richness and subtlety that actually exists within our feelings and needs. (See sub-section: 'A rich language', from page 157.)

Empathy and open, respectful intent

The analytical and interpretation forming ability of our minds is a glorious thing and has enabled many human accomplishments. To use NVC, there is no need to turn that part of our brain off; on the contrary, we simply tweak how we use it. By using our own experience and intelligence we can take what we observe in someone else and try to find what they *might* be feeling and needing. In this way we can 'translate' any judgements we might hear and achieve a deeper empathy. By then focusing more on the aspects of feelings and needs, unhelpful judgements can be further bypassed. At that point we can use our intelligence to find the best strategies to meet the needs of everyone involved.

Here's a before and after example: A couple arrange an important meeting with friends and one partner is late, as they often are. After some initial words the partner left waiting says:

A) "You *always* do that, *showing me up* by being so late! How do you think I felt sitting there alone? *Did you even think? It seems like you don't care. You give me so much stress, you know that? Is it too much to ask for a little support? I don't know why I even bother.* Do it again and *I might just leave.*"

B) "When we've both agreed to spend time with friends and you're late I feel *frustrated* and *embarrassed,* because I'd like more *support* and *reliability.* I also want to feel *respectful,* as a couple, to our friends. It's really important to me to find a way of meeting my needs and also understanding what's going on for you. Can you tell me what you understand by what I just said?"

Version *A* might help to off-load pent up emotion and give an impression of the seriousness of feelings, but it's not particularly conducive to developing understanding and a peaceful outcome. Version *B* is still firm and assertive but without the blame or judgement. See how the open honesty of it gets to the core of what matters to the person saying it?

Without the barrier of threat or judgement both the feelings of the partner and *why* they're feeling that way are more clearly presented. Thus there's much more opportunity to empathize and respond in a constructive fashion. In this way disputes can more easily be focused on finding mutually agreeable solutions, instead of simply defending and attacking and going around in circles.

Notice in the above example, that in version *B* the expressions of needs could easily be turned into (or interpreted as) personal judgements: "I'd like more support and reliability.", "I also want to feel respectful, as a couple, to our friends." → "You're un-supportive, unreliable and disrespectful." But by turning the expression of needs into accusations the communication tends to get less constructive. Obviously if we're really thinking in terms of accusations under the surface then eventually it will come through, however 'nicely' we put it. But if we truly focus on just identifying our needs – without a sense of fault, blame or what someone else 'is' – then it leads to a different frame of mind and a way of being that genuinely reflects this absence of judgement.

When we try to understand someone else's feelings and needs, we're not trying to diagnose them, rather just to have a respectful and constructive empathy with them. With practice we can find many ways to express this intention.

It often works out well for us, where we have the option, if we first try to understand, before trying to be understood. That's because people often want to know that you care about what's going on for them, *before* they're willing to listen to what's going on for you. Empathy begets empathy.

Questions to aid mutual understanding

To relate observations to feelings, this simple pattern might be useful: "When I see/hear/remember/imagine *state observation* I feel *state emotion(s)*". E.g. "When I hear you say *that you don't care in that tone*, I feel *sad* and a little *confused* ..." you can then go on to share what needs you have which are, or are not, being met: "... because I have a need for *clarity* that is not being met and I'd like to feel some *affection* from you."

It's important to relate your feelings to your needs as above. Otherwise our words could simply be taken as meaning: 'when you do ... you make me feel ...', which is not the intent with NVC. Thinking of someone else as 'the cause' for our feelings robs us of our power to take charge of our own inner state (see section: 'Responsibility').

One risk of expressing your needs so directly is the other person(s) thinking that you expect them to meet your needs, or see them as responsible for doing so. Again, this really isn't the intent with NVC. Like with feelings, the idea is we're responsible for meeting our own needs. If there is confusion, saying something like this could help: "I'm telling you what my needs are, not because I want you to feel any pressure to meet them. I just want us both to understand each other more clearly. I'd like to see if there's a way for us to help meet each other's needs, but without us feeling *responsible* for doing so. How does that sound to you?"

Similarly we can try to understand the other person:

"Are you feeling *state guessed emotion(s)*" or "It looks/sounds/ seems like you're feeling *state guessed emotion(s)*." You can then follow that by "Is that because you have a need for *state guessed unmet need(s)*?" or "Do you want/Would you like more *state guessed unmet need(s)*?"

You may be thinking: Why not just ask "What are you

feeling? What are you needing?" This can work well in some circumstances. But if there is tension between you and the person you're talking to it can easily sound like you're adopting the position of a shrink, analysing them. It also lacks the degree of effort to understand them, that making a guess at what's going on for them shows. If someone sees you're genuinely trying to understand them (without judgement) they tend to be more willing to open up.

It's really not so important that we guess correctly first time what's going on for the other person (or if it takes us multiple guesses). Mistakes are OK! If our intent is to respectfully form a deeper understanding then the other person will often help us out and give us a clue about what they're feeling or needing.

If we want to get clear on what someone is reacting to *before* discussing feelings we can simply ask: "Are you reacting to *name specific action/event?*" But be careful it doesn't slip into: "Are you *feeling ... because I ...*". 'Reacting to' something is not the same as 'feeling because of' something – and it does no-one any favours to claim responsibility for someone else's feelings. Getting clear on what stimulated a particular reaction, however, can help you identify the likely feelings and needs.

When you're trying to understand what's going on for someone, stopping them for clarification if you're getting lost can be very helpful for everyone. A simple: "Excuse me, are you saying that you're feeling ... about ... because you're needing ...?" can work wonders. Section: 'Assertiveness' talks more on the subject of interrupting.

Making requests and hearing requests

Requests are most effectively made and received after a sense of mutual understanding of feelings and needs is reached. Often, after we share what's going on for us, there's some specific action or 'thing' we'd like to follow from that. If so, we have the helpful option of a request (rather than a demand).

To encourage someone to say what they'd like to happen, requests may be invited in many ways. Two examples are: "Is there something you'd like to request of me?" and "What can I do to make life more wonderful for you?"

A simple and clear way of making a request is: "Would you be willing to ... ?" Or, to first see how an idea sits: "How would it work for you if ... ?" Understanding how our request might affect someone else's needs helps things to stay collaborative.

It's useful to remember that requests are *strategies* to get a certain result which meets one or more needs. *There are almost always multiple strategies for achieving any one result and many results which can meet a need.* This means it's often counter-productive to get attached to any one particular request being accepted and carried out. There is most likely another way.

Requests have the best chance of being accepted and carried out if they are: specific, positive ('to do ...' rather than 'to *not* do ...') and physically actionable. The table on page 147 shows some examples.

Have you ever had someone talk with intense feeling to you and a sense of expectation, but been completely unclear about what response they'd like from you? Or perhaps there have been times where you wanted someone to take some action and were sure they would just know what to do without you spelling it out, but somehow they didn't seem to have a clue?

This happens because when feelings are running high it's easy to forget that others don't have the same understanding as we do, even if they know us well in many ways. Also, when we're already experiencing pressure and confusion, it's harder to relate to someone else. So for this reason and to avoid needless upset for everyone, if something really matters to you it's a good idea to make a specific, positive and actionable request. Suppose you'd really like some support from your partner, for instance. What specific thing could they do that would really help you? How could you make that a request?

Specific, actionable request	Non-actionable or vague request
Would you be willing to:	*Would you be willing to:*
Tell me what I am doing that you appreciate?	Appreciate what I'm doing? *(requesting a feeling – not 'doable')*
Give me some hugs/tell me I'm OK/acknowledge that you accept my independence/trust me and let me cook tonight/etc.?	Love me? *(requesting a feeling, and one which could mean quite different things to each person)*
Listen to me say what I want to say now?	Take some interest in what I have to say? *(vague, suggests lack of interest)*
Wash up for half the meals and take turns to hoover on Sundays?	Do more cleaning? *(actionable, but vague)*
Spend more time with me when we're both at home, on a few evenings of the week?	Not spend so long in your study? *(vague, due to negative clause)*
Replace my bike that was stolen when you borrowed it and left it unlocked?	Take responsibility for my stolen bike? *(vague and could be confused with an accusation of blame)*
Tell me what you would have liked/would like me to do?	Tell me what I should do/have done? *(requesting a judgement of right-doing and vague. 'Right' according to and for who?)*

NVC isn't really about 'getting what you want', it's about finding a way of meeting everyone's needs as far as possible. Keeping that in mind, if we get a 'no' response to a particular request it simply indicates that our chosen strategy (the requested action) is leaving some of that person's needs unmet. Either that or they have a more present need to be heard and understood a little better, or want reassurance that your request isn't really a *demand*. No-one likes to have their freedom stepped on.

One particularly useful request is for a reflection on what was heard by the other person(s): e.g. "Would you mind telling me what you heard me say?" or "Could you tell me what you understood by that?" While it may seem a little odd, it's extremely useful in finding out if we've been able to communicate clearly. Sometimes even when we do our best to express observations, feelings and needs, the other person(s) doesn't really hear this, but instead interprets our expression as judgement of various kinds. Just getting to the point where we hear each other clearly is so valuable that it's really worth checking.

When we make a request for reflection, it's not that we're testing the other person's ability to hear or understand. Our intent is to test our *own* ability to communicate clearly enough in that moment. If someone reacts as if you're interrogating or analysing them when you make this request, try to express the above intent.

When making any request be as clear as you need to be that it *is* a request and not a demand in disguise. (This is an example of where asking for reflection can be helpful.) If there is any doubt, be positive that there is no intended obligation or implied guilt, shame, or punishment for not accepting and fulfilling the request. Obviously if someone is used to hearing demands this may take some effort and time until they start hearing the request in the request.

Here's an NVC example that starts from a request being heard as a demand:

Adie: "Would you mind getting some groceries for dinner tonight please?"

Bill: *what you're *really* saying is if I don't I'm a cheap-skate and you'll give me a guilt trip for it, so do I have a choice?* "OK, sure I'll go." *(said reluctantly)*

Adie: "Wait a sec. It sounds like you're less than happy about the idea. Can you tell me what you heard me say?"

Bill: "You think I'm a cheapskate and that I should buy more food around here. Even though you asked 'nicely', I know you'll make me feel guilty if I say no."

Here, what Bill heard in their mind was actually more of a demand since they perceived an implicit threat of guilt if they didn't comply with what Adie wanted. Uncovering this creates the opportunity to explore those feelings and whatever unmet needs there are in Bill. Note that Adie picked up on Bill's initial reluctant agreement. Agreements that result from a sense of coercion often lead to far more trouble than they were worth.

Adie: "So you're feeling pressured and maybe a bit resentful because you think that I think you're not spending fairly and you'd like me to see things differently, is that right?"

Bill: "Well, yeah I suppose, except I don't really feel resentful. I feel miserable, because I worry that maybe I don't spend enough on food here and that you're right."

Adie: "Oh, I see, thanks. So you'd like to feel a sense of fairness in your contributions and you worry that they might not be fair and that I think they aren't?"

Bill: "Yes."

Adie: "I'm really glad that you could tell me this and that I understand better now what's been bothering you."

At this point, after Bill's feelings and needs have been understood and separated out from judgements, Adie can share more of what's going on for them. That might be that they really have no issue over fairness, or that actually they would appreciate a little more contribution from Bill. Options for getting a greater sense of fairness for everyone could then be explored in this non-judgemental style.

How can you hear a request, even when judgemental or demanding language is being directed at you? To do this it's essential that you first get clear on what the feelings and needs are of the other person(s). This works in two ways. One, when they have a sense of being deeply understood they can more easily relax and be less demanding. Two, when you have that understanding you can translate what you hear into words like: "You'd like me to *guess what they're 'requesting'* because that would help to meet your need for *guess their need(s)*. And you're feeling desperate/frustrated/angry/anxious/... because those needs aren't being met and you want to be sure that they will be." We'll talk more about dealing with anger shortly.

If, in any situation, we hear a request that we're less than happy to agree to, how can we say 'no'? A straight "no/no thanks" can work well, but sometimes more information/feedback is useful. In this case a 'no' can be a simple matter of reflecting what we heard and stating our feelings, relating to which of our needs are not met by the request (or the idea of agreeing to it). E.g. "When I hear you ask me to stay in tonight I feel slightly restless, because I have a need to get some exercise and fresh air." Otherwise, or additionally, we might reply with a suggested alternative that includes the other person. E.g. "I'd prefer to go out tonight, but if you'd like to join me, I'd enjoy your company."

Of course, when we *are* happy to agree to a request, saying what needs of ours are *met* by it can really aid mutual appreciation.

Dealing with anger and aggression

Firstly, let's consider what anger means and where it comes from.

Is it possible to feel anger without also perceiving that something has happened that *shouldn't* have happened, that there has been a *wrong* committed? It seems that this is a pre-requisite of the feeling – along with a sense of *threat* to you or something you value.

What then does anger achieve? It obviously serves a valuable purpose since it can be seen not only throughout human history but also in other animals that have a sense of social order. According to the research of Dr Brosnan and Dr de Waal[14], for example, Capuchin monkeys show their displeasure if given a smaller reward than a partner receives for performing the same task, like a piece of cucumber instead of a grape.

Anger is a strong sign that some of your needs are not being met and it gives you a certain power. If you don't suppress it, it drives you to take *action*, which may help you to protect yourself or that which you value. (Sometimes this action can be used constructively for self-change, where it's channelled more into determination

---

14 Sarah F. Brosnan & Frans B. M. de Waal (2003) "Monkeys reject unequal pay"
 Nature 425, 297-299

and learning.) If you do suppress – rather than *transform* – anger, it will degrade your well-being, while still leaving clues for others to pick up, as in passive aggression. Eventually you may snap and let it all out in one go.

Anger also allows you to prompt feelings of fear, guilt and shame in other people, which can either lead them to do as you'd like (removing the perceived threat), or instead fight back (increasing the perceived threat). Because of these factors, experiencing anger can be seen as a signpost which reads "Welcome to 'threat-focus' country" – it's very hard not to be in this mode of conflict when feeling anger.

Just about everyone loses their tempter sometimes and simply venting it may seem like a good way of releasing the tension. However, anger can be transformed into more effective (and less violence or resentment fuelling) self-expression through getting more in touch with your unmet needs that are *causing* the anger and communicating those needs. This opens the path to empathy. Often the fullest way of releasing anger is to take this approach. (This is the case whether our anger is directed inward or outward.) If empathy is not gained, the best strategy may then be just to take some time out before trying again.

How can you be peaceful if you're trying to empathize with someone who is very angry or agitated? By developing a deeper understanding – not engaging with unnecessary or alienating judgement – there is *opportunity* to focus on a collaborative resolution rather than threat. If you can see the needs behind their feelings there's less impetus to be defensive; they're not acting *against* you, they're acting *for* their needs, which tends to mean less stress or anxiety. Obviously doing this can be pretty challenging if you think you're in personal danger.

Aggression (violent behaviour) is an expression of anger with an intent to harm or punish. Sometimes it is possible to address aggression through empathizing and sometimes it is necessary to use protective force, which we discuss in a later section.

Using the above understandings, let's see how we can address anger or aggression when it's directed at us. Imagine two people in a close relationship, Sam and Ali. Sam tends to be overbearing during arguments. Ali tends to walk away or get defensive by shouting back or capitulating and admitting fault, none of which leads to a happy ending. In this scenario, Sam asked Ali to pick up some shoes they were having fixed. Ali agreed to do that, but forgot, which will now cause Sam some inconvenience. Sam loses his/her temper and starts shouting. But this time Ali decides to do something different. (To get a good flavour for how NVC can work in such situations we'll explore this scenario in some detail.)

Sam: "I asked you to do one simple thing and you forgot! How could you do that?" (*shouting*)

Ali: "I can see you're really upset about it."

Even though Ali's distressed by the shouting, here he/she is just trying to reflect back the feeling they sense in Sam, so that Sam can begin to feel understood. This and the rest of what Ali says, is said with a *calm tone of voice and posture*. (Congruent body-language is crucial.)

Sam: "Uh, no kidding! How do you expect me to trust you in future for something really important if you can't be relied on for such a simple thing!?" (*shouting*)

Sam's clearly very upset and it seems like the shoes may have a symbolic significance for other issues. Ali could get defensive here: "What are you talking about? It's just a pair of *shoes*, that I *forgot* to pick up *for you*. Now you're talking about not being able to trust me in future? Get a bloody grip!" - but resists the temptation. Ali could instead try to diagnose: "I think you're over-reacting. You've got some issues here that aren't my problem." But that can easily have an inflammatory affect, so Ali carries on trying to empathize.

Ali: "It seems like having me pick up those shoes was really important to you. And that you'd like to be able to rely on me for important things but when you saw I'd forgotten the shoes you were lead to question whether you could."

Sam: "Well, how should I know? I was relying on you and you let me down. Since I'll need them in the afternoon, now I'll have to miss my lunch break tomorrow and cancel a meeting with a friend to pick them up. Great." (*calming down slightly, but still annoyed*)

Now Ali can see that Sam had a strong need for reliability that wasn't met and also understand the inconvenience that perhaps contributed to Sam's anger.

Ali: "So it's really important to you to feel sure that if you ask me to do something and I agree, that I'll do it. I'm sorry that my forgetting is leading you to cancel your plan to meet your friend. I wish I hadn't forgotten."

Note that Ali's not claiming to be the *cause* of Sam's feelings, only that their actions led to certain unwanted external consequences for Sam. (We'll discuss this point more later in section: 'Responsibility')

Sam: "Well thanks for apologising. Since it was your mistake, if you wanted to make it up to me you could pick them up first thing tomorrow. Can I trust you to do that?"

Now this is a pivotal moment in this conflict. On previous occasions Ali, because of feeling guilty, or afraid of more shouting, might quickly agree to do what Sam wants – even though he/she still feels hurt after being shouted at. Although Ali would like for Sam to trust them, to be calm and be able to meet his/her friend tomorrow, this time Ali doesn't want to act out of fear or guilt. Ali also knows that they would feel a lot better about agreeing to Sam's request if Sam understood their hurt feelings and needs for respect and calmness.

Ali: "I'd like you to trust me and for you to meet your friend tomorrow, but I don't want to act out of fear or guilt."

Sam: "What do you mean?"

Ali: "Right now if I agreed to pick up your shoes tomorrow it would also be because I was afraid of you getting angry and shouting at me again. It would also seem like I was admitting that I did something 'wrong' when I only intended to help."

Sam: "So what? Is it my fault you forgot? Is it my fault you got upset because I raised my voice slightly?" (*said angrily*) "Fine. I'll pick up the shoes then, it's obvious I have to rely on myself, so forget about it." (s*aid with a clipped tone*)

Here it seems like Sam interpreted what Ali said as an invite to feel guilty, then claimed it was all 'fine' in a tone of voice suggesting quite the contrary. When this kind of response goes unchecked, ill-feelings are likely to fester. Ali, feeling proud that they were able to stand up for themselves so far in a way that didn't mean attacking the other person, perseveres.

Ali: "Whoa there. It seems like I didn't express myself clearly. I'm not trying to blame you for anything Sam. I'm trying to let you know that I care about your feelings and needs and at the same time I'd like you to understand my feelings and needs. I'd like you to know that when I hear you raising your voice in the way you did I feel hurt and upset, because my needs for respect and calmness are not being met. Can you tell me what you heard me say?"

Sam: "Why?"

Ali: "I'd like to know that I've expressed myself clearly."

Sam: "If you insist. You said when I raise my voice you feel upset and hurt because you want respect and calmness. You care about my feelings and needs and at the same time want me to understand yours. And you're not trying to blame me." (*calmer*)

Ali: "Thank you. I feel so much better hearing you say that, it seems like you understand."

Now all that effort to empathize and avoid judgements seems to be paying off. Sam is now able to see things from a slightly different perspective.

Sam: "I'm sorry I upset you by raising my voice. I was just so frustrated and angry. I've been awful."

Ali: "It means a lot to me that you can understand how I feel and are sorry that I was upset, despite how much me collecting your shoes meant to you. But I wish you wouldn't judge yourself. I really don't want you to feel awful. And I'd be happy to get your shoes tomorrow morning."

Sam: "Thank you."

Ali: "There's just a couple of things on my mind. I can't be sure I wont forget something again one day, my memory isn't perfect and sometimes I get distracted, even though I fully intend to do what I say I'll do. I'd like for you to be able to accept that but still be able to see me as someone you can trust with important things."

Sam: "I'll try. It's difficult for me."

Ali: "Thank you. I know it's been difficult for you."

Sam: "So what was the other thing?"

Ali: "I'd also like to know if you'd be willing to find a gentler and more calm way of expressing your feelings towards me in future, rather than raising your voice."

Sam: "OK, I'll try. I see now how it affects you."

Ali: "Thank you, I'm so glad we could talk like this."

What started out as enmity is transformed into harmony through empathy, honest sharing and a focus on working together. There are lots of ways this dialogue could have gone, and lots more it could continue, but hopefully the above has demonstrated some of the 'active ingredients' of the NVC process and some common pitfalls to avoid.

One such pitfall would have been for Ali to dwell on Sam's angry judgements (instead of digging deeper for the underlying needs). If Ali had done that they might have come away thinking they were 'unreliable', 'stupid', 'over-sensitive' and feeling very guilty. Of course, it takes practice to engage on a deeper level than personal judgements.

On the subject of 'raising your voice' (less of a judgement in conversation than 'shouting' which is open to interpretation), it's a type of emotional vent that can be used to express many feelings, including: anger, desperation, frustration, pain and disconnection. When it's a case of losing your temper with someone, that may or may not be an issue in individual instances, but shouting (as they see it) at someone close to you habitually *will* be a destructive force in that relationship.

What about, in other arguments and other scenarios, getting responses such as: "I shout at/hit/otherwise punish you, *because* I care/want to help/love you"? Let's assume that it's, at least to some extent, their way of expressing some feelings that you value – albeit a destructive way that's really a tragic strategy for meeting some of their needs like: significance, certainty, connection, respect, etc. It's *very* important to separate strategy from feelings and needs here, and not fall into the trap: "Oh, since their feelings are good, and believing they feel that way helps meet some of my needs, that's OK then. *I'll just have to accept it as their way of showing their feelings and get used to it.*"

Instead, acknowledge the feelings: "I really appreciate/value that you care/want to help/love me." But be clear that their strategy isn't working well: "Even though that means a lot to me, when I hear/see/feel you ..., what I actually feel is pain/sadness/fear/terror/confusion/... I have a need for safety/respect/tenderness/calmness/..." In this way there's a chance that you can help them find a more compassionate way of expressing their feelings and meeting their needs, as well as saving yourself suffering.

Situations like this can be very difficult and sometimes communication doesn't lead to an acceptable resolution. However, applying the ideas of NVC should help you make the most of what hope there is in communicating. I say communicating and not just 'talking' because NVC is also very much in our body and voice. These channels convey our inner state even more strongly than the words we use (see sub-section: 'What is your body saying?' from page 137).

A similar approach as above can be tried where someone is taking out their emotional pain on themselves in a harmful way.

Just a clear expression of your emotional response to your observations of what they're doing and your needs/wants to support/protect/heal/understand (but without blame or other judgement) is a great start. If someone in such a vulnerable state thinks they're being negatively judged they're likely to close down to you. On the other hand it may be tempting to offer positive judgements about them, to try and raise their self-esteem. But, unless you have incredibly good rapport, this approach will also often result in them closing down, because in their mind you're not seeing what they really are, you don't *understand*. From my Samaritans experience, I know how valuable sticking to exploring their feelings is. See also, section: 'The role of judgements'.

A rich language

Because of our conditioning and the roles we sometimes settle into within relationships, it may take repeated efforts before making observations, expressing feelings and needs and exchanging requests becomes fluent, or even comfortable. A lot of people aren't used to doing that without making the kind of judgements we've talked about; even just finding the words you want can be a struggle initially. Persevering here, however, will enrich all your relationships.

One common reaction when you start trying to communicate differently and more directly is that people think you're trying to control them or be superior. E.g. "Why are you speaking to me in that weird language? Are you some kind of psychiatrist all of a sudden? Do you think you're better than me now? So, not only do I have to put up with your usual behaviour now, but I also have to deal with you patronising me? This is just too much!" The thing to do here, as well as empathizing, is just to keep coming back to your *intent* for trying out a different way of communicating. For instance, you might respond to the above (if it feels sincere to do so) with something like:

"I'm trying to communicate differently because I'd really like us to have a more peaceful and loving connection and I'm really tired of us fighting so much. I'd like you to know that I respect you deeply and that I just want to get to what matters without us judging each other. I want to give this a chance, because I don't know what else to do. How does that sit with you?" If you can be honest and straightforward with your positive intent then there's a greater chance that you'll be trusted. Fortunately, NVC is something you can introduce in small increments to your life. To get a taster of the benefits, you needn't leap right in from the start.

I've found that some people also have the fear that using this kind of language will take the excitement out of a relationship; imagining some kind of oppressive calm or scrutiny of words. It really depends on your approach. Since I started using NVC in my relationships, I've noticed that it leads to more excitement not less. By focusing on the core intent of honesty and respectful empathy, seeing the method only as supportive structure to build on, it becomes easier to reach those moments of deep connection and authenticity. (Obviously, a mechanical or insincere use of NVC methods gets rather different results.)

As an aid for ideas when using NVC, I've included a short list of feelings and needs on the following pages. Both lists are subjectively grouped into rough 'families' (with some repeats). As an exercise you may wish to extend and reorganize them. Even just looking at these small lists it becomes apparent what a rich field our feelings and needs are and what subtle hues of emotion and realization of our nature we can experience.

The needs list is inspired by Manfred Max-Neef's work on universal human needs. Needs are repeated where they seem to fit into multiple groups. Indeed needs are very interrelated things. They also have no strict hierarchy, except perhaps for basic survival, or subsistence and personal safety, but even that can be overridden by needs to protect, love, contribute, etc.

Needs can seem like tricky things to pin down. When is a

'need' really just a strategy, desire or belief? Sometimes needs seem pretty close to feelings, and other times just like values. I think the critical aspect of a need is that it encapsulates a quality of being or experience, that leads to an enriched and more fulfilled existence. There is also a reciprocal element to needs, i.e. they are inherently about sharing or they have a giving and receiving side to them (e.g. to give *and* receive support/affection/ knowledge/trust/hope/etc.) By experiencing both sides we gain the fullest fulfilment of that need in our life.

The process of looking for our needs, especially in relation to our present feelings, is helpful because it empowers us. It makes our inner state more self-contained: *'I feel ... because I need ...'.* We are then freer to make choices and take action that assists in meeting our identified needs – resulting in the feelings we'd *like* to have.

Needs
Subsistence, health, vitality, rest, movement, air, food, water, shelter, touch
Safety, protection, security, stability, trust, well-being
Affection, connection, love, intimacy, sexual expression, touch, passion, desirability, companionship, tenderness
Nurture, care, support, giving, protection, companionship
Identity, sense of place, respect, integrity, authenticity, honesty, separation, independence, self-expression, acceptance, mourning
Purpose, significance, contribution, meaning, hope, mourning
Participation, connection, belonging, fellowship, cooperation, acceptance, appreciation, respect, companionship
Leisure, relaxation, peace, calm, harmony
Understanding, clarity, certainty, trust, knowledge, mastery
Creation, change, variety, adventure, spontaneity, challenge, discovery, learning, growth, stimulation, inspiration, exploration
Freedom, choice, space, independence
Joy, play, humour, celebration

Feelings resulting from: met needs (left) and unmet needs (right)	
Affectionate, loving, tender, warm, connected, playful	Aversion, animosity, hostile, repulsed, appalled
Confident, empowered, proud, open, strong	Afraid, panicked, terrified, desperate, suspicious, wary, dread, worried,
Safe, secure, certain, centred	Vulnerable, insecure, fragile
Engaged, focused, absorbed, entranced, intrigued, alert	Angry, livid, resentful, incensed
Inspired, wonder, amazed, awed, illuminated, admiration	Confused, lost, puzzled, dazed, bewildered, hesitant, overwhelmed
Excited, aroused, eager, energetic, enthusiastic, surprised, passionate	Disquiet, alarmed, restless, upset, shocked, troubled
Blissful, exhilarated, ecstatic, thrilled, elated, radiant	Embarrassed, ashamed, guilty, mortified, self-conscious
Grateful, moved, appreciative, respect, fellowship, connected, honoured, admiration	Fatigued, lethargic, sleepy, tired, weary, exhausted, listless
	Disconnected, distant, numb, distracted, bored, isolated, lost
Hopeful, encouraged, expectant, optimistic	Pain, agony, grief, hurt, lonely, torment, remorse, regret
Joyful, happy, jubilant, pleased, amused, playful, merry	Sad, despair, forlorn, hopeless, melancholy, gloomy, wretched, disappointed, depressed
Peaceful, calm, content, still, trusting, relieved, relaxed, centred, grounded	Annoyed, dismayed, exasperated, frustrated, flustered, impatient
Refreshed, recovered, rested, enlivened, revived	Tense, nervous, anxious, edgy, stressed, cranky, jittery
	Yearning, nostalgic, pining

In the above list of feelings you may have noticed some conspicuous absences, like:

'entitled, accepted, manipulated, superior, inferior, beautiful, ugly, put down, taken for granted, violated, used, victimized, clever, stupid, unheard, judged, wronged, threatened, humiliated, vengeful, contempt, envy' (The list could go on for pages.)

It's true that we can have a very strong *sense* of items in the above short list, however, they are not strictly *just* emotions. They also involve interpreting someone's intent, thoughts, actions or ability. Such judgements may be accurate or not, but the aim here is to separate out the emotions, so that we at least have the option of communicating without the judgement. It's by no means an exact science and there's no point in getting tied down in semantics; something can be a 'feeling' in the sense that it is experienced and that it has a distinct flavour to it. But the idea is that, that experience is composed of *underlying* feelings which can be separated out from judgement – regardless of any role the judgement had in the origin of a feeling.

Let's take 'unheard' as an example. You might *think* someone is not hearing you or not listening (and it could be true). But the emotion or *feeling, as distinct from judgement* might be one of disconnection or distance and frustration. Hence 'unheard' is feelings + judgements.

How about a particularly strong impression like humiliation? Humiliation is where you are put down and feel hurt because you deem being put down as a violation. So there may be thoughts that someone wanted to hurt you, show you to be deficient, flawed or gravely at fault, as less than them or less than you *should* be, etc. All this combined with a sense of undeserving, victimisation or disrespect. Powerful stuff. What feelings can be distinguished from this? Perhaps: torment, shame, despair, vulnerability, being overwhelmed, resent, anger. There may also be a sharp *loss* of the feelings: self-respect, pride and confidence.

One clue that feelings and judgements are getting unintentionally mixed together is using language like:

"I feel *that/like/as if/you/they/I* ..." or "I feel ... *by you.*"

For instance: "I feel *like* you did that on purpose." → "I think you did that on purpose." or "I feel threatened *by you*" → "I think your intentions towards me are detrimental and I feel unsafe around you now."

It seems, in connection with needs, our judgements have an

immediate effect on our own feelings. When our interpretation of the world changes, so does our position in it, our sense of meaning and so too in the broadest sense our relationships. Thus we get an emotional response. So, by *changing the personal meaning of our experiences*, judgements determine how and whether we experience our needs. By using observation in place of judgement where we can and shifting what's left more to *value-judgements* we open our inner world up to deeper truth and empathy.

That pretty much concludes the introduction to NVC. I can recommend "Nonviolent Communication: A Language of Life" by Marshall B. Rosenberg, as a good reference. Some of the following sections will now build around the principles of NVC.

Practice time and pausing for thought

To help you really put NVC into practice in your life, if you would like to see the difference, here are some exercises to try:

Translating: How can you translate the following statements into observations, feeling, needs and (optional) requests? I'd like to invite you to translate each statement three times: First as if you were saying it to someone else, then as if saying it to yourself, then as if hearing it said to you by someone else:

"That was your fault that ..."

"I want you to do ... right now."

"You're making me feel ..."

"That was the most silly suggestion I've heard you make."

"By doing/not doing ... you're being inconsiderate."

"Your feelings about ... are inappropriate."

"The trouble with you is you don't think before you speak."

For each statement pick a context that is relevant in your life for the translation. E.g. "That was your fault that *you dropped the plate, because you were rushing about.*" *(saying to someone else)* → "When

I saw you moving at the speed you were and then dropping the plate I felt annoyed and slightly tense because I have a need for peace and quiet right now. How can I help, so I can have that this evening?" *(saying it to yourself)* → "When I dropped the plate I felt impatient and disappointed in myself because I would like to have been more careful and leave the house sooner." *(hearing it said to you)* → "I guess you had a sentimental connection with that plate, and if so I can understanding why you'd be feeling upset or angry and would have liked me to take more care with it before I dropped it."

When thinking of a translation pay close attention to your intent. Are you thinking about how everyone's feelings and needs can be accepted (and not alienated by judgement)? You may also like to think of a few of your own statements to translate as above.

Recognize the judgement: In this exercise I'd simply like to invite you to pay extra attention over the next week to what you're saying, particularly when you're feeling strong emotions. First try to notice when your observations are getting mixed in with judgements and perhaps pause for thought and ask: 'Is what I'm about to say an observation or a judgement?' E.g. "making a fuss" or "jumping up and down and raising your voice"? See how that alters the responses you get.

Next, do the same with feelings and needs. Notice when you're mixing judgements in with what you're saying. E.g. "I feel used", instead of something like: "I feel sad/suspicious/insecure/resentful/aversion/... because my needs for respect/trust/appreciation/protection/... are not being met."

Finally, repeat this process with requests. E.g. you might say: "Would you be willing to play your music at a more reasonable volume?" and then notice, ah 'reasonable' was a judgement – maybe they have a different understanding of 'reasonable'. We might say "down, so I can't here it across the road" or "below 90db after 10pm" instead. Notice your intent and when you're not so willing to accept a no for an answer. Is your request hiding a demand?

You may find when you're doing this exercise and you're faced with a particularly challenging confrontation, that taking a moment of mindfulness is very helpful. Sometimes it takes only a fraction of a second, looking inward and just observing (without grabbing hold) what thoughts and feelings are happening, to be able to find your anchor and gain empathy with yourself.

The role of judgements

So far we've hopefully shown some of the potential obstructive effects of judgement in conflicts – a risk of it resulting in defending and attacking and dialogue which fails to get at the real feelings and needs involved. However, judgement of others, including criticism and the placing of responsibility, sometimes seems like a practical necessity.

Judgements are not 'bad' things, they just have certain consequences. In practice we make many judgements from day to day – they help us make decisions and build up a sense for how things work. They can also form some of our most closely held values and beliefs (see section: 'Untangling values, beliefs and desires'). Some of the judging we do is going to be about other people. The *purposes* of those judgements about other people include:

- Value projection and categorisation: "They're not worth spending any more time with.", "You're a "pillar of hope"

- Reward: "You did very well, you should be proud of that.", "You're very good/clever/beautiful/strong/..."

- Punishment: "That was bad, you shouldn't have done that, you should be ashamed.", "You're stupid."

- Asserting authority: "I know what's best, this is what we

should do.", "Just do what I say, don't ask questions."

- Making moral judgement: "That is right/wrong/good/bad/...."

- Giving advice, comforting or diagnosing: "I think you should ...", "Don't worry, it's OK", "The trouble with you is ..."

- Assessing someone's ability and encouraging: "You're just not capable of this.", "Come on, you can do it!"

- Setting a boundary: "That was not acceptable, I can't let you do that again."

- Making use of the idea of 'fault': "That was your fault, so you must fix it.", "Don't worry, it wasn't your fault."

- Stating thoughts about another's reasoning or belief: "You do that because ...", "You think ...", "You knew that I ..."

- Fuelling violent conflict: "They are wrong and unjust, we are right. They are not like us. They have what rightly belongs to us and therefore they are the enemy, which must be defeated and punished."

By making these types of judgement we're highlighting one perspective and closing off others. In this way we steer events and alter our own or someone else's awareness.

The above cases can often be 'translated' into non-judgements without losing what was useful and avoiding the judgement downsides. We'll now look at each use of judgement in the previous list – and a (suggested) alternative strategy for each one – in more detail. As it's a fairly lengthy process you may wish to skip ahead to the 'Responsibility' section, if you don't immediately see any of the above uses of judgement as creating problems for you.

Value projection

Value projection is where we take how well or poorly someone provides some of the things we value (our needs) and turn it into a judgement, which we then treat as an *attribute* of that person. With the example: 'They're not worth spending any more time with', the (lack of) worth we sense in spending time with someone may, for instance, reflect our unmet needs/valuing of joy, connection and growth. We *project* our value-judgements onto another person so we can categorise them simply. Pragmatically we might make such judgements to save time, help us to be decisive, or sum up someone's character. In other words, saying "You/they are *categorising judgement*" becomes a kind of rough short-hand for expressing a value-judgement about how someone meets (or otherwise) some of our needs and what feelings result. Value projections occur frequently in other uses of judgement such as reward, punishment (including criticism) and moral judgements. Value projection can also be directed inwardly and form habitual internal dialogues, e.g. "I'm just annoying/stupid/boring/nobody/great/perfect/superior/..." Some of these dialogues, as discussed in section: 'Internal dialogues and identity', can cause serious havoc in your life.

Alternative strategy: Instead of doing the above, supposing we were clear on our feelings and needs here and focused on those? E.g. continuing the example about spending time with someone: 'When I'm with this person I feel bored and withdrawn and sometimes exasperated because my needs for joy, growth and connection are not being met.' Putting things like that – identifying what drives us – we may feel able to be even more decisive about how and with whom we spend our time. Some categorisation may still be there: 'you are someone who when I spend time with I tend to feel ...', but now this is a category based more on *observation* than judgement.

Supposing you had a friendship where you felt like the above. Despite previously spending time and doing things together which you both enjoyed, sometimes friendships fade, but one person doesn't understand and tries to maintain the relationship as it was. In this situation, if we share the above identification of feelings and needs sensitively with the person concerned, they now have an opportunity to better understand why we may not wish to spend more time with them. E.g. "I'm enjoying doing … less than I used to. Maybe there's another way for us to spend time together that meets your needs and gives me more of a sense of connection, enjoyment and growth? I'd like it if that was possible, and I'm wondering how that is for you to hear?"

It could even be that just sharing something like the above, as uncomfortable as it may be, helps you both to see ways of continuing the relationship in some form, while meeting everyone's needs better. If we simply act on the thought 'you're not worth spending any more time with' we're more likely to create hurt and a sense of personal judgement, without a sense of understanding. Thus we get far more positive results from our effort to be clear and avoid simplistic value projections.

Reward

The motivation behind rewarding someone may be to show appreciation, to give what is due, or to reinforce desired behaviours. The latter can easily lead to the objectification of people as we discuss in section: 'Manipulation'. The idea of giving what is due, if it comes from a sense of obligation, places a strain on spontaneity. But what could be the issue with simply complementing or expressing our appreciation with a judgement? After-all the expression of appreciation is such a fundamentally important part of relationships. The dangers with judgemental appreciation or praise are:

a. The potential for there to be confusion and disagreement over the same judgement term. Is my understanding of 'great/ kind/caring/...' the same as yours? Do I *deserve* your praise? What will be expected of me? Am I *superior* to or *separated* from you now that you've given me this label?

b. Using it to appease someone in a disagreement – making it less heartfelt. "Maybe you're just saying that so I'll be quiet." or "Are you just trying to make me feel better?"

c. Such reward being an incentive for someone to do what we want, because our judgement affects their sense of identity: 'You are *good/smart/generous/funny/etc.* when you do ...'. Such a pattern of showing appreciation for someone can lead to their dependency on the judgement to feel OK. Unhealthy approval seeking tendencies can then arise.

Alternative strategy: So how can you fully express your appreciation for someone without such risks? By focusing on whatever it is they did or are doing *means* to you. E.g. "The way you acted in that situation just filled me with joy, awe and respect. I really admire the kind of ability you showed." or "The time and care you took to help me showed me how things could be different. I'm truly grateful to you, thank you." Expressing yourself like this helps to create more of a personal *connection* than, say: "You're so masterful/compassionate/..."

This 'express the personal meaning' idea also works if it's you who seems too attached to approval, or positive judgement. Ask: what does this positive judgement say about how this person has been *affected* by something I have done or am doing? Simple questions like: "I'm curious to know, how did that affect you?" and "How does it make you feel?" can help establish a more rich and personal understanding, beyond basic 'liking', 'approval' or various opaque labels. While gaining approval can be useful sometimes, consider, when someone says "well done!" to you, what means the most and stays with you the longest? The words, or the sense of joy, pride, warmth or admiration in their voice or expression?

Punishment

Punishment – to cause harm or suffering for the purpose of deterrence or retribution – has similar foundations as deciding to use force to control someone (in a non-protective way). Even with the desire to educate someone, if that goes with seeking to make them feel 'wrong', guilty or shameful, then we are still effectively trying to coerce that person. Since a decision to punish someone involves judging them as going against our sense of 'right', it calls for both a moral judgement and one that we are entitled to have some authority over that person.

Alternative strategy: Can you get away entirely from using punishment in the real world? I don't know. But there are a few things I do know that suggest it's worth trying. Firstly, the world provides pain and deterrence aplenty without us trying to top it up. Generally when something we do contributes to the pain of someone we have an emotional connection with, we will feel a portion of that pain too. This is the natural negative feedback process of empathy. Secondly, punishment often begets resentment and retaliation, along with regret. Punishment is typically at odds with intimacy. Thirdly the choice to seek *mutual* empathy, free of any judgements of wrongdoing, offers a very full and thorough way of resolving grievances and reaching a peaceful resolution.

Delivering punishment can simply be an indirect strategy for meeting a need such as respect, being significant/cared about, self-protection, etc. The beautiful thing about *empathy* is that it embraces all of those needs, giving them the attention they call for and the best chance of being met long-term.

Anger, of course, is often a big part of deciding to punish someone. We discuss this factor in sub-section: 'Dealing with anger and aggression'.

What do you do in those situations where someone shows little concern for others despite the best of efforts to empathize with them and they present an immediate danger? Then there is the option of *protective* use of force, which we discuss below.

Asserting authority

If your authority is already well established then sometimes making authoritative decisions affecting others is a very efficient way of bringing about collective action. However, if you're having an *argument* and you try to assert authority in this way, as with getting angry, one of two things can happen: the other party capitulates, or they resist and it becomes more of a fight.

There are certainly people who get a sense of safety and order around other people who 'take command', even in arguments. The thing to remember about claiming authority in this way is that it invites people to give you *responsibility* for whatever consequences your judgements bring. This may not be what you want. Also, when someone complies out of fear, the bitterness of defeat will accumulate under the surface. That's definitely bad news for any enduring relationship.

Alternative strategy: It's my belief that authority is often given according to two things: the gentle strength of our actions and the clarity of our thought. This happens without the need for us to make any judgement about our entitlement to that authority and without trying to take anyone else's authority over themselves away. Thus an alternative is simply to focus on those two things: the gentle strength of your actions and the clarity of your thought.

The only use of force over someone else that I can think of which has no preferable substitute is to *protect* someone from *imminent* danger. E.g. restraining a child who is about to play with a sharp knife, or disarming someone who is at the point of injuring you or someone else. See also, section: 'Assertiveness'.

Making moral judgement

There are different meanings of the word morality, but generally in practical usage it refers to a code of acceptable conduct relating to fairness, honesty and respect. What is acceptable, or expected, is 'good' (or 'right') and what is not acceptable is 'bad' (or 'wrong'). 'Acceptable' meaning what is socially tolerated, with 'bad' acts resulting in ostracism, or active punishment where a serious threat is perceived. The utility of 'good' and 'bad' then is to map out acceptable and unacceptable behaviour. It seems there are some elements of morality that are more innate and universal: "It's bad to kill", or "It's wrong to steal", while others are more dependent on culture and society, such as: "It's *wrong/perfectly fine* to *be homosexual/get drunk/use profanities/be naked in public/get high/*..."

One of the dangers with moral judgement is confusing the moral position of an *act* with the moral position of a *person* – which tends to have a more striking and permanent impact. (It's the same kind of 'convenient' simplification of value projection.) If you've done something 'bad' and you take it as '*I* am bad', this tends to amplify feelings of guilt (regret + sense of personal wrongdoing) and shame (guilt + hopelessness, sense of inadequacy or intense disappointment). Regrettably, this feature of moral judgement makes it very effective as a means of coercion.

Another risk of moral judgement is failure to see either the wood or the trees, instead realizing only whether or not what's in front of you matches with your impression of what it *should* look like. Moral judgement forces us to file down the complex curves of reality to straight edged blocks. Certainly when used as a personal guide, it can be useful, helping us to make a decision in difficult situations. It could be argued though that this kind of use is really just a covering layer of an innate morality that results from our ability to empathize and tendency to have a positive regard for the well-being of others.

Perhaps the biggest difficulties with moral judgement arise when judging other people. Reality is complex, it's hard enough to get to the bottom of why *we* do things. So then, what are the chances of us understanding the causes and circumstances surrounding another person's actions, well enough to make a sound moral judgement? It's so easy to misunderstand. This is the reason why moral judgement tends not to go down too well during a conflict.

***Alternative strategy*:** One alternative to moral judgement is to break it down into steps. What are the accompanying judgements or assumptions about someone's motives or circumstances? Turn them into questions: "Did you do ... because *say what you guess was their intention or drive for doing it*?", "Were you feeling *guilty/angry/hurt/gleeful/hopeless/numb/distant/bored /panicked/tormented/...*, when you made that decision? What was it like for you?", "What did you think the effect of your actions would be?" See how your assumptions match with their view of reality. Alternatively, where play in earlier life, or otherwise practising empathy in later life gives us the opportunity to understand moral behaviour at a gut level, we might do without explicit moral judgement altogether.

Rather than having moral codes imposed upon us, cultivating *awareness* of our potential influence on the well-being of others, may be more effective in creating a fairer, more compassionate society. If as Charles Darwin suggested, moral action is action with the greater good of all at heart, or as 19th century philosopher, Arthur Schopenhauer, said "compassion is the basis of all morally", then 'moral rules' present a dilemma. When some authority tells us what we must do, are we more or less able to listen openly and allow empathy to develop in a challenging situation? Is there not a tendency to disengage or lose personal connection and just 'follow the rules', where we feel pressured too? And if that's the case, how can we be truly moral, with our empathy – that foundation of compassion – obstructed? It could be said then that we're most at danger of our natural moral fibre atrophying when we allow rules (however well meaning) to obstruct the process, learning and practice of empathy.

Giving advice, comforting or diagnosing

Advice allows us to share knowledge and help each other. I'm personally extremely grateful for some of the advice I've received over the years, I don't know where I'd be without it. I also believe I've been able to offer useful advice from time to time, which also makes me feel grateful and connected and gives me a sense of being valued.

What's the issue with advice then? Misunderstanding, both on the part of the person hearing it and of the person giving it. Firstly, does that person really *want* advice? If not it can seem like someone's trying to order them about, or just not understanding their situation. Even if someone wants it, do we understand their situation accurately enough to give appropriate advice, and are we clear enough so that our advice isn't misinterpreted?

During my Samaritans training we had it drilled into us: "Don't give advice." When someone calls in distress, very often it's the last thing they want; all their friends and family give them advice, they just want someone to *listen and understand*. Simply doing that can bring such a relief and sense of acceptance, it's a wonderful thing to be able to offer. It's a sad fact that a lot of people *avoid* calling their friends, family and loved ones when they have a crisis, because they think they wont be given space to really share their feelings or have them accepted without judgement. Often, just talking through a situation, a person is able to find their own solutions.

Alternative strategy: The benefits of advice are generally possible without the: "I think you *should (because I know how things are for you)*" judgement, by swapping it for: "I think maybe you *could*". So then 'advice' becomes: "What if you ..., how would it be if you did that?" Otherwise we could try: "If I was in a situation where *reflect the situation you think someone asking for advice is in* I might do ..." or "I've tried doing ... in the past and it's worked for me, maybe you could try it too?" It's true sometimes people want to have a decision made for them, e.g. "I'm stuck, just tell me what to do!" Perhaps sometimes there's no problem in doing that. But other times, by telling someone what they should do, you may be inviting responsibility or aggravation you'd rather not have.

Often with advice comes a judgement of 'good' and 'bad', either in a moral sense, or in terms of what will help meet needs and what won't. This latter use of good and bad is hard to avoid in conversational discourse. The word good appears over 130 times in this book, for example. If its meaning is restricted only to an *opinion* of what is and isn't helpful in meeting specific needs in a specific context then I believe the use of 'good' and 'bad' is fairly innocuous. It's when these words are used or taken as more permanent, absolute and objective judgements involving people that problems arise.

Comforting: "Don't worry, it's OK" is a common example of making a judgement about what someone's situation is in order to console or comfort them. Again, sometimes that's what people want to hear, but when it's not, it can easily create distance and even anger, leading to responses like: "How can you tell me not to worry? Of course it's not bloody OK!" (whether verbalized or said inwardly), or "They just don't understand."

Alternative strategy: How can you comfort someone without making a judgement? Simply by being supportive, listening and trying to empathize. An offer to help can also work very well, e.g. "I'm really sad to see you so upset, I'd really like to help you if I can, is there something I can do?" In *some* situations other effective approaches include being specific and offering new understanding, e.g. "Don't worry, I know this problem well, if you do XYZ it will be fine", or offering alternative perspectives and humour. Other times a simple hug is all that's wanted.

Diagnosing: When we diagnose we present ourselves as an expert. Obviously there are some circumstances where diagnosis is very valuable. But if we're *not* an expert (or at least not in the other person's view) or a diagnosis is not desired, friction and the idea "you think you're superior to me" result.

Alternative strategy: The alternative (if you're not a doctor diagnosing a patient, or such like) is as for advice. Help the person explore their own situation, ask questions and offer ideas just as ideas, not judgements. If someone truly wants your diagnosis they will be prepared to ask for it. But even then be aware of the responsibility they may want you to take.

Assessing ability, encouragement and discouragement

There could be many reasons for assessing someone's ability (deciding if someone is capable of doing – or not doing – something), such as: avoiding danger to yourself or others, being responsible for some outcome or process, protecting reputation, being concerned that everyone's needs are met, wanting to help someone's potential be reached, protecting social structure or hierarchy, etc. Related to this assessment/judgement is the desire to encourage or discourage someone in a particular pursuit or course of action.

With this judgement of ability there are the usual risks of misunderstanding and disagreement. Sometimes there is also clearly an overlap with this use of judgement and others, such as asserting authority, value-projection, reward or punishment.

We can have very positive intentions when making this kind of judgement, even when it's that someone is not capable of doing something. E.g. "Sweetheart, interior design isn't your strong point, why don't you let me choose the colours?" *could* reflect an intent for their partner to avoid anxiety, frustration or confusion in this activity, or to serve them by doing a really good job. Of course, there are other ways of seeing it and that's often the problem. E.g. "Oh, so I'm not entitled to choose the colours of the walls I'll be living with then? Isn't it a matter of personal preference? Doesn't my taste count?"

So a particular risk of sharing what you think someone else can or can't do, or is good or bad at doing, is of it being heard as a dictation or diagnosis. Another risk is the bounds of that judgement not being clear, e.g. "You're just not good at singing" → *I'll never be a good singer*. The typically static nature of judgements causes a lot of problems in relationships.

Alternative strategy: The obvious way of avoiding some of the above risks are to express your intent along with your judgement and to be more specific. E.g. "Sweetheart, I think interior design isn't your strong point. I don't want you to get stressed over it and I think I could do an amazing job with the living room, so why don't you let me choose the colours? Of course if you feel strongly about any of them, please let me know." Or "The choir decided that currently your singing isn't at the standard they're looking for. But maybe with practice you could improve it." But usually we can do without the judgement altogether, replacing it with either an observation or a guess about feelings: "Sweetheart, it *seems like you don't enjoy* interior design. I don't want you to get stressed over it ..."

Encouragement and discouragement: What about using this kind of judgement to encourage someone, e.g. "Come on, I know you can do it! Don't give up!" Encouragement is very valuable, it can give us a lot of conviction and confidence and, as usual, there are different ways of giving it. In the context of a clearly defined relationship within a certain situation and with good rapport (trust + sense of commonality and mutual understanding) this sort of judgement can be very effective. Otherwise, if someone feels hopeless or very doubtful and thinks that you don't understand their situation then they are less likely to be receptive to your assessment. Instead, what you may intend as encouraging may lead to feelings of disconnection or could be heard as: "Don't make a fuss, just get on with it." or "I don't have time to understand your problem."

The potential pitfalls for encouragement are compounded for discouragement. It's an unpleasant feeling – unless you have a crystal clear sense that the motivation behind it is loving, has your well-being at heart *and* you happen to agree with the judgement.

***Alternative strategy*:** If you first listen and develop empathy and *then* say something like "I know how hopeless/doubtful/ frustrated/... you feel, but if you just persevere I know you can do it.", then you're more likely to be listened to. If someone understands your feelings and situation and *still* thinks you can achieve what you want to achieve then maybe they're right. This is why people naturally seek advice and thrive on encouragement from other's who have had similar experiences, because that sense of *understanding* is already there. Developing empathy is another way of getting both that understanding and receptiveness.

With discouragement (as with encouragement), the alternative really depends on your motivation. If it's not with a positive regard for the well-being of the other person then sub-sections 'Asserting authority', 'Punishment' and 'Fuelling violent conflict' may offer more handy ideas.

If your motivation does come from a positive regard you may be trying to protect the person you're discouraging. Here the practice of 'loving detachment' can be very helpful. The idea is that after fully sharing your concern, your needs to care and protect, and your reasoning, you *allow that person to take full responsibility for the natural consequences of their actions*. If this is done with a loving desire for that person to grow stronger, wiser and more independent, then it is not neglectful.

If you believe someone's actions will result in grave harm to them and that they're not in a position to understand the risks or accept responsibility (such as a toddler crossing a busy road) then you might obviously consider the use of protect force.

Setting a boundary

What about those important times where we want to set a personal boundary for our own integrity or safety? Using a judgement of another person we might say something like: "That was totally unacceptable and wrong, I can't let you do that again." However, that may lead to more conflict over whether they agree with your assessment, and whether they will let you tell them what they can or can't do.

Alternative strategy: Compare the above to something like: "This is my boundary. I will do whatever I need to make sure it's not crossed" perhaps followed by "I request that you acknowledge and respect that." By bringing the situation home to *you*, you can actually get a greater sense of *control* over it. Once again, identifying your feelings and unmet needs in that situation can further empower you to do whatever you decide. (In some situations, particularly if there's the threat of violent conflict, first helping the other party to have a sense of being understood can be the best way to protect a boundary.) See also sections: 'Responsibility' and 'Assertiveness'.

To make use of the idea of 'fault'

The idea of fault or mistake is an interesting one. We can be mistaken or inaccurate in what we think we observe (as is obvious when you look at an optical illusion). We can also have mistaken judgements, but what does it mean to be at fault in our *actions* and told 'that was your fault'?

Alongside an indication that someone disagrees with an action we've taken, there is often an implicit invitation to accept responsibility, together with fault. One clear use of finding fault is indeed blaming people. Blame is a way of pushing around responsibility and accepting or passing on punishment.

Alternative strategy: The alternative is to focus on responsibility rather than fault. As responsibility is such an important issue there is a whole section on it later.

Stating thoughts about another's reasoning or knowledge

This is a fairly common occurrence in arguments, e.g. "You only did that because you want ...", "You knew how that would effect me." or "You think I'm a fool!" We might be trying to show understanding and express feelings at the same time, but this way of doing it often sounds like diagnosis or fault finding and tends to result in similar judgements back (voiced or not).

Alternative strategy: In the context of play (discussed later) we can more easily explore this kind of communication with less risk of exacerbating a conflict. Otherwise it's generally more fruitful to focus on the underlying drives of feelings and met or unmet needs. If we definitely want to understand someone's thinking, we can check it out with a question, e.g. 'Are you thinking ...?", rather than a statement.

Fuelling violent conflict

The discussion of asserting authority over others and punishment – and the inherent judgements – ties in with violent conflict between people, communities or nations. What would a conflict be, without asserting authority over others or punishment? And then there is the alienating effect of seeing other people as 'not like us'. This breaks our natural, default ethical or compassionate tendency towards those people, opening the doors to violence. The above factors are both the symptoms and causes of violent conflict.

Obviously there's often some material factor involved, like limited resources or access to sources of wealth. But it is the presence of the three elements: alienation, claiming authority, and punishment or control, that allow conflict to ignite and spread. There's no doubt that those three elements can also be used as a recipe to start up a conflict:

1. *The material factor*: "They have something we need and they don't want to give it to us." or "They are stopping us from getting something we need." *(That 'something' could range from attention or affection, to a sense of normality or conformity, to resources such as food, water, diamonds and oil.)*

2. *Alienate*: "They are not like us. We are good/just/normal/ righteous/superior and they are bad/unjust/strange/wrong doers/inferior. We would not do as they have done."

3. *Claim authority*: "It is our right to have what we need. They are wrong to deny us. Thus we are justified in taking any necessary measures to get it."

4. *Punish/control*: "They deserve this punishment or control, until they change or give us what is rightly ours."

Alternative strategy: Whatever step of the above four-point list you're at, reclaim your responsibility (discussed later) without passing or accepting blame. It's important to realize that this is not about denying suffering, or forgetting the dire consequences which resulted from certain actions. It's about reclaiming self-control and escaping the mobius strip of right-doings and wrong-doings. With this progressive perspective, empathy can be developed and reconciliatory actions *willingly* taken by each party. At this stage, even the original material factor of the conflict may dissolve with the benefit of deeper understanding and creative collaboration.

Finding strength in openness and a paradigm shift

Now that we've considered quite a few of the common reasons for making judgement about other people and discussed less problematic alternatives, it seems surprising that we still make those judgements. In a few cases, judgement is without much useful alternative, e.g. protective use of force, expert diagnosis and giving instruction where authority is accepted. But aside from these uses, why do we keep doing something that doesn't lead to much lasting happiness, especially in conflicts? We've already looked at the threat-focused drives for making judgement, but there is also a convenience and conditioning aspect to it.

Judging others is a kind of short-hand for expressing our thoughts and summing things up while avoiding the effort or *risk* of more personal expression. With judgement rich language we can be very directive and appear powerful while covering up our feelings and needs. So we form boundaries.

Conversely, sharing your feelings and needs can also show the appearance of great strength and power. Think of the person you've met in your life that seemed the most in touch with their inner state, who was at peace with it because they took responsibility for it and who was not afraid to share what was going on for them. If there is someone who comes to mind, I wonder if you can you think of anyone stronger? Where being judgemental can suggest authority over others, acting in this way demonstrates authority over yourself.

However, if you're at all out of touch with your feelings and needs, judgement language is simpler and more concise and so takes less *effort*. The more used to this style of communication we are and the more our peers share it, the harder it becomes to break free. The situation is self-perpetuating.

Perhaps another significant factor in our choice of judgement rich language is the air of *objectivity* it lends. Being 'objective' has a certain cachet, it's associated with powerful entities in society like law and science. When what's at hand is inherently *subjective*, pursuing objective expression can actually lead us further away from the truth though. In relationships which we are a part of, the truth is our own experience – which sometimes may cross over the bridge of empathy. The very meaning of our relationships is rooted in our feelings and how our needs are met. Thus the most fruitful and *truthful* language for expressing ourselves in relationships will be one that embraces our subjective truth rather than concealing it.

Finally, after reading this sub-section, to think 'ah, so judgements are generally bad then' would be to miss the point. Language rich in feelings and needs, together with empathy, offers a paradigm shift; we simply need not think in terms of 'good' or 'bad', 'should' or 'shouldn't'. Morality can be strong and responsibility taken readily, quite naturally without relying on these judgement concepts.

The use of force and young people

I've separated out part of the previous discussion on asserting authority over others, as I believe the treatment of young people deserves special attention. The way adults treat children can be a real window into their underlying beliefs and values, especially as children are apt to ask searching questions and behave in ways we find challenging. Those beliefs and values also have a tendency to rub off. Thus it's also worth sparing some thought to our relationships with children in general, even if we are not parents.

Consider *imposing* your authority against another person's will, thinking 'my way is the right way, you will do as I wish'. Obviously between adults this idea is generally considered abhorrent – it shows a lack of respect for a person's liberty and flies in the face of the United Nations declaration of human rights. It's interesting that when it comes to young people there's a point at which this common attitude often changes.

When we (speaking as an 'adult') see a young person doing something which affects us and which we consider as misbehaving, if our attempts at reasoning fail, resorting to forceful coercion can seem appropriate. Doing this can achieve several things: teach that young person how to use force when they don't get their way, instil some boundaries for them to either accept or fight against, and lastly meet our objective to change their behaviour or lead them to feel regret with minimum short-term fuss. What if we could use deeper understanding – empathy – as we've discussed throughout this section, to reach a mutually agreeable and peaceful solution? At what age is a person capable of attempting to see things from another's point of view and of sensing what someone else is feeling?

It's now common thinking amongst developmental psychologists that children generally have the ability to recognize both the emotions and preferences of other people at 2 years of age or less, sometimes even before they can walk reliably. Between age 3 and 4, most children have a fully developed 'theory of mind' (the ability to attribute mental states – beliefs, intents, desires, pretending, knowledge, etc. – to oneself and others and to understand that others have beliefs, desires and intentions that are different from their own).

The strategies of communication children pick up in those early years are instrumental to how in touch with that innate empathic ability they tend to be in later life. While change in later life is certainly possible with enough effort, naturally we'd all prefer to get off to a good start.

What about asserting force, even to cause pain, with the intent to educate but without a judgement of wrongdoing? Is it possible that doing this could sometimes have the same motivation as the protective use of force? I offer the following as an example to ponder: you restrain a child who doesn't yet understand the danger of hot things from touching a very hot fire poker. Is it acceptable to wait until the poker has cooled a little and then touch their hand to it so they can learn from the pain but without injury?

History has shown that people adapt to how they are treated. Thus, treat someone 'like a child' and they may start behaving like one, if it somehow offers the clearest chance of meeting their needs. How much, then, of the challenging behaviour young people sometimes present is simply an adaptation to the way they're treated?

Responsibility

Responsibility is a powerful idea. It can frighten or embolden, trap or free, all depending on how you understand it. The core of responsibility is about ownership; being in charge or possession of something, an object, situation or outcome. Responsibility is also having the burden of action to change whatever that something is, if we want it changed.

To 'be responsible' for something first requires that you accept responsibility for it. That may seem obvious, but it's a key point. It means there is a difference between being 'held responsible' – another party thinking you *should* be responsible and taking steps to make you accept it, and actually 'being responsible' – acting with and accepting responsibility for something. Let's consider now what 'being responsible' is not, but is often confused or *associated* with. It's not:

'Being the cause'   *'Being to blame'*   *'Being at fault'*

You may think you are any of the above but that doesn't automatically make you responsible – and being responsible doesn't necessarily equate to you being any of the above.

If you can be clear on what you are (and *want* to be) responsible for and what you're not, then it becomes easier to make the best use of your time and energy. When there is a conflict in your relationship it will also be easier to resolve it, knowing where responsibility – not cause, blame or fault – lies.

Responsibility for feelings

If we're not careful about the scope of responsibility we try to give someone, or accept ourselves, it can be very disempowering for us. Let's take 'feelings': it's certainly true that within a close relationship the actions of one person will affect how the other feels (their emotional state) – that is after-all what *makes* a relationship close. This *may* mean someone wants to make things better if something they did prompted you to feel unhappy, but ultimately the *responsibility* for that feeling can only lie with you (and vice-versa). Who else could really take ownership of your emotional state, other than you? Who else ultimately has the burden of action to change it?

Returning to what responsibility is not, the idea of 'blame' is an interesting and formidable one. Essentially it means to try and pin responsibility, cause and fault on someone: "It's *their* problem and they need to sort it out, they *caused* it and it was their *fault*." Ouch.

This leads to the conclusion that we're rarely, if ever, to *blame* for our feelings, but we can be entirely responsible.

Though someone may have been *part* of the cause of your feelings (or a trigger for them), so is your perspective and subsequent interpretations. Those things are up to you. But surely, if someone is part of the cause of your feelings they *should* share the responsibility? Here we have to recognize the fundamental difference between feelings and actions. When it comes to *your* feelings, it's only really possible for you to be responsible – they're your feelings, you own them. Thus taking a leadership role and taking charge is the way to go. Blaming others – or yourself – for feelings you experience simply takes power from you, because it gets in the way of the true responsibility taking process.

On the question of cause, here are two perspectives:

You feel what you feel because of who you are, the choices you make and the views you take.

You feel what you feel because you are affected by others you care about, or who have power over you.

Both are true, both are important. I believe cause – what leads to a certain outcome – is always distributed. It can never be located at one single point, there are always multiple factors, each one influencing the combined effect. When you strike a match, for instance, is it you who causes it to combust? Or is it the materials of the match, or the striking surface, or the air being above a certain humidity? So when we talk about 'specific cause', it's never quite the whole story.

On an emotional level, sometimes, especially when you're younger, the balance of power may lie with other people where you're dependant on them. It can be that if certain of our needs – like love, nurture and acceptance – were not met then we are left with a feeling of helplessness and despair or anger. This can lead to us wanting someone else to take responsibility for our inner turmoil. However, as you develop self-awareness you can become increasingly emotionally secure and self-directed, realizing your own power over your inner state.

As for 'fault', when applied to feelings, as in "It's your fault I feel this way", the focus is on a perceived wrong-doing, but really it's another way of trying to pass on responsibility, which we've already discussed.

In summary, recognize the role in your feelings (both wanted and unwanted) that other people play. But remember your own responsibility for those feelings and your power to change them. (See sections: 'Fear (and general emotional turmoil)' and 'Untangling values, beliefs and desires' for some more ideas on how to do that.) Being clear on that, and also avoiding language like "You make me feel ..." or "I feel ... when you ...", can help you to not play the victim when you needn't, and help someone else to avoid guilt. Similarly, the other person in a relationship is responsible for their feelings, despite what influence you may have. (While of course you remain responsible for your actions and *intent* towards that person.)

Thinking we're responsible for another's feelings, especially in 'serious' relationships, can easily lead to us feeling trapped by an urge to sort someone else's problems out before our own. It is still possible to be kind and considerate, but without wearing that chain which ultimately helps no-one. A big warning sign you may be entrapping yourself is using language like: "you feel sad/angry/bored/disappointed/worried/... because *I* ...", instead of: "you feel sad/angry/bored/disappointed/worried/... because *you* wanted/needed/hoped/would have liked ..."

Disputes where *all parties acknowledge their own emotional responsibilities* can be resolved more quickly and satisfactorily – because you're not carrying that extra weight. Also if you have a sense of being in command of your feelings then it's easier to share them.

The question of wanting someone else to tell you what's right and wrong, because you don't want or think you're able to take responsibility yourself, is touched on in section: 'Get your fresh roles here'.

Responsibility for actions

Taking responsibility for your actions is about being aware of your influence, having concern for how you affect others and, where your actions do affect others, being willing and able to take steps to look after their interests as well as your own. This seems pretty central to a healthy, loving relationship.

But how can we stop the above sensitivity and positive intent from slipping into "I'm responsible for your happiness" territory? By focusing on three things: what responsibility actually means, what your intent towards that person was/is and what your own needs are. Also consider how valuable a skill it is to learn to be more self-sufficient. If your sense of self-worth is lower than what you ascribe to others, then you might find it hard to respect your own needs. If so, section: 'Fear (and general emotional turmoil)' and others from the first part of this book, may be of some help.

The act of taking responsibility for your actions can be a very satisfying and empowering experience, where there is no sense of obligation or blame. This is true regardless of whether the consequences of that action were favourable or unfavourable.

How can you appeal to someone to take responsibility for their actions, where those actions have been detrimental to you, without using blame and shame? A good start is to use the NVC method: explain the situation in terms of your observations, sharing how you feel about it and what needs of yours are not being met. Then, simply make a specific, actionable request (free from implied obligation or threat), that if they carried out would enrich your life. Then proceed to engage in dialogue. As is often the case, trying to express understanding of their situation and needs before sharing your own may work out even better for you. The challenge is to be assertive, while retaining respect for the other person's needs and without resorting to blame.

Here's an example of a request to take responsibility:

"Look, if you think about it rationally, you'll see that it is only right that you take remedial action for what you did. You caused me a lot of hardship and distress when you … I'm sure you had your reasons and there's no shame if you take responsible action now to redress your mistake. Here's what I'd like you to do: …"

It may sound 'reasonable' but it's crammed with judgement and the threat of shame. Instead, we could try:

"I'd like us to understand each other better. I'd like to understand your feelings and needs surrounding your actions *provide specific observational details*. I also wish to share my feelings and needs relating to those actions. I hope you will be willing talk about this." Followed by something like:

"I guess you *summarize what you think their feelings and needs might be relating to the actions in question (without blame or diagnosis)*. When I saw/heard/experienced/learnt about you doing this I felt alarmed/afraid/angry/despair/… because my needs for understanding/trust/safety/respect/… were not being met. Since that time *talk about how their actions have affected your situation and ability to meet your needs*. Would you be willing to tell me what you understand by what I've said?"

When you get to the point where you're actually hearing each other's feelings and needs, without the distraction of blame or other judgement, requests are more likely to be successful:

"Would you be willing to *say what specific measures you'd like them to take*? If you did that is would *say what difference them fulfilling your request would make to you*." Even if your exact request is not agreed to, there's a fair chance that by following this process of empathy you get to a better position than you were in before, or what you could have reached with the old judgement and threat-focused method.

If after gaining a mutual empathy and getting to some agreements your mood is more collaborative than threat-focused, you might even say something like: "Is there anything I can do that would help you take the action you've agreed to?" This reinforces the idea that you'd like to work together with – rather than opposed to – them for mutual benefit.

Notice in the above example there wasn't actually the direct request to 'take responsibility'. If there was a prior discussion on exactly who is responsibly for what, then you can refer to any agreements made. But in many cases, to say "I'd like you to take responsibility for your actions" after the fact, can easily sound like blame. As previously discussed, blame can get the results you wanted, sometimes, but it moves away from the longer term approach we're exploring here. As Dr. Martin Luther King said "Peace is not merely a distant goal that we seek but a means by which we arrive at that goal."

Apologize without blame: the fault free way

How does the idea of taking responsibility for your actions fit with apologies? While essentially an expression of regret, apologies are used for several things:

- To accept responsibility
- To accept fault or blame (usually along with taking

responsibility and requesting forgiveness)

- To express sympathy, e.g. "I'm sorry for your loss."

Taking responsibility is obviously pretty important and it's natural to express regret when we feel it, as it shows understanding and concern for others. For this reason apologies can be very useful things. In regard to accepting blame, it's said that apologising is an art. If so then it's one that few would choose to master. Who likes to be 'wrong'? I'd like to suggest that it's the very idea of being wrong, or at fault, that gets in the way of more people taking responsibility for their actions and showing genuine regret.

So how do things normally function, with apology being synonymous with fault or blame? We get by with this approach because taking responsibility isn't always a decision that we fully own or feel at peace with.

A person can be lead to feel compelled to 'take responsibility' through judgements of wrongness and the resulting feelings of guilt (regret + sense of wrongness) or shame (guilt + intense disappointment, sense of inadequacy or hopelessness). In this system, there's the idea: the more at fault you are the more you should accept responsibility → The more you accept responsibility the more at fault you must have been. This actually serves to give you more painful emotional energy to spur you on through the motions of taking responsibility. You're acting to atone for your fault and rid yourself of guilt or shame; you're acting to free yourself from suffering. But there's only so much you can put your heart into doing something to improve someone else's life if you yourself are suffering. Apologies that result from this model of thinking are often fraught with inner conflict, misery, a sense of defeat or being manipulated or forced.

What are the most valuable parts of an apology where there is regret for actions taken? Surely it is the showing of that regret and the *intent* to take responsibility (including planning how to avoid similar outcomes in future)? If that's the case then perhaps there's a way of making them which is free of the idea of fault? Before we investigate further let's consider more closely the idea of 'fault'.

If when adding up two numbers you produce a result that disagrees with the rules of counting, then what you have done is clearly 'at fault'. But there, in the world of counting, everything is exact and well defined, the laws are mathematical and absolute. What sense then does it make to think of 'fault' in a world with no such laws or well defined rules, where there is no limited set of factors, no final answer, or even a clear beginning? We *could* pick someone else's idea of right and wrong and try to conform to that, but then whose to choose? And if we make that choice we're giving up our independence and opting to be submissive. If we're able to freely choose our own general sense of right and wrong, then what more can it really mean than: that which helps to satisfy our needs ('right') and that which doesn't ('wrong')?

Surely then it's smarter to stick to the knowable facts when you do something that you regret. That is, you regret your actions because they didn't produce the outcome you would have liked, or led to an outcome that upsets you – *because your needs were not satisfied*.

How would apologies work, if we just showed regret and intent to take responsibility for our actions? What would it be like to be able to sincerely apologize and take responsibility without being riddled with shame or saddled by blame?

Here are some basic tips on apologies, which are also compatible with the fault free, blame free idea:

- By being *clear* and *sincere* in what you are apologising for you are both making it easier for yourself and improving the chances of the apology being accepted.

- Show that you know what it was you did, being clear about your regret and *why* an apology is being given. E.g. consider the scenario where someone you're cooking with is very upset because you put several times as much chilli in the soup than they wanted: "I'm so sorry for making the soup so hot. I didn't take your advice to measure the chilli out first from the packet. I know you're hungry and the ingredients were expensive and I know you're also upset about it because you wanted to serve some to your mum this evening. I'd really like to make it up to you if I can." is probably a bit better than: "I'm very sorry for making the soup a bit too hot. I know you're upset about it. Is there anything I can do?" The first apology shows more *appreciation* of the action and of the consequences for and feelings of the other person.

- If you do want to explain why you did or didn't do something, wait until the other person asks or at least *after* they've had a chance to respond to the initial apology. This shows more appreciation of the other person's feelings and less emphasis on excusing yourself or getting forgiveness.

- Apologies that are conditional: "I'll be sorry for that, if you ...", mixed with excuses: "I'm sorry, but I only did it because ...", uncertain: "I'm sorry if my actions hurt you.", reluctant: "OK, I suppose I should apologize then ..." or demanding: "I'm sorry for ... Satisfied now!?"; these are all great ways of being counter-productive. Such apologies are compromised by reluctance, insincerity, aggression, lack of understanding and apparent *avoidance of responsibility*.

It's easier to make a good and genuine apology if neither you or the other person are 'threat focused' – there's less risk (or threat) of negative repercussions. This pretty much rules out the use of blame.

Actions can be a fantastic way of apologising, they can show understanding and sincerity in ways that words alone can't. Even something as simple as a hug and a kiss, or small gift of some other kind can make a big statement.

Obviously there could be a big difference between an action that serves as a touching token of apology and the action that is required to take responsibility for the consequences of the original action. Imagine, for instance, a situation involving three people: *Adam* makes a somewhat indiscreet remark to *Clare*, relating to a private business of *Bob*'s. This causes *Bob* embarrassment and changes the way *Clare* thinks about *Bob*, maybe resulting in some social or financial cost to him. It's one thing for *Adam* to take *Bob* to lunch to apologize, but that's no substitute for *Adam* speaking to *Clare*, explaining the situation, accepting responsibility and doing his best to sort things out, as far as seems appropriate.

If you're dwelling on feelings of guilt or shame, try to separate out the *regret* from the *fault*. Why do you regret what you regret, aside from any sense of being wrong? What needs were or are not being met? Then allow that *regret* to transform into a *focus* on meeting those needs, as far as possible and seems appropriate. Take what action you choose, *then move on*. Where you take action, what was once regret can become *celebration* of how what you're now doing will enrich someone's life. Notice too, that thinking in terms of guilt, wrongness or shame, tends to hinder you taking positive action.

If you want to try using words other than: "It was my *fault* / I was *wrong* / I *shouldn't* have", try (along with empathizing) substituting the words: "I would like to have acted differently / I wish I'd acted differently" – followed by "I will take responsibility", according to the situation – and see how it feels.

If we follow this idea of fault free apology to it's conclusion, then *apologies are never owed*, only freely given and received. Even requesting an apology becomes a strange concept, since it's requesting that someone feel a certain way (regret) and that's not really an actionable request. How can you just choose to feel a certain way? Of course, behind a request for an apology may simply be a desire for empathy and possibly the taking of responsibility for certain actions. In any case, it's worth clarifying what is really wanted.

When you receive an apology, clarity is also the key here. If someone's actions have had an impact on you, be clear on your feelings and on what needs were met by the apology and what needs may remain unmet.

Forgiveness

Is someone wanting forgiveness from you? If so they're probably holding onto guilt. If you were blaming them and feel ready to let that go, let them know; it could lift a tremendous weight from their shoulders and yours. Looking at forgiveness as the letting go of blame, it really is a healing gift. If someone is wanting forgiveness but you held no blame to begin with, again, let them know that there was nothing to forgive. They might even appreciate you sharing some of the ideas in this section.

In connection with guilt and thinking about how good it can feel to be forgiven, I'm reminded of a story that I was told by Kanakabja Das, a then Hare Krishna monk who I enjoyed spending time with some years ago: "There was a man who one day decided to start wearing shoes that were far too small for him. He would wear them all day long, his poor feet crying out for mercy. His friends saw this and felt sorry for him, but they also noticed that he seemed to be emotionally attached to the shoes, so for a while they said nothing. But the man's suffering went on and eventually one of his friends said: "Dear friend, please tell me why you do this to yourself? Why do you wear these shoes that obviously don't fit you all day and cause you such pain?" The man replied: "I go through this suffering because when I get home at the end of the day and I sit down and take these shoes off, it feels so good, it's like I'm in heaven!"

The story was intended to make the point that what we think of as the pursuit of pleasure in life is often really only the temporary relief from pain. It occurs to me though that it also applies to pointing to the relief of forgiveness as a good reason for having guilt and shame. You can see a *kind* of sense to it, but it's kind of crazy too. The tragedy is when we don't realize there is a pair of shoes to just stop wearing altogether. The natural needs for acceptance and peace can be met without first being blamed and feeling guilty.

Play conflict: fighting, arguing, joking

Going back to the main topic of conflict, there is a certain type of conflict quite distinct from the rest and common amongst a large fraction of the animal kingdom. *Play* conflict, in the case of people, takes the form of fighting, arguing, criticising, insulting, mocking, etc. With it we have a unique context in which to explore ideas, express ourselves, demonstrate understanding and practice various social and threat-focused fighting skills that may protect us in the future.

Play conflict allows us to gauge whether someone can be trusted when we are in a vulnerable position. It also lets us see how someone understands social rules and boundaries – not just whether they conform to them, but also whether they can demonstrate mastery of them, by breaking them in acceptable and exciting ways. Consequently this type of play can feature heavily in courtship.

Plato put it aptly: "You can discover more about a person in one hour of play than in a year of conversation."

There are other forms of inter-personal play which are not conflict or competition orientated, where the focus of play is more directly on working together. E.g. building a sandcastle, making music or dancing together. But here we focus on conflict.

Within the context of *mutually accepted* play, the words and actions of conflict are acted out, without the seriousness of intent of genuine conflict. So long as those playing give some cue that their intent is playful and they avoid attacking with intent to harm then play conflict is a uniquely valuable type of role-play. With play conflict we must pay close attention to the emotional state of the other(s). This creates a mutual understanding and degree of empathy, which is often accompanied by a sense of 'fair play': cooperation between players to make sure everyone is enjoying the play and is given a chance to compete. Indeed, play conflict *can* provide a lot of fun, excitement and mental as well as physical exercise.

Applications and advantages

It can be easier to joke about something important than talk seriously about it. In the same way, the mock argument can allow the significance of certain subjects to be explored and mutual understanding to be found, where debating it calmly might feel awkward, less effective, or at least less fun.

Imagine that your partner, or someone close to you, is rather anxious about doing 'something wrong' and prone to unnecessary apologies. They apologize to you for squeezing the toothpaste tube from the middle, it's the fourth worried apology that day for something equally trivial. Instead of gently telling them not to worry, again, you decide to start an 'argument':

"I'm sorry, I'm going to have to not see you any more. The toothpaste was the last straw. I'm sure you did it deliberately. I mean you might as well have spat in my face. I will leave immediately. Please pack my things and remember to fold everything perfectly. Do you have anything to say for yourself?"

The idea here is to suggest how silly worrying about such small things is, by blowing an already inflated importance out of all proportion. If the person is able to see this and laugh at your reaction, the new understanding may sink in deeper. (It might even be that by expressing this kind of playfulness you encourage the other person to explore that way of expressing themselves too.) It's worth being aware though that some people really struggle with play arguments or sarcasm in general. Also there can be quite a fine line between play and perceived aggression or ridicule, so use with caution.

If we wanted to respond to the above kind of 'toothpaste scenario' non-verbally, we might, for instance, pretend to transform from Dr Jekyll to Mr Hyde[15] for a few seconds, followed by a quizzical smile, as if to say 'Come on, do you really think this is so important to me?'

The physical play fight has particular relevance in courtship. It is a way of transgressing physical boundaries in a playful way to gauge another person's interest, both in play *and* in physical contact. The heightened levels of awareness and blood flow in this state can be compared to what happens with more amorous arousal. In new and established couples, play fights can often have a sexual tone to them.

Another handy use of the play fight is working out aggression or pent up energy safely – providing the person receiving it feels safe and understands the situation.

Teasing or making fun of someone *can* have a positive meaning. It can show that we understand what's really going on with someone, that we can see when they're pretending and what they're really trying to say. What's more it can do this in a light hearted way, while demonstrating confidence and well developed social skills. Consider, for example, someone you're close to is pretending to be ill because they want to avoid making a presentation to friends or colleagues. The thought of it fills them with anxiety and fear of embarrassment. You might say:

"Hmm, you look pretty ill there. I can only imagine how upset you are that you'll have to cancel that presentation you were so looking forward to making. Did the dog also eat your notes by any chance?"

If this is delivered coldly then it will probably appear as a

---

15 Referring to the famous story by Robert Louis Stevenson, where the respectable Dr Jekyll transforms into the monstrous and debased Mr Hyde after drinking a potion.

sarcastic verbal attack, lacking in any sympathy. But if such words are delivered with a friendly and conspiratorial smile then the affect is very different. Even if you said directly: "I think you're pretending to be ill because you don't want to make that presentation", it might not show the same degree of understanding. It might even seem condescending or evoke embarrassment or shame, where joking as above shows you know their way of thinking as if it was your own.

The use of this kind of joking really depends on the level of rapport you have with someone and your ability to show in your body-language that you're not trying to cause them suffering. If you can do that, then it can deepen a sense of mutual understanding and help someone shift their perspective and explore different ways of relating to and acting on a troubling issue. Showing understanding with a – not necessarily conflict orientated – sense of humour can also avoid fears that you may be diagnosing or looking down on someone, opening a path to more trusting conversation. In other words, if you help someone to see the funny side of an emotional problem, that problem often becomes easier to resolve or at least easier to talk about.

To continue the previous example about feigning illness, if the joking is taken well, that person might respond: "OK, was it that obvious? I just can't face it, I go to pieces when I have to talk to groups, I always have. I feel terrible about it." If you wanted to stay with a sense of humour to help the person re-evaluate their situation you might respond with something like: "So does it seem like your audience will be out to get you? Will there be bowls of rotten veg for sale at the door to throw at you? Hecklers?" At this point the person may relax about their engagement or be more open to discussing the issues. If you get the response: "You just don't understand!" then you've probably lost the warm-heartedness from your connection and they're seeing only ridicule. (Anxiety issues can reflect deep self-beliefs. See section: 'Untangling values, beliefs and desires'.)

When 'play' isn't just play

In play conflict, acting in ways that would normally be considered judgemental, insulting, spiteful or aggressive can be perfectly acceptable – because of the understanding that it is play. Obviously things can get out of the play zone though, especially when behind the play is a battle for 'social advantage'. This is a common form of what seems to be play conflict (although it's debatable how much play it really is). Within the framework of play we can compete for seniority in a social group or hierarchy; a victory in play is then taken in place of what might result if the conflict were acted out more seriously. Thus all parties can accept the results without risking greater injury from an all out conflict.

That's all fine, evolutionarily speaking, but this form of play conflict, where for someone there is a real sense of being put down, can be very detrimental to relationships. Where empathy or positive regard is lost, play fights, play arguments or even joking can easily cross over into intimidation and bullying.

Joking is particularly apt for this type of not-quite-just-play conflict. Let's look now at this use of joking which has a less positive meaning. Consider those situations that start off as someone 'only joking' and end up with someone else being quite upset and an argument ensuing. This could be a case of 'over-sensitivity', it might also be an indicator of a tendency to joke at another's expense (for the sake of being dominant or otherwise making yourself feel better).

If you think you might be prone to making this type of joke (or you've been accused of being so), spend a week taking notice of the jokes that you really do make. Pay particular attention to how they frame the person you're joking with. If that frame tends to be one that portrays them as: *silly, stupid, odd, subservient, inadequate, inferior, at fault,* etc. then I suggest you have a problem worth fixing.

Certainly there are situations where making fun of someone in good humour can be acceptable and everyone is able to have a laugh – with 'give and take' of course – and understand the positive intent behind it. But if there is a *trend* of joking that portrays the person you're sharing the joke with in the above listed negative ways, then you're sending a powerful message. That message says that you put yourself above them and that you see them as worthy of ridicule or contempt – even if your jokes, when taken individually, seem to be good humoured.

If you do joke like this it could be that you don't really identify with the above message, that it's just a bad habit you've acquired, but the message sent remains the same. This will naturally tend to start arguments and will certainly be a big spanner in the works of any relationship.

Peace bringing approaches to humour

It might be hard to find other ways of being funny, if you're used to joking by exposing people's flaws. In my school days, I was known in the playground for my sharp wit. I can see it now as a way of carving out a place in a social hierarchy and a way of looking after myself. It took me awhile though, to learn that I could use my wit fully in ways that didn't put people down.

I have to admit, watching a lot of comedians it seems like being funny is easier for a lot of them too when they're making fun *of* someone. But it is possible to be very funny and not have to do that (Bill Bailey is a personal favourite who demonstrates that fact rather well). For a start, if you must make fun of something, why not begin with yourself? Then move on to 'ideas', conventions (not just the comic-book kind), customs (while being sensitive to present company and cultural diversity), institutions, film genres, fictional characters, politicians, etc., avoiding directly targeting other individuals entirely. (There's still a chance you'll offend someone who identifies with those things, but it's at least not as direct.)

The element of surprise is a key one in humour; just doing something quirky and unexpected is often enough. Then there's word play, innuendo and physical humour. We have then quite a fertile bed of 'funny seeds' to draw from when it comes to humour, that don't involve making others the butt of your jokes.

Humour can be used effectively to diffuse conflict, if it shows understanding and an underlying calmness and positive regard for the other person(s). However, if there's even a slight apologetic or fearful element to the humour, or an apparent lack of understanding then the effect will be less favourable. In the latter case it can be taken as an attempt to make light of something serious or avoid responsibility. From a threat-focused perspective, it easily becomes an invite for further attack, e.g. "You think this is a laughing matter? Are you taking me seriously? You obviously have some big issues with taking responsibility!" The question to ask is: Are you joking to try and run away from a conflict or to address it? If it's to address it, do you understand the situation and can you make a joke with an inner sense of calm and positive regard?

Imagine someone is expressing what seems like a lot of displeasure towards you and is applying pressure to get you to do something. If you think it might be coming from desperation and fear, trying to empathize with them may be the best way to go. E.g. "I can see you have a great need to express your feelings right now. Are you feeling desperate or frustrated because you wanted/needed/hoped ...?" But sometimes it takes the rediscovering of common ground before someone is willing to open up about their distress. Without it, allowing themselves to be more deeply understood might seem like a *vulnerability* which you could exploit.

Humour can help your commonality be remembered. Imagine, for instance, there was a misunderstanding between you and a close friend. They believe you were disloyal and have a strong sense of being betrayed. You talk for a while, but they're being passive in their anger: "If you can't admit that you betrayed me, then I don't know what we have to talk about. I don't see the point in 'sharing our feelings', when the plain fact is, what you did was dreadful. It was below what I thought you were capable of."

One example of using humour to restore a sense of commonality in the above scenario might be: "It's funny – your need to get clear on the truth is just like my need to get clear on the truth and I know we both value our friendship, otherwise we wouldn't even be trying to have this painful conversation. Yet, somehow, here we are, finding it so hard to communicate. Were we always this stubborn with each other?" The idea is to think of what you have in common and is currently important to both of you, including your underlying positive intent and then contrast that with the fact that you're *still* fighting each other. There's a funny side to that. If everyone can appreciate it then strategies such as where you each talk for five minutes, uninterrupted, while the other person listens, can be very effective.

Otherwise, what if it seems more like someone wishes to assert dominance over you in a more 'status orientated' way (which itself may be underpinned by fear)? Then *assertive* use of humour can work well – especially where they refuse to engage with you directly on the level of feelings and needs. For instance, perhaps someone close to you is upset with a meal you've made for them: "These carrots are underdone and the meat over-cooked. I expect a little better than this, what's wrong with you today?" One way you might respond with assertive humour is: "Oh, I'm so sorry master, it was unforgivable. Would you like to whip me now, or later?"

Rather than talk about food, or what is or isn't a 'reasonable' expectation, this kind of response addresses the much bigger issue of the person's attitude towards you. It shows you're wise to what's going on – and that you're not OK with it. Remember: be calm in your delivery with a positive regard for the other person for maximum effectiveness.

Obviously, if someone is dead-set on being 'the boss', or

testing out whether they can be, then you may have a fight on your hands. Using humour to be assertive is one option to try and steer the conflict or tension more into the domain of play.

Let's take another example, where someone is asking the impossible of you and is not seeing that fact: "Please could you to run a little shopping errand for me today, and also do the cleaning and book the holidays, before you cook dinner later? I'd really appreciate that, thanks!" After reasoning fails, you might try: "OK fine, I've decided that it's possible for me to do all that, but I'll only need half the time, because in the other half I'll be solving world hunger." If someone is able to laugh with you, it's hard for them to maintain what can seem like an 'against you' attitude, or one that is insensitive to your reality.

To compromise or not to compromise

Supposing you've come to a point where your serious disagreements are expressed in a mutually respectful and fairly non-judgemental fashion. Where, despite the very best of efforts, you can't find a solution such that everyone's needs are met fully and you don't wish to agree to disagree or go your separate ways, compromise is another option.

Why compromise can be smart and healthy

If things have come to a head and you don't wish to give way, agree to disagree or part, but to continue trying to get your way, then it will probably mean someone else making a compromise to make that possible. If they resent doing that even slightly, it then becomes pretty hard not to fall into a 'threat-focused' or fighting style of conflict; someone is 'winning' or being dominant, someone else is 'losing' or being submissive. Therefore, in situations where neither of you wish to agree to disagree or go your own ways, a *willingness* to compromise helps you keep a collaborative focus in disputes. Such willingness also shows maturity, goodwill, a generous spirit and flexibility – especially if you're prepared to take the lead with showing it. Of key value though, is the attitude we compromise with.

Conflict arises because people have their own minds, perspectives, experiences and needs. It's natural, even between people with similar interests. We can't always get what we want either and sometimes what someone else wants seems more, or just as, important to us than what we want. When things seem that way out of an unforced willingness to give, show appreciation or care – without a sense of obligation, threat or shame – then compromise is a natural and healthy part of a relationship. Compromise where there *is* a sense of obligation or coercion of some kind tends not to sit very well and can easily lead to resentment and further conflict down the line.

If you are open to compromising, considering the bigger picture, is there a *balance of give and take* in the relationship? Can you let the other person know that something is especially important to you and they'll be willing to compromise gracefully where they feel less strongly and vice-versa? It takes trust and respect to have this kind of *mutual flexibility*, and the result is a more resilient relationship. There's no end of possibilities but some examples of compromise are: changing the date, place or cost of some arrangements, missing an activity sometimes which you look forward to or making an extra effort to get on with a relative or dear friend of someone close.

Do it gracefully, acknowledging the choice

A key point here, once you've shared your feelings, explored options to meet your needs and then decided to make a compromise, is to do it *gracefully*. That is, after you've agreed, without a big sigh, or making a huge point of what a pain it is or continuing to let them know that they 'owe you'. It spoils the agreement and suggests resentment. Compromise because, all things considered, including your value of the other person's needs, that is what you felt was the *best possible thing to do*, and you *want* to do the best thing possible. Own your decision.

If you make a choice to compromise on something and you're finding it especially hard to do it gracefully, or you're wondering whether it was the right decision, then ask: "Given my options and all the things I care about, is this really my best option?" If you answer 'yes' then try this exercise. When you think about the compromise, tell yourself repeatedly: "I'm doing this because I *have* to." Now compare that to how you feel when you say: "I'm doing this because I *choose* to." Which feels better and helps you to feel more at peace with your decision? When you think about it, actually everything we say or do is a choice. Sometimes it might be a choice between a rock and hard place, but the choice is still there.

Liberating entrenched conflict

Long standing disagreements, tiffs or feuds can be especially hard to break, because the resolution of conflict goes against entrenched positions. Each party has a catalogue of stories to support their position and to change it would be to compromise on what they felt was right, risking pride, the forgetting of injustice or even further injury. The more habituated a conflict is the harder it is to make what seems like such a big compromise – a change of position, or perspective. But if there's something to be saved in the relationship, whether it be between family, long time friends or partners, this willingness to compromise – in the form of changing perspective (and thus approach) – is precisely what is required.

It's not that you're 'giving in' to someone else, but simply to inner transformation. Without the stories that are built up around old judgements, our long standing disagreements could not last. Thus those stories and judgements must first be acknowledged and then laid aside for reconciliation to happen. It's about stepping outside of established roles. (The process of doing that may involve some unravelling of your values, beliefs and desires, see section: 'Untangling values, beliefs and desires'). Then it's a matter of keeping our focus in the *present* (what needs are alive right now, not bringing up old stories) and sharing feelings and needs without blame or other judgement. Section: 'Get your fresh roles here' explores one such example.

Agreeing to disagree and over-compromise

It's a fact that not all disputes can be resolved such that everyone gets all of their needs met to the extent they had wished. None-the-less, sometimes agreeing to disagree and finding a way of working around a point that you both strongly differ on is the most favourable decision. By accepting each other's differences and not trying to force a change, it's still possible to end such a dispute peacefully and respectfully. Such an outcome may not be one where everybody gets all that they wanted. But it is one where everybody accepts the outcome as the best that could be hoped for – *at the time and all factors considered*. It is one where feelings and needs were heard, and shown to be heard, and possibilities allowed to be explored.

A simple example of agreeing to disagree might be a couple going shopping together. Alice and Bob both enjoy going into to town together to do their shopping but for different reasons. Alice would like Bob to join her when she shops for clothes, because it meets her need for togetherness and gives her reassurance that what she's getting is pleasing to Bob. Bob, on the other hand, would prefer to do his clothes shopping independently and spend more time looking at camera equipment, say, because it meets his needs for efficiency and excitement. But he likes walking in town with Alice and sharing a drink together in a café after shopping, because that also meets his need for togetherness.

Alice and Bob respect each other's needs and try to find a compromise, such as limiting the amount of time they each spend doing what they tend not to enjoy when shopping together. But whatever they try it seems to lead to stress for both of them. Eventually they agree to disagree on the subject and decide to go into town alone to shop. It's not exactly what they both wanted, but it seems to be the best option for them. It is, in a way, another type of compromise.

It's important to remember that agreements to disagree in personal relationships are not contracts, nor are they necessarily permanent. They are simply an agreement to accept each other's differing values, beliefs and desires – even if that makes *some* of our needs challenging to satisfy. However, *this does not mean you have to forget about those needs*, rather that it's necessary to investigate other situations, ways and times for meeting them. In the case of Alice and Bob that might be, for instance, looking at a short-list from a clothes catalogue once in a while and going for more walks together.

The process of agreeing to disagree is much easier if you stop thinking: "I/you/we/they *should* ...". The less you do it, the easier it gets. Another factor that makes the process easier is getting over your fear of rejection, as explored in section: 'Fear (and general emotional turmoil)'. Really acknowledging the fact that you don't see eye to eye on a matter important to you and someone you're close to can raise such fears. But then, if that difference is a worry, how else can you lay it to rest?

Is it possible to be over-compromising with things that are important to you? Yes. Four signs that this is the case are:

- You notice a drop in your sense of daily enthusiasm for and absorption in what you spend your time doing.
- You feel less of a sense of purpose in your life.
- It seems like your freedom of self-expression on a daily basis has been hampered.

- Your general health suffers.

Ongoing compromises that lead to the above are almost certainly not good for you. Setting boundaries for yourself in this respect is a smart choice. But before it even gets to the point of such over compromise, if we come back to the idea of *holding our own needs as equally important to the needs of others*, then saying 'no', when we're not truly willing to compromise or agree to a request, becomes easier.

A 'no' does not mean rejecting the needs of others. When we say 'no', we're taking responsibility for our own well-being – and allowing someone else to take responsibility for theirs. A "no" (or a "I'm not willing/I'd prefer to ...") can be an incredibly valuable response to give in a relationship, and not just for our sake. It helps the other person to understand our needs more and know us better. It also helps a natural balance of give and take to be found, which is ultimately good for everyone. See also, page 150.

Criticism, 'over-sensitivity' and the wall

Here we discuss various types of and responses to criticism. So what about that common catalyst of conflict, criticism? The previous discussion of sharing feelings and needs without judgement applies in as much as criticism is a *type* of judgement. Criticism, however, is specifically about making a challenge and actually finding fault – or at least room for improvement.

Taking criticism, the 'good' and the 'bad'

If you find criticism hard to deal with, here is a tip that may help: ask yourself, what's the intent of the person 'criticising'? Do they want to help or obstruct you? Then behind that, can you see the underlying positive intent to meet their needs, through their criticism?

If their overall intent seems to be constructive, or at least *wanting* to help, remember, sometimes criticism can be a favour. Look for what you can learn. Indeed, some people value those they're close to being willing to criticize them, as it shows an assertive frankness which they respect and trust. It can also show a willingness to risk a negative reaction in order to give you some information *they believe* will be valuable to you; a sign that they care. See how we can remould the idea of criticism? If the criticism is phrased quite negatively, try to re-phrase it more positively. E.g. "You're doing it wrong. If you want to stop losing you need to XYZ" → "So you're saying, if I try altering my approach/technique to XYZ, then I'll be more successful?"

Otherwise, if the intent seems more to punish or to be obstructive, again look for what you can learn: are they in pain and angry? Are they trying to compete with you? Do they want to be important or in control? Is their challenge really an invitation for play? If it's along those lines *it's not really about the criticism*. You can then respond with sensitivity (feeling less emotional threat yourself) more directly to their unmet needs.

The more aggressive, mean or bitter criticism is, the more suffering is buried underneath it. Often criticism, including name calling, is a way of expressing anger and pain, or an attempt to defend against blame or punishment – so addressing those possibilities can help get to the root of the issue.

Tending to see judgement and threat where none is made or intended

Some people have a tendency to take what is chiefly a dispute or comment about something independent of them as a reflection on them or a deliberate veiled personal judgement. This can be bought on by judgemental language, e.g. "Did you see those tatty old shoes that person was wearing? Pretty clear they have no pride!" → "Hey, I have a pair of shoes a bit like that and I quite like them. What does that say about me then?"

Sometimes though, it is just a case of having their attention focused on potential judgements or threats – to the exclusion of what's actually being said. (See section: 'The glass melon dichotomy' for ideas on redirecting your attention.)

Even using the most sensitive and non-judgemental of language, just articulately expressing your feelings relating to something you disagree on or making a genuine request will still lead to some people having a sense of threat. There are thoughts like: "You're challenging me because you think *I am wrong*, even if you don't say it directly." or "I know you're really blaming me for how you feel." or "You're trying to control me." These thoughts can lead to very emphatic responses like: "No!" or "This conversation is over!"

There is the confusion between having differing opinions or needs and finding personal fault, and between the goodness of a strategy and the goodness of themselves. Or, there is a fear that you will use your unfamiliar way of expressing yourself, which they're not comfortable with, to manipulate them (as perhaps they've been manipulated a lot emotionally in the past).

Where someone seems to be hearing criticism or other judgement and fearing manipulation, despite no such intent from you, here are some things to do: try to develop empathy with them, emphasize your respect and be *very* specific about what your position is. In the case of disagreements, be clear, even if you don't agree with their opinion, decision or strategy, you know that they have a positive intent to meet their needs. In the case of a request, be clear that you don't wish to take their freedom away from them.

If you'd just like to have your feelings heard, where normally you would be cut off, something like the following may help: "I want you to know that I don't blame you for my feelings. They are totally my responsibility. It would really mean so much to me just to have you hear my feelings, without you thinking you were wrong in any way. Would you be willing to try that and hear what I have to say?" You may get a very positive (and relieved) response to this request, but guilt, or fear of it, can be a hard thing to let go of. E.g. "But when I hear you talking about your unhappy feelings I just can't help feeling guilty, so I just don't want to hear it. I'm sorry." could be another response. In such cases, gentle attempts to understand more can help, e.g. "When you feel guilty, is that because you blame yourself for something you've done or not done, or because you think *I'm* blaming you?" followed by reassurances that you're not interested in finding any wrongdoing, and that you really do just want to be heard.

Despite repeated attempts to understand and reassure, if someone close to you is steadfastly refusing to listen to what you'd like to say in terms of your feelings and needs, then it could be time to ask the question: "How do you see this relationship continuing?" This isn't about threatening anyone, but simply honouring your own needs alongside theirs. Re-evaluating what you each mean to one-another and what you're each getting from the relationship can help you both gain some clarity and momentum to connect in empathy.

Denial and avoidance

For most people there are times when it's tempting to avoid facing a conflict, or simply to deny its existence: "What's to talk about? There is no problem, everything is fine." At the heart of it is often the fear that we won't be able to cope or that we're helpless to change anything and that talking about it will only worsen the situation. So we erect a wall around the issue.

If someone adopts the above strategy of avoiding conflict it could be that they think by talking about a 'problem' they have to accept personal fault or responsibility. In the previous sub-section on page 210 there was a suggestion for helping someone to hear you if they have these concerns. This may also help where someone is denying the existence of difficulties that have come between you.

If someone is already under stress in their life, then facing 'yet another problem' isn't going to be that appealing. It might not even be that they're worried about you judging them, it could be that they're judging themselves and want to avoid the shame involved in facing those judgements head on. For instance, let's consider some stereotypical gender roles. If you believe that to 'be a man' you have to be the 'self-sufficient, problem-solving breadwinner', but you currently don't see much hope in being that, you might prefer to be tarred and feathered than talk about anything that might expose the issue. Similarly, if you believe to 'be a woman' you have to be the 'home maker who also works, yet has time to organize the holidays and the energy to make love on any given night', you may prefer to struggle on than to talk and face what you see as a personal failure.

If a person is thinking in terms of avoiding problems (or denying personal failures) then shifting away from the problem perspective might open up communication. Be clear that you don't want to talk about 'problems', but rather what is true for you and them at this time. Be clear that you'd like to know how you can *support, help or serve* each other in this situation, while respecting each other's needs and limits. Doing the above may relieve some of the stress they're feeling, so they're then comfortable enough to talk more openly.

Manipulation

Related to the subject of conflict and compromise is manipulation. Faced with conflict, compromise, or indeed a lack of compromise or acceptance, it can be tempting to manipulate someone, to bring about a 'better' situation. To manipulate is to control or handle an object or person in a skilful or artful manner.

While it may involve deception, I feel the key point is the objectifying effect of manipulation. If through trying to achieve what we want, we start to ask 'How can I get this person to do XYZ?', we *depersonalize* them (much as with possessiveness), in as far as they become like a 'thing' to be controlled to satisfy us. From time to time most people show some elements of manipulative behaviour, for instance coercing with a promise, feigning injury or ignorance to get attention, or flattering to get favour. Sometimes manipulation is innocuous, other times it's far from it.

Manipulation can, for instance, be an attempt to meet needs for significance: *"I'm important because I can control you."*, certainty: *"If I handle you skilfully I can be more sure about things."* or respect: *"You will have to respect me because I have power over you."* Meeting such needs, then, presents the choice: to treat the other person as someone to potentially *collaborate* with in meeting them, or as a *threat* to those needs to be conquered, contained and transformed. Manipulation is not necessarily about having someone wrapped around our finger. It could be that we've found more sincere approaches less effective at meeting our needs in the past, or that we're simply afraid of exposing our true feelings and vulnerability.

If what we desire is relationships founded on *mutual respect* and *understanding* perhaps the thing to focus on is noticing when our view of others begins to grow object-like, or tinged with fear, and thus inherently further away from what we really want.

Assertiveness

We've already touched on the subject of assertiveness in different areas, from anger to responsibility to humour. Here I want to bring the ideas together and ask, 'What does it mean to be assertive and how can I do that while being respectful and sensitive?' Firstly, if you're sensitive, a good listener and care about other people's feelings, are you also a pushover, someone who is dominated by others? You needn't be. The sensitivity of empathy is a choice which does not mean forgetting about your own feelings and needs. Rather it means having a clear understanding of someone's emotional state and what needs might be in play. It has nothing to do with being overly 'nice', passive, not standing up for yourself or being apologetic for your own feelings and needs – all things which have more to do with your self-beliefs.

We're capable of having empathy with ourselves as well as with another person in any situation we're in. Having this balance, remembering that what you do is a *choice* and not over compromising, it is possible and natural to give joyfully when you are truly willing; and express with sensitivity *and* strength, when you are not. As discussed on page 208, it can actually be very helpful to say 'no'.

The empathy and honesty centric style of communication explored in this book allows you to be extremely assertive – without being aggressive, critical or demanding. That's because it's based on inner strength. One cornerstone of this strength is responsibility. Being in touch with ourselves, really knowing what we feel and need – and then taking responsibility for it – actually makes us far stronger than we would otherwise be.

The kind of assertiveness we want, then, is about asserting full authority over ourselves, rather than over anyone else. It's about knowing what's going on for us and what we'd like, owning it and being perfectly OK with sharing it (respectfully), when we feel an inclination to.

Assertiveness skills are useful in many parts of life, one area in particular being long lasting relationships. Assertiveness is a bedrock for mutual understanding and respect. Moving in with someone, for instance, can be a make or break test for how effectively we can communicate our own needs, while continuing to work well together. The quicker we learn to be assertive (in the way previously described), the easier spending a lot of time with someone tends to be.

The kindness of interrupting

Part of being honest is saying when you *don't* wish to listen (or to give in another way), e.g. "It's hard for me to hear you right now because of how tired/annoyed/angry/hurt/overwhelmed/... I'm feeling." Being genuinely willing to listen can be a way of showing kindness and sensitivity. But to continue to listen when you *don't* feel willing (but do so out of fear or obligation) is easily misleading and a recipe for misunderstandings and imbalance.

Is it rude and inconsiderate to interrupt someone? You *could* make those judgements and in some contexts it would agree with the judgements of social convention. But sometimes interrupting can be the kindest thing to do. Sometimes people carry on talking because they feel an obligation, or they're afraid of silence, or they're struggling to express themselves clearly and are going around in circles. There are many reasons why interruption can be a relief to the person talking and a way of saving the life from fading out of the connection.

Interruption *could* reflect an intent to take the stage from someone for ourselves. But if we instead make use of it to make sure we're not misunderstanding and to honour our own need for clarity and engagement in the moment, then interruption can be assertive as well as respectful, kind and honest. A simple: "Excuse me, are you saying that *summary of what you guess they might be feeling and needing/wanting/hoping/etc.*" can help everyone avoid boredom and frustration. Another, to the point interruption which can work well is: "Excuse me, I'd like to understand you, but I'm feeling overwhelmed by the detail. Would you mind summarising your point, or letting me know what kind of response you'd like from me?" Page 227 discusses interrupting non-verbally, which could also be a great option.

Sometimes it's you that needs a good listening to and it's OK to assert that, e.g. "I'd really like you to listen to me right now. Would you be willing to do that?"

The effect of focus and self-interest

The power of focus has been a key theme throughout this book. The diagram on page 217 integrates the topics discussed in the previous sections on conflict, showing how patterns of conflict reinforce themselves, according to how we focus. (See the parallel here with the CAP idea from page 31.)

Do you need to protect yourself from serious danger? Is your goal worth the loss of peace, mutual understanding and respect? Otherwise, the more fruitful path seems clear!

Nature has endowed us with the ability to operate in both a threat-focused mode (seeing no common interest of working together, or superseding it with a perceived threat) and a collaborative mode (placing a primary importance on the common interest and working together). This applies to *any* kind of conflict, minor or major, voiced or unvoiced.

Are you stuck in crisis management?

In the previous pages we've explored both modes of conflict and their traits a fair bit. Subsequently, it seems like threat-focused mode (given its heavy costs to intimacy and peaceful relations and thus its relative inefficiency in achieving mid to long-term goals) is most akin to an emergency back-up or crisis management mode. It's a fail-safe that kicks in when things like survival or reproductive success are at stake.

Without this level of threat it's interesting to note that the mode most singularly focused on self-interest is least likely to serve it, especially in the case of healthy, loving relationships. It seems self-interest is normally best served when focused on as a *collective* objective. But for many people, operating in this emergency back-up mode of threat-focus (with the judgement-heavy thinking that fuels it) seems to be the norm, even when they are materially secure. They are constantly in a kind of crisis management. The reasons for this, I believe, are to do with our social conditioning and environment (see sub-section: 'Education and employment', from page 270 for more on that). It's a self-perpetuating state, but, as I hope these sections have shown, one that can be positively transformed.

Contrasting modes of conflict

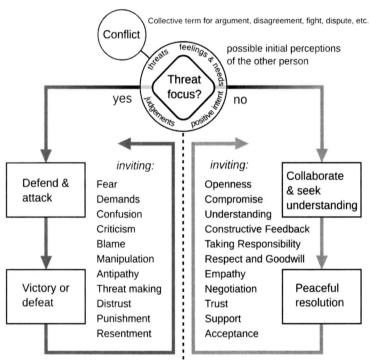

The experience of each approach provides fuel for taking the same approach for future conflicts.

Can threat to reproductive success (dealing with competition or not being attractive enough to get the mate you want) explain why a lot of people spend so much time in threat-focus mode? Yes, possibly. But does it mean we have no alternative? No, of course not. Just like every other kind of conflict in relationships, when you're faced with rejection or someone taking a strong sexual interest in your partner, you have a choice of focus. How could you focus on the common interest with the intent of finding a peaceful outcome? Just by treating the person who could represent a threat with the same respect, honesty and openness to empathy you'd have for anyone else. This approach demonstrates a lot of inner security and strength – besides the usual benefits of empathy – and so, ironically, is often very effective at avoiding potential rejection or competition.

When it comes to competition for the attention of a mutually desired person, why is it that some friends (or even family members) sometimes act with apparent total disregard for that friendship? By understanding just how separate a way of thinking threat-focus mode is from collaboration, we can gain a potentially more constructive perspective.

It can be saddening, even shocking to see a friend you trust and respect suddenly make you the butt of jokes or give you the cold shoulder in attempts to gain someone's affections. But when this happens it's fairly likely they're feeling a little conflicted, since in their mind (now operating in threat-focus mode) you've just become a 'threat to be defeated'. If it's a very ingrained behaviour they may not even realize that what they're doing is undermining the friendship. It doesn't necessarily mean your friendship is not genuine or important to them. But in either case, the issue is probably worth addressing with them. Getting clear with them about your feelings and needs, and theirs, and if necessary the status of your relationship, may help to wake them up in future situations. It can be an awkward subject to broach later and addressing it at the time often works out easiest. (Reviewing the sections on responsibility and play conflict may be of use here.)

The smarter way

So hopefully it's clear by now, that all this talk of not judging, taking responsibility for your feelings and actions, seeking to collaborate and being willing to compromise sometimes, is not about becoming some kind of saint. Really it's self-interest.

Seeking deeper understanding, peace and personal responsibility liberates and *empowers* you to transform unhappy feelings into happier ones, form closer bonds and to *get more from your relationships*. It's easier to trust someone if you know them better. It's easier to love if you feel peaceful and have the freedom and confidence that comes from positively taking responsibility just for your own feelings and actions. It's easier to avoid stress and have a mutually supportive and long lasting relationship with the willingness to compromise. It's easier to build create things together if you're always open to possible collaboration. So I think of this collection of perspectives and habits as 'the smarter way'.

Making the switch to using 'the smarter way' takes a certain braveness and determination. It could be those close to you are set in a more combative or defensive style of communication and resist efforts to 'switch modes'. It could be you risk embarrassment, stumbling over words or even initially ridicule by altering the way you communicate. This is something that gets easier with practice and the more you adopt the elements of the smarter way the more peaceful and in control of your own state of mind you will be. Not only that, but your company will tend to bring more joy and contentment to others.

Of course, the principles of the smarter way (and much of the previous sections) are about more than just 'dealing with conflict'. They also serve as a more general approach to embracing life and promoting inner and outer harmony.

Practical tips and further considerations

This part of the book explores in more detail various aspects and stages of relationships, from that first connection and getting to know someone, through to sex and potentially building a partnership. Along the way we'll discuss different attitudes, approaches and perspectives that are of practical use in all of the above, drawing from earlier material in the book.

First contact and conversations

Getting back to brass tacks, what can be said about the initial contact? There's quite a bit going on at this time; opinions forming, lots of new information and rapidly branching possibilities. You're discovering a new person, or rather what parts they're sharing. You might be in the same place as them for hours or just a few minutes.

As far as advice in a sentence goes, mine is: walk your talk, start as you mean to go on, listen with your whole being and remember, relaxed self-confidence, good humour and congruent communication makes for rapid rapport. The essence of what I believe makes the most beautiful connections is contained in the section: 'The five keys'.

If you find meeting and creating that first connection with people you're attracted to quite challenging, the next few subsections are for you. Otherwise, you may wish to skip ahead a few pages.

Initial attitude and keeping it in the moment

One of the very first and most important connections you'll make with someone, eye contact. Your emotional state and attitude comes through in how you make it. Page 78 discusses eye contact from the perspective of connecting with someone you're attracted to. The process of practice described there can be applied to building confidence, rapport and intimacy with friends, family and colleagues too. eye contact brings you into the present, which as we discuss more soon, is a valuable thing.

There is typically a certain crossing point where eye contact goes from being a sign of interest, confidence or trust, to one of either dominance or sexual intent. That point will depend on a person's character, whether they are the same or opposite sex as us, the culture and the context of the situation. If your cross-over point happens sooner than for the people you communicate with, it may create the impression that you're insecure or submissive, or otherwise disinterested in connecting with them. If your cross-over point happens later, you may be seen as dominant, imposing, or sometimes, depending very much on how you do it, quite seductive. If you'd like to change how you use eye contact so that it's more in tune with the person or people you're with, mirroring (see from page 83) and 'modelling success' (from pages 23 and 41) are good places to start.

Obviously, the way you make eye contact is crucial to the result you get. The surest way to improve how you make it is to examine your intent behind it, and shift accordingly. For instance, if you want a peaceful result, let peaceful thoughts and feelings build up inside you as you make eye contact. As for the most *attractive* kind of eye contact, in my experience this comes down to being playful, relaxed, and non-threatening. For playfulness, think about being a little bit cheeky and daring (see also page 255). Being relaxed means feeling OK in yourself about making contact. Now, combining those two qualities while being non-threatening is about nudging up against their cross-over point, but not charging over it. Allow your eyes to scan elsewhere and then return, trying to stay in tune with that person.

Moving on, what attitude do you tend to take when

approaching someone to begin a conversation? For instance, is it more one of wanting to openly explore possible connections, or more one of wanting to prove something about yourself? There's not necessarily a right answer, but this initial attitude will affect the sort of connections you develop. If it's not working, change it!

The above obviously leaves a lot to the imagination – which is where your *imagination* comes in. If you're comfortable expressing the attractive qualities previously discussed in 'The five keys', it hardly matters what you say initially. A simple, "Hi", "Hi, how's it going?" or "Hi, how's your day been/going?" is fine. A lot depends on the other person – especially their mood and ability to handle the unexpected. So simply take in their response with an open heart and mind.

Initial talking points could be something they're wearing (only pay compliments you mean – and if they're especially beautiful, go easy): "That's an interesting ...", something you observed about them: "I noticed when you ...", or something you'd like their opinion on: "Hi, can I ask your opinion on ...", a comment or question on something going on around you: "Did you notice ...", or about something interesting that happened recently in your life: "You wouldn't believe the/It's been a funny ...". Get creative. Before dialogue starts, and during, practice the principles of the beautiful connection. The words are often incidental.

Notice above, I didn't give any example of asking someone what they do, or where they're from. It's fine to ask these things, if it feels important to know or you're really interested. However, they are very *expected* questions that we've all answered a thousand times over, so you run the risk of putting someone in autopilot – and consequently not really engaging emotionally with you.

If you say or do something that brings people into a more fresh, exciting state of feeling and thinking they will start to associate that state with being around you. If you can bring them right into the living present, even better! This is one reason having a good sense of humour and generally being spontaneous and confident in a sensitive and playful way is so attractive. With this emotional engagement it can be more meaningful to then ask things like "What do you do?"

Observing an interest and getting involved

I'd like to give a quick example of using what you observe about someone to start a conversation. It can be a particularly natural way of doing it, especially when what you observe is currently something significant to the other person. It shows that not only do you pay attention to what's around you, but that you paid attention to something which that other person to some extent cares about. Here's the example:

You're on a train and you notice that the rather attractive person you sat down opposite to is trying to solve one of those problems in the puzzle page of a newspaper. They're frowning with a hint of frustration (they're also wearing headphones, but you don't let that put you off). You lean forward to catch their attention and say with a relaxed smile "A tough one huh?" Now, if they have any interest in talking to you, there are many ways for them to respond: say how it's been frustrating them for the last half hour, ask whether you're any good at those puzzles, or say how it's just that square there they need to solve, etc. Ideally you know something about and also enjoy the puzzle and you offer to help. At this point you're now working together on something of *mutual interest*, during which you can get to know each other better.

Of course you could do a similar thing with someone who is reading a book ("That's an interesting looking cover. Is it a good book?"), writing in a notepad ("Hello. How's the work going?") or looking out the window at a nice view ("What a beautiful view. Do you know this place?").

Beyond the small talk, enjoying discovering

Let's say that, whatever the scenario, you've made that first step, started a conversation and things are going well. What now? Now you enjoy the experience of discovering who they are and sharing who you are. The more we've developed and accepted ourselves the more we'll have to share, and the more things we've experienced the more we'll have to talk about.

What are your thoughts about some of your values and beliefs? Turn it into a conversation: "What do you think about the idea of creating your own destiny/deception in relationships being a natural tendency/compassion being at the heart of love/ morality being innate/...?" You can show interest in theirs just by asking something like: "What are your strongest beliefs about or values in life/relationships?" The values or beliefs we think or say we have aren't always the ones we act on, but it's at least a good talking point!

In conversation sometimes leaving out details or not answering directly can create opportunities for the other person to enjoy the process of *discovering* you. It also helps you see what interests them, by what questions they ask.

Saying goodbye for now and hello

Now supposing you're having a good first meeting and you'd like to meet again, but time is limited or perhaps there are several people you'd like to talk to there. Or maybe the conversation was going great, but shows signs of exhausting itself and you want to end it on a high.

Providing you've both enjoyed the other's company you simply need to give some clear indication of the fact and suggest meeting again, e.g.: "I've really enjoyed meeting you. I'd like to meet you again" or "I feel like there's a lot more we could share", if you've had an especially strong connection. If they respond positively: "Great, let's swap contacts!" or arrange a time there, if convenient. You can then say sometime like: "Thanks for the good conversation/time/company/..., I look forward to next time/ meeting you again/seeing you next week/...!" These are just a few suggestions, alter to your needs.

Before you part company it's generally a good thing to touch and offer a kiss on the cheek. (Of course, if there is no reason to part, then run with it for as long as it feels right.)

One thing I've learnt about kissing is not to rush. It can lead to uncomfortable collisions and a general feeling of awkwardness. Also if you are relaxed and unrushed you will find some people would like to kiss you straight on the lips. If you're not OK with that for any reason, just smoothly navigate around. It's nice to have the option! (See also page 120 and for a related idea for overcoming blocks to sexual intimacy, 236)

Within a few minutes of meeting someone we often know if we'd like to meet them again. So, if after this point, with a good rapport, either of you would like to move on, simply swap contact details then. You needn't wait.

If finding the words to suggest a place to meet up is difficult for you, try something like: "There's a place/view/exhibition/... that I'd like to show you. How about tomorrow?" Or just simply: "Would you like to grab a cup or tea with me sometime this week?" The better the rapport you have, the easier this part will be.

As for where to meet people you find attractive, the answer is, anywhere you see them! Public transport, supermarkets, parks, parties, the gym, classes – it's all good! I recommend places you enjoy being anyway.

For some people it literally is the saying hello part or even making eye contact that fills them with fear. I can relate, I spent many years shouldering that fear – and from time to time it still pokes up, to remind me to let go of self-judgements. Much of this book is about addressing self-judgements. There are different, complementary, areas to start addressing them from, one of the simplest is your habits of body. I recommend the eye contact habit on page 78. When you get comfortable doing this, don't be surprised if people start thinking that they already know you from somewhere else. It seems to be a natural consequence of being so relaxed when you first meet someone. Now *that's* a great place to start a conversation from.

Balance, humour and body language

Going back to conversations, one basic point about them is they're generally more mutually rewarding if there is a balance of dialogue and a variety of tones and emotions. So, not one person doing 90% of the talking or someone's whole life story right off the bat and not a drone of monotone. Also avoid habitual contradictions like "Yes, but...", which tend to undermine what someone is saying.

If you want to query some aspect of an idea someone is expressing you can use a question like "How does that work in the case of/allow for XYZ?" Otherwise if you really do disagree, do it directly: "I don't agree with that ..."

Ask open questions, like: "How do/would/did you feel about...?", "What will/would you do about/if ...", etc. If someone is reluctant to share their feelings/thoughts for lack of confidence, then gentle encouragement, that doesn't push too far beyond their comfort zone, can help.

This is also the case for good natured humour delivered with a friendly smile and some contact: "Er, do you need a moment alone? Should I come back in a minute?" Delivery is very important when you're saying something that, if you said it deadpan, could lead to hurt feelings or awkwardness. Let your body and voice communicate warmth.

If you help someone smile and laugh about something they've found a source of anxiety, it's then much easier for them to relax, because they've, at least temporarily, changed the way they relate to that issue. Laughter is a powerful transformer of anxiety and stress.

When you're talking to someone who's perhaps a little shy, offer more relaxed space for them to respond than you would a confident conversationalist. Don't feel the need to fill the gaps all the time. Silences can be beautiful.

Conversely, if someone is talking for their country and shows no signs of stopping to give you a chance (and you'd still like to continue a conversation) you can elicit a pause by touching them. This can be more effective than simply butting in, and done with sensitivity can help restore balance to communication. It could be they're just nervous and feel the need to keep talking to fill the space. A touch can be like saying "Hey, it's OK, I like you, lets share a moment of calm together." Often, if someone is worrying whether you like them, a simple hand on the shoulder or hug and a warm smile does more than words can.

Eye contact should be relaxed, free and unforced. Pay attention to your posture and what you're doing with your hands and feet. What does it say about your emotional state? If it's not what you want, change it! Similarly, if you muffled the words, what would your *tone* of voice be saying about you? Allow the qualities you want to show to come through these channels.

Now take all these points about your body language and voice tone and see what you observe in *theirs*. It could be they're sending you a message, knowingly or not. The non-textual is always a significant part of a conversation whenever you can see or hear someone.

Expressing attraction

There are limitless ways to express attraction. But when you do, do so in a way that doesn't require telepathy to understand and do it as if it's the most natural thing in the world – because it *is* the most natural thing in the world.

Expressing feelings of attraction is really just a form of appreciation mixed with desire. We'll focus on this particular form now and discuss appreciation more generally shortly.

Overt verbal expression of strong attraction is a bit too much for some people initially; it can lead to anxiety, even (or especially) if they are attracted to you. It's often better just to start with more physical contact (hand, shoulders, back, waist, knee, hair) and skip the words until later. Being affectionate is a big part of expressing attraction. See also pages 126-128.

In the context of talking to someone you find particularly attractive – and have a good rapport with – if you did decide to verbalize your interest you might say something like: "I find you very attractive/beautiful/intriguing/..." Done with a sense of ease, it can show a lot of confidence and if they have a favourable view about you then things could easily and quickly get more intimate – if that's what you want. But if awkwardness ensues (if you misjudged their feelings, or they're not at ease with their own attraction to you), you can diffuse the situation with something like: "Do you always take compliments so well?", light-heartedly, or just: "How are you feeling?" and continue from there.

Sometimes if we express our interest in terms of a judgement ("you're beautiful/captivating/so attractive...") it can create disagreement and confusion in the person hearing it. One alternative is to express more directly what the way that person is or what they do *means* to us, in terms of our feelings and needs, values or desires. We discuss this idea more in sub-section: 'Reward' from page 167.

Compliments, how to take them

Genuine complements are about reaching out and showing appreciation. Take compliments with gratitude, do not negate them. If you tend to negate them it can indicate that you don't trust what the person giving them tells you, or you don't value it. How would that make you feel in their place? This behaviour can suggest that you have a low self-opinion, which can be hard work emotionally to be around. You can opt to be humble, without dismissing or negating. Better yet, find out what you've done means to them and how they are affected by it.

Related to not accepting compliments is habitually belittling or devaluing yourself in front of others. Please stop it, now. It projects neediness and unhappiness.

Show your appreciation

From the first meeting on, practice sharing the various different things you *appreciate* about each other. E.g. "I like how you walk, it's so graceful" or "I really love how you touch me, it's so expressive and sensitive". If you'd like to express more directly what a certain quality means to you personally, try substituting feelings and values in place of labels or judgements. E.g. instead of "I love how you talk, it's so eloquent." we might say: "The way you talk often gives me such a sense of clarity and grace. I really enjoy and appreciate that." (See from page 167)

Hearing this appreciation – or otherwise being clearly shown – makes a big difference to our sense of being valued in a relationship. It doesn't have to be a big conversation, you can just say or show it when you feel it. In the same way, show your appreciation for the things you *do* for one another. A simple "Thank you" can do wonders.

Good meetings and good meetings

If the first meeting goes well, just carry on getting to know each other. Ask yourself: "What complementary differences and similarities do we have?" (See section: 'The five keys'.) What activities and conversations can help you discover and share these? This is how relationships develop.

Along with this general approach, three indicators of character that I find useful are: how someone is around their other friends, how they are around children and how they deal with the unexpected. As well as a good test of any pretences, these scenarios provide opportunities for someone to express desirable qualities, such as openness, resourcefulness, inner-calm, kindness, patience, playfulness and more.

If that first meeting or two doesn't go so well, consider that it was just a few of many millions of moments in your life, which though minute, present a learning opportunity for both of you – and in that sense also a good meeting.

Sex and the emotional impact

This section takes a multi-angle view on sex. Just why is it so important to most of us and what functions does it serve other than making babies? Some key considerations for before, during and after are offered along with various strategies for overcoming common obstacles.

What does sex mean to you?

There is often great emotional and social – as well as physical – significance to sex. There is also, in general, a powerful drive for having it. Because of these factors, just the idea of sex, as much as the reality, can be a great holder and releaser of emotion.

Sex can be a consummation of love, desire and trust. It can carry with it social status. It can also alter our self-image and outlook, release stress (or create it), promote emotional and physical health (or degrade it), and it can often lead to pair bonding behaviour. Sex, in a nutshell, is very flexible and multi-functional. While ostensibly the most intimate act and the fullest bodily expression of attraction, much like love, sex is really what we make it.

Why we get so hung up about it and ways of dealing with imbalance

Sometimes, due to our tangled VBDs (values, beliefs and desires), we can become quite unbalanced in how we think and act around sex. So much so that the slightest overtones of sexual feeling can cause major anguish and inner conflict, sometimes even leading us to denying the sexual aspect of our nature. On the flip side, the way we relate to sex can also lead to us completely obsessing over it at the expense of the quality and longevity of our relationships and our general health. Sex can be highly addictive, not simply because of the pleasure giving chemicals it releases but because of its ability to channel, vent and mask emotions. It can be a place to hide and forget, as much as one to act out emotional knots and unhealthy self-beliefs.

The kind of obstacles that lead to such imbalances are the same kind that impede healthy and fulfilling emotional connections with people in general. Whatever the obstacle is, it may be specifically anchored to sexual expression and so not present so much in other contexts. However, in as much as it is a collection of self-beliefs and physical and mental habits or conditioned responses that sabotage our balance and happiness, the obstacles in our sex lives are the same as in other areas of relationships. So then the solutions are also similar.

What about brain chemistry? Can chemical imbalances explain why our sexual behaviour can become unhealthy or destructive? We've discussed previously how there is a very strong link between behaviour and emotions (see sections: 'Internal dialogues and identity', 'Untangling values, beliefs and desires' and the exercise on page 68). Neuroscience is also showing a correspondence between certain chemicals and certain kinds of emotions – if you feel a certain way there is likely to be certain chemicals running around your brain. So, while brain chemistry can influence our actions, by deciding what actions to take (and what thoughts to focus on) we can also influence our brain chemistry. The loop runs both ways.

Perhaps issues tend to come up for you with new sexual partners, or perhaps it's a case of never having had sex before. I'll share a little of my past troubles that you may be able to relate to either some of your own difficulties, or those of someone close to you.

For a long time I had a major hang-up about sex. For me it was tied up with proving that I was not unlovable, or somehow irreparably emotionally flawed, both of which I suspected. Sex was an assertion of validity, acceptance and my own manhood, all things I felt lacking in myself. Therefore sex (or the lack of it) had a massive significance to me. It was tearing me up inside. Every time I saw a friend enjoying the physical affection of a partner it bought it home to me what I apparently was incapable of having (spot the negative internal dialogues) and feelings of bitterness and inferiority flooded through me daily.

Naturally the huge significance I placed on sex made me tense – and thus others also tense – and the feelings I had around it made me depressed and inhibited my confidence. Quite a viscous cycle! It took discovering and consistently working on the attitude shifting ideas discussed in this book repeatedly pushing myself outside my comfort zone, to get myself out of this rut.

For me, losing my virginity was a big deal and it wasn't until I was 25 that the day came. The symbolic and emotional significance was huge. I felt the accumulated weight of years lift from me and sensed a new power of self-determination. It wasn't that all my issues about sex then vanished, of course not. It took having a number of sexual partners and a further deepening of self-confidence and increased comfort with *emotional* intimacy before sex took on a different meaning. It became then less a 'self-proving achievement' and more simply an intimate moment of togetherness with my focus in the present. Perhaps this is the challenge, for a more fulfilling sex-life, however sexually experienced you are; to focus on the present moment togetherness.

A common block to natural sexual expression is *shame*. Sex is somehow 'wrong', 'sinful' or associated with being inadequate. This could be to do traumatic experience, gender identity issues or religious conflicts. Many pages could be written wrangling with scripture, so I wont do that. Instead I'll assume shame is a feeling you'd like to get rid of, at least around sex. In that case I suggest looking at the judgements and underlying needs or innate values that are *behind* your shame/sex conflict. Sections: 'Conflict' and 'Untangling values, beliefs and desires' may be helpful here.

If shame focuses around the element of *desire* (e.g. "The fact that I want sex means I'm bad/wrong/sinful"), then consider the difference between desiring sex and desiring, say, a nice cool drink on a hot day. Is one more or less natural than the other? What specifically is it about desiring sex that leads to shame? Getting clearer on that and searching for the underlying innate values as mentioned above will help you find better strategies for dealing with your feelings.

It's very sad that shame, a feeling that seems to hinder love, caring, understanding and acceptance – of ourselves and everyone else – is as common as it is around sex. Focusing on *giving* those four qualities to ourselves and others, seeing sex as simply one manifestation of love, caring, understanding and acceptance, may help to overcome some of the shame you may be feeling.

For many people, sex is a healthy activity that plays a significant role in their intimate relationships. Just how significant a role, differs from couple to couple. On the subject of balance within a couple, everyone has their own libido. Sometimes a significant difference in one partner's sex drive from the other's leads to major stress. As with personal imbalances the key is to explore the roots and different strategies for meeting the underlying needs. Stress or anxiety can be reduced simply by coming to an understanding that because your loved one may not want sex as much as you sometimes, that does not mean they don't love and cherish you being in their life. Similarly just because your loved one seems to very often have sex on their mind doesn't mean they don't also love and cherish you for other reasons.

Sexual desire can be fairly independent of any other quality in a relationship, although sexual intimacy often serves as a bond-strengthening process. Testosterone has been shown to increase sex drive, so since men tend to have more of it than women it's not that surprising they tend to be a little more focused on sex (accept approaching menstruation, where a woman's testosterone levels peak, driving up libido). Of course there are plenty of exceptions and there are many influencing factors on sex drive, including: stress levels, time of day, self-image, fatigue, degree of positive affectivity, relating beliefs and values, your strategies for getting affection, regularity of sex, hormonal balances and competition.

For the above reasons, our sexual attraction to a person can come and go from day to day, or from hour to hour. This means that during your moment of arousal, someone you usually have a strong chemistry with might be feeling fairly under-heated, or vice versa. While arousal can often be triggered as described in the 'Foreplay and dealing with pressure' sub-section, sexual desire is frequently an unpredictable thing. Accepting that makes relaxing easier.

Seek out what works

If you feel that the role of sex in your life is out of balance (either taking up too little time and energy, or too much), what are you doing about it? If it's not working then I suggest taking a different approach. Start by writing down your VBDs around sex. This will help you see any conflicts more clearly. Ask yourself: "What does 'sex' mean to me?", "What does it give me?", "What does it allow me to give?" Then have a look for some context specific role models. Who do you know who seems to have a really balanced and healthy attitude to sex and the kind of sex life that you'd actually like to have? Approach them and find out more about their VBDs and related strategies in that area. This needn't be such an embarrassing process. You might say, for example:

"Excuse me, I'd really like to get your view on something, would you mind? ... I've noticed you seem to have a very relaxed/confident/healthy/... way of being affectionate or physical/communicating sexually/flirting/talking about sexual things/... I want to be more like that and I was hoping you'd be willing to tell me a bit more about how you see things. I could really use some help."

Most people enjoy sharing knowledge in an area they're confident in and will be willing, even honoured or flattered, to help if you ask nicely. By getting not just one, but a variety of perspectives from different people who seem to demonstrate different qualities you'd like to have more of, you'll begin to build up some 'alternative strategies' that can help you. (See section: 'Our attitude to change'.)

As discussed in section: 'Lack of resources', external factors (like money or good looks) are no guarantee of happy relationships. Neither are they a guarantee of a desirable sex life. But it's only natural to play to your strengths. For this reason picking a role model who has some similar external factors will help you focus on the critically important shifts in self-image and outlook and play to your own strengths. (The 'Obstacles and new perspectives' part of this book covers ways of getting the necessary self-understanding and conviction you need to do this kind of thing.)

Overcoming blocks to sexual intimacy

Differences in sex drive within a couple and influencing factors on arousal are discussed on page 233. So, there are many reasons why sex with your parter may not be as fulfilling or regular as it once was. Section: 'Observing, feeling, needing, requesting' offers an approach to talking about sensitive issues that could help you get to the root of this issue and find ways of resolving it.

What if, prior to being in a relationship, you have some blocks between having good verbal rapport and having good *physical* rapport, that has a sexual energy to it? Towards sorting these things out it's often useful to have smaller, clearly defined interim goals, so here's one on goodbyes (or hellos) you might like to make your own:

When you say goodbye to a group of women or men, some of which you find sexually attractive, make a habit of having physical contact with those people – major point – people by and large love it. Many people these days are starved of physical affection and those that aren't tend to enjoy it! So, make it a friendly hug and a kiss. (It helps a lot if you're clean and smell nice.) Now, this is the challenge/goal: to feel comfortable and make space for that kiss to be a kiss on the lips. How does that work? Just by not rushing and feeling confident and affectionate. Stay relaxed and allow them and yourself the *opportunity*.

The situation is you're saying goodbye, you have just spent good time with them and it's a natural and common thing to hug and kiss in such situations. I suggest a group because the fact that other people will probably be doing this too will make it easier to do the same. But doing this when it's just you and one other is great also! If you need to, just start with a good hug and move on from there.

The reason I suggest starting with a 'friendly hug' and not a 'I'd like to have sex with you now hug', is so you can check out the other person's openness to you, without so much risk of them having a sense of being invaded. Pay attention to their response.

Sometimes you may find a person is less comfortable making contact than you are. That's OK. It could be for any number of reasons, many of which are not related to you. Remember you're just saying goodbye and it's just a friendly hug and kiss.

Once this habit becomes second nature, doing it between the hellos and goodbyes becomes easier – don't feel like you have to wait! Some attitudes that might trip you up here include:

"I should maintain respectful distance" – and other antiquarian ideas. Not forcing someone to hug or kiss you is being respectful, but not giving them a friendly invitation and opportunity can come across as cold or disinterested – be the brave one!

"They probably don't want to" – how would you know if you don't give them a chance? Just as likely they're thinking "they probably don't want to" about you! (See section: 'Internal dialogues and identity'.)

We'll now discuss other kinds of specific blocks to sexual intimacy, such as anxiety or pressure. The gist of this sub-section is that, whatever the block, if you look for ways of tackling it from the root and a little bit at a time, then the whole thing will get easier to overcome.

A natural arrival and dealing with pressure

Through your touch, movement, voice, breath, smell, taste and eye contact, sex is a wonderful opportunity to carry on communicating and discovering more about each other. (It's not simply a mechanical pleasure giving activity, nor does it have to be a performance test.) Looking at it this way, it can be an extremely natural progression from talking to touching to kissing and having sex.

Sometimes it doesn't feel so natural though. If you're in a relationship where it seems like you're being pressured to have sex and you don't wish to, one thing that can help is to talk frankly about it. Express clearly your feelings and any concerns you have about them, their intentions or sex itself. It will hopefully help them understand the situation better and also relieve you of some pressure. What does sex mean to them? Do they take it more lightly than you'd like, or do you see too many strings attached? Talking about it openly should at least help you know each other better. We listed earlier some of the many reasons that affect libido, so it needn't be that anyone is 'at fault'.

On the subject of pace, if you're all hormones and raging to go, remember to check in with how the other person is feeling. If physical intimacy doesn't progress at a pace comfortable for both people then it will probably stop progressing, or there wont be the emotional closeness, or pleasure there could have been. It's just one of those things that's very useful to be understanding of – that people heat up at different rates. We discuss foreplay shortly.

Sometimes the best way of helping someone feel good about sharing sexual intimacy with you is to pause yourself or even draw back a little when things are heating up. You could see this as teasing a little. In any case it does several things: it gives the other person a chance to express themselves and reciprocate, it shows you're in control of yourself and it creates anticipation and stokes desire.

In general, to naturally arrive at the point where you and someone you like want to have sex together, practice the five keys of the 'beautiful connection' (see section: 'The five keys'). Practice especially spontaneous playfulness and relaxed confidence – with progressive physical contact. Note, it would be an error to see the five keys as just some recipe for seduction. While you *could* use a pile of breeze blocks to make a dolls house, it's not such a smart use of them, and might end in personal injury. I'm not speaking out against 'casual sex' here or even seduction per se, just the idea of using some 'system' to objectify and emotionally and physically manipulate people. It will end in misery for everyone.

Foreplay

Play is an especially powerful and transformative process in many parts of a relationship. Foreplay (the play that takes place before sexual intercourse, or heading in that direction) can be thought of as an emotional and physical preparation for sex. Sometimes only the briefest of preparations is desired by each of you. Other times a more gradual, anticipation building process is needed, or at least strongly desired.

Sometimes by initiating foreplay, what started out as disinterest in sex, can grow into intense desire. In a sense, any kind of play with someone we're physically attracted to, even just a wink or lingering smile, can be seen as foreplay.

Types of physical foreplay that work well for a lot of people include: kissing, stroking, licking, sucking, pressing or gentle biting of common *erogenous zones*. Besides the genital areas, these include the neck, nipples and generally anywhere where the skin is particularly soft and near major blood supplies, like the inside leg and the back of the knees and elbows. Pay attention to the quality of touch. Some places are usually best treated with softness (such as the clitoris and forehead of the penis), while other places like to be grabbed. Really the message here is to explore and see what works for you and your partner. The very act of being explorative and playfully seeking to find ways of pleasuring your partner can be a big turn on.

Curiosity and especially generosity in foreplay goes a long way to improving the quality of your sex life, and consequently the health of your sexual relationship. (But avoid falling into a sense of obligation in foreplay, which isn't so helpful.)

Anxiety, 'over-excitement' and emotional intimacy

Moving on to 'the act itself'. With sex as with love; the understanding and trust shared between you can grow as you spend longer together.

Spontaneity is a great thing during sex, however it's worth also reading up on some sexual anatomy/technique to give you some ideas about how to give the most pleasure to your partner. People will differ in what works for them most, but there are a few things that tend to work well for a lot of people, some of which are listed at the end of the previous sub-section. Foreplay can also be 'during-play'. Often, keeping things simple works well.

While generally not having any problems with getting to this point and appreciating the positive value of sex, you might still have difficulties. Three interrelated factors that present problems are: anxiety (from a lack of experience, bad experiences, or shame), over excitement (possibly also due to a lack of experience) and a lack of emotional connection.

Anxiety and over-excitement (in the sense of climaxing very quickly, to the detriment of mutual satisfaction) can often both be addressed by slowing down. Take your time over what you're doing and feeling. There are no rules and there is no rush. It's different with everyone, remember to breath, and if you're uncomfortable, say so and talk through it if it helps. It's pretty difficult to hide feeling tension in this situation, so if it persists, you may as well get it out in the open voluntarily.

It doesn't have to be a straight road to the end. Fixating on a particular outcome can invite anxiety and frustration. Actually it's the twists and turns and changes in pace that can make the experience of sex more beautiful (and less tense) for everyone. Also fulfilling sexual experiences don't always have to involve intercourse, or orgasm.

Aside from slowing down, if what's causing problems during sex is shame – over your desires, body, or the idea of sex itself – then the ideas near the start of section: 'Sex and the emotional impact' may help.

Broadly speaking, emotional closeness during sex is about acceptance of, understanding and responding to each other's needs and desires. Sometimes what you both want is tender and gentle (including holding each other after intercourse). Sometimes it is more animal and primal (it doesn't have to be soft and sweet all the time), sometimes cheeky and playful, etc. On those occasions where you both have similar needs or desires and respond to those, you'll tend to feel very close. If you want different things, sometimes you can still have that closeness by showing understanding. Other times either a compromise is called for, or acceptance that sex is just not going to work well for both of you at that time.

Stay respectful and open to being playful and you can't go far wrong. Realize too, that *people often like to be enjoyed as much as to enjoy* – and of course one is often in the other!

Orgasm and ejaculation, for men and women

Orgasm. This psycho-physical, or even spiritual, experience is one of the most intense joys that we can feel. Yet the idea or pursuit of it can obstruct our connectedness, relaxation and pleasure during sex. One particularly obstructive idea is that if you don't have an orgasm, or if you don't bring your partner to orgasm, there is something 'wrong' with you or what you are doing. Ironically, if you can avoid thinking that way, you'll be more relaxed and more likely to have – and help your partner to have – one. The same goes for fixating on climaxing together; it's great when it happens, but it's perfectly normal (and far more common) to climax at different times.

Just as with libido, there are many factors influencing whether (and when) we orgasm or not on a particular occasion. Part of it is just physical – knowing the specific places to touch and how to touch them, for your partner. Part of it is psychological – feeling attracted, attractive and free of performance related pressure. Your partner may use some affirmation from you, that you find them attractive during whatever it is you're doing and that, whatever it is they're doing is just fine with you. Needless to say, faking orgasms, as expedient as it may seem, creates barriers to get over later on.

Contrary to common belief, men can orgasm without ejaculation and women can ejaculate with orgasm (and also without). The consequences of this are more full-body orgasms.

What do I mean by 'full-body orgasm'? Waves of intense pleasure flowing over your body, euphoria, increased affection, involuntary muscle contractions and vocalisations and increased heart rate, temperature and skin sensitivity. These are some of the symptoms. And they are all possible during sex and foreplay, without ejaculation. On the flip side it is also possible to ejaculate, without any of the above orgasmic experiences, accept for the necessary muscle contractions for the ejaculation.

For men, avoiding ejaculation opens up the possibility of multiple orgasms – along with the ability to satisfy your partner for longer. By having the option to avoid ejaculation, men can also conserve energy, letting more of the invigoration of sex carry on into the period after intercourse. To be clear, if as a man you're totally satisfied with climaxing along with ejaculation, that's absolutely fine. I do not mean to say there is anything 'wrong' with it – it's a truly wonderful and natural sensation – simply that there is an alternative you may like to explore, that may open up even more pleasure.

So, how is the above done? It's essentially a process of shifting focus and relaxing, while developing control of certain muscles. The first thing is to work on elevating pleasure, without crossing the 'point of no return'. In doing that, it may help you to stay focused on the shared experience between you and your partner, rather than to lose yourself in your own physical sensations. (Yes, it is tough to make that shift when the pleasure seizes you.) Maintain full, relaxed breathing and relax the front of your body. Practice getting closer to orgasm but reducing stimulation at progressively later points. You will notice that orgasm actually begins before the ejaculatory spasms. Now by drawing in your pelvic floor (contracting the pubococcygeus muscle that goes through your scrotal, genital area), with practice, you will be able to avoid ejaculation while having a full orgasm. You will also be able to maintain arousal and a full erection after orgasm. You may find the above easiest to experience at first, while you're lying on your back with your partner on top.

A similar process as above, of relaxation and 'teasing the peak', can be used by women to achieve multiple orgasms. But even though technically easier for women, multiple orgasms are still not such a typical experience. Indeed in several studies (including the ground-breaking work of Shere Hite) 50-70% of women do not have a single orgasm during sex, let alone multiple ones. Many women require stimulation of the clitoris in order to orgasm, or are greatly aided by it. Yet, sadly, there is a common belief in both men and women that if a woman doesn't orgasm from penetrative sex then there is something wrong with her, or what the man is doing. Really it's about experimenting and finding out what works for you and your body. If, as a woman, you'd like to experience orgasm from intercourse, it may help to allow more time and to find a position that also stimulates your clitoris (such as where you and your partner's pelvic bones rub together) or 'G-spot' (by changing the angle of your hips, or where you are entered from behind).

When it comes to female ejaculation, for many people, sadly, it's another source of confusion, anxiety and shame. In fact, it's a totally natural function that has been well known in many ancient cultures and documented in anatomical studies almost 400 years ago. It's even been discussed in marriage guides, such as the famous 1926 guide "Ideal Marriage: Its Physiology and Technique" by T.H. Van de Velde. Yet, oddly, it remains a contentious subject in much of the world today.

The substance, sometimes mistakenly thought to be urine, is expelled from the glands around and including the urethra and comes from the female prostate. It has a composition similar to the seminal fluid produced by the male prostate gland. Women that are unaware of their natural ability to ejaculate, may suppress it, or cause the ejaculation to go backward into the bladder. Of course, when these natural sensations are accompanied with anxiety or shame, sexual pleasure is dampened. As with male ejaculation, it can be very pleasurable and accompany orgasm. The key seems to be to relax the pubococcygeus muscle and to apply medium or firm stimulation to the urethral sponge or prostate, often referred to as the G-spot. If you are worried about peeing (as the initial sensation can feel similar) go to the toilet first.

The books on sexual health and fulfilment by Mantak Chia, talk more about orgasm and multiple organisms for both men and women.

Solo pleasure

Masturbation is an activity that humans share with many other animals, including: apes, dogs, cats, horses, birds and even porcupines, walruses and vampire bats[16]. It's a natural thing. Besides providing pleasure, stress relief and self-nurture there are also reproductive advantages[17]. Masturbation boosts sperm fitness for men (when ejaculation occurs). It also increases the chances of conception for women, when done close to sex, and reduces the likelihood of cervical infections.

Masturbation is another area of sexual pleasure that is subject to shame. Yet, when done with respect for our body, it can be a very healing, releasing and invigorating experience. Masturbation is a handy way (excuse the pun) to explore our own sexual nature, which has the knock-on benefit of helping us give and receive more in our sexual relationships.

---

16 Bruce Bagemihl (1999) "Biological Exuberance" ISBN: 978-0312253776, p.71,209-210
17 http://en.wikipedia.org/wiki/Masturbation#Evolutionary_utility

After sex and seeing through the haze

Finally, there is the question of what to do *after* sex. Sometimes it's already known between you. Especially in the case where it's the first time you've been together, I strongly suggest talking to gain clarity on the situation and see what you both want.

If there were any expectations of what sex would mean for you both that slipped by previous discussions, discovering them afterwards can be tough. Sometimes it happens, that one person assumes sex would equate to a kind of love and commitment that the other person doesn't necessarily attach to sex. A lot of confusion, stress and turmoil can result – that's why it's a good policy to be clear on any expectations (or absence of), *before* the fact.

Sex can do funny things to your brain chemistry, which often results in a kind of romantic love. Try to keep a foot on the ground and avoid language that places people on a pedestal (e.g. "she's/he's so perfect"). It's not about denying your feelings, more about associating words with them that have some room for movement as you grow to know someone more – without shattering hopes that had been placed upon them. So instead of 'perfect' you might say: wonderful, fascinating, sensitive, caring, passionate, funny, intelligent, etc. As we saw in section: 'The role of judgements' though, any kind of labelling can create unwanted effects.

If we grow too idealistic in how we see and talk about the person we're interested in or involved with, this can create a divide. If someone started attributing you with qualities you either don't have, or have but not in such superlative quantities, you might think they weren't really seeing you, but rather what they *wanted* to see. You might also have a sense of being pressured to live up to something you couldn't be. Do these thoughts incline you to get closer to someone?

One way to express strong feelings of appreciation and

attraction, without risking the above is to separate the *feeling* from interpretation or *judgement*. So if, for example, you were over the moon about someone's smile, instead of saying something like: "You have the best smile in the world, I love it, it's just perfect." you could say something like: "I feel so happy when I see you smile. My heart responds so strongly, in that moment I want for nothing else." See the difference? Strong feeling, but no judging or labelling ("best in the world", "perfect"). For more on the idea of expressing what matters to us, without making judgements, see section: 'Observing, feelings, needing, requesting'.

In sections: 'Love and life in the clouds' and 'But what is love?', the emotional impact of romantic love is discussed further.

Attitudes and the other's shoes

As the title suggests, this section is about putting yourself in the other person's shoes (trying to see things from their point of view) – and the attitudes that help, both in doing that and in making a bridge between wherever you both stand. We focus here mainly on the context of making a good first impression, but practising these perspective-taking skills will make it easier to understand someone's feelings and values in many different situations.

Evaluating appreciation: nice ≠ interesting

Just as every coin has two sides, every quality that a person has can be viewed from at least two perspectives.

You can probably recall having the experience where you said something to someone you'd just met, meaning well and got a response you really weren't expecting, or found quite confusing. This is an example of the same words or even the same *idea* having a different meaning or significance to different people.

But so what? A lot of these 'mis-communications' can lead to a good connection being cut off, even before its had a chance to really develop. Thankfully, a lot of these instances are predictable, which means we have a chance to avoid them.

Bringing it back to relationships, what often draws us to people? Beside the interest they might have in us, there is usually some quality or attribute (e.g. their looks, confidence, talent, intelligence, kindness, etc.) that *stands out* about them.

If that quality (or several) is one that they're usually noticed for, when you express your appreciation of it, your expression will be evaluated in the context of *all their accumulated experiences of how other people related to that quality*. Where it's a quality that a lot of people are *attracted* to, this can raise questions like: "Is this all they want from me?", "Can they appreciate the whole me?".

Being presented with so many choices also creates *competition* – and thus a shorter window of opportunity, to show them why they might like to get to know you. How do you stand out from the crowd? Even if someone is enjoying how you're expressing your appreciation of them, if you're doing it in the same way the last 100 people did, it doesn't really help you. *'Nice' does not equal 'interesting'.* (One of the most unhelpful and uninteresting kinds of 'nice' is the sort that can arise from an anxious need for acceptance or approval. It suggests fear and self-concealment.)

Fuller acceptance and bucking the trend

Let's now explore in detail some perspectives for a common attention-drawing attractive quality and then see how the same ideas apply to other such qualities. (Showing and responding to confidence is discussed on page 116 and elsewhere):

Consider for a moment you are a stunningly beautiful man or woman. How would that shape your view of yourself and the opposite (or same) sex? It could be that you're an extremely well balanced person and your appearance is just one of many qualities you value in yourself. It could also be your initial view of those attracted to you is equally non-judgemental and balanced.

On the other hand it could be your whole world revolves largely around your appearance. You might then, for instance, feel empowered in this situation as you get so much attention and people give you power over them. Or you might feel trapped because the attention you get depends on and is focused on this one quality and you want to connect in other ways.

There are many possible perspectives. In most cases, however, being approached sometimes 20+ times a day by people who have apparently fallen in love with you at first sight (or otherwise seem to want your close attention) will colour your view slightly. You could, reasonably, start to develop ways of letting people know quite quickly that their company isn't wanted – since otherwise you'd soon have no free time at all. You might learn to judge them soon, just in order to try and have a 'normal' life. You could even start to believe people are interested in you *only* because you look a certain way (which could lead to all kinds of insecurities) and will say anything to sleep with you, or be seen to be with you, until proven otherwise.

You might find ways of quickly *testing* how people are affected by your appearance, because you'd like to find someone who is genuinely comfortable in themselves around you. E.g. making clear eye contact and smiling flirtatiously, to see how they handle it, or by seeing how they'll react to requests to act like your servant. (It may be you also do that because you're so used to people going out of their way to try and please you.)

The truth is a lot of people will have strong reactions to your appearance. Some will be simply enchanted or overwhelmed, others may want to conquer it, some may be threatened or afraid (because it challenges their self-control, or makes them feel weak or inferior, or reminds them of their perceived lack of beauty). Over time people's reactions will influence your own beliefs and behaviour.

Now, how would you feel if someone you recently met just engaged with you on an emotional and intellectual level without bringing your appearance into the foreground? Wouldn't that be a refreshing change? Even if your appearance is at the centre of your world, someone – who you may expect finds you attractive – behaving in this way demonstrates an unusual self-control, sensitivity and depth. They are able to convey a fuller interest in who you are and thus they stand out. Of course it might be *nice* to be appreciated for your beauty, but almost certainly better if this is in balance with other types of appreciation. So by engaging with the whole person and making an effort to not focus so much on what most people would, we do ourselves a big favour.

(A little note on fixating on someone's appearance. Sometimes it's hard not to. Personally I've found in the past it's been useful to imagine the same personality in the body of an old woman, or with plus 12 stone, or wearing a clown outfit. Choose whatever works for you. With practice such mental tricks aren't needed.)

The challenge of standing out (both for those that do and for those that don't) and the importance of a fuller acceptance and appreciation, applies to any attention drawing attractive quality. E.g. fame, intelligence, power, talent. There is also an element of boldness that helps overcome the barriers that can build up around such people. Let's briefly consider some of those attention drawing qualities and some potential useful perspectives.

Supposing you are someone who is remarkably articulate and good at analysing things. While you enjoy connecting in this way, you might find many people seem to be intimidated around you. Perhaps what you'd like, much more than praise for being smart (which leads you to feel distant), is to find someone who would just give you a good hug when they felt like doing so?

So once again, by engaging with the whole person and making an effort to not focus so much on what most people would, we make it easier to connect meaningfully with someone in a way that brings them (and you) into the present moment.

Suppose now you're a very powerful person. Maybe what you'd really like is for someone to stand up to you or just be totally relaxed around you and show you that they appreciate your other sides too? What a breath of fresh air that might be. What if you're very talented or famous? Again, knowing that someone isn't phased by that and would enjoy your company even if you weren't so popular might really touch you. See how it works?

Seeing the opportunity in challenging behaviour

We mentioned the possibility of being presented with tests or challenging behaviour – where someone wants to see how we're affected by whatever quality they tend to get a lot of attention for. How do you deal with that? With good humour and by challenging their assumptions of you. Such challenges are often an invitation for you to qualify or prove yourself in some way or act in a servile fashion. Of course, that's the test, to see if you feel the need to do that. This behaviour might indicate that the person sees themselves as above you in some way, or merely that it's a habit they've developed to cope with the attention they get. They may even be unaware of doing it.

You can show that you *understand* what's going on by saying something like: "I expect most people do *state what you'd expect most people to do* when you say/do that." If it's your style you could be a little sarcastic with it: "Oh, sure, I'll hold your drink for you/be your servant/try to win your approval, I can also clean your shoes if you like." or "You must be mistaking me for someone who thinks *state what most people seem to think who try to qualify themselves*..." You could also turn it into a question: "I'm curious, what do most people do when you say or do that?" In any case, avoid being harshly judgemental in your response and keep it fairly straightforward and light-hearted.

Take the opportunity to show in your body and actions how you're comfortable just doing things in your own way and don't readily slot into the common category or usual role they're offering you. Avoid being so predictable.

Challenging behaviour can sometimes be more a sign of fear, than a test (conscious or otherwise). I've lost count of the number of times I've expressed interest in a woman and got an initial response that *could* be interpreted as aversion. But I almost always find that behind that reaction was a fear for their own emotional security. It's like if someone takes you by surprise and you raise your hands for protection. It's an involuntary action, especially if you're feeling a little vulnerable anyway or used to being upset when people get close to you. In fact it's not unusual for someone to be *more* on guard if a person they find attractive pays them attention – how much more painful would rejection or ridicule be then?

Let's walk through a real example of the above phenomenon. I was at the supermarket checkout and the young woman about to serve me had quite striking silver hair. I detected a slight discomfort in her making eye contact with me. 'Probably shy' I though, 'also maybe she noticed me appreciating the woman ahead of me in the queue and is comparing herself'. It came my turn to pay:

Me: "I like your hair."

Her: *(slight recoiling of head and showing of teeth)* "Thanks."

At this point my mind started serving up all kinds of interpretations: *'she doesn't like you', 'she doesn't know how to take a compliment', 'maybe there's something strange about me', 'do I have something stuck in my teeth?'* etc. Instead of grabbing an item from the never ending conveyor belt of judgements I continued to observe, *looking beyond my reflections*. I registered that her nervous seeming reaction might simply be the best way she knew of dealing with unexpected attention. So I smiled warmly.

Me: "Well, have a great weekend, take care."

Now something changed in her. What seemed like aversion was now more like surprise and then a moment later pleasant surprise.

Her: "Thank you, you too."

Her eyes followed me as I stepped away with my shopping and she had a big, friendly smile on her face.

So the challenge in these kind of circumstances (as discussed in section: 'The glass melon dichotomy') is to delay the making of judgement about what someone thinks and just stay with your positive intent. The *'What's the alternative interpretation?'* question, discussed on page 70, can also help you here.

Other ways of standing out

Some people feel ill at ease precisely because they feel they don't stand out. They haven't discovered how they are unique, or special yet. Of course there's a difference between 'standing out' to people in general and standing out to someone you already have a strong loving connection with. This connection in itself makes those in it stand out (besides our intrinsic uniqueness), since the feelings you have with the other you will not share with most people.

Supposing that you meet someone and what draws you most to them is not what they're usually noticed for, but the qualities that aren't quite so easy to notice straight away, like loyalty, respect for others, ability to really listen, or reliability?

If these qualities represent important values or beliefs of that person, think, what could be some of their sensitivities around them? (In the case of the four above qualities, these might include: others being fickle, not treating them with the respect they were given, talking over them, or not keeping closely to their word.) We may not have so much to go on in terms of how most people would react, but then competition is usually less of an issue. Still, the same principles of engaging with the whole person and demonstrating that you're at ease around them, still very much apply.

Hang-ups and insecurities

This idea of looking at the possible flip sides of qualities/ attributes we find attractive in people can be applied to qualities people feel others find *unattractive* (e.g. someone who is usually considered 'gorgeous' having an extra toe, or someone who wishes to identify themselves with the archetypal masculine male, who has a lisp or slightly feminine features).

If we find the quality charming or endearing, then expressing that can put someone at ease. In this case we can help them see the flip side. If though we find this quality or attribute of theirs really doesn't bother us either way, then we can say to them how what they mean to us is simply not affected by whatever it is they're worrying about. Simple stuff really, but all too easily forgotten.

Sometimes someone's self-image is very different from what you'd expect. Old experiences can lead to very distorted perspectives. Sometimes it only takes a few comments from someone we care about or who had power over us to seriously affect how we see ourselves for many years after.

From school on into the beginning of my twenties I was convinced that I was 'ugly'. A few kids, as is often the way in the playground, picked up on my birth mark and the fact I had quite prominent teeth and made it a subject of amusement and ridicule. In my mind 'I' became 'ugly'. It wasn't really until I started learning the stuff I write about in this book and got a lot of positive, contrary evidence from women that I managed to get rid of that destructive message. Sadly, lots of people out there give credence to such early, unhelpful messages late into their life. If you've met one it may take a few goes to get through to them.

Talking about it

The perspectives and attitudes someone has to the qualities we find attractive about them can be a good subject of conversation. Not only does it help us learn more about them, it also gives them a chance to talk about two things: themselves and something they've probably already spent a lot of time reflecting on. Both of which people generally enjoy doing, if they are relaxed. Additionally, if we show sensitivity and understanding to a matter which also occupies someone's heart and mind, that person is likely to feel more close to and trusting of us. A simple way to ask might be: "What's your perspective on beauty/ intelligence/power/talent/humour/kindness/honesty/respect/loyalty/ ...?" or more focused on how they feel others see them: "How do you find people usually react to your appearance/intellect/...?"

Of course what someone says or even thinks they believe is not always the same as the beliefs they act on. Still, it's fun to talk about, providing you already have a good rapport.

Attentiveness

Finding out about someone's perspectives on the qualities you find attractive in them is one benefit of putting yourself in their shoes. Another is being more sensitive to their needs in the present moment. It helps us to be *attentive* and to show that we care.

There is an important distinction between attentiveness and being ingratiating or appeasing. The former is about being caring, sensitive and observant; so having the option of helping someone get a sense of being appreciated, heard, loved, understood, etc. While the latter comes with a sense of inadequacy, fear, weakness, inferiority or manipulation.

There are two key components to attentiveness: awareness and compassion. To awareness, there are several approaches. Having a clue about what someone is thinking and putting yourself in their place (the subject of this section) is one. Shifting how we make use of judgement and identify with our needs is another (see section: 'Observing, feeling, needing, requesting'). Learning to be more inwardly still and developing better habits of observation is yet another (see section: 'The glass melon dichotomy'). Naturally, body language gives us a lot of clues here about what someone is feeling or wanting. Putting yourself in their shoes, ask yourself: "What would I be feeling if I was acting that way?" The other component of attentiveness, compassion, is discussed below and on numerous other pages.

Playfulness and a light heart

Besides putting ourselves in their shoes, what attitudes can help to build a good connection with someone, even with all the assumptions and different perspectives that might be in effect? Playfulness and light-heartedness really help – as does expecting nothing from your gifts of time and attention, other than common respect. By 'playfulness' I mean using your spontaneity to make a mutually enjoyable game out of something in your environment or that is understood between you and someone else. This can, and often should, involve physical contact as well as eye contact. Laughter is an important element here (there's nothing else that helps us relax and see things from new perspectives quite like laughter does) don't hold it back, but be aware of people's sensitivities.

Being playful brings people into the present, shows confidence and social intelligence. We discuss several types of play (and non-play) in section: 'Play conflict: fighting, arguing, joking'.

Issues for all and compassionate authenticity

On the subject of distorted perspectives, one thing that's been helpful for me to realize and remember is: For every neurosis, fear and strange social way of one sex, the other has a similar one, if differently expressed. Although our roles (and the marketing we're subjected to that appeals to them) sometimes distinguish us, man or woman, we're basically in the same boat, issues and all, just people. We have the same basic needs for love and affection, understanding and expression (and many more besides, see page 159), even though our outlooks can differ greatly.

Being aware and respectful of someone's outlook is to be distinguished from bending into their expectations or perceived desires. If we try to bend in this way we risk neglecting our own needs and development. We're strongest when we act in accord with our own values, and so then all the more likely to be recognized and appreciated.

Whatever someone's outlook, there's something about comfortable, *compassionate authenticity* that shines through a great deal of jaded opinion, fear and doubt, opening a path to connection.

Compassion is that deep concern for another's well-being that springs from a sense of oneness or fellowship with them. Being authentic, or 'straightforward', is about acting congruently with how you feel and what you really believe. Authenticity gives a sense of personal freedom and strength, which can be very attractive. (See section: 'Our attitude to change', for more on 'being true to yourself'.)

By recognising the things people have in common with each other, if not at the same time, then in our collection of life experiences, it's easier to act with *compassionate* authenticity. By being mindful of the things we all struggle and rejoice over – finding who we are and our place in the world, love and being loved – we can see ourselves in other people (and other people in us). This makes us care more. It gives us confidence too!

Lastly, while it's very useful to put ourselves in someone else's shoes, beware of the danger of thinking we're doing this when in fact we're projecting our own self-beliefs far more than the direct observations we make of the other person. See section: 'The glass melon dichotomy'. Remember also, *there is always an alternative interpretation.*

Evolution, competition and deception

Everything I've written so far hasn't really touched on the role of evolution, or how competition and deception affect the formation and course of relationships.

Predisposal is not predetermination

The theory that how people select and treat their mates is strongly influenced by successful strategies which evolved over many generations and which are carried on through our DNA, carries some weight[18]. This needn't be a bad or deterministic thing for you. All our potential for shaping our own life as we wish still remains.

There are many ways to show interest for and feel an interest from someone – and it is truly a cornucopia of elements: circumstances, preferences and in-the-moment choices that bring people together. Considering then the vast scope of human character and couplings, our evolutionary 'guidelines' for mate selection, such as how strength or fertility is demonstrated, must be quite flexible.

The work of Prof. Dean Ornish et al. has shown that actually the choices you make about your behaviour and lifestyle have a very real and rapid effect on gene expression[19]. What you feel and experience, changes your hormone and chemical levels, which directly alter your gene activity. Thus the 'genetic nihilism' of "oh, we can't help the way we are, it's in our genes" needs to be re-examined, from behavioural traits to health complaints. But whatever the genetic or evolutionary pre-disposal, competition and deception are realities that we all experience.

---

18 Matt Ridley (2003) "The Red Queen: Sex and the Evolution of Human Nature" ISBN: 978-0060556570

19 Ornish D, et al. (2008) "Increased telomerase activity and comprehensive lifestyle changes: a pilot study" Lancet Oncology

Deception and a look at fidelity

The thing about deception (at least when it comes to deceiving other people) is that it's always a choice – most often made to make our lives easier or manipulate others.

Of course, deception can be useful. It can even be a great thing in humour or play – the important question is, are we honest with the things that really matter to us, like our true feelings for someone and our intentions – and if not, how is that affecting us and the people we care about?

Often at the root of the decision to deceive (outside of playing) is a sense of threat within a perceived conflict. We discuss this type of thinking in sections: 'Distinct modes of conflict' and 'Manipulation'.

Luckily, the more crap we clear out of our own head, the easier it is for us to see what's really going on for someone else. Our bodies, face, voice and behaviour leave a long trail of clues about our true inner state, (embarrassing as that is sometimes).

Let's look now at the perennial issue of broken fidelity. Why is infidelity so common and what does it mean? As we'll see, various factors and inner conflicts can be involved.

Clearly there are natural drives in both men and women for physical and emotional intimacy with multiple partners. Clearly there are also natural drives for forming long lasting and loving couple relationships. Aside these factors, and polarising them, there exists societal pressures to conform to certain ideals. Deception is often an expedience to accommodate these powerful elements.

We can take a biological view and consider EPCs (extra-pair copulations), or 'sex-on-the-side':

For women, EPC is a chance to optimise the fitness of their offspring, separately from the suitability of their home making partner. This allows the best of both worlds: the fittest, strongest, most successful and attractive male available for sex – to increase the chances of her babies turning out that way – and a caring, supportive, loyal male who is also strong and protective to help raise them. Doing this may also get her additional food or support from interloping males, whose babies she *may* be raising.

For men, with plentiful supplies of sperm, if EPC is available it generally helps to increase the success of their genes; as does initiating EPC, even by creating a false impression of availability for a social pairing. If a woman is fit, has large breasts and a certain hips-to-waist ratio (or has other traits strongly favoured within a society that confer status) the more social pairing offers she'll get. This makes her a prime target for EPCs, because any baby she has is likely to be looked after, by a duped (or sometimes willing) partner.

For men and women then, while it's natural to seek sexual monogamy in a partner – from a biological viewpoint – it's not *quite* so natural to practice it oneself ("it's OK for me to sleep around, but not for you, sorry"). Therefore keeping up appearances of unswerving faithfulness helps.

Society influences our perception of mating success and desirability. There are also risks involved for both men and women with EPCs, of punishment by (or loss of) their own or the other's partner. But the potential genetic advantages of EPCs are strong. Studies have repeatedly shown nature, in most of the animal kingdom, to agree; *sexual monogamy* is actually a rare thing, even where *social monogamy* (having only one home making partner) is normal. This is especially true for the genital-to-body and male-to-female size ratios of humans. In fact, even in that age old symbol of life-long monogamy, the swan, infidelity is common[20].

This discussion of EPCs perhaps sheds some light on why those who are 'hard to get' – not always available and have 'options' – are often found sexually attractive. By the same token

---

20 Kraaijeveld K, et al. (2004) "Extra-pair paternity does not result in differential sexual selection in the mutually ornamented black swan (Cygnus atratus)" Mol Ecol. 13(6):1625-33

it could be part of the reason why some people go for 'bastards' or 'bitches'; being 'in control' and dominant, even to the point of lacking respect for others, representing a perceived power or status advantage. (There are many other, deeper and more wholesome ways of demonstrating strength, of course.)

Looking at things in this manner it's easy to become jaded. Although it would be extremely foolish to say we're beyond the influence of evolved behaviours/strategies in our mating habits, remember as humans we do have some conscious choice over our actions. We have values beyond the success of our genes, and honesty and personal fidelity is something deeply cherished by many.

From a social perspective, we connect in different ways and satisfy different emotional and physical desires with different people in our lives. As we grow we often want to test different options and experiences. Sometimes, despite a solid commitment and a high value placed on loyalty and honest love, we're seduced by the chance to explore and express different parts of ourselves with someone else; or we're just swept up in the desire for pleasure. Sometimes we make the choice to try and hide the fact, where it involves a breaking of trust and understanding.

So it's not always a question of someone caring little for or not respecting their partner. But whether we rationalise it, are racked with guilt or simply care very little about the deception, there is a price to pay.

What is that price? The pain and confusion caused when it's uncovered can take a long time to get over and can make it hard to trust again. On the one hand you have the betrayal of trust – that foundation of deep intimacy – and on the other you have the message: "you didn't satisfy me in all the ways you were lead to believe you did" and perhaps also "I allowed myself a freedom that I wouldn't give you (i.e. we're not equals)". For the deceiver there is often retribution or the loss of their partner to face.

Even if there was no such intent or thought in the guilty

party, it's easy for the deceived to think they were made a fool of. Indeed, if you end up raising someone else's baby having thought it was your own, or being left to look after a child alone, it can take a profound inner peace to look on the bright side and just get on with it.

What about when such deception is not discovered? The cost then (besides any guilt or stress you experience) is to the *quality* of intimacy. You can only be so close to someone if there remains a lie between you. In those moments of deflection or falsification you move apart.

With a deep acceptance, understanding and trust in love, there is no need or space for hidden infidelity. You can't have both at the same time. Being that close to someone can be pretty scary and more than some people want (or can find). For many, a degree of affection, support and understanding that isn't especially compromised by secret sexual affairs (that remain secret) feels like a good balance; in which case this cost might not figure much.

Deception or not, under the harsh light of close examination, sexual fidelity in society at large seems like a bit of a sketchy compromise. Sometimes we're sexually monogamous because it feels completely natural and right (especially in those early months), but often it's because we feel we need to be, or the risk of not being so is too high; otherwise we just pretend to be, with all the costs that deception brings. Could there be a way of integrating better our natural drives with our personal, moral values?

The open alternative

Is it possible for people to be socially monogamous (having one home building/life partner), where they wish, while being openly sexually polyamorous at points in their relationship? Just vaguely entertaining this idea there is immediately a blow to the ego and a sense of risk: "If some of the risk of having other sexual partners is removed, is it more likely they'll find someone else they prefer as a life partner?" It's not totally clear that would be the case.

Since those who would wish to 'sleep around' may do so anyway on the sly, despite the risks of deception, it would be ridiculous to say: "You can have sex with other people, but you can't get emotionally intimate." It could be though, the act of trusting someone, accepting their nature and giving them this freedom – without the condition – inspires a deeper connection and emotional loyalty. (Obviously there's a world of difference between giving something because you feel you *need* to and giving it because you *want* to, the effect will be very different too. The former tends to show weakness, the latter strength.)

The potential avoidance of pain and confusion this idea brings by removing the appeal of false fidelity is huge. The trouble is, it requires swapping a potential big pain later on, for a more likely, but smaller one now. On paper it looks good, but in practice people tend to choose deferring the bigger pain. Jealousy and insecurity are kept in a box before we let them go; a box monogamy helps keep shut.

Perhaps the biggest challenge to this idea is stomaching the thought that we might not always be enough to fully satisfy our partner in every way. There is the *expectation* that if two people are in love, each should want for no more than the other – and if your partner does then there's something *wrong* with you. Only, this idea is at odds with both the evolutionary and the social reasons for straying outside monogamy. There commonly *is* a desire for intimacy with more than one person and it doesn't mean there's anything wrong with you, because it's normal and natural. If someone wants to be intimate with you (and you, them) it means there is something right with you. It's just that, in their eyes, it might not be *all* the kinds of 'right' that you'd like. Such is life.

Of course there are practical considerations. We only have so much time and energy and the more people we're involved with the less time and energy we have to go around, particularly for the people that matter most to us.

Taking a step back, beyond questions of true sexual exclusivity, how does deception affect relationships? As with fidelity, the choice to deceive about significant things ensures an emotional divide. Where it's discovered there's often an emotional injury, which undermines *trust* and *respect*. There are few bigger gambles in a relationship, at least for those qualities.

To sum up this cursory look at deception; it's built into nature and many relationships, but the cost is often high and maybe there are alternative ways to explore of honouring both our nature and the virtue of honesty.

Competition

Competition is the rivalry that occurs where there is a common object of desire and an unwillingness to collaborate or compromise (or alternatively a desire to play). In the case of someone competing for the affections of a person you're close to, or would like to be close to, often the best way of addressing it is to not engage directly with it. Avoiding getting wrapped up in competition confers strength of character (because we feel no need to prove ourselves on someone else's terms), a very attractive quality!

Competition can come at every stage of a relationship, and be in various forms: other people, other interests, physical, aggressive, friendly, resource related, status related, etc. In general, dealing well with competition – where you need to – is largely about being strong in your internal state. That means being relaxed and confident in your feelings while having a clear mind about what you are doing and wanting (so as not to be derailed). Let that inner state be reflected in your actions and the way you communicate. Being strong in this way, using humour to diffuse competitive conflict and focusing on building a beautiful connection, it's difficult to be threatened. The 'Conflict' sections, in particular: 'Distinct modes of conflict' and 'Assertiveness' detail ways of keeping a strong internal state.

On the subject of groups, if there's someone you're interested in with a group of friends and you approach to talk, be aware of the group dynamic. Acknowledge everyone there and realize that some friends will be quite protective/possessive. If they don't like what you're communicating they will give you a *lot* of competition. Make time to build rapport with them as well.

In the case of someone joining a group all of the opposite sex, if you're adding value to the group with your energy/humour/ individuality/appearance, you could soon find *your* attention is being competed for!

When you speak in a group there's no need to feel pressure to entertain everyone (or indeed anyone). Have you ever noticed how people tend to gravitate to interesting sounding, emotionally alive conversations between just two people? It's a good thing to involve others, but it only takes two to *engage* a whole group.

On the flip side of competition, how do you deal with the situation where you feel drawn to someone who is currently in what appears to be an exclusive, loving relationship? Our responsibility, as one adult to another, is not so much for the lives of others, but for the impact we see our decisions having on them. We can never predict exactly how things are with people or how things are going to work out, but sometimes, if we take a moment to think, we have a good idea – please act responsibly!

The fact of competition is further reason why having a broad perspective and developing a rich life outside of any relationship is a good idea. Not only does it make you more attractive, it also makes you less vulnerable, and more able to give to those special to you.

Get your fresh roles here

In our day-to-day lives we have many different 'roles' that are a part of who we are, or what we 'identify' with. Just a few examples: the mature adult, the professional, the novice, the loving son or daughter, the parent, the teacher or student, the lover, seducer or seduced, the confident or shy one, the always funny or serious one, the rescuer, the rescued, the masculine male, the feminine female, the dominant or submissive, etc. Our roles define the kind of relationships we can have.

What is a 'role' and why do we have them?

In this book there have been several examples of learning new roles (and changing old ones) and making them part of who we are. 'Role', here means a certain set of attitudes and demeanour that come into effect in a certain context to serve some purpose. A role's context could be any *type* of situation we deal with, like being at work, talking to a certain relative, meeting someone new, or dealing with an emergency. We naturally develop roles as we find ways to communicate our needs and emotions in different situations. Roles are essentially sets of strategies that together have a certain 'character'.

Some roles are usually in effect most of the time, for instance, our gender identity role, which tells us what is or isn't acceptable behaviour for our gender (not always agreeing with natural inclination). Other roles are very situation and person specific, e.g. stairway conversations with an irritating neighbour.

The roles we fall into are the product of how we see ourselves and, to a variable extent, how we think other's see us. But our roles also *predispose* us to acting and thinking a certain way. When we are in them, we may think "I am ...", even though they are just a *part* of us, or our way of doing things. While a role may have an associated 'story' (of the world the role operates in and of you, the player of it), being 'in a role' doesn't mean we're 'acting', or pretending, just that we are expressing a particular aspect of ourselves.

It's quite possible to get stuck in an habitual role, but also to break free when we have sufficient awareness, or an intense enough experience which the role doesn't deal well with.

Having said that, roles can be very helpful to us, giving a sense of place and certainty. They are part of our character and identity. In fact we'd find it pretty hard to go through life as we know it constantly taking in each thing in front of us with no role based responses, or without honouring the responsibilities adjoined with certain roles. Imagine, for example, if a close friend calls, obviously distressed about some problem they're having and seemingly in need of a supportive voice and instead we respond with our true thoughts in that moment: "I want to help you, but I don't think I can. When I hear you cry I feel scared and lost too, and you're not making much sense anyway." Indeed, our roles can be very useful.

Compatibility issues

For a lot of people a relationship based on strongly defined roles works very well, because how they relate and how their lives fit together is very clear. However, 'fitting well together' isn't necessarily a wholesome, or constructive thing. Unfortunately some people end up in relationships that are very unhealthy, precisely because their pre-established, destructive roles fit so well together.

Some people are attracted to those who have a very clear and strong view of the world and the way people should be in it, because it gives them that sense of certainty, purpose and place, that they otherwise lack. Authority figures can be very helpful at some points in life. But they can also present an impediment to our personal development if we continue to rely on them – as comfortable as doing so may be.

Let's look at an example of where acquired roles create challenges in the relationship between two siblings. Rory and Chris grew up with an emotionally distant and critical father figure. They each developed slightly different 'roles' to try and meet their needs (or innate values) for acceptance and nurture. Rory became the perfectionist, super demanding of themselves and fixated on pleasing others. Chris became the aloof rebel, set on fighting those who would put them down, to win acceptance. (Again, these are 'roles' not in the sense that Rory and Chris are pretending, but in that their collection of strategies have a recognisable character to them.)

The result is that Rory and Chris grow to antagonise each other. Chris sees Rory as trying to be superior, judgemental and needy. Rory sees Chris as uncaring, impossible to please (just like dad) and also a little lacking in various personal standards. The tragedy is, that two siblings with a shared past come to have such stressful tensions between them, only because of the roles they've adopted and the stories that build up around them.

Setting the scene and the moment

In general, how do roles affect our relationships? They set the scene. Roles are like rooms we build, with a certain décor and view (which reflect what goes on in that room).

Fortunately, unlike the bricks and mortar variety, we can quickly rebuild these rooms, altering the décor and the views we have from them, borrowing elements from other rooms as we wish. Now, the liberating thing to realize here is that when you meet someone, they typically don't care what room you were in last week or last year. The room they're in right now, with you, is far more important. Are you comfortable in it?

When we meet someone, we generally want to be as open minded as possible, so we can better understand them, without our projections obscuring too much (see section: 'The glass melon dichotomy'). What we want, then, is more like an open-top space, decorated with our best attitudes and ways of being. The challenge, especially when we already know someone, is uncluttering that space.

Once we begin to see our roles as things we can pick up or put down at will, there is a lot of opportunity for playfulness, in the broadest sense of the word. With a *mutual* understanding that a certain way of relating *is* an 'act' and that there is an underlying respect, roles that might otherwise be uncomfortable or repressive can sometimes be had fun with in certain moments.

It's not unusual to relate to someone we're close to through several roles. For instance, if we have a life partner, they may also be like a sibling, parent or child to us at times. This 'role shifting' can be a source of friction, where it arises from old patterns of conflict and unmet needs that result in one person relating to the other, not as they are now but as if they were a figure from their past. But being open to exploring different roles can also be a beautiful and fulfilling experience where it helps to meet everyone's needs for connection, self-expression, nurture, love and understanding. For instance, a woman I met on the train (I'm in the habit of starting conversations on trains), 17 years married, described to me recently how she also considered her husband as the brother she never had. That seemed to work well for everyone, but she was less happy when he treated her like a mother, which tended to happen when they argued, where he'd 'revert' to the role of 'naughty boy being told off by his mum'.

Gender roles

Some roles are set deeper than others and some have a biological basis, such as what it means to be a man or woman. Beside cultural conditioning, there are hormones, brain-chemistry, physiology and our genetic heritage at play here.

Historically there have been stronger forces than exist today shaping classical gender roles. Before so called civilised society (or even agriculture) a man's physical prowess and willingness to fight and be dominant would really affect his success in hunting and how able to protect himself and his mate he was. Similarly, in such times, a woman's charm, physical attractiveness and gathering skills would make a big difference to her success and safety. At least that's the theory. Of course, intelligence and social skills would also be factors for both sexes, as hunting, gathering and child care tend to be group activities – working together is how to survive. Leisure time too would be chiefly spent with other group members. (Interestingly, there are a few known hunter-gatherers, such as the Aeta people, where these gender roles are reversed – the men gather, the women hunt – or even shared.)

In more recent times, where career prospects were heavily weighted in favour of men, women were perhaps more dependent on them than ever for security – reinforcing the idea of men being the providers and protectors and women being the nurturers and caretakers of the home. This disparity in earning potential still exists in many parts of the world.

Without such strong influencing factors as above, these divisions of gender role seem to grow less important. Of course, not that there is anything wrong with a mutual choice to adopt such archetypal roles.

Femininity and masculinity have various qualities or traits associated with them: soft vs. hard, yielding vs. unyielding, gentle vs. firm, etc. (This is particularly apparent in languages with grammatical gender.) Together these aspects are complementary, they form a more complete and able whole. In reality, no man has only 'masculine' qualities and no woman has only 'feminine' qualities.

It's fairly common within healthy and long lasting relationships for each person to be flexible with what jobs and responsibilities they take on, in order to be mutually supportive – even if that means doing something not stereotypically masculine or feminine. *Working well together takes precedence over conforming to expected roles.*

It's worth opening up gender for discussion, e.g. "What does 'being a man/woman' mean to you?" Obviously it helps to get to know each other better, but also a lot of conflict can arise when we pin our self-worth to our gender role and someone or circumstances make it hard for us to stick to that role. Through discussion we can explore the *assumptions* we may be making about our own and the other's gender, that are facilitating such conflict.

In section: 'Distinct modes of conflict' we talked about 'threat-focused' and 'collaborative' approaches to conflict. It's by choosing to focus on what you might create together, rather than what threat you pose to each other, that a lot of stress and suffering is avoided. With a collaborative approach, conflicts can more easily become opportunities for deeper understanding, and uncertainty can be faced together and openly. This approach allows the personal nature of gender roles to be embraced and a balance to be found, where there are compatible personalities.

In conclusion, gender roles are fluid and vary according to culture. Embrace your individual nature, but recognize too that much of our gender roles are merely society's manifestation of our collective desire to conform to norms and produce new generations that will fit well together in couples. As an individual you may fit very well and happily into these standard roles, or you may not. But in any case your life is yours to live. There are also few characteristics that are more attractive than being truly at ease with your own nature and personality, whatever it is. Not only does it demonstrate confidence and inner strength, it also tends to help other people give themselves permission to be like that too, which is what we all want really.

Education, employment and entertainment

How does our education and employment impact the roles we develop in our personal relationships? Since we spend the most formative years of our life in education and the most active hours of our days thereafter in employed work, it's fair to expect the impact will be significant.

I was struck recently by one of creativity expert, Sir Ken Robinson's talks[21] on education. He described how the global main-stream education system was designed at the dawn of the industrial age and how, to a large extent, it still functions as it was then. Four points in particular resonated with me: at school we're generally taught that *there is only one right answer*, that *it's bad to make mistakes*, that *we shouldn't be too different*, but that *it's bad to copy others*. Those beliefs are practically in direct opposition to our most powerful and natural ways of learning; copying and then adapting what others do (or 'modelling success' as it's referred to in this book), and exploring freely what doesn't work ('making mistakes') so we can better understand what does. Those school learnt beliefs also increase fear of stepping outside norms and degrade our natural ability to be creative. So it's then harder to consider the alternative interpretation (see page 70), a habit which helps avoid many of the mental tangles we get ourselves into with relationships.

Forming and maintaining healthy, loving relationships is fundamentally a creative process. It's rather unfortunate then that for much of our eduction, our natural creativity is hamstrung, rather than being nurtured and celebrated.

For the most part, employed work is an ideological continuation of main-stream education. With a small minority of exceptions, we're employed to be cogs in the machine; standardized, managed and compensated. Not that such work can't be enjoyed and a sense of contribution gained from it. Also, there are many jobs in society that, while considered 'low status', are essential to our health, safety and liberty (and vice versa). This is not a critique of any particular job, but a view of the over-arching system.

We are able to play different roles in different parts of our life. But the way we *identify* with ourselves in work and through

21 http://comment.rsablogs.org.uk/2010/10/14/rsa-animate-changing-education-paradigms/

education will naturally spread to other areas, just because much of our learning about and forming of relationships takes place while in education, or at work. (Institutional religion also has a significant impact, where it's part of the culture, but has been in a global decline for generations).

Taking a step back and looking at these two cornerstones of society (education and employment), how does their current form reflect our approach to *conflict* or problem solving, i.e. how we all meet our various needs in a world of limited resources? It seems as if the way these cornerstones function is currently much more threat-focused than collaborative (see section: 'Distinct modes of conflict').

If we look to the entertainment industry, we find more clues about how we view the above conflict. In his book "Information is Beautiful", David McCandless shows how an increasing proportion of the most financially successful films are either based around a violent story or have significant levels of aggression and fighting within them. This trend suggests that films *(a prime source of role-models)* are one outlet for the frustrations and anger that result from our needs not being met in our daily lives. Sometimes the 'entertainment' value of them is really a kind of relief or catharsis. The situation is even starker with computer/video games. In the US, more than 67% of households play them. In the UK it's probably closer to 75%. When "Call of Duty: Modern Warfare 2" was released in 2009 it had global sales of over $550m in its first five days – more than the *combined* value of the global music and film industries for that period. A record since broken by the title's sequel the following year. The general media and TV culture could equally be viewed (in part) as frustration/anger outlets.

We could read the previous paragraph and say 'well, violence is part of human nature, so it's natural that our media and entertainment should embrace it'. The question for me is not whether violence is part of our nature, but under what circumstances does our *potential* for violence manifest? The clearest answer I can find is that violence – and the attraction to it – comes about when we're under pressure or threat and struggling to meet our needs. Violence is not a need in itself. The history of conflict and the historical and present alternatives[22] to our threat-focused culture demonstrate this.

Nonetheless, it's quite understandable why, in many cultures, the roles people adopt in relationships have varying degrees of violence towards one another. If our culture itself creates the above conditions for violence to manifest, then violence becomes part of our 'normal' way of doing things; it becomes part of our paradigm. The good news is, since this way of existing isn't that deeply fulfilling, the potential for change is strong – if we can catch a glimpse of what lies beyond that paradigm.

A full discussion of how the powerful role-forming parts of our life previously discussed might be restructured would make for a much longer book. But in brief, as Gandhi put it "Be the change you want to see in the world." If you apply the content of this book (or whatever else works for you) and others see how it improves your life, they might be curious to know how you've done it.

Stepping out of role

Having a clear awareness of your roles makes it easier to adopt models of success. Knowing that you are in a certain role, you can then go from saying "this *is* me" to saying "this is a *part* of me, which I have a *choice* over", or simply "this is how I'm choosing to be". Because roles boil down to sets of established strategies born from certain values, beliefs and desires, the same

---

22 Douglas Fry reveals many notable examples of peaceful, more 'collaborative' cultures in his book: "Beyond War: The Human Potential for Peace". But whatever culture you live in, if you're interested in practising more peaceful and sustainable methods of conflict resolution (for instance, NVC) in every-day life, there could be some local groups with the same focus. If there isn't, maybe you could start one?

approaches used to untangle them can be used here.

Be aware that some people are uncomfortable communicating outside of their habitual roles. It requires effort and unfamiliarly is associated with risk. It's a choice for them to make. Perhaps this is one reason why those first moments of meeting someone are so influential, because we often, quickly decide what role to be in, which plants us in a certain emotional landscape.

On the other hand, we tend to feel more emotionally involved with people who bring us more fully into the present moment and out of our habitual roles. It can bring some of the wonder of the world and being alive back home to us, if we were starting to lose touch with it.

Continuing the earlier example of the sibling tensions, supposing Rory adopts the kind of strategies shared in the sections on conflict? Rory would really like to have better connection with Chris and decides to be open about it when Chris next drops by. Chris is sitting on the sofa reading a magazine and keeping themselves to themselves, as usual:

Rory: "How are things going?"

Chris: "Oh, fine thanks, can't complain."

Rory: "Great." then, after a long pause "How is it that you don't ask me how I am?"

This is a big step for Rory, because it means putting aside the role of the long suffering sibling whose not cared for by their brother/sister – and all the stories supporting it.

Chris: "Er, I'm sorry. How are you?" (*laboured tone*)

This is difficult for Chris too because to them – playing the role of the long suffering sibling who's brother/sister expects too much and thinks poorly of them – it seems like another case of Rory putting pressure on them and being needy. But next Rory decides to stay in the present.

Rory: "It seems like you're irritated after my question."

Chris: "No, I'm fine."

Rory: "Are you reluctant to share your feelings because you'd like to have some space and don't want to be judged?"

Chris: "Yes. You're always so judgemental and trying to be superior. It's like you need to remind me there's something wrong with me. Maybe that's why you're always pressuring me to spend time with you?"

By focusing on developing understanding of what's going on with Chris in the present, Rory has encouraged Chris to share more of how they're really feeling. Although the challenge is to focus on the underlying feelings and needs and not the judgements they are expressed through.

Rory: "I guess you're feeling angry and frustrated because you'd like more acceptance, respect and independence in our relationship."

Chris: "Yes. And I'm sad you can't accept me for who I am. Why can't we just have a normal relationship?"

Rory: "I'm so happy that you said that much to me. I can see how the way I've expressed myself in the past has made it hard for you to understand my feelings and I'm very sad about that. I want you to know that I do accept and respect you and I'm so proud to have you as my brother/sister."

Chris: "Er, thanks."

This is a fairly unfamiliar way of communicating and Chris isn't sure what to say, but the fact that this much has been shared openly is testament to the progress made.

Rory: "I understand your need for independence and I respect that. At the same time it would mean so much to me if you expressed more interest in my life when we spend time together. Would you be willing to do that, knowing that I accept your choices?"

Chris: "I guess so. So long as you don't start judging me."

It's easy to feel fragile and wary, stepping outside of established patterns of relating to others, so it's important that Rory and Chris support each other by following through on what they express a willingness to do in good faith.

Commitments and goodbyes

So, you've met someone, you've been spending time together and have a really beautiful connection. Now those thoughts of building some kind of partnership together come into the foreground. What do you do? A relationship grows on the strength of communication in it, so sharing these thoughts is generally a good thing.

Hopefully from the start you've kept an idea of what the other was looking for, as the relationship progressed, but as your feelings develop it's wise to check up on that.

Getting clear about commitment

After having that conversation about how you'd like to continue your relationship, you may be feeling a number of things, such as joy, surprise, disappointment or fear. These feelings often revolve around the idea of commitment – typically exchanging some independence for some security or assurance of togetherness and mutual support.

The positive side of this exchange is that it helps you to build things like trust and intimacy, a family or a shared home – the risks are mitigated by the strength of a solid commitment in a relationship. Commitment can help shared value to grow, and through a strong, mutually supportive bond, you may both become more than you would have been without it.

On the flip side is the risk of it being mistaken as a requirement to take responsibility for each other's problems. Commitment can also be seen as a means of possessing someone, or as a sign that your partner only has eyes for you, which (even despite everyone's honest intentions) is often a few shades from the truth.

Commitment can be a beautiful thing and if what you want is a genuine partner in life, then certainly some commitments will be necessary. However, for some people the idea of a healthy, loving relationship does not really include much independence-exchanging commitment, where personal freedom is of prime value. Commitment can also be understood as an extension of identity, as indicated by the term 'my other half'. So then it could be the question of independence doesn't come up so much, if as a couple you really function well as a unit, and commitment comes more from a happy willingness than a sense of duty. In any case, the exact nature of commitment will differ from couple to couple, according to each person's sense of personal balance and what 'being together' is.

Whatever your feelings about commitment, the clearer you can be in this 'about our relationship' discussion about your needs, values and desires the better! Then, however you decide to go on, compromise or not, the commitments to each other of honesty and respect should be there.

Staying respectful when we don't want commitment

How can we be respectful and considerate to someone we feel close to in the case where we do not wish to compromise on or give up certain freedoms? Sometimes the best we can do is to show that we understand another person's needs or desires, while being clear, in a sensitive way, that we do not share them. Let that person know the great things about them that you value and respect and acknowledge their feelings, while at the same time saying how important certain values and freedoms are to you.

Allowing false impressions to develop and persist, more often than not results in greater pain than being clear from the start. A similar approach as above can be used when someone wants to make a friendship a more intimate relationship and you don't share that feeling.

The strength in compromise

It may seem odd to use the word compromise about commitment, but that's what it often is; the choice to do (or not do) one thing, even though we have some inclination for another course of action. Compromise used to be a dirty word to me. I was tied to my ideals. But I learnt compromise is really just a kind of flexibility that stops you getting stuck in a gilded crevice. It's also a strength, letting you meet someone halfway, to build a bridge. So compromise may manifest commitment – the *structure* that can support the growth of a relationship.

Looking at it this way – as a supportive structure – some people might only require honesty (more than simply not lying, but openly sharing true feelings) and respect, in way of commitments, while others may require a certain amount of regular time together, or an assurance of exclusive physical intimacy. To an extent it comes down to what you want to build together. For this reason it might help to talk about what you each want commitment *for*, as well as what commitment means to you.

Fear of commitment and voicing your hopes

You may be reluctant to bring the topic of commitment up if, when you did so in past relationships, it seemed to put a spanner in the works. It's true, some people have a particular, almost irrational, fear of commitment. Maybe if you just delay talking about it, they'll eventually give you the sign you're looking for?

The risk with this attitude is that they simply might not be looking for the kind of relationship you are and the longer you spend living in hope without sharing your feelings, the bigger the shock could be when things finally become clear. So how can you get that clarity without necessarily using the 'c' word? The trick is not to apply any pressure and focus on the other person's feelings. "What are the most important qualities in a relationship for you?", "Is there anything you'd like us to share more in this relationship?" or "How do you feel about the word commitment?" Asking questions like this can help you get a good idea of where the other person sees your relationship going or at least their feelings for commitment. If their answers indicate a positive attitude to commitment you can then go on to talk more specifically about the sort of commitment you'd like between you.

It could be that you or they feel that, although the relationship works really well on some levels, there isn't (currently) enough compatibility, chemistry or common goals to warrant it being a 'life partner' type of relationship (if that's a goal of yours or theirs). Naturally things can change, but if you're ever wondering how things stand, now is usually the best time to find out.

Do you feel like you want a life partner but are afraid of commitment? If so, consider that most commitments are non-binding, you can try it out and see. Also, talking about your fears *before* they build up will reduce feelings of pressure.

One of the biggest issues with commitment (or 'serious' relationships, or ones where you say 'I love you' to each other) is the idea: "If we have a serious relationship, then it seems like I'm somehow responsible for making sure you're happy, which makes me feel trapped and hide my own problems." Section: 'Responsibility' explores ways of overcoming such fears.

Possessiveness

What are the distinctions between a strong desire for commitment and possessiveness? Essentially the former turns into the latter when you take steps to impose another's commitment, or you do not take into equal consideration their needs and values on the matter. If we begin to objectify someone we are involved with, thinking "they are mine", or give ourselves the right to control their behaviour we go beyond seeking commitment and become possessive. A person loved makes a more healthy and fulfilling companion than an object controlled. Being possessive is actually de-personalizing – making it harder for mutual love to grow.

Underlying needs for significance and appeasing our fear of losing someone special can be more successfully addressed by working on ourselves; so that we are someone our partner *naturally wants* to commit to a relationship with. It is this willing and happy choice to 'act as a couple' (as you both define it) that indicates a sturdy commitment – while a freedom stepped on is a desire fanned. We can be very clear about what we're looking for without being manipulative or controlling. Open discussion about what commitment means to each of you will help everyone be clear on what kind of commitment they currently, naturally want to give and how things can go forward.

Reasons for it ending

Alas, relationships don't always work out 'happily ever after', despite everyone's best intentions. People grow apart, what they want from life or a relationship may change, mutual acceptance and support can become a struggle, or someone else they feel more strongly about arrives. Factors such as distance, work or family might also come into play. Whatever the particulars may be, things happen that lead to our connection becoming something that one of us doesn't want to maintain with the same commitment.

We'll talk about how to deal with this eventuality shortly. But firstly, it needn't be taken as a personal failure. There are always factors outside of your control, and the reasons why blaming (yourself or them) is not such a smart strategy, is discussed at length in section: 'Responsibility' and elsewhere.

Being open with issues and helping them move on

If it's you wanting the break, foreseeing the pain of the other person, it may be temping to just walk away without trying to explain, but this can make it *much* harder for them.

There's only so much you can talk, but if you can let them know they're still valued and cared for, but that you can't give them that love you once had (elaborate more if it helps them make sense of things), this can save a lot of anguish. By being kind and *clear* you will help them move on. Another approach that can be very helpful when you *first* have issues or doubts, is to address them then with your partner, rather than try to brush them under the carpet and let things pile up. Sometimes it's a conflict suppressed that drives people apart.

What if you're having trouble letting someone go even though being with them isn't fulfilling you in the way it once did and you don't see much chance of that changing? There's a multitude of reasons why that might be, including: not wanting to disappoint expectations (theirs, other people's, or even your own), not wanting to 'make someone feel rejected', feeling obligated or indebted to carry on a relationship, being afraid of being alone yourself, wanting some 'security' while you wait for a better match, or wanting a lighter commitment and over-compromising because you lack confidence.

In any one of those cases, when the other person gets a sense of your reservations or dissatisfaction it will cast a shadow over what light there is in the relationship. The common factors of feeling dissatisfied, fearful and trapped will undermine everyone's sense of well-being. That conversation where you share your feelings will be hard, but in the interests of mutual understanding and respect I would say it's a conversation worth having. (It may be that with feelings out in the open there is a way for the relationship to continue – perhaps in a new form – with a new understanding of both of your feelings and needs.)

Recovering from a break up

If you are that person trying to make sense of things when you learn your partner's feelings have changed, it can be tough. How is it that they felt so much for you and now they want to part? The first thing to accept is that, for whatever reason, their feelings *have* changed – and that doesn't mean those feelings were never there, or that they don't still feel affection for you and cherish the beautiful times you shared together. For me, two things really helped: searching for what constructive things I could learn from it, and then taking responsibility for changing any feelings of pain and anger. With time you can look back at those memories with a smile, not a tear, and feel gratitude. As discussed in section: 'Internal dialogues and identity', the words we choose and the way we frame the situation, makes a big difference to how able we are to learn and move forward.

Is there any hope in the relationship working again? That depends, of course, on what the issues are for it not working (at least for one person) the first time. I've noticed though, that when one person, *A*, wants some distance or is not feeling as strongly attracted as the other person, *B*, there's one common reaction that doesn't usually help *B*. If *B* responds by pushing more, sharing more and trying to close that emotional gap themselves, the usual result is *A* moves *further away*, to try and maintain the *distance* they want. So *B* gets the opposite effect they were hoping for – and has a further way to fall when the connection finally breaks. (Note how this is different from simply reassuring someone of your feelings.)

The best you can do is to be clear about your feelings, without demeaning yourself or pressuring the other person to reciprocate. Be open about what you want, try to talk about it – and then *give them the space and time they need*. If there is mileage left, they will let you know. In the mean time be sure to take care of yourself and get out and spend time with other people. It will only help.

Getting a handle on over-commitment

Before it comes to saying goodbye, what can we say about over-commitment? If it's a case of being dependent on or addicted to someone then you must first address that imbalance as much as possible. (See sections on fear, love, what relationships mean, and our attitude to change.)

Where it's a case of, in retrospect, just putting too much time and energy into making relationships work, or compromising too much, the best guidance I can give is this: keep your commitment roughly proportional to what the relationship *currently is*, not what you'd like it to be at some point in the future. This means assessing the level of commitment of the other person and what you both currently mean in each other's lives. If your level of commitment is found to be overshooting, you might consider scaling it back. This in turn could give your relationship breathing space, so it can grow more naturally, without the need for propping up.

Nurturing commitment and responsibility

When it comes to making commitments in relationships for the sake of our own or another's happiness it may be helpful to remember this: while relationships can enhance our lives immeasurably, and relying on people sometimes is just part of being human, ultimately we are each responsible for our own happiness. By claiming our responsibility and letting the other person claim theirs, we actually become better able to serve each other in a healthy, loving relationship.

Giving and receiving support of all kinds is one of the beautiful aspects of a committed relationship and just the act of being supportive can strengthen commitment. It's so much easier and joyful to share support when we know we're not being held responsible for someone else's feelings. Thus, by avoiding that situation, we're helping to nurture the commitment in our relationship(s).

Commitment is strengthened by continuing to touch each other, emotionally and physically, and by helping to meet each other's needs. So, if you do have a strong mutual commitment in a loving relationship, nourish it by doing things *together* that play to your strengths and passions, that allow you to contribute, learn, and feel more alive. In closing, allow your affection to be spontaneous, practice acceptance and honesty, value your differences, and appreciate the simple moments of togetherness.

Final words

Is it possible to say which relationship is (or was) 'successful' and which is not? While what you're looking for will make a difference, is there some common measure?

It is not the length of a relationship, since people can be miserable together for many years. It is not the lack of arguments, since they can lead to greater understanding and closeness. Neither is it how much your friends or family like your partner, since that makes little difference to the quality of time you spend together. I think the simple answer is:

A relationship that welcomes you to be you and them to be them, but in a way that helps you both be more than you could have been alone. In what way 'more'? Simply more of what you want to be, in your sense of self and togetherness, in receiving and giving. It is synergy that makes a success.

I believe it is this support of self-expression and growth that is the mark of a healthy relationship; and the willingness to value someone else's needs along side your own that marks a loving one.

While the mutual benefits of such a relationship may multiply over time and with commitment, the success of it can live on long after you part company. It is loving empathy that makes relationships like this possible.

The road to healthy, loving relationships can be paved with many prototypes. You may learn a lesson many times before you imbibe it. You may think you've exorcised an unhealthy attitude or fear, to find you slip back into it when things get stressful, or you stop doing the things that move you forward in your way of being. Perseverance and being a friend to yourself is the key.

My journey of development in the area of relationships could be summarized something like this: growing self-awareness and development, being part of something bigger, feeling OK about being different, but being ready to change, taking small steps often, finding my passions, building confidence and happiness through self-expression, feeling the strength in openness, contributing to others, learning about rapport and attraction (watching and listening, reading around the subject, modelling success, practising as much as possible), practising empathy and playfulness. Making mistakes and learning from them. So if you're feeling stuck, just keep going and keep allowing yourself to grow and experience new things.

At this point the classic advice "just be yourself" starts to make a lot more sense. Find yourself, develop yourself, then just share that which emerges!

For me, adopting the view that the initial outcome of any one connection is not so important (in the sense of you being OK whatever happens), was essential. More useful than thinking in terms of 'success' or 'failure', is just to see it as a learning process of mutual discovery and appreciation. If you continue to be drawn to each other and it feels good to, then run with it, otherwise let it go with gratitude and welcome the next connection. Commitment to giving things (and yourself!) a chance of being what you'd like them to be, whatever that is for you, is important – just as not over-committing is.

If you practice the principles of the beautiful connection here, then any time or place becomes a great time and place to meet people that attract you: trains, supermarkets, libraries, bookshops, passing someone on the street, gyms, parks, cafés, classes, queues, online, just about anywhere. (Even in those places where the music is too loud for comfortable conversation and half the people are drunk, i.e. nightclubs, it could happen.)

When you find someone to potentially have the kind of relationship you'd like with, naturally it's just the beginning. It's a process of ideals and hopes meeting reality and a mix of two people's changing feelings and needs, with luck, finding a happy balance.

If the nature of relationships is to connect, then it stands to reason that different relationships will be inter-connected. The more I think about this subject and the more I live, the more it seems that *all* our relationships are connected. What we get from one, we bring to another. Friendships tend to develop into social groups and partners tend to be connected to our social groups. Even relationships that seem disconnected, e.g. professional and personal, are connected through the inner state of being that we carry from one to another. Even just making eye contact with a stranger can affect how we act with the next person we happen to meet. And all of these relationships exist within the context of how we relate to our environment and ourselves, and also our close inter-dependence as members of a modern society. So then the question is raised – how can we attend in the best way to one relationship, without also attending to the others?

This inter-connectedness is complex and part of what gives life its richness. Reflecting on it can help us be more open-minded and sensitive. Conceptually, all personal relationships are connected because we all have a common set of needs or innate values. But, depending on our view, this inter-connectedness can also be very restricting. Not wanting to 'upset the balance' or to be judged, creates a strong pressure to conform to other's expectations. While some conformity allows for social cohesion, change is one of the few constants in life. Sometimes the only way to really live is to take some risks and be the one to make that change and express your individuality.

The inter-connectedness is also within any one relationship. Each little moment of connection combines to make a whole greater than the sum of its parts. A long and happy partnership seems like such a solid thing, but it would not exist without all the little moments of togetherness that fill it. A conflict in one area can easily spread to others; just as feeling each other's love can mend many conflicts. Even within ourselves, our deepest values overlap and sometimes appear to be different facets of each other.

In connection with lasting success in relationships, the work of Dr Martin Seligman on 'happiness' comes to mind. His rigorously tested research shows what some people have known for a long time: contribution (being a positive part of something bigger) and flow (full engagement in the present moment) lead to the deepest, most long lasting happiness. While the 'good life' (material success, popularity and an active sex and social life) actually leads to *comparatively* less and more short lived happiness. But also that these three types of happiness (contribution, flow and the 'good life') *together* make for the richest life experience of all. With the right approach, your relationships can help you have all three.

Finally, though it might seem the be all and end all, if you're not in one, or have felt alone for very long, loving relationships are just one wonderful part of the crazy magic of being human. I've found it useful to keep that in mind – and of course having other pursuits and passions in your life that really make you feel alive is something that will help attract someone you can be even happier with.

Wishing you health and love,
Joe Hudson

Ps. I'd really like to know how you find this book! Please send all feedback to: comments@healthylovingrelationships.com

Subsection list

Obstacles and new perspectives...1

What relationships mean to us........1
Many ways to connect, but what for?..........1
Clarify and acknowledge what you want 2
Personal boundaries: supports or impediments?..3
The spice of life..3
A balance of give and take..........................4
The weight of expectations.........................5
Strategies are not needs............................6
Outside the 'what you should want' box......7
Relationships never happen in a vacuum....8

Lack of resources............................9
What is it about the way you look?............12

Untangling values, beliefs and desires...13
Judgement and the tree of actualization....17
Getting to the root: innate values...............19
Beliefs, the gatekeepers to fulfilment.........23
Knots not to keep...27
Why does this keep happening to me?.....31
Breaking the pattern....................................34
VBDs, the foundation of your relationships
....38

Our attitude to change....................39
Your outlook makes choices for you..........39
Giving away your power through blame....40
Studies have shown your brain is plastic...41
Being 'true to yourself' and 'behaving as if'
....41
Making change stick....................................45
What's to lose, what's to gain?.................47

Internal dialogues and identity.......48
Strategies for transformation....................50
Your body, an emotional organ..................53
Your words become what you see.............54

Projections and prophecy...............55
The ripples of our outlook..........................55
Smart projections..58

Fear (and general emotional turmoil)
....**59**
Define your fear 61
Rejection, the truths and the unknowable..62
Knots, self-love and taking action.............64
When your fears happen............................66
Fears about openness and intimacy..........68
A curious experiment..................................68
The alternative interpretation....................70

A life changing journey.................72

Spirituality and personal development 73

Self expression...............................75
Release, recognition and unity 75
Find what makes you feel alive, then share it
....76

Experimenting with ways of being and discovering the art of attraction
....**77**
Small steps, taken often 78
I don't need you to like me........................79
It's OK to experiment (but keep moving forward)...79

The power of contribution, modelling success and building rapport........80
A valuable tool box, body and mind aligned
....82
Look into the mirror of rapport...................83
Contribute your way to fulfilment..............84
Know what you want, and that you can get it
....85

Putting things into practice and the strange world of PUAs....................86
Taking a risk and welcoming opportunity...86
Who wants to be a pick up artist?............87
I'm positive until proven otherwise 89
Authenticity is always possible..................90
Congruence is the key...............................90

Love and life in the clouds 91
The painful blessings of separation..........92

Echoes of the past......................................93

But what is love?............................94
Opportunity and the rewards of
perseverance..97
Possessiveness..97
If you loved me then you would 98
What's in a word?......................................99
A blinding flash of love..............................101
From cynicism and familiarity to continued
freshness..102
Making sense of love that ends...............103

The beautiful connection............104

The five keys....................................104
And the secret ingredient is......................107
Contribution and gift giving......................107
What does blame give you?.....................108
Something for every relationship (accept
where three is a crowd)............................109
Applying and re-examining the five keys. 110

The glass melon dichotomy..........114
Don't miss the melon for the glass...........115
Projection is an invitation.........................117
Acceptance, from acknowledgement to
disputes..118
... and even while kissing..........................120
The connection of inner and outer
acceptance..120

Practice makes perfect (virtually). 121
Success is where preparation meets
opportunity..123
Exploring qualities you wish to express...125
Support and affection...............................126

Conflict...129

Conflict in a nutshell......................129
You already know the solution.................130
Arguments...133

Distinct modes of conflict.............134
What is your body saying?......................137

**Observing, feeling, needing,
requesting.......................................138**

Empathy and open, respectful intent.......142
Questions to aid mutual understanding...144
Making requests and hearing requests....145
Dealing with anger and aggression 150
A rich language...157
Practice time and pausing for thought 162

The role of judgements..................164
Value projection...165
Reward 167
Punishment..168
Asserting authority....................................170
Making moral judgement..........................170
Giving advice, comforting or diagnosing..173
Assessing ability, encouragement and
discouragement...175
Setting a boundary...................................178
To make use of the idea of 'fault'.............178
Stating thoughts about another's reasoning
or knowledge 179
Fuelling violent conflict.............................179
Finding strength in openness and a
paradigm shift..180
The use of force and young people.........182

Responsibility..................................184
Responsibility for feelings.........................184
Responsibility for actions.........................187
Apologize without blame: the fault free way
....189
Forgiveness..194

**Play conflict: fighting, arguing,
joking..195**
Applications and advantages...................196
When 'play' isn't just play.........................199
Peace bringing approaches to humour....200

**To compromise or not to
compromise.....................................203**
Why compromise can be smart and healthy
....203
Do it gracefully, acknowledging the choice
....204
Liberating entrenched conflict..................205
Agreeing to disagree and over-compromise
....206

Criticism, 'over-sensitivity' and the wall...208
Taking criticism, the 'good' and the 'bad' 208
Tending to see judgement and threat where none is made or intended.......................209
Denial and avoidance 211

Manipulation..................................212

Assertiveness 213
The kindness of interrupting 215

The effect of focus and self-interest 216
Are you stuck in crisis management? 216
The smarter way.....................................219

Practical tips and further considerations...............................220

First contact and conversations...220
Initial attitude and keeping it in the moment 220
Observing an interest and getting involved 223
Beyond the small talk, enjoying discovering 224
Saying goodbye for now and hello..........224
Balance, humour and body language......226
Expressing attraction...............................227
Compliments, how to take them..............228
Show your appreciation...........................229
Good meetings and good meetings.........229

Sex and the emotional impact.......230
What does sex mean to you?...................230
Why we get so hung up about it and ways of dealing with imbalance..............................231
Seek out what works...............................234
Overcoming blocks to sexual intimacy....236
A natural arrival and dealing with pressure 237
Foreplay...239
Anxiety, 'over-excitement' and emotional intimacy...239
Orgasm and ejaculation, for men and women...241
Solo pleasure..244
After sex and seeing through the haze....245

Attitudes and the other's shoes....246
Evaluating appreciation: nice ≠ interesting 246
Fuller acceptance and bucking the trend.247
Seeing the opportunity in challenging behaviour..250
Other ways of standing out......................252
Hang-ups and insecurities.......................253
Talking about it..254
Attentiveness...254
Playfulness and a light heart...................255
Issues for all and compassionate authenticity..255

Evolution, competition and deception......................................257
Predisposal is not predetermination........257
Deception and a look at fidelity 258
The open alternative 261
Competition...263

Get your fresh roles here..............265
What is a 'role' and why do we have them? 265
Compatibility issues 266
Setting the scene and the moment..........267
Gender roles..268
Education, employment and entertainment 270
Stepping out of role.................................273

Commitments and goodbyes 276
Getting clear about commitment..............276
Staying respectful when we don't want commitment..277
The strength in compromise....................277
Fear of commitment and voicing your hopes 278
Possessiveness.......................................279
Reasons for it ending...............................280
Being open with issues and helping them move on..280
Recovering from a break up.....................281
Getting a handle on over-commitment.....282
Nurturing commitment and responsibility.283

Final words....................................284

Index

Acceptance 52,5,26,51,105, 114-121,261

Addiction 97,101

Adopted-strategy 31-38,41-47

Affection 125-128,58,236-237

Alternative interpretation 70-71,271,89,252,123,50

Anger 150-157,59,179-180

Anxiety 226,123,51,95,228, 151,237-244,175

Apology 189-194

Appreciation 229,167-168, 106,110,112,246-247,131,159

Arguments 119-120,129-212

Assertiveness 213-216,136, 143,139,50

Attraction 1,9-13,55-58,124, 77-114,247-256

Authenticity/Being yourself 41-47,75-80,90,104-107,158,237-242,251,256,265-275

Beliefs 13-38,39,48,114-121, 246-250

Belonging 74,108,159

Blame 40,64,109,119-119,129-219

Boundaries 3,178,181,195, 208,197,182

Boredom 166,215,187,111, 28,172

Collaboration 134-137,216-219

Commitment 276-283,102, 12,28,260

Compassion 255-256,94,98, 107,254,140,172,179,156, 168,224,138

Compatibility 112,266,270,279

Compliments 227-228,167-168,246-247,222,251,77

Compromise 203-208,102, 277,261

Confidence 104,44-46,256, 83,116,220,61,89,88,74,255, 124,77,219

Congruence 2,256,137,220, 87,31

Contribution 84,107,128,75, 86,29,159

Criticism 208,141,164,29

Cynicism 102,56,28

Deception 43,257-263

Dependency 5,28,283,97,

Desire 13-38,140,240,94, 262,90

Empathy 9,130-144,219,71, 126,246,23,195,284,25,106

Equality 5,136,85,279,260

Expectations 5-6,84,255,108, 102,256,28,101

Eye contact 220-221,78,119, 106,255,37,237,117,251,248, 123,226

Fear 59-70,27-37,256,278, 100,128

Fidelity/Faithfulness 278-258-263

Forgiveness 40,108,194

Freedom 39-48,61,68,261-263,265-276

Gender differences 268-270, 96

Generosity/Kindness 108,204, 239,95,20,215,39

Gifts 107,255,192

Guilt 98,4,153,171,194,148, 186,140,211,151

Honesty 41-45,68,105,112, 281

Hugs 127-128,99,227,174, 236-237,13,147,17,249

Humour 104,223,220,198, 200,200-203,226-227,250,20

Identity 13-55,59,117,265-276

Inner-conflict 13-55,59-70, 134-138,258-263

Intimacy 68,276,109,230, 236-239,261,260,76,128,67, 216,169,65,28,30,159

Jealousy 135,97,262

Judging 129-219,16,39,105, 98,245-246,67,61,116,63

Kissing 120-120,236,225,239

Listening 114-120,105,125-126,134,210

Loneliness 128,64,86,56,29, 27,103,160

Love 91-103,15,256,219,64-66,127,254,262,56,233,4,28, 95,55,279

Loyalty 4,102,252,99,262,201, 259,28

Manipulation 212-213,61, 135,210,90,5

Meeting people 220-230,246-257,104-125,86-90

Mental or physical violence 7, 49,60,129-161,199-203

Mindfulness 53,114-121,67-68

Modelling success 24-27,34-38,41-45

Moving on/Leaving 280-282, 103,92-93

Needs 138-164,19-23,71, 255-257

NVC 138-164,119

NLP 80-85,

Open relationships 261-263

Outlook 1-70,134-137,114-120,246-257

Playfulness 255,195-203,104, 268,241,239,83,197

Positive-attitude 9-59,62,70, 134-137,104,220-229

Possessiveness 97,279

Pressure 277,237,7

Punishment 168-170,148,151, 156,259

Rapport 83-91,220,236,225, 264

Rejection 62-64,56,46,218, 36,32,28

Requests 145-150,188-189, 163,210

Rescue 5,28

Responsibility 184-194,219, 283

Reward 167-168

Roles 265-276,82,117,136

Romance 91-93,97-97,101- 102,227

Saying no 150,208,214

Seduction 87-91,260,238

Self-expression 75-77,104- 110,129-219,220-246

Self-image 1-70,73-92,265- 276

Sex 230-246,97,258-263

Shame 59,171,169,189- 194,231- 244,151,148,212,161

Shared value 19-23,106,276

Sharing 68,74,93,75-78,104- 108,277-278,67,57

Spontaneity 104,223,255

Support 126-128,159,277- 280,146,142-143,219,266, 269,259,212

The smarter way 219-219,137

Threat-focus 134-137,216- 219

Togetherness 112,283,118, 286

Touching 125-128,236- 244,120-120,87,74,227

Trust 68,68,83,204,136,195, 209,93,60,218,55-59,39,176, 27-31,152

Understanding 118-120,130- 144,126,195,66,83,90,219, 246,43

Value in differences 106-112, 269

Values 2,13-38,129-162

Joe Hudson has also written:

Frottage Triage - *Frottage Triage is a collection of poems and verse, diverse in scale, style and emotion. You will find poems about love, grief and revelation amongst studies of every-day social minutia and chance encounters. Expect passion and exploration, along with a good dose of humour. This work is motivated much more by a need to expose and examine, rather than celebrate or castigate, although there is a sincere sense of searching for what is important and of pragmatic evaluation.*

For more information about this book,
or to buy more copies, visit:
www.healthylovingrelationships.com

Lightning Source UK Ltd.
Milton Keynes UK
UKOW021334051011

179805UK00010B/56/P